FILIAL PIETY

CONTRIBUTORS

Akiko Hashimoto
Charlotte Ikels
Roger L. Janelli
Brenda Robb Jenike
Jun Jing
Sung-chul Kim
Eric T. Miller
Clark Sorensen
John W. Traphagan
Danyu Wang
Martin King Whyte
Dawnhee Yim
Hong Zhang

Filial Piety

PRACTICE AND DISCOURSE IN CONTEMPORARY EAST ASIA

Edited by

Charlotte Ikels

STANFORD UNIVERSITY PRESS

STANFORD, CALIFORNIA

2004

Stanford University Press
Stanford, California

© 2004 by the Board of Trustees of the
Leland Stanford Junior University.
All rights reserved.

Printed in the United States of America on acid-free,
archival-quality paper

Library of Congress Cataloging-in-Publication Data

Ikels, Charlotte
    Filial piety : practice and discourse in contemporary East Asia /
edited by Charlotte Ikels.
        p.   cm.
    Includes bibliographical references and index.
    ISBN 0-8047-4790-3 (cloth : alk. paper)—
ISBN 0-8047-4791-1 (pbk. : alk. paper)
        1. Kinship—East Asia.   2. Family—East Asia.
3. Households—East Asia.   4. Parent and adult child—
East Asia.   5. Filial piety—East Asia.   6. Adult children
of aging parents—East Asia.   7. Aging parents—Care—
East Asia.   8. East Asia—Social life and customs.
I. Ikels, Charlotte.
GN635.E18 F55   2004
306.85'095—dc22   2003013738

Original Printing 2004

Last figure below indicates year of this printing:
13   12   11   10   09   08   07   06   05   04

Typeset by Heather Boone in 11/14 Garamond

Contents

List of Tables and Figures   *vii*

List of Contributors   *ix*

Introduction   1
CHARLOTTE IKELS

1. Ritualistic Coresidence and the Weakening of Filial Practice
    in Rural China   16
    DANYU WANG

2. Filial Daughters, Filial Sons: Comparisons from Rural
    North China   34
    ERIC T. MILLER

3. Meal Rotation and Filial Piety   53
    JUN JING

4. "Living Alone" and the Rural Elderly: Strategy and Agency
    in Post-Mao Rural China   63
    HONG ZHANG

5. Serving the Ancestors, Serving the State: Filial Piety and
    Death Ritual in Contemporary Guangzhou   88
    CHARLOTTE IKELS

6. Filial Obligations in Chinese Families: Paradoxes
    of Modernization   106
    MARTIN KING WHYTE

7. The Transformation of Filial Piety in Contemporary
    South Korea   128
    ROGER L. JANELLI AND DAWNHEE YIM

8.   Filial Piety in Contemporary Urban Southeast Korea:
      Practices and Discourses   153
      CLARK SORENSEN AND SUNG-CHUL KIM

9.   Culture, Power, and the Discourse of Filial Piety in Japan:
      The Disempowerment of Youth and Its Social Consequences   182
      AKIKO HASHIMOTO

10.   Curse of the Successor: Filial Piety vs. Marriage Among
      Rural Japanese   198
      JOHN W. TRAPHAGAN

11.   Alone in the Family: Great-grandparenthood in
      Urban Japan   217
      BRENDA ROBB JENIKE

      Glossary   245
      Notes   251
      References   267
      Index   291

Tables and Figures

Tables

1.	Living Arrangements of Zhongshan Elderly Parents, 1993–1994	66
2.	Zhongshan Elderly Parents Living Alone and Availability of Children	68
3.	Percent Distribution of Main Provider for Physical Care and Household Assistance in Baoding and Urban Taiwan	119
4.	Comparison of Attitudes of Taiwan Elderly and Baoding Elderly	121

Figures

1.	Residences of the elderly in Zhongshan, Hubei	69
2.	Newer housing in Zhongshan	77
3.	Paper goods for funeral rituals near Guangzhou	94
4.	More funerary goods, including paper cell phones	95
5.	Guangxiao (Glorious Filial Piety) Temple in Guangzhou	100
6.	The rural-to-urban transition in Kimhae, Korea	163
7.	Age distribution for Akita, Iwate, and Miyagi Prefectures	202
8.	Age distribution for Japan and Tōhoku	203
9.	Group exercises at a day care center for the elderly in Tokyo	230

Contributors

Akiko Hashimoto (Ph.D., Yale University) is associate professor of sociology and Asian studies at the University of Pittsburgh. Her publications include *The Gift of Generations: Japanese and American Perspectives on Aging and the Social Contract* (Cambridge University Press, 1996) and *Family Support for the Elderly: The International Experience* (Oxford University Press, 1992). She is currently working on a book-length study of cultural identity and national memory in post–World War II Japan and Germany.

Charlotte Ikels (Ph.D., University of Hawaii) is professor of anthropology at Case Western Reserve University and an associate in research at the Fairbank Center for East Asian Research at Harvard University. She is the author of *Aging and Adaptation: Chinese in Hong Kong and the United States* (Archon Books, 1983) and *The Return of the God of Wealth: The Transition to a Market Economy in Urban China* (Stanford University Press, 1996), and is a coauthor of *The Aging Experience: Diversity and Commonality across Cultures* (Sage Publications, 1994).

Roger L. Janelli (Ph.D., University of Pennsylvania) is professor of folklore and ethnomusicology, and East Asian languages and cultures at Indiana University. He coauthored *Ancestor Worship and Korean Society* (Stanford University Press, 1982) and *Making Capitalism: The Social and Cultural Construction of a South Korean Conglomerate* (Stanford University Press, 1993) and coedited *The Anthropology of Korea: East Asian Perspectives* (Japanese National Museum of Ethnology, 1998).

Brenda Robb Jenike (Ph.D., UCLA) is a visiting assistant professor of anthropology at the University of Notre Dame. Her research interests include contemporary Japan, the cultural context of aging, intergenerational relations, gender ideology, social welfare, and person-centered ethnography. Her previous publications examine the perspective of family caregivers in Japan.

Jun Jing (Ph.D., Harvard University) is on the faculty of the City University of New York and of Tsinghua University. He is the author of *The Temple of Memories: History, Power, and Morality in a Chinese Village* (Stanford University Press, 1996) and editor of *Feeding China's Little Emperors: Food, Children, and Social Change* (Stanford University Press, 2000).

Sung-chul Kim earned his doctorate in anthropology from the University of Washington. He is currently on the faculty of Inje University in Kimhae, South Korea.

Eric T. Miller is a doctoral candidate in anthropology at the University of Pittsburgh and administrative coordinator of the China Law Center at Yale Law School. His primary research interests in China are aging, intergenerational relationships, and popular religion.

Clark Sorensen (Ph.D., University of Washington) is associate professor of Asian studies at the Jackson School of International Studies and director of the Korean Regional Studies Program at the University of Washington. He is author of *Over the Mountains Are Mountains: Korean Peasant Households and Their Adaptations to Rapid Industrialization* (University of Washington Press, 1988) as well as numerous articles on East Asian family organization, social stratification, social change, and values.

John W. Traphagan (Ph.D., University of Pittsburgh) is assistant professor of Asian studies, research associate of the Population Research Center, and research affiliate of the Institute of Gerontology at the University of Texas at Austin. He is the author of *Taming Oblivion: Aging Bodies and the Fear of Senility in Japan* (SUNY Press, 2000) and coeditor of *Demographic Change and the Family in Japan's Aging Society* (SUNY Press, 2003) and is editor-in-chief of the *Journal of Cross-Cultural Gerontology*.

Danyu Wang (Ph.D., Brown University) is a staff member at MIT Sloan School of Management. She has published papers on family change and household survival strategies in (post)socialist China.

Martin King Whyte (Ph.D., Harvard University) is professor of sociology at Harvard University. He has conducted research on a large range of features of grassroots social life in contemporary China.

Dawnhee Yim (Ph.D., University of Pennsylvania) is professor of history at Dongguk University in Seoul. She is the author of the Korean-language *Explorations in American Culture* (P'yŏngminsa, 1995) and coauthor of *Ancestor Worship and Korean Society* (Stanford University Press, 1982) and *Making Capitalism: The Social and Cultural Construction of a South Korean Conglomerate* (Stanford University Press, 1993).

Hong Zhang (Ph.D., Columbia University) is assistant professor of East Asian studies at Colby College, Maine. Her research interests include family and gender relations, kinship and marriage, social transformations, changing patterns of eldercare, and new family-building strategies in contemporary China. She was guest editor for a special issue of the *Journal of Chinese Sociology and Anthropology* on "Eldercare Issues in Contemporary China" (2001–02).

FILIAL PIETY

Introduction

CHARLOTTE IKELS

This volume had its origins in a panel entitled "The Practice of Filial Piety in Contemporary China" organized for the annual meeting of the Association for Asian Studies (AAS) in San Diego in March 2000. Although anticipating a modest turnout for the inauspiciously scheduled early morning time slot, the panelists were surprised by a turnout that far exceeded expectations. Furthermore, the questions raised by the discussant (Myron L. Cohen) and by members of the audience following the presentations revealed a tremendous interest in the meaning and practice of filial piety in China today. Consequently the panel organizer (Ikels) decided the topic merited a more thorough treatment and a broader audience than was possible in the annual meeting format. She also believed that we could better understand what was happening in China by examining what was happening in other East Asian societies as well.

To this end, additional scholars working on filial piety in China or in other East Asian settings, specifically the Republic of Korea and Japan, were invited to address the issues raised at the AAS meeting. Four of the chapters (those by Miller, Jing, Zhang, and Ikels), all considering the state of filial piety in China, represent extensive revisions of the papers presented in San Diego. Of the remaining seven chapters, one (by Wang) also deals with China while two (one by Janelli and Yim, the other by Sorensen and Kim) investigate the state of filial piety in contemporary Korea, and three (those by Hashimoto, Traphagan, and Jenike) investigate its state in contemporary Japan. Only one chapter (by Whyte) is explicitly comparative, addressing the question of whether the practice of filial piety has survived better in Taiwan or on the mainland. While the authors of the various chapters do make reference to Confucian scriptures and to efforts of national governments to promote aspects of filial piety as a patriotic duty, their primary aim is not to study attitudes or normative behavior but to document actual behavior. All the contributors are experienced fieldworkers, anthropologists or sociologists, who speak the language relevant to their field site and have firsthand knowledge of the settings and the people involved in their research.

We do not argue that there is, or ever was, a single version of filial piety that can be said to characterize all of East Asia nor that particular versions can be said to characterize entire nations. Rather we argue that beyond a shared core of understandings the actual practice of filial piety, both its delivery and its receipt, is situationally dependent and shaped by local circumstances of history, economics, social organization, and demography and by personal circumstances of wealth, gender, and family configuration. The multifactored nature of this dependence means that definitions and expectations of filial behavior are subject to contestation even within the boundaries of a single community. In order to enhance reader appreciation of this variability the editor chose two strategies: (1) inclusion of multiple sites within a given country, and (2) recommendations to authors to consider the import of the above-mentioned variables within their own sites. With regard to the first strategy, the editor sought out for each country not only researchers who worked in rural areas but also those who worked in urban areas. In addition, in the case of China the editor attempted to assure regional representation. Each of the six Chinese studies took place in a different province: the four rural studies in Liaoning, Shandong, Gansu, and Hubei, and the two urban studies in Hebei and Guangdong. With regard to the second strategy, each author provides basic historical and economic background data necessary for understanding the contemporary situation in the community or communities they studied. Depending on their own research interests, authors then focus on the variables of interest to them, for instance, family configuration, gender, wealth, or social class.

Filial Piety: What Is It?

The most basic meaning of the concept of filial piety is succinctly illustrated by the character *xiao* 孝, which is used to write it. (The same ideograph with the same meaning though different pronunciations is used in Korean and Japanese. Chinese is privileged here because it is the language of the original Confucian writings that serve as the concept's ideological basis.) The character *xiao* is composed from two other characters: the top half of the character *lao* (old) and the character *zi* (son). When combined to constitute *xiao*, the element derived from *lao* rests on top of the character *zi*, that is, the "elder" is on top of the "son." This ideograph communicates multiple messages of which the officially preferred one is that the old are supported by the young(er generation). However, it could also be read as meaning that the young are burdened by the old or even that the young are oppressed by the old—the interpretation Hashimoto (Chapter 9) offers for filial piety in contemporary Japan. Or, more benignly, hearkening back to the fact that Chinese was originally written from top to bottom, simply that filial piety is the continuation of the family line, that is, the father produces the son. Indeed, in the classics and in popular thought, support, subordination (or obedience), and continuing the family line have all been touted as the essence of filial piety.

According to the *Classic of Filial Piety*, Confucius (551–479 B.C.) said, "In serving his parents, a filial son reveres them in daily life; he makes them happy while he nourishes them; he takes anxious care of them in sickness; he shows great sorrow over their death; and he sacrifices to them with solemnity" (Chai and Chai 1965: 331). Yet elsewhere Confucius himself acknowledged that children often did not carry out their duties with the proper attitude: "The filial piety of nowadays means the support of one's parents. But dogs and horses likewise are able to do something in the way of support;—without reverence, what is there to distinguish the one support given from the other?" (Legge 1933: 16). Nearly 200 years later, Mencius (372–289 B.C.) declared three things to be unfilial of which "to have no posterity is the greatest" (Legge 1933: 725). According to James Legge, the other unfilial acts are to encourage one's parents' participation in immoral activities and to be unavailable to serve them. Having no posterity is worse than either of these because it affects not only one's parents but the entire ancestral line. Later Mencius expanded his examples of unfilial behavior.

> There are five things which are said in the common practice of the age to be unfilial. The first is laziness in the use of one's four limbs, without attending to the nourishment of his parents. The second is gambling and chess playing, and being fond of wine, without attending to the nourishment of his parents. The third is being fond of goods and money, and selfishly attached to his wife and children, without attending to the nourishment of his parents. The fourth is following the desires of one's ears

and eyes, so as to bring his parents to disgrace. The fifth is being fond of bravery, fighting and quarreling so as to endanger his parents. (Legge 1933: 763–64)

Over the centuries these and similar scriptural guidelines, both positive and negative, have shaped the expectations and behavior of countless parents and children. Yet in itself the relentless insistence on the value of filial piety in premodern official discourse suggests the existence of a counterdiscourse, one that said the elderly are a burden and it would be better to be rid of them. Indeed this thought is given voice in the Japanese folktale dealing with Oba-suteyama, "Throw-Out-Granny Mountain," a grisly version of which was made into a film, *The Ballad of Narayama,* by Imamura Shōhei in 1983 (see Chapter 11). As Laurel Cornell (1991) has shown, the documentary evidence provides no support for the notion that the elderly who had reached a certain age or outlived their usefulness were carried up mountains and abandoned by their children. There are neither archaeological data to support the film's images of a bone-littered summit nor cross-cultural ethnographic data to support the idea that abandonment of the elderly was common among settled agricultural populations. As our contributors on Korea point out, there is a very similar and widely known Korean folktale with the same theme except that in that version the practice, and not the parent, is abandoned when people realize that otherwise their own children will do the same to them.

Filial Piety: What Motivates It?

Tradition alone is seldom sufficient to motivate people to behave in certain ways. While many people subscribe to the notion that filial piety is "natural," that is, an unreflective response to the care one received from one's parents, calculations of self-interest and sanctions against unfilial behavior are surely influential determinants of behavior also. Let us consider self-interest first.

SELF-INTEREST AS A MOTIVATOR

As the chapters in this volume reveal, the practice of filial piety has and has had direct consequences for a person's psychological, social, and economic well-being. As Hashimoto, for example, points out, a Japanese child is taught from its earliest days the primacy of obedience: a good child is an obedient child. This and a host of other filial piety–promoting attributes, such as gratitude, are so thoroughly inculcated in the home and the school that the Japanese adolescent simply cannot disentangle him- or herself from these attributes. To feel otherwise, to experience the urge to be disobedient or ungrateful, amounts to a violation of the self. The individual who has been trained well accepts the willingness to practice filial behavior as a key indicator of a mature, well-adjusted adult.

This characterization has social consequences. In the eyes of fellow community members a filial person is a reliable, trustworthy, and honorable person. As Janelli and Yim point out, filial demonstrations testify to a person's moral worth and provide him or her with a form of symbolic capital that accrues not only to the self but also to the lineage and the village. One is reminded here of the structures erected in Chinese villages in honor of chaste widows, whose dedication to their parents-in-law as much as to their deceased husbands was the object of memorialization and whose filial actions reflected glory on the whole community. Justus Doolittle (1865) makes it clear that just as filial behavior could bring honor to a community, unfilial behavior could bring dishonor and shared punishment. In the extreme case of the murder of a parent, the miscreant "would not only be beheaded, but his body would be mutilated . . . his neighbors living on the right and left would be severely punished; his principal teacher would suffer capital punishment; the district magistrate of the place would be deprived of his office and disgraced" (Doolittle 1865: 140). In other words, the practice of filial piety was everybody's business.

Scarcely mentioned in the scriptural justifications for filial behavior are economic incentives. Yet the link between providing care and inheritance is or until very recently has been explicitly recognized in the law codes of China, Korea, and Japan. In China, for example, the 1985 Inheritance Law allows a testator to leave property to whomever he or she wishes subject only to a proviso that disabled dependents be left a requisite share. However, in the absence of a will, the guidelines for allocating the estate provide that the larger share should go to those who have "fulfilled the principal obligation to support the decedent" while "either no or a smaller share should be allocated to heirs who had the ability and means to provide support [but] did not" (Ikels 1996: 107). In Korea, it was not until the early 1990s that the law entitled all children to equal shares of their parents' property. Previously the eldest son, as the primary successor and supporter of the parents, had been entitled to two shares, younger sons to one share, unmarried daughters to one-half share, and married daughters to only one-quarter share. Although the law has changed, the cultural understanding that differential inheritance is conditioned by level of support has not (see Chapter 7). In Japan, the formal abolition of the *ie* (household) and of the designation of the eldest son as the successor occurred in the early postwar period. Nevertheless, the societal expectation that the eldest son will assume primary responsibility for elderly parents remains so strong in rural areas that firstborn sons generally have much more difficulty obtaining brides than their brothers (see Chapter 10).

SANCTIONS AS MOTIVATORS

As indicated above, failure to live up to local standards of filial piety can result in damage to one's own self-image, to loss of reputation in the community, and to loss or diminution of one's inheritance. Equally important, one's own children may note these shortcomings and file them away for future reference.

Since the costs to parents of children's failure in the performance of filial piety are substantial and may even be life-threatening, most parents have given considerable thought to how to deal with this problem. The strategies chosen usually reflect the relative position of the parents. Those with valued economic resources, such as land or a residence, attempt to use them as bargaining chips. Unfortunately for most rural parents in Japan and Korea, and increasingly in China, these chips are no longer valued by the young who prefer nonagricultural employment and urban living. Parents lacking economic resources must utilize other strategies, such as reversing the traditional roles of mother-in-law and daughter-in-law. Whereas in the past members of the older generation envisioned being "served" by the young, they now find that the tables have been turned. Today the old "serve" their daughters-in-law who are employed outside the home by providing assistance with childcare, marketing, cooking, and cleaning. Both Miller in Lijia and Zhang in Zhongshan found parents who chose to live independently in order to avoid having to do such chores and to have more freedom. Should the strategy of providing extended assistance not motivate children to reciprocate, parents have the option of "going public" with their grievances. In Lijia, support problems are often resolved by the signing of a household division contract that distributes household property among the sons in exchange for specific and usually equal amounts of support. In Zhongshan, the act of living apart from one's sons is both a statement to the community that coresidence has not been working out and a means of compelling children to take equal responsibility for providing support.

The ultimate sanction a parent holds over a child's head is the threat or act of suicide. Margery Wolf (1975) was one of the first to note that between the 1920s and the 1960s the peak in female suicides in Taiwan had moved from the first years of marriage to old age, suggesting that the later stage of life had become the most stressful. Zhang (in Chapter 4) reports that between 1991 and 2000 nine elderly in Zhongshan committed suicide, but she suspects that the toll could be higher as elderly deaths are not usually investigated. Suicide functions as a sanction in two ways. First, according to Wolf, blame is assessed, and people, especially the deceased's natal kin, will want to know who is responsible, who drove the victim to take such a drastic step. Second, a suicide produces a vindictive spirit that will return to take vengeance on the person(s) responsible. More broadly, the ancestors will not be pleased that one of their own was so tormented that dying was preferable to living. Ancestors expect respect from their descendants and can make their displeasure known by inflicting disease or misfortune upon offenders. Under these circumstances the threat of suicide can be a powerful weapon.

Filial Piety: Why Is It Likely to Be Changing?

Researchers, policymakers, and advocates for the elderly generally assume that the practice of filial piety in East Asia is not what it used to be. We will not attempt here to assess the extent to which filial piety has or has not changed (nor the extent to which it will or will not continue to change); rather we will present the arguments used to explain why change is to be expected. These arguments variously emphasize population dynamics, "modernization," and the role of the state.

POPULATION DYNAMICS

According to projections of the U.S. Bureau of the Census (1999), between 1960 and 2000 the populations of China, Korea, and Taiwan doubled or nearly doubled. China's population grew from 650 million to 1.256 billion;

Korea's, from 24.8 to 47 million, and Taiwan's, from 11 to 22 million. More recently, however, the fertility rates in these locations have been declining as a result of both individual and state decisions to reduce births. Because Japan underwent its fertility transition earlier, between 1960 and 2000 its population increased by only one third, from 94 to 126 million. As a result of declining fertility, the average age of all these populations has been rising as the elderly (those 65 and older) make up ever larger proportions of the total population. Again, according to the U.S. Bureau of the Census (1999), in 1998 the elderly constituted 6.4 percent of the population of Korea; 6.6 percent of China; 8.2 percent of Taiwan; and 16 percent of Japan. As national averages these figures do not reveal the enormous variation within these countries in the geographical distribution of the elderly. For example, because of the greater success in enforcing the one child family policy in urban areas, China's cities have older populations than does the countryside. Shanghai, considered China's oldest city in terms of population structure, has become the national leader in developing innovative programs for older people. Yet because the Chinese population as a whole is largely rural, the great majority of the elderly actually lives in the countryside. In other countries, such as Japan, the rural population is older than the urban due to high rates of out-migration.

While the above figures on population change might not seem alarming—after all, several European nations have higher percentages of elderly than even Japan—they are alarming to policymakers for two reasons: (1) the rate of change, and (2) the availability of resources to cope with them. The proportion of the elderly in these East Asian populations will continue to grow. The U.S. Bureau of the Census (1999) estimates that by the year 2025 those 65 and older will account for 13 percent of the population of China, 16 percent of the populations of Taiwan and South Korea, and a colossal 27 percent of that of Japan. Chinese policymakers already worry about the future unintended consequences of the one child family policy, envisioning an inverted pyramid with eight grandparents at the top, four parents in the middle, and one adult couple at the base responsible for supporting them all. Japanese policymakers worry more about the shortfall in the labor force that could threaten its economy, already in a recession, and thereby the tax revenue on which support programs for the elderly depend.

Not only have the absolute numbers of elderly and their proportion of the total East Asian population increased, but the elderly are living longer than they used to as a result of improvements in nutrition, public health, and access to advanced medical technologies. In 2001, life expectancy at birth for females averaged 73.6 years in China; 78.7 in South Korea; 79.5 in Taiwan, and 84.1 in Japan. Male average life expectancies ranged from almost four years less than female in China to nearly eight years less in South Korea (Central Intelligence Agency 2001). More significantly, the life expectancy of people who have already reached 65 is also increasing as a look at the most longevous of our four populations, the Japanese, demonstrates. In 1995, the life expectancy of a 65-year-old Japanese woman was 21 years, that is, on average she could expect to live until 86, while that of a Japanese man was 16.5 years. By 2025, however, Japanese women who have reached 65 are projected to have a life expectancy of 23.2 while their male counterparts are projected to have a life expectancy of 18.2 (Calhoun 2001). Jenike (in Chapter 11) notes that despite evidence to the contrary the general perception in Japan is that women who have already reached these advanced ages are in poor health, and there is as yet no role for them.

Governments view the prospect of millions or even tens of millions of people in their 70s or 80s as highly problematic. Even if all work together, how can the state, society, and family possibly support such a large number of elderly whose needs for financial and medical assistance will strain entire economies? It is in this context that any faltering in the performance of filial piety is regarded as a disaster. Not everyone, of course, subscribes to an apocalyptic view of aging. In the United States, for example, most elderly live independently, managing their own affairs into their 80s. Far from being in poor health, they are providing care to others, volunteering, or otherwise contributing to their communities. However, the United States is an affluent society, and its population has aged more slowly than any of the populations under consideration here. This relative slowness has allowed Americans to recognize the desirability of accumulating resources for their own support in old age and has allowed federal, state, and local governments the necessary time to develop appropriate programs to assist not only elders but their family members who provide care as well.

In most of East Asia today the family remains the primary and sometimes the only resource on which the elderly may rely, but families are now being asked to provide care for much longer periods than was generally the rule in the past. Even if an elder is in reasonably good health, he or she might nevertheless require years of financial support (however modest), possibly leading to friction among descendants. When elders require not only financial support but also personal care, such as help with bathing, eating, and toileting, adult children and children-in-law, who themselves are often elderly, can easily become exhausted. Elderly who are immobile, incontinent, or severely impaired cognitively are highly susceptible to infections via bedsores and the respiratory and urinary tracts. In the absence of antibiotics, they would normally die from these infections in a few days, but with the advent and availability of antibiotics they can now overcome them. Antibiotics can preserve life, but at the cost of preserving also the state of immobility, incontinence, or cognitive impairment that contributed to the infection (and to likely future ones) in the first place.

"MODERNIZATION"

Modernization theory has been offered as an explanation for the presumed decline in the status of the elderly in their families and communities for decades (see, for example, Cowgill and Holmes 1972, and Goode 1963). As societies change from predominantly rural and agricultural to urban and primarily industrial, the elderly are said to lose a host of status-enhancing attributes. First, their land, the source of much of their influence over the young, is no longer the only means of gaining a livelihood. Young people may choose to migrate to work in factories in nearby towns or cities and live economically independent lives. Second, as literacy becomes widespread with the development of compulsory education, knowledge is no longer the special property of age, and the rural experience of the older generation becomes less relevant for solving the problems of urban life. Third, with urbanization young people are exposed to a broad range of ideas; they no longer have to accept uncritically the ideas and values of their parents, including ideas about the proper relationship between the old and the young. Fourth, physical separation of the home community and the workplace allows young people to escape the prying eyes of their neighbors and to evade gossip and other community-level sanctions should their behavior be found wanting. Fifth, the nuclear family comes to prevail over the extended family as young people become attached to the conjugal family of spouse and children at the expense of their relationship to their (distant) natal family of parents and siblings. Thus, ultimately, what began as a change in the mode of production ends in intergenerational estrangement or, at least, in a shift in relative advantage.

That modernization theory has an intrinsic popular appeal is manifested in two recent films produced in East Asia. In the first, *Shower*, produced in China in 1999, modernization is personified by the older son of the proprietor of an old-style communal bathhouse, who leaves his father and mentally impaired (but endearing) younger brother behind to seek his fortune in the Special Economic Zone of Shenzhen, an ultramodern metropolis in south China. Incorrectly believing his father has died, the older son returns to his crumbling neighborhood, soon to be demolished as it is on the planned site of a shopping mall, to arrange his father's funeral. The viewer soon learns that the old neighborhood and its engaged residents represent urban life in the recent idealized past when people understood the meaning of community and family. Although the father is gladdened by his older son's return, he is also ambivalent, sensing that he represents everything old and unglamorous that the son has rejected. Fortunately, though the father dies during his older son's visit, their relationship has been restored. The older son abandons plans to return to his selfish wife in Shenzhen and vows to look after his younger brother and keep the bathhouse open until the wrecking ball falls.

The second film, *Home Sweet Home*, produced in Japan in 2001, stars a retired opera singer who no longer has any role in either his family or society. He lives with his son and daughter-in-law above the son's small restaurant and has become a major burden to his family since he suffers from dementia and wanders. One day, in a physical struggle with his son, he accidentally knocks his son down the stairs, leaving his lower body paralyzed. As a result of this catastrophe, his son and daughter-in-law can no longer look after him. Then, in another modern version of the Obasuteyama story, the old man is dropped by one of his granddaughters in the dead of night on the doorstep of a home for the aged out in the countryside. Fortunately this is no ordinary home for the aged. It is operated by a very sympathetic proprietor who felt sorry for old people and decided to establish a home in the full sense of the term. Everyone has a role, and the residents support—and annoy—one another, just as in a real family. As the only male, the retired opera singer thrives under all the attention and appreciation he is given. When his guilt-ridden family members come to the home intent on bringing him back to live with them, they are amazed at his transformation. Witnessing this, his son admits that he has been transformed too. Sitting in his wheelchair, wondering whether there was any point to continuing his efforts at rehabilitation, he came to understand his father's sense of loss and disorientation. Seeing his father's recovery in this beautiful natural setting, he realizes that the competitive, self-aggrandizing lifestyle of the city is meaningless, that the real basis of life is caring and community. He will not return to his restaurant in the city; instead he will spend the rest of his life cooking wonderful meals at the home where his father is so comfortable. The failures (and eventual recoveries) in the father-son relationships depicted in these two films are emblematic of the dilemmas of modernization. How can a people modernize and yet retain the core values epitomized in filial piety that are so essential to national cultural identity?

Modernization theory has been critiqued on many grounds—that it is too simplistic; that it idealizes the past; that it overgeneralizes by failing to differentiate among the elderly, for example, the well-to-do versus the poor, the healthy versus the infirm, those with kin versus those without, men versus women; and that it fails to take into account the multidimensional nature of the concept of status. Modernization theory is revisited in Chapter 6, with Whyte directly tackling the question of the impact of modernization on the practice of filial piety in his comparison of China and Taiwan. The authors of the two South Korean chapters also consider the significance of modernization by concretely examining the economic and social changes in the communities they studied and linking them to the changes in the discourse and performance of filial piety.

THE ROLE OF THE STATE

The role of state policy in supporting or undercutting the practice of filial piety is considered in most of the chapters in this volume. In terms of official rhetoric, the governments of all of the societies under study here are firm supporters of filial piety, but of a much reduced version of it. The emphasis previously placed on obedience and the production of descendants as signifiers of filial piety has been nearly completely overshadowed by the emphasis on supporting elderly parents. This change is a direct consequence of government efforts to do away with the prewar family system.

Since the end of the Second World War, East Asian governments have utilized constitutional reform, legislation, and other means to replace the "traditional" family with a modern democratic one. The effort has been most extreme in China, which, under Chairman Mao, was determined to destroy the "feudal patriarchal family" with its age- and gender-based inequalities, but even the national governments of South Korea and Japan undertook constitutional and legal reforms aimed at democratizing the family, for example, weakening the power of the head of the household over the younger generation, modifying inheritance laws, and emphasizing love as the foundation of marriage and as the reason to have children. Fearful of runaway population growth that would compromise economic recovery and further development, governments promoted smaller families and made contraception and/or abortion readily available, thus weakening the filial motivation to reproduce. In China, of course, excess reproduction was (and remains) forbidden and penalized.

Traditionally, providing a grand funeral for one's parent was one of the most important public expressions of filial piety, but in all of the societies under study here grand funerals (among those who can afford them) have become more the exception than the rule. Secularization, migration, and five- and six-day work weeks have all intruded on the ability of families to assemble large groups of kin for extended periods. In Japan and South Korea, changes in funeral ritual have occurred more or less independently of any efforts by the state. In China, however, the state has for decades attempted, with particular success in the urban areas, to reduce the religious elements and economic display characteristic of traditional funerals. Unlike Japan, which has a thriving commercial funeral industry (Suzuki 2000), China even after more than two decades of economic reform has steadfastly maintained a state monopoly on almost all aspects of death ritual (corpse handling and transport, viewing and memorial service, cremation, and final disposition) in the urban areas. In rural areas, kin and neighbors remain the primary functionaries, and, though subject to certain restrictions, they have gradually restored some elements of the old-style funerals.

As discussed above, although specific state policies democratizing the family, reducing family size, and circumscribing death rituals have more or less restricted the practice of filial piety to providing support to elderly parents, other state policies, though not aimed directly at the family, have also had an impact on the ability of family members to provide such support. For example, governmental decisions to develop an export-oriented economy or to declare certain regions as suitable for industrial parks provide alternative employment for the young and encourage their migration. Decisions regarding pension eligibility and the nature of the calculation of pension payments affect the ability of retired workers to support themselves.

Decisions to offer (or withdraw) subsidized health care and medical insurance to workers and their dependents affect the costs of dealing with a parent's long-term illness. Similarly, housing policy and real estate pricing affect family decisions about the relative merits of coresidence. Most obviously, governmental decisions about whether, when, and how much they will encourage the development of programs and services that facilitate or complement family caregiving can be absolutely critical in determining how successfully families manage their filial responsibilities.

Filial Piety: How Is It Changing (or Not)?

Suicide was mentioned earlier as the ultimate sanction available to an aggrieved individual, young or old, in East Asia. For this reason a review of suicide rates in the societies considered here should shed light on the relative satisfaction of the elderly with their circumstances. Yow-Hwey Hu (1995) addressed exactly this issue, utilizing rates from the early 1980s for Japan, Singapore, Taiwan, and Hong Kong and comparing them with those from the same period for the United States, Canada, and five Western European nations. Three facts stood out: (1) the elderly (65+) in the Asian sites committed suicide at a rate triple (double in the case of Japan) that of the young (25–44), whereas in the Western sites the rates were just about the same; (2) although in all sites the rates of elderly females were lower than those of elderly males, in the Asian sites the gender disparity was minimal compared to the Western sites; and (3) the average of the rates of the elderly in the Asian sites exceeded the average of the rates in the Western sites by a factor of 2.5. Hu concluded that "suicide as an indicator does not support the orthodox supposition that the elderly in the East Asian system are better off than their more independent western counterparts" (1995: 203). Focusing on Taiwan and noting that rates were higher in rural than urban areas, Hu suggested that the configuration of the patrilineal family, with women receiving care from a daughter-in-law rather than a daughter, was a primary source of distress.

More recent data (from 1996–98) for China, Japan, and Korea (but not for Taiwan) are available from the World Health Organization (2001). Because the set of countries is different and the data are presented differently (in ten- rather than twenty-year intervals), direct comparisons with Hu's work cannot be made, but the findings are nevertheless supportive. First, suicide rates of the "young" elderly (aged 65–74) in all three countries are substantially higher than those of the young (aged 25–34): in China by a factor of 3.0 and in Japan and Korea by a factor of 1.7, with the "old" elderly (aged 75+) having even higher rates than those 65–74. Second, although in all sites elderly males have higher rates than elderly females, the relative differential is less than in most Western countries. Third, the elderly suicide rates in the three East Asian countries are generally two to three times higher than in the comparison Western countries (in this case the United States and Sweden). All of these findings are consistent with those of Hu. Furthermore, an analysis of the rural-urban differential among the elderly in China indicates that, just as Hu found in Taiwan, the rural rates are four to five times higher. Ji Jianlin (1999) notes that some writers attribute these high rates among the rural elderly to mental and physical illnesses, life crises, and social and economic problems. But Ji also believes that the breakdown in the rural health care system and in the traditional extended family make life extremely difficult and that the elderly who live alone, particularly men, simply cannot look after themselves.

Is the situation of the elderly as unbearable as these figures suggest? Is the practice of filial piety in contemporary East Asia "endangered" and perhaps facing extinction? Or do these figures represent only the most extreme cases? If so, what then are the experiences of ordinary elderly men and women in the villages and cities of East Asia? Are they hapless victims of their adult children or skilled agents crafting their own futures? And how do younger people view filial piety? Do they labor under the heavy burden of traditional expectations, including their own, or have they redefined the meaning of filial piety to fit the new social and economic realities? These are the questions addressed by the contributors to this volume.

CHAPTER I

Ritualistic Coresidence and the Weakening of Filial Practice in Rural China

DANYU WANG

The process of household formation for newlywed couples in rural China has changed drastically in the past fifty years. In the past, living with the parents and joining the parental household economy was a matter of course for newlyweds.[1] Since the 1980s, instead of pursuing the old ideal of a large complex household, rural families have turned to a new practice—early household division.

The practice of early household division is exemplified in the case of Lun of Stone Mill, a village in northeastern China where the research for this chapter was conducted. Lun is a typical young man who married in the 1990s. Upon his wedding, Lun's parents had prepared for him and his bride a separate housing unit of three rooms within the family house. The bridal room, which was festively decorated with red paper cutouts of the Chinese symbol for happiness, was set up in their new apartment by Lun's parents. Although they lived in their own apartment, Lun and his wife were not considered to have their own household before the formal household division. After the wedding, the couple ate at their parents' apartment, an important symbol that the couple were members of the parental household. A month after the wedding, Lun and his wife hosted a stove-warming party, which marked and celebrated the beginning of their new household. Unlike the traditional household division, which involved a complex division of the joint family property, this division simply served as a formal recognition of the conjugal assets—from large pieces of furniture and modern electric appliances to small items, such as utensils—that had been set aside for the newlyweds at the time of their wedding. (Examples of division contracts are presented in detail in the following chapter.)

In Stone Mill since the 1950s, the tradition of newlyweds settling in the parental household has gradually lost its status as a normative practice, and the once-cherished ideal of a multigenerational household has increasingly become a faded memory (Wang 2000a). Since the 1980s, an increasing number of newlyweds in Stone Mill have lived with their parents only for a very short time. In the 1990s, the majority of the newly married couples in the village moved out of the parental household within a year. The village of Stone Mill was not alone in shifting to a new practice of early household division. Ethnographic studies in villages in northern, central, and southern China (Cohen 1992, 1998; Harrell 1993; Johnson 1983; Judd 1994: 173–81; Parish and Whyte 1978: 131–34; Potter and Potter 1990: 196–224; Selden 1993; Danyu Wang 1999; Yan 1996: 176–209, 1997) have demonstrated the recent practice of early household division to be widespread. At the national level, demographic studies have shown a substantial decline in the duration of postmarital coresidence since the 1980s in many rural areas of China (Lavely and Ren 1992; Zeng et al. 1994). What was noticeably consistent in these radical departures from the custom of settling in the parental household was the retention of a short period of coresidence with parents after marriage. That this short coresidence lacked any real practical function or economic advantage revealed it to be primarily ritualistic.

Six decades ago, before the establishment of the People's Republic of China (PRC) in 1949, having generations of family members living under the same roof had been a symbol of social-familial success and self-fulfillment. Complex households were the embodiment of the sons' filial loyalty, as well as the family living regime in which filial practice could be carried out through everyday life. The understanding and practice of filial piety in contemporary rural China have changed substantially. With early household division putting an end to the old regime of practicing filial piety within the household, how did rural families find new ways to address and practice filial piety in this particular stage of family transition?

In this study, using the village of Stone Mill as an ethnographic case, I examine, in the context of the Chinese family tradition and the state's reformation of the family, the changing intergenerational dynamics of rural families, as well as their complex views on intergenerational relationships. Even though the ideal of filial piety has remained constant in a general sense, the means of achieving filial piety have changed in the postsocialist period. Rituals and ritualistic performance have been an important element of rural community life, especially where direct intervention from the state is weak. Ritualistic transitional postmarital coresidence is the new solution by which rural families reconcile filial piety in the ideal sense with the weakening of filial piety in practice. Living in the paternal household after marriage has thus been transformed from a customary stage of adult family life to a rite of passage in the household formation process.

Before proceeding to an analysis of filial piety in ritualistic coresidence, the following brief introduction to the village and my field research there provides the ethnographic and methodological context in which this study was developed. The village of Stone Mill is located in Dalian Prefecture, Liaoning Province, in northeast China. In 1997 Stone Mill was an average-size village, with a total population of 2,300 people and 730 households. The village is in a basin surrounded by hills, on which generations of villagers have planted fruit trees, raised livestock, and buried their deceased. A river passing through the village has provided the water with which villagers have irrigated their orchards and fields; on the banks of the river, women have washed clothes and exchanged neighborhood news. The hills and river are still there, and the rural way of living has remained; however, the village community has begun to change. Apples and other fruits have been the major source of income in Stone Mill, but during the 1980s and 1990s, villagers—especially young people—began to explore economic opportunities in urban areas. Since the 1980s, the younger generation has begun to bring back earnings as substantial as, if not greater than, those of their parents.

I went to Stone Mill in 1997 to conduct fieldwork, primarily on family change. I interviewed individuals of different ages and family backgrounds and of both genders who had had different family experiences in different historical periods. I also conducted a survey of 315 couples born after 1930 to collect information on family history and villagers' views of family life. In order to learn about the community, I interviewed individuals in the village who were knowledgeable in certain areas, such as local history and family rituals. While experiences and perceptions are limited by the individual's family experience and the time in which he or she lived, by interviewing a wide spectrum of individuals I was nonetheless able to gain a general understanding of cultural ideas about the family and changes in family customs. By collecting archival materials from various sources, including county annals (*xian zhi*), local newspapers, and folk literature, I situated individual cases and

Stone Mill as a whole within the political-cultural context of the Dalian region and the PRC state.

Navigating Tradition in Light of Family Life in the Past

Collective memories of local family lives, as well as classic Confucian discourses on the family, were the local cultural foundations on which Stone Mill villagers built their ideas of family tradition. In popular culture, filial piety, which had been the highest family value, permeated every corner of daily life and extended to the realm of rituals and ritualistic performance. Filial sons were generally defined as those who served their parents kindly and rightly when their parents were alive and observed the mourning rites when their parents died.

Among the paths to filial piety in everyday life, maintaining a multigenerational large household was one of the most important. Indeed, partitioning the parental household was socially disapproved of and was considered notoriously unfilial. The prevailing stigmatization of household division in many areas of China and the family pride gained from maintaining a multigenerational household (see, for example, Ahern 1973; Fei 1939; Freedman 1958) had once been everyday realities, and are still vividly remembered by elderly residents of Stone Mill. In leisurely chats and nostalgic recollections of the "good old days," older villagers have passed on stories of the past to the young. The following story told by an elderly man is one of the many family anecdotes that constitute the oral history of Stone Mill families.

> After years of hard work, my family was wealthy enough for my father and uncles to split the property and start their own households, but no one dared to propose this. Whoever caused the family partition won himself a bad reputation for breaking up the unity of the family. One would have to live with this bad reputation for the rest of his life. My father and my uncles, who were regarded in the village and in neighboring villages as obedient, filial sons, waited until a few years after the death of my grandparents in 1929. . . . The year when my grandfather died, the big poplar tree in front of our house suddenly fell down. Every event is foreshadowed by an omen sent to us by the heavenly god (*laotian*), and I believe the fall of the poplar tree was the sign for the splitting of the household. I also heard a similar story from elderly family members—that

one lunar New Year, the plate that contained buns served to our ancestors broke into four pieces. In that same year, my grandfather and his three brothers divided the household.

The social disapproval of family partitioning was strong in the area, such that this and many other oral histories of Stone Mill families have often emphasized various justifications (for instance, supernatural indications or family misfortunes) for the division of the household.

While men practiced filial piety by maintaining the unity of the parental household, women practiced it by helping their husbands fulfill their filial duties and by fulfilling their everyday duties as daughters-in-law. Daily household chores in complex households were tedious and never-ending, requiring round-the-clock compliance with filial codes. A local folk lyric, written as a dialogue between a young woman and her sister-in-law (her brother's wife), describes the local codes of women's everyday behavior.

. . .

When you get married and become a daughter-in-law,
Be submissive and well behaved.
Be able to weave and sew clothes.
Do not forget the three rules of obedience and the four virtues.[2]
Being filial to your parents-in-law is of utmost importance.
When you cook, ask your parents-in-law what dishes and soup they want.
When the meal is ready, you set the table.
Set up two pairs of sandalwood chopsticks for your parents-in-law.
When you serve the rice, serve it elegantly with the bowl eight-tenths full.
When you serve a dish, make sure you drain the extra sauce.
When your parents-in-law are dining, wait beside the table but do not join in
     their conversation.
When your parents-in-law finish their meal, hand over the mouth-wash soup
     right away.
Clear the dining table and serve cigarettes to your parents-in-law.
If your parents-in-law praise you, it is to the honor of us, your natal family, as
     well (Wang et al. 1987: 102).[3]

Detailed descriptions of housework etiquette not only instructed women how to serve their parents-in-law, but also prescribed ways of serving that manifested a daughter-in-law's filial respect for her parents-in-law. The practical end and ritualistic manifestation of a daughter-in-law's filial piety were thus intertwined in every detail of everyday life.

Indeed, serving parents in everyday life was considered merely ordinary and rudimental; it was not sufficient to establish one as a filial son or daughter-in-law, nor to express one's devout filial loyalty. Filial piety could only be eloquently, legitimately, and formally addressed through the performance of ritualistic acts (often involving physical suffering) or elaborate family rituals (for instance, death rituals). Family rituals occupied a significant position in the conception of filial piety. (See Chapters 5, 7, and 8 for further discussion of the importance of death ritual as markers of filial piety.) As addressed in the teachings of Confucius, "Today, when people call a man filial they mean that he is supporting his parents. But he does as much for his dogs and horses! If he does not show respect for his parents, how is he differentiating between them and the animals? . . . When the parents live, serve them according to the rites. When they die, bury them according to the rites and make the offerings to them according to the rites" ("As One Learns," see Ware 1955: 26, 22).

Through family rituals, such as mourning for deceased parents and providing splendid funeral ceremonies, sons demonstrated to the public their filial piety (Ebrey 1991: introduction; Kutcher 1999). This can be illustrated by the legend of three Stone Mill brothers told by an elderly villager.

> There used to be two kinds of funeral rites—the grand funeral rite, which lasted seven days, and the small funeral rite, which lasted three days. Average families usually observed the small funeral rite, whereas only rich families could afford to observe the grand funeral rite. In the early 1930s, three sons from a wealthy family held a splendid grand funeral for their father. They hired a band to play day and night for the mourners and for the funeral rituals. They provided one pig each day at the funeral feasts for the guests; even passersby and beggars were invited to join the feast. . . . After they buried their father, the brothers were broke. They had to sell their farms to pay for the funeral expenses. With almost no land left, they divided the household. It ended up that two migrated to the northern frontier in Manchuria and one migrated to a city to look for a job.

Public and ritualistic expression of filial piety could go to such extravagant lengths as to result in the depletion of one's wealth and the loss of one's socioeconomic status. Both in Confucian classics and popular culture, filial piety was supreme beyond any other social or political aspirations or obligations. The true practice of filial piety required giving up one's physical well-being, material interests, public obligations, and political ambitions when such sacrifices were required in order to serve one's parents. No doubt, traditional family culture had set a high standard for the performance of family duties, as well as a high family-based standard for judging the social achievements of every man and woman. This foreshadowed its repositioning in the new family regime as China began to transform itself into a modern nation-state.

The State's Promotion of the New Family Regime

Whereas the late imperial states and the Republican state officially supported filial piety and ancestral rites, the successor PRC endeavored to revolutionize them (see Kutcher 1999; Watson and Rawski 1988). The primacy of filial loyalty to parents was a threat to the integration of individuals into the political-economic system of the new socialist state; ancestor worship contradicted the state's demand for public belief in Communist ideology. Because of the drastic transition from an imperial state to a modern nation-state, it was imperative for the PRC to take a position on the traditional family regime, which it condemned as a feudal, patriarchal marriage–family system.[4] From the framework of the Marxist theory of social evolution-development, the state viewed peasant culture as backward, superstitious, and a living representation of the feudal past (Kipnis 1995). Consequently, it disapproved of a range of beliefs and practices, such as the kowtow, and regulated some family rituals, such as funerals and ancestor worship (see, for example, Kipnis 1995; Whyte 1988). Along the same lines, the state proposed to revolutionize the feudal patriarchal marriage–family system through socioeconomic reforms and legislation, as well as through the official cultural discourse.

In the PRC, the individual, and not the lineage, family, or father, was legally entitled to civil rights and was legally bound by civil obligations. Both civil law and marriage law clearly stipulated a person's right to decide on his/her marriage partner, a woman's right to property, and women's civil equality with men. In addition, in the last five decades a series of structural transformations in the family, mainly involving property ownership, household production, and wage labor, in response to state reforms and socio-economic development, such as land reform, collectivization, and globalization and marketization, have greatly influenced intergenerational relationships in rural China (Greenhalgh 1994; Parish and Whyte 1978; Wang 2000b; Yan 1996, 1997).[5] In northeastern China before the PRC, land, the most important family asset, was owned by the father and was the basis for the children's dependency on their parents. In the PRC, during the periods of both collective production (1950s–70s) and household farming (1980s–90s), land became the property of the collectives and was distributed to collective production teams or individuals by the state (through the collectives). Land is no longer the major component of family wealth or the basis for children's economic reliance on their parents. In addition, early household division has enabled children to acquire a substantial amount of parental wealth at the beginning of their marriage. While the younger generation has increasingly gained its socioeconomic independence at a younger age, the older generation has been economically depleted due to heavy expenses for its children (especially their weddings), being left with little or no savings by the time the children are all married. With no state retirement pension, social security, or savings, parents in rural China have had no other choice but to rely on their children in their old age. Parents have not only fallen into economic reliance on their children, thereby losing power and authority, but they also have begun to rely on their children for the fulfillment of their aspirations for the family, which is to live in a household surrounded by filial sons and daughters-in-law.

Even with the socialist revolution's goal of revolutionizing the feudal patriarchal family, the state's reformation of the family has been selective and sometimes contradictory. Scholars have argued that changes in the family and women's status in the PRC have not been what the state has claimed them to be (see, for example, Johnson 1983; Stacey 1983; Wolf 1985). In order to mobilize peasants to participate in political movements and socialist reforms during the period of collectivization (1950s–70s), the state even fell back on the patriarchal family ideology as a motivator (Stacey 1983; Wolf 1985). Similarly, various studies have confirmed both the improvement of women's family status and their return to traditional family roles in the post-socialist era (see, for example, Jacka 1997; Rofel 1999). Other scholars, examining changes in family organization and the household economy, have found both the continuation of tradition and significant change in the family in the (post)socialist state (Whyte 1992). Some elements of the traditional family system became targets for abolishment or reform, whereas others were left untouched or implicitly endorsed. Contradictions were brought about by the state's endeavor to dismantle the feudal family system on the one hand, and its reliance on traditional family relationships on the other. For example, the state took a strong stand against patriarchy and for women's liberation, while simultaneously enforcing filial respect and filial submission (*xiaojing, xiaoshun*) as family virtues.

It is worth noting that filial piety, the moral and political basis of the traditional family system, is not under direct attack in (post)socialist reforms or ideological discourse. The state has not directly regulated generational equality (vs. patriarchy) as a basic expression of its position on the equality of the individual. On the contrary, in order to compensate for the lack of social welfare and public services, the state has urged adult children (especially women as caregivers) to support their aging parents. It has reinforced, through official media, the renewed individual civil (and family) obligation to take care of elderly parents, and promoted the "socialist family virtues" of respecting, supporting, and caring for the elderly. Thus, among the traditional dual set of everyday and ritualistic filial behavior, caring for the elderly has in this way been elevated to be the primary traditional Chinese family virtue as well as a virtue of citizens of a socialist state. The story of Junqing, reported in a local newspaper under the title of "A Heart of Gold," is representative of the official promotion of modern virtuous women.

> In the summer of 1993, while Junqing was on maternal leave, her 75-year-old mother-in-law suffered a stroke. . . . In order to avoid having her husband be distracted by family problems, Junqing single-handedly took over the task of taking care of her paralyzed mother-in-law. Every morning, she got up at four o'clock to help her mother-in-law go to the toilet, eat breakfast, and take her medication. She then got her daughter dressed and prepared her breakfast and sent her to a neighbor for daycare. . . . In less than a month after her mother-in-law's stroke, Junqing lost a lot of weight, and the rheumatism she got after giving birth to her daughter got worse and worse. . . . Seasons came and seasons went, and two years later, because of Junqing's patient care, her mother-in-law was able to walk again. With a heart of gold, Junqing created a miracle that brought a glowing sunset in the life of her elderly mother-in-law. (*Dalian Daily*, July 29, 1997)

In promoting new family virtues, the state has drawn from and relied on the cultural tradition that underscores filial obligation to one's parents. The difference is that the traditional filial figures, like those in the well-known *The Twenty-four Tales of Filial Piety* who sacrificed their political careers and who were often males, are no longer in the forefront. Instead, much-feminized filial figures have emerged in the official discourse. In the official mainstream culture, the central concern of filial piety has been translated into the caring for and supporting of the elderly, in which women are the primary agents. The official representation of model women is molded on traditional virtuous women as wives and daughters-in-law. They are portrayed as women who compromised and sacrificed their own comfort and well-being to take care of aging or ill parents-in-law. These mass educational materials were aired through national and local television stations, and printed in national and local newspapers (for example, *People's Daily, Peasants' Daily, Dalian Daily*) and popular magazines (such as *Chinese Women*), which are readily available to average rural families.

Some other traditional family practices, including the custom of household division, were not actual targets in the state's program of reforming the family. However, they were indirectly influenced by the official discourse of the new family regime, as well as by structural changes in the family over the last five decades, as discussed above. Interestingly enough, although not surprisingly, the new custom of early household division has not appeared as "news" reported in local or national newspapers, nor has it drawn the state's approval or disapproval.[6] However, with decades of exposure to the state's influence, Chinese villagers have revised their vision of family relations and their sense of what "filial piety" ought to mean.

Conflicting Expectations

The complexity of state-initiated change in the family was echoed by similarly complex and conflicting expectations of intergenerational relationships found in Stone Mill, where both the young and old generation showed a strong consensus about the basic meaning of filial piety.[7] They agreed that children should show "filial respect and filial submission" to their parents. In gratitude to their parents for bearing and rearing them, children should repay their parents in every way possible. More specifically, children should care about their parents and treat them kindly; children should not dishonor their parents or make them unhappy.

Yet as villagers elaborated upon their expectations and interpretations of intergenerational relationships, it became clear that their concerns and opinions were sharply segregated by generation. Parents shared a common practical concern over being supported by their children, hoping that their children would provide them with food, clothing, and household necessities. Moreover, they hoped that their children would not make them unhappy by doing what they disapproved of or treating them in an unfilial manner. They typically hoped their children would not quarrel with them and would visit them regularly. The parents' expectations in receiving actual material support from their children proved to be modest. However, they were angry at and disappointed by the social messages sent through the poor parental support provided by their children—namely, that their children were losing the traditional virtue of filial piety. One parent remarked, "I don't complain if they cannot serve me delicious meals. As long as they give us the same kind of food they eat, instead of 'one family, two kinds of food,' I will be happy."

Along the same lines, parents were seriously concerned about their children's lack of submission and obedience to parental authority. Although arguments between daughters-in-law and parents-in-law, or sons and their parents, have become common in the village, they are still socially unacceptable. Any semblance of argument with one's parents was considered a public statement of one's disrespect and disobedience, which was definitely a humiliating blow to parental prestige.

While the older generation struggled to cling to the traditional standard, the younger generation's viewpoints diverged clearly from traditional ideas and echoed the state's promotion of the new family regime. The younger generation pushed for new intergenerational relationships in the hope that their parents, instead of giving them orders, would discuss family matters with them as equals. They strongly resisted absolute submission to parental commands and hoped that their parents would have some understanding of their concerns and difficulties. They also expressed the expectation that parents not interfere with their family lives, allowing them to be independent. The conflict between acknowledging the basics of filial piety and aspiring to a new mode of intergenerational relationship was expressed in the comment of a young villager:

Sons and daughters-in-law should have filial hearts. Our parents have done a lot for us and cared for us; we should do our best to let them not worry about us. We should be obedient to our parents and not make them angry. On the other hand, parents should understand us, and not overly interfere with our lives or meddle with our household matters. We should have our own minds because society is changing so fast, and we need to learn new things and adapt to the rapidly changing, modern society.

The discrepancy between the expectations of the two generations was striking—as the older generation strove to maintain the basics of filial piety, the younger generation pleaded for change. (See Chapter 10 for a very similar intergenerational debate in Japan.) Another discrepancy in the family life of Stone Mill villagers, as shown below, lies between the doctrine of filial piety and the weakening of filial practice in everyday life.

Weakening of Filial Practice in Everyday Life

The realization of the younger generation's aspiration for independence has been purchased at the price of the elder generation's failed expectations. For the older generation, parental domination and authority in deciding household matters has become a nostalgic recollection. Although memories of traditional family life still provide villagers a vision of what a filial son (or daughter-in-law) used to and ought to be like, everyday life in Stone Mill since the 1980s reveals a rather different picture.

In opposition to parents' desire for filial submission from their children, by the 1980s young people began to openly disobey parental orders or disagree with parental opinions. Various forms of confrontation with one's parents, such as arguing or retorting, used to be regarded as disobedient and ill-mannered. This perception has not changed, yet quarrels with one's parents have occurred more and more frequently and received very little social reprimand. Conflict between generations in Stone Mill, as well as in other Chinese villages (see Yang and Chandler 1992; and Chapter 4 in this volume), has revealed not only the tension between generations, but also the resistance of the younger generation to parental domination. Moreover, conflict publicly marked the young people's abandonment of absolute submission to parental domination in everyday practice. One mother-in-law in Stone Mill commented with bitterness,

In the seventies, many daughters-in-law fought with their parents-in-law. I heard my neighbors quarreling very often. Now early household division has "solved" the problem. Families are relatively peaceful again. But it is not that we don't have conflict anymore, but that they [daughters-in-law] don't have to encounter us [mothers-in-law] every day on every little thing. They live in their own house, and they go ahead and make their own decisions. We are no longer in charge of our daughters-in-law, as my mother-in-law used to be in charge of me.

The new custom of early household division is a significant change in the family that weakens filial practice and deals a deadly blow to the older generation's hope of having their family living under the same (that is, their) roof. Needless to say, socialist reforms and socioeconomic development have fostered the younger generation's desire for independence and generational equality. Moreover, dividing the household had been the means for the younger generation, especially daughters-in-law, to gain independence in family life in the past and it remains so in the present. Earning income on the basis of individual labor contributions during the collective period had begun to enable the younger generation to gain economic independence from their parents (Wang 2000a). Since the 1980s, vast wage labor opportunities, more lucrative than farming, have favored the young, who are better educated in marketable skills and of course physically more capable of hard labor than their parents. Young couples have thus transformed the power of economic independence into the power to gain family independence through separation from the parental household. The dream of generations of daughters-in-law for a household of their own has been realized; on the other hand the dream of generations of parents for a large household composed of filial sons and daughters-in-law has been lost.

In order to cling to the ideal of family unity and to keep children geographically as well as emotionally close to them, parents have made concessions to their children. In accordance with the practice of early household division, parents now build two-door houses to meet the expectations of their future daughters-in-law. As in other rural communities (Judd 1994; Potter and Potter 1990; Yan 1996), young women in this area have begun to consider the availability and quality of housing as a primary criterion for selecting a future husband. Since the 1980s, houses in Stone Mill have gone through a change as parents adjust to the new tradition of early household division. The style of houses has changed from the traditional complex, consisting of four surrounding row houses with one door and one common kitchen, to the new style consisting of a single row house with two doors and two separate kitchens. The old complex, which had six or more apartments, enclosed a family space in which daily activities—cooking, sewing, dining, child care, leisure activities (especially for women), and so on—were communal. The new row houses built during the collective period of the 1950s–70s omitted the side rows. The households of the parents and married sons divided the courtyard space into two sides, on which each household built its own pens for its domestic animals. The two households still shared the same gate and courtyard such that they had a common space for daily family activities and social life. The new two-gate row houses built after the 1980s, in contrast, prescribed not only socioeconomic division, but also the full separation of the living space of the two households. This new housing structure projects the reality of separate living right at the time of the wedding. The parental family has thus dispersed into several households and decentralized its socioeconomic activities into spatially segregated dwellings.

Living separately, however, has not changed the reliance of the older generation on the younger. This reliance is not only material, but also social and ideational in that everyday contact with their children is the embodiment of the older generation's aspiration for family unity. In an attempt to maintain the unity of the family in the age of early household division, members of the older generation have made efforts to reach out to their children—especially daughters-in-law. Similarly, mothers in other rural communities have adopted "the new uterine family strategies" of taking care of grandchildren or helping daughters-in-law with their household chores so that they can maintain the family bond with their children (Judd 1989, 1994: 192–202). In Stone Mill, what parents have done for their children has, to an extent, taken the place of what children were expected to do for their parents in the past. For example, raising sheep to provide the family with milk has recently become popular. One woman, Qiaoer, raised two sheep and provided sheep's milk to the family of her youngest son, who lived next door. However, this resulted in some friction with her older daughter-in-law, who lived elsewhere in the village. Later, when a lamb was born, Qiaoer gave it to her older daughter-in-law. Thus Qiaoer has not only helped both of her daughters-in-law, she has also managed to treat them equally and avoid angering either one.

In reflecting upon her family life, another woman, in her late 50s, revealed her concerns and dissatisfactions:

Nowadays, daughters-in-law are like our ancestors. My mother-in-law used to give me orders to cook delicious meals for her. I can hardly believe it, but the situation is reversed! Now when I have some good food, I've got to wait to share it with my son and daughter-in-law when they come to visit. I cook a big dinner now and then and walk over to their house to invite my son, his wife, and my grandchildren back home to have a family get-together. [She sighed] Sometimes, my daughter-in-law doesn't even feel like coming.

During this time, the idea that traditional modes of expressing filial piety should guide contemporary practice in Stone Mill was nearly subverted. Measured by the standard of filial piety teachings and family traditions in Stone Mill's past, the younger generation's performance was undoubtedly a great disappointment to their parents, a situation that also imposed further social pressure on young people themselves.

Saving the Filial Heart Through Ritualistic Coresidence

Indeed, both generations felt the tension between the reality of their everyday family life and the community's expectations of proper filial behavior. Members of the younger generation were eager to seek reconciliation between community expectation and their filial practice. Members of the older generation, although disappointed with their children, were also anxious to seek a remedy to compensate for their unmet expectations in everyday life and save themselves from being embarrassed by their children's lack of filial piety. Both generations yearned to bridge the gap between filial practice and filial expectation, thereby salvaging their belief in filial piety.

In discussing the invention of tradition in modern world history, Hobsbawm and Ranger commented: "It is the contrast between the constant change and innovation of the modern world and the attempt to structure at least some parts of social life within it as unchanging and invariant, that makes the 'invention of tradition' so interesting to historians of the past two centuries" (1983: 2).

The attempt to structure some parts of family life (such as postmarital coresidence) to maintain local tradition, the goal of Chinese peasants, has been of considerable interest to observers of Chinese society. In examining the new popularity of old customs and rituals in many local communities after the 1980s, some scholars have noted the restoration of ritual practices as the revival of tradition after the cultural repression of the socialist era (see, for example, Potter and Potter 1990); others have emphasized that the "recycling" of tradition involved the renewed use of local customs to adapt to the new socioeconomic conditions brought about by the reforms after the 1980s (see, for example, Siu 1989a, b). Still others have pointed out that by restoring tradition (for instance, the kowtow), Chinese peasants intended to make a statement about their peasant/Chinese tradition and to resist the mainstream representation of peasants as feudal and backward (Kipnis 1995). These studies provide empirical evidence that in the Chinese context the (re)use of old customs involved various cultural and political processes, and that rituals were an important medium of local community life.

In fact, studies of imperial China and the PRC have demonstrated the importance of local mechanisms (for instance, "informal justice," Huang 1996: 51–75; and "a rule of rituals," Fei 1992: 94–100) in maintaining social order and enhancing the political-cultural regimes of the local community (Dean 1997; Fei 1992; Huang 1996; Madsen 1984, 1990). More specifically, rituals and ritualistic actions are an important and expressive idiom of Chinese culture; they give voice to one's identity, political stance, and emotions (Potter and Potter 1990: 180–95; Zito 1997). In the past, for commoners such as those in Stone Mill and imperial rulers alike (see, for example, Rawski 1988a), performing rituals had been an effective medium for addressing one's filial piety, and therefore legitimately establishing one's identity as a filial son (and thus a ruler of the state in the case of emperors). In the 1990s, when the everyday practice of filial piety in the traditional sense was in crisis and when there was a lack of direct state intervention in this issue, a ritualistic approach to filial piety became especially important to families in Stone Mill.

The problem of not meeting the standard of filial piety, which has created social-moral pressures for both generations, is compounded by the implicit family disintegration at the marriage of the son because of the practice of early household division. Thus coresidence as a symbol of family unity has become salient as well as critical in this particular stage of family transition. Marrying in the parental home assured the membership of the bride in the parental family and established the fact that the newlyweds' family life started from within the parental household. Moreover, marriage involved the incorporation of a new member (the daughter-in-law) into the family and the creation of a new family unit. As the family was at the stage of incorporating a new member (the bride) and a new conjugal unit, living together symbolized the family's continuing unity and the young couple's filial loyalty to the parents. These cultural connotations of coresidence were implied in the postmarital arrangement in the pre-PRC period. However, they were enhanced by a longer duration of coresidence and were not threatened by the lack of filial practice in everyday life. The conventional celebrations of lifecycle transformations (for instance, weddings and funerals) at times of family (re)integration have traditionally served as public statements and affirmations of one's filial piety. Now the rapidly accelerated separation of the newlyweds from the parental household has endangered the sociocultural significance of coresidence. As a result, there has grown a need for a ritualistic expression of one's filial loyalty to satisfy the family as well as the community at the very beginning of the new conjugal union.

The practice of temporarily living in the paternal household with no intention of forming a collective household economy is ritualistic. Although the villagers of Stone Mill have not identified it as a ritual, the ritualistic quality of postmarital coresidence became overt when the duration of coresidence declined sharply from as long as several decades to as short as several days. The ritualistic aspect is particularly manifested among couples who have planned to settle in a different place within or outside the village. These couples set up their fully furnished bridal wedding rooms in their parents' houses as if they were to live with them, yet move to the new location within a week or a month after the wedding.

In fact, postmarital coresidence, which symbolizes the newlyweds' membership and unity with the parental family, has never disappeared. As villagers have expressed it, "it just would not look good or feel good" if the couple did not marry in their parents' household. As one villager elaborated, "besides, if the couple didn't live with their parents, neighbors would say the family did not get along, and the family would lose face." It would be a shock to the village community and a shame to the family if the newlyweds did not live with the parents for a least a few days. As reviewed earlier in this chapter, nationwide statistics as well as ethnographic studies in many areas of the country have all demonstrated the remarkably shortened, yet persistently practiced, period of living in the paternal household. For the younger generation, a ritualistic coresidence has become an important medium whereby they can make a statement about their filial piety that they otherwise would fail to make in everyday life. For the older generation, this short period of living together allows them to maintain their "face" and prestige as respected parents and to celebrate filial piety.

At the birth of the new conjugal unit, a temporary period of living in the parental household has become a solution to dilemmas in rural family life. The disappointment of parents in their children has been redressed; the filial piety of the young couple has been addressed and expressed; and the shared belief in filial piety of both generations has been sustained and celebrated—all in a ritualistic manner.

CHAPTER 2

Filial Daughters, Filial Sons: Comparisons from Rural North China

ERIC T. MILLER

Old Age in Rural China

In the face of a rapidly aging population of staggering size, the Chinese government is continuing to place primary responsibility for care of the aged on adult children. Because of the Confucian tradition of filial piety and the ideal of family members living together in intergenerational households, many consider the family to be the culturally appropriate locus of care for the aged. This arrangement is viewed as especially true for rural China, which is thought to hold to more traditional values than urban China and where only a small minority of people receive pensions. At the same time, due to the birth-planning policy, often misnamed as the "one child policy," the aged of China's future will rarely have more than one son, and many families will have no sons, but only daughters or no children at all.[1] Though traditionally daughters were not responsible for the support of their birth parents, under current legislation daughters share responsibility equally with sons for the support of their parents in old age. This chapter examines the nature of support provided to aged parents by sons and by daughters in rural China through a case study of Lijia, a village in central Shandong Province where I lived and conducted fieldwork from autumn in 1997 to near the end of 1998.[2]

There are three major types of support provided by children: that provided by sons who have brothers, that provided by sons without brothers (referred to in this chapter as "only sons," though they are not necessarily only children and may have sisters), and that provided by daughters. Support by brothers and by only sons is characterized by the fact that it is expected and discussed publicly. Such public discussion helps to ensure that sons will indeed provide support. At the same time, however, it sets not only the minimum level of support but also tends to set the maximum. Support by brothers is usually detailed in family division contracts, while that provided by only sons and by daughters is not. These contracts serve to ensure not only that support will be given, but also that it will conform to and not exceed the requirements written in the contracts. Support given by daughters is neither contracted nor expected. Daughters may provide nothing for their parents or may give gifts exceeding the support given by their brothers. Besides the nature of the sibling set, location of residence is another major factor determining support. Children living within the village or in nearby villages often give valuable assistance to parents in the form of services. Daughters who live nearby often contribute significantly to the care of frail and ailing parents. Children who live in towns and cities, on the other hand, are usually able to provide considerably greater financial support.

The strength of traditional ideals of filial piety and support for parents cannot be taken as a given in rural China. Shandong is the birthplace of Confucius, and so I arrived naively hoping that the influence of Confucianism would be stronger there than in other provinces and might be reemerging more visibly in the post-Mao era. Yet there was little evidence of a reemergence in the area of Lijia. Lineage temples had not been rebuilt, unlike in Gansu Province, as Jun Jing reports (1996). Nearby mountains that were named for temples now had only empty slopes; I once saw columns from one former temple that had long since fallen into disrepair being recycled to construct new buildings. Not that filial rituals had vanished. Sacrifices were made at ancestral graves on holidays and death anniversaries, and they were performed openly by everyone, including village leaders, and were shown in local and provincial television reports and in magazine articles about my research. Ritual specialists were few in number, though one villager was well read in traditional practices and had a genealogy stashed away that survived the fires of the Cultural Revolution. Pictures of the stove god and Buddhist deities were present, and people spoke of occasional trips to sacred Mount Tai, perhaps as tourists, but undoubtedly as pilgrims as well. The traditions are by no means dead, but lack the depth and richness seen in some other regions (Watson and Rawski, 1988). The most visible religion in the area, after grave sacrifices, was Christianity, to which about 8 percent of the population subscribed. A Catholic missionary had established a church in the village before the People's Republic was founded, and a new Protestant church had recently been built atop a nearby hill. Christian converts often clashed with family members when they refused to participate in sacrifices to the ancestors, but considered themselves filial, since Christians are to "honor their father and mother." There was, then, some ritual support for filial piety, but less ideological support. Villagers tended to view filial piety in practical, not theoretical, terms. During the Cultural Revolution of the 1960s and 1970s, the idea of filiality was attacked as feudal, but has since been rehabilitated.

Filial piety is viewed as a virtue that will help avert a crisis in eldercare and serves current government policies of relying on families to provide for the aged. Also it is highlighted as an aspect of Chinese uniqueness that distinguishes China from other socialist states and from developed nations. Traditionally in China, strong lineage organizations, marriage and funeral rituals that emphasized family hierarchy, laws, and the ownership of property contributed to the power of elders over their children and encouraged support of aged parents (see especially Ahern 1973; R. Watson 1988). As pointed out by Deborah Davis-Friedmann (1991), the position of the aged continued to be quite strong throughout the early Maoist period and into the reform era that followed Mao's death. While communism attacked Confucian ideologies and land was collectivized, the aged were given a place within the community, and their contribution of work points and childcare to the family made it difficult to ignore their needs later. After the disbanding of the collectives that followed Deng Xiaoping's rise to power, the position of the aged in the 1980s remained strong largely because of general economic improvements in the countryside (Davis-Friedmann 1991). However, as overall wealth increases, the contributions of elders to the family income usually become less significant while at the same time the costs of supporting them, especially if they require medical care, increase. In Lijia the levels of wealth are still insufficient to prevent the costs of supporting an aged parent from being a burden to most families.

Although children, including daughters, are mandated to support their parents in old age in China, the main incentive in the village for sons to provide support is social and cultural, not legal. While filial piety is part of this mix, definitions and expectations of filial piety have changed through time and vary from place to place across China. Daughters are not expected to support parents, but the villagers of Lijia feel that it is morally imperative that sons support parents when parents are no longer able to care for themselves. Reasons people give that sons should support parents differ, but the first reaction is often that it is simply the way things should be. The support of parents by their sons is a cultural norm, and it is often accepted without further justification as natural and right. Sons are in many cases the only source of support people can expect to have in old age, and for this reason people prefer to have sons rather than daughters. Yet they feel that daughters can be filial, and daughters do, in fact, often provide significant support for parents. Pushed to give a deeper explanation, villagers would often point out that support of parents is appropriate reciprocation for the raising of the sons. "I took care of them when they were children, they will take care of me when I am old." They do not apply the same logic to daughters. Although most villagers said that the filiality of daughters was the same as that of sons, they did not feel that daughters had an obligation to support them in old age. Filial piety itself was not the first reason villagers would give that sons should support parents, but it was an idea many would bring up after further questioning and thought. Filial piety is the virtue of reverence of the father by the son which was advocated by Confucius and succeeding generations of literati as the quintessential virtue upon which all others were modeled. Traditional concepts of filiality often included ideas of unquestioning obedience. To the people of Lijia, though, filiality has been distilled to its barest essence. It is about immediate needs and relationships. When applied to sons, filiality is primarily about support. Additionally and when applied to daughters, filial piety is about visiting parents on holidays and bringing gifts. It is also about not creating conflict in the family.

While it might seem evident that a concept of respect for elders would be clearly beneficial for the aged, filial piety is played out in specific ways in rural China that defy the expectations of Westerners, urban Chinese, and even the villagers themselves. Anthropologists often point out that there is nothing essential about anything. Filial piety does not exist in a platonic world of the ideal, ever untouched, but rather exists in the ideas of the villagers, their memories, and relationships. When I came to Lijia Village in 1997, I was in part looking to discover what this concept meant in the lives of the people of one village. Though I knew in theory that filial piety did not mean that the lives of China's elders are always ideal, especially in contemporary China, I was nonetheless struck by how marginal the lives of the aged often seemed in the village. Even physically, the aged in Lijia often lived off to the side of a household, or alone on the edges of the village. (See Chapter 4 for further observations of the marginality of the rural elderly.) In most cases, they took turns living with different sons, changing every six months or every year. (See Chapter 3 for a contrasting situation with regard to rotation of the elderly among their sons' households.) Filial piety continues to be or is once again important in structuring intergenerational relationships in Lijia, but it is not the most important factor.

This filial piety of Lijia contrasts sharply with the ideal filial piety of the Confucian *Liji*: "On getting where [the parents] are, with bated breath and gentle voice [the son and his wife] should ask if their clothes are (too) warm or (too) cold, whether they are ill or pained, or uncomfortable in any part and if so they should proceed reverently to scratch the place. . . . In bringing them the basin to wash . . . they will beg to be allowed to pour the water" (Legge 1885: 62). In a nearby town, a temple immortalizes a filial daughter-in-law who, braving the dangers of bandits and wild animals, endured great hardship by going to a distant well to bring back water. As a reward for her selflessness, a spring suddenly issued forth near her home, at the site where the temple now stands.

In Lijia, people are aware of such lofty examples of filial piety, and nearly all believe that it is important, but they define it much more modestly. As they describe it, the filiality of sons is simply to provide basic support and to not create conflict.

Lijia Village and Its Elders

Lijia is located in central Shandong, in Zouping County, far from the province's coasts. It is nestled at the foot of a small mountain at the opposite end of the county from the Yellow River. It is not representative of villages in other parts of China, or even other parts of the township, as I was to discover, but it is possible to identify the sources of Lijia's differences. The way the aged are cared for in Lijia and the role that filial piety plays in specifying that care can be understood as the result of broad social and cultural forces enacted in a specific context. The village is not especially wealthy for the county or the province, though it is in one of China's wealthiest provinces. Due to its mountainous location, the village is exempt from the normal requirement to produce grain. Instead, the villagers raise fruit: primarily apples, peaches, and grapes, and purchase grain to pay the tax. Most villagers still spend the majority of their time and earn most of their money in agriculture. Since the paving of the road leading to the village in 1992, the village government has created two village-owned enterprises, but these have met with only limited success. A small factory to produce woven plastic bags had been shut down while a stone works continued to employ fifteen people. While I was in Lijia, profits were down, and the village was looking for alternative ways to earn money. Where successful, such village-owned enterprises are the main source of income for the village government and for social services. As a result of the poor performance of its enterprises, Lijia provided very little for the aged, unlike nearby villages with stronger enterprises. Those villages were able to offer such benefits to the aged as housing and stipends for the childless, a cash gift annually on Old Persons' Day for everyone over sixty, and a commons room for the elderly to gather in and play chess in bad weather. Village enterprises can also greatly enhance the status of elders by providing pensions to retired workers.

Another difference from other villages in the township is that Lijia had few entrepreneurial families. Older people who had established successful businesses were able to pass on a significant inheritance to their children and to greatly increase both their children's indebtedness to them and obligation to support them. Unlike Lijia, other villages also allowed the building of two-story homes. Parents would build these homes then live on the ground floor while a son's family lived on the second floor. Lacking two-story homes, the elders of Lijia had to cede their homes to one of their sons. They themselves would move into a side room of the house and often would rotate between the homes of the sons. The aged were spatially marginalized, and no longer had homes of their own. Lijia's lack of entrepreneurial families and the village policy limiting houses to one floor of a standard-sized lot also greatly affected the lives of the village aged, mostly by limiting their contributions to the household, and, therefore, their power within it. Across China, villages are more likely to be like Lijia in their lack of successful entrepreneurial families and village enterprises than like Lijia's more successful neighbors.

Traditionally land was the most valued resource. In China today most, if not all, villages lack privately owned land, thus eliminating a potentially powerful bargaining chip that elders could use to encourage children to be filial. Emily Ahern (1973) reports that inheritance of land was sometimes taken away from children who gave inadequate support to parents. Instead, people would give land to their other children. In Lijia, parents may pass responsibility for fields over to children or continue farming it themselves, but they cannot pass land on to their children, nor can they establish larger holdings. While parents remain alive, sons may take over the task of farming their responsibility lands, but after the parents die, the land is returned to the village to be reallocated to others. As noted, the ability to pass on to children the control of family enterprises, which have begun to spring up in China over the past two decades, creates in the children a greater sense of indebtedness and gives the parents at least some bargaining power. Wealth generated by the senior generation can also be parlayed into greater influence in old age. Villagers in Lijia who had retired from state-run enterprises included a retired banker, a postal worker, a naval officer, and six men who had worked in a Tianjin factory. These individuals did collect pensions, were more likely to continue to live in the main room of the house, and expressed greater satisfaction with their children and with the quality of their lives. Most did not, however, receive any financial support from their children and noted that their pensions were more than adequate. Several of those who received pensions actually gave money to their children, and one contributed to his grandson's schooling.

Theoretically, it could be argued that support of elders would be better in China's rural areas than in its cities because people are more traditional and have been less influenced by modernization and cultural forces that would tend to elevate the status of the young (Counts and Counts 1985). In reality, the lack of economic resources seems to have resulted in a lower status for the aged in rural China. Another indicator of the lack of power of Lijia's elders in family relationships was the frequency with which elders indicated that they preferred the independence and freedom of eating apart from children or in some cases even living apart in separate housing. A few elders lived in small homes built on the families' responsibility lands. These were technically not regarded as homes, but as shacks built for "watching the fields." A small number of the aged lived in them during the summer or year-round. People under the age of sixty never lived in them. While these elders appeared on the surface to be the most marginalized in the village, and others at times pointed to them as examples of people whose children were unfilial, all indicated that the move to the fields was their own preference. This arrangement was a way of living their lives on their own terms. They expressed this in concrete terms, noting that they could come and go as they pleased, eat what they wanted and when they wanted, and throw trash, seeds, and cigarette ashes on the floor without being bothered. (See Chapter 4 for similar statements by rural villagers from another province.)

Lacking power, the elders of Lijia had little basis for demanding filial behavior from their children. Lacking resources, however, they were at the same time very dependent on the support of their children. As a result, Lijia's elders had to do what they could to ensure that children would provide at least adequate support. Part of this strategy was to not ask for too much, and many elders expressed a reluctance to bother their children with their needs and instead to be grateful for whatever support and gifts they did receive, however minimal. Others took to criticizing the inadequacy of support their children gave them. Because the law mandates support, it was possible to appeal to the village leaders. The assistant village head told me that this did sometimes happen, but explained that people rarely asked for such help because it would be embarrassing to admit family problems to others. Also, he said that such cases were not always decided in favor of the elders. The parents may not feel that they were receiving enough money, he explained, but as long as the village committee felt that it was adequate to meet the basic needs of the individual and fulfilled the terms of the family division contract, they would do nothing. Even if they did intervene, it was only to mediate and try to persuade the children to fulfill their obligations.

Sons Versus Daughters

Most people agreed that sons were the best source of support in old age. Many added that more sons were, of course, better. I spoke with one woman who was, by this measure, quite fortunate; she had four sons. She told me that she wished she had had daughters instead.

"My sons," she said, "are useless."

"Are they filial?" I asked.

"Oh, yes," she said, "but they don't do anything for me."

"But they give you grain, coal, and spending money?" I prodded.

"Yes, but I'd prefer to have daughters."

Here was a woman who seemingly had achieved the ideal, yet she believed she would be better off with daughters even though her sons lived up to the local standards of filial piety. They provided basic support, paid her medical bills, and did not argue. Most people treated similarly by their sons expressed satisfaction. There was no evidence, however, that people with several sons were actually better off than people with fewer sons or with no sons at all.

Daughters, however, marry out. Echoing people elsewhere in China, the residents of Lijia often asked me rhetorically, "What good are daughters, they will no longer be at home?" In spite of this, they believe that daughters can also be filial and that filial piety is the same for daughters as for sons. Closer questioning revealed, however, that, unlike sons, daughters are not expected to provide support. To be filial, daughters need only visit sometimes and not bring conflict when they do. The key difference between filial sons and filial daughters is that of support. Sons must provide support; daughters are not required to do so. Daughters may, however, give substantial gifts, provide loans, or offer help with work or care for a sick parent.

In interviews, it was difficult to determine the value of gifts given by daughters. People stressed that these gifts were optional. When asked how much money daughters gave them, they would say "It's not 'how much'— they just bring a little." In contrast with support and gifts from sons, people were generally reluctant to discuss support of this kind. One woman waited until after the interview had concluded to lean towards me and whisper, "Actually, my daughter gives me more money than my sons." In cases where people did express an amount, however, the amount given by daughters often exceeded the amount given by their brothers. In a village where cash allowances given to parents by sons averaged 5 yuan a month, a cash gift of 200 yuan from a daughter was quite large, especially if repeated on two or three occasions during the year. The few yuan they receive each month from sons does not go far, especially for those who like to buy treats for grandchildren or cigarettes and liquor for themselves. Most of the elders expressed a lack of interest in such things, and many pointed out that old people do not smoke or drink, but those with pensions indulged in such things daily. Generally individuals who had only daughters also expressed satisfaction with their situations. One very real benefit for the sonless in Lijia is that they would continue to have their own home, while those with a son would have to turn over control of their home to one of their sons.

Family Division Contracts: Support by Sons

The support of sons differs from that of daughters in another important way: it is documented in the family division contract. Family division contracts have a long history in China, as described by Myron Cohen (1976, 1998), Reginald Johnston (1986), and David Wakefield (1998). The contracts of Lijia demonstrate characteristics similar to those of northern China in the post-collective era described by Cohen (1998). Most significantly, property is divided equally between sons, rather than giving preference to the eldest son. Also, the contracts reflect the fact that a new house is expected to be built for a newly married son, as noted by Cohen (1998). All married couples in Lijia without married children are entitled to a plot for a house, which is usually built some time after they are married. During my field research, I was able to collect a sample of fourteen household division contracts from randomly selected households. I requested contracts from twenty-five households randomly chosen from the household register. Eleven of the twenty-five households did not have a contract either because they had no more than one son or a contract had not yet been drawn up. These contracts were drawn up over two decades, from 1975 to 1994. In most cases, these contracts are drawn up when the eldest son marries because each married son is entitled to his own 16- by 14-meter lot for building a house. One of these plots is the home belonging to the parents and is usually given to the youngest son. In drawing up the contracts, fathers would often point to their increasing frailty and inability to manage family affairs as the main reason for the division. The economic forces pushing for division differ markedly from those noted by Cohen in Taiwan (1976), but the basis of the decision appears to be practical and economic as in Taiwan. The support of only sons in Lijia is usually not contracted since the family is not divided. In interviews, I asked whether the family had divided. Those who were only sons or had only one son would usually respond with the question, "Divide with whom?" In fact, only one of the fourteen contracts in my sample is between a father and his only son. Likewise, those with more than one son usually do write a contract, but not always. In this regard, only sons are more like daughters, though unlike daughters they are still expected to provide support for their parents. The division contract was normally seen as a division between sons, not between generations, though in fact the parents would form their own household as a result of the division.

All contracts in the sample deal with the division of the household itself. Most concern themselves with care for the parents including food, coal, and medical fees; who will take over the responsibility for the parents' responsibility and leased lands, and debts; and the division of the parents' furnishings and tools. Notably absent is any division of the parents' money. Contracts also often deal with who will be responsible for costs of marriages and building houses for younger, unmarried brothers.

Family contracts were often mentioned in interview questions about support for the aged. While all contracts address care for parents, however, they do not necessarily focus on it. The main purpose of the contract is to establish an equitable agreement between sons. In general, all property, debts, and responsibility and contract lands are divided equally between sons in these contracts. While most define support for the parents in detail, one of the sample contracts puts off most aspects of care for elders to the future: "The [eldest son] will give mother and father 300 jin of wheat and 1,000 jin of coal. While they are able to work, they will pay other fees by themselves. When they can no longer work, we will make another agreement."

Li Qi, a native of Beijing who helped me decipher the handwritten contracts, commented that if she were one of the parents in this contract, she would not have signed the document.[3] Another contract also clearly focuses elsewhere than on the care of the parents. It concludes with this line: "Important: The courtyard wall will be used by mother and both households. When mother dies, the wall will be used by Yuzhou," reiterating a division described at the beginning of the contract. The fact that these contracts are drawn up between sons does not, thereby, render them irrelevant with regard to care for parents. After all, to a certain extent the support of elders is dependent upon a harmonious relationship between sons. The contracts minimize chances that a son will feel slighted in the distribution of property or saddled with an unfair share of responsibility for parents. Clear, written agreements can make it less likely that the parents will become entangled in a future dispute between sons. Also, parents do sign these contracts and may enter into the negotiations to a greater or lesser degree to ensure that the provisions for care are at least adequate to their needs or wishes. The care outlined in all cases is modest, and the amount of money received monthly from sons in the contracts is 10 to 40 yuan per month compared to 50–200 yuan per month from pensions.

As noted, where care for parents is discussed in detail, the purpose is to set up equal support by all sons. In one of my earliest examples, a contract signed in 1975, care for the mother is outlined in more detail than in later contracts:

> Every year, each son will bring mother two carts of coal, each cart being on average not less than 400 jin. If mother does not want it, they do not need to bring it, but they should still offer. Each son's family will pay for the coal themselves.
>
> Mother will pay for cloth for her clothes herself. The sons' households will share mending and washing her clothes. Every year, the two households each will give mother two pairs of summer shoes and will each give her one pair of winter shoes. The two households will be equally responsible.
>
> The money from the brigade's forest will be enjoyed by mother while she is alive. After she dies, the two households will divide it equally.
>
> Every year, mother will dry sweet potatoes. When she cannot do it anymore, the two families will share drying them.

More recent contracts are less detailed and often focus only on material support for the parents. Today the old women are more likely to make shoes and clothes for themselves. Here is an example from 1984:

> Care of parents: The parents' land will be tended equally by the two brothers. Costs for medicine and other fees and taxes will also be divided equally. Every year, each son will give the parents 250 jin of wheat and 800 jin of coal. Every month, each son will give the parents 2 yuan of spending money, which will be increased to 5 yuan in 1990.

This contract is unusual only in having a built-in increase in the amount of money given. Later contracts do not offer labor for parents such as making and washing clothes. Later contracts also usually specify that children will divide their parents' medical costs. In most cases, division of support is strictly equal in contracts from both the 1970s and 1980s. In one case a son who lives outside of the village is not expected to contribute foodstuffs, but is required to make up for it with an equivalent cash payment.

The above examples also indicate economic changes. In the 1975 contract, individuals were allocated a share of income from the collectively held and farmed lands. By the end of the decade, land was instead allocated to each individual under the responsibility system. Parents would at some point turn over this land to one or all of their sons who would then benefit from this land as long as the parent lived. As indicated earlier, at that point the land would revert to the village to be turned over to others.

Following is a translation of the entire text of a division contract that contains the standard elements of contracts written after decollectivization:

Division Contract A

Wang Zhaomin, because he is weak and he has no strength to manage the affairs of the family, has agreed with all the members of his family and with the village committee that his four sons, Yucai, Yuhe, Yushui, and Yujin, will live separately. It has been agreed as follows:

Care for the parents: Starting in 1993, the three brothers except Yucai will each give the parents 10 yuan each month. Each year, they will give 1,000 jin of coal for the parents' use. If mother or father becomes sick, the four brothers will share the expenses. Before Yucai marries, the parents will live in his home. Afterwards, the four brothers will all be responsible for the parents' residence.[4]

Division of property: Whatever is in the rooms will stay in the rooms. There will be no other change. Father's lease fee for the orchards will be divided equally by the four brothers starting in 1992.

We write this so it will not be empty words.

Division Contract B, below, is also fairly basic, but includes a bit more detail and deals with the fact that the home allocated for one son has not yet been built. It also has some elements unique in the sample:

Division Contract B

Li Lihua

Because of advanced age and my inability to manage household affairs, all the members of my family have made this agreement along with the brigade and team leaders. I would like to live separately and independently from my eldest son, Li Lihou, and second son, Li Limei. This has been agreed upon as follows:

1. Division of the house: It is decided that the north five rooms of the new house all go to the oldest son, Li Lihou. The old rooms will be divided equally by the two brothers. Before we build a new house for Limei, the parents and sisters will continue to live where they are now. There is no reason the oldest son could find to not let us live there. After Limei builds the new house, mother and father can live where they choose. The brigade and team have the right to intervene.

2. Care for the elders: We have decided that the parents' responsibility fields will be farmed by the brothers. Each person will give the parents 300 jin of wheat and 200 jin of maize each year. It is up to them to decide how much of other kinds of food to give. After Limei marries, each month each son will give the parents [unreadable] yuan and each year give 500 jin of coal in addition to the grain. For everything else the brothers will be responsible equally. The leased orchards will be as agreed upon; for thirty years they will be held completely by second son Li Limei, and Li Lihua will pay the fee for it. When Limei builds a new house, Lizhun is not responsible for anything but should contribute 300 yuan. When younger sister marries, the brothers will equally pay the expenses [of the wedding], and they will equally share the gifts received.

3. Division of other property: The trees in the old house will go to second son Limei. The trees at the new house all go to Lihou. The lumber all goes to Limei. The furniture and tools can be divided by the brothers by agreement. We write this so that it will not just be empty words.

In this contract, the reference to the brigade and team's right to intervene and to the eldest son having no reason not to let the parents and siblings live with him are not usual and imply that problems are anticipated. Some people in the village told me that this couple, now in their seventies, had trouble with one of their sons. Conflict with this son may have also contributed to their decision to move into the village offices while I was in the village and for Mr. Li to work as the watchman for the compound and for his wife to work as my cook. In other respects, though, this contract is quite typical.

Division Contract C, below, is unusual in several respects. First, it gives reference to ideological reasons for caring for parents. Second, it is very specific about deadlines for providing required support, perhaps because, as in Contract B, problems are anticipated. Third, it is also unusual in making arrangements for sons to provide not only money but also, via their wives, nursing care for ailing parents. Daughters who lived in the village would often be called upon to provide this kind of support. This contract also reveals parental plans to live with one son, citing that one of the sons is having some sort of troubles. Equality between brothers is sometimes qualified in these contracts by circumstances. In other cases, a son who lives outside of the village is often expected to give additional money in lieu of having his parents live with him for a time.

Division Contract C

Executor of division contract: Wang Yuguang

In order to protect the elder's legal rights, develop the virtue of respect for the aged, care for the aged, and love for the aged, establish good socialist moral practice, and make the parents' later years happy and peaceful, now at my, Wang Yuguang's, suggestion and through discussion with my wife, and with Wang Guangzhi, Wang Guangyong, and Wang Guangli, from now on my affairs and living will be properly arranged for the rest of my life. Moreover, we have consulted with the village political office, the village committee, and our production team's leaders. All of the requirements in this agreement to care for the elders should be implemented every day.

1. Living quarters: According to agreement with the parents, they will live with Wang Guangli year-round. But if Wang Guangyong's family conditions improve the parents also have the right to choose where to live.

2. Living support: Guangyong and Guangli will divide and farm the parents' responsibility land. They will pay the annual tax. Each year, each will give the parents 230 jin of wheat. They will give the grain every year on the first of the fifth lunar month.

3. Expenses: The three brothers each month will each give the parents 15 yuan. Payments will begin from 1996 in the fourth lunar month, each month at the beginning of the month. From after the sixth month they can give half a year's coal. The three brothers each year will give the parents 500 jin of honey-comb briquettes and 200 jin of heating coal. If conditions change, then it is appropriate to make adjustments and purchase more.

4. Medical fees: If the parents get sick, no matter how much it costs the three brothers will share the costs determined by the clinic or hospital bill. On odd days of the lunar calendar, Guangyin will be responsible for providing nursing care and on even days Guangli will be responsible for care. Moreover they should care for household affairs: The two brothers will be responsible for New Year's and holidays in turn and they will receive the guests.

The above agreement on care has been agreed with by the village committee and I myself have agreed. From now on I hope the sons will follow the agreement so we can have a peaceful, happy old age.

The last contract viewed here, Contract D, is an early one, presenting a detailed description of care for the mother including arrangements for the celebration of her birthday. This contract specifies that the unmarried son will not be responsible for care for his mother until he marries. Like contract C, this contract specifies deadlines for when grain and coal should be provided. This is the only other contract in the sample to do so.

Division Contract D

An agreement about Wang Yujun's, Wang Yuhe's, and Wang Yuxiang's family division. The three brothers—Wang Yujun, Wang Yuhe, and Wang Yuxiang—have discussed this matter and with the agreement of the leaders of the brigade and team have agreed as follows:

1. Division of rooms: The two small north rooms of the east house, the outer room, and the kitchen go to Yuhe. The three rooms of the large north house all go to Yuxiang. In addition, the small north room of the west house that was earlier given by Yuzhun to Yuxiang also goes to Yuxiang.

2. Division of property: Yujun is not part of the division. The small cart, table set, and the trees given by the brigade all go to Yuhe. All of the other furnishings go to Yuxiang.

3. Care of the parents: Before Yuhe marries, he has no responsibility to take care of mother. Yujun and Yuxiang will equally divide the responsibility of caring for the parents. The two brothers will divide and farm mother's responsibility land, and each year, each will give her 170 jin of wheat, 20 jin of millet, and 10 jin of beans, and each month will give her a 5 yuan allowance. Before the end of the ninth lunar month they will give her 1,000 jin of coal. Each year, each will give mother a set of clothes and a cotton sheet. Each son will be responsible for mother's birthday for a year. At Spring Festival, each person will give 3 jin of meat and 3 jin of oil. Medical bills will be divided equally by the two sons. Before Yuxiang builds a house, mother will live in Yuxiang's rooms. After he builds a house, both sons will have equal responsibility for her housing. If the brigade does not claim their land in the north section, Yuhe can farm it.

For parents, household contracts specifically outline exactly what support will be given, and so function to ensure that a certain level of support is given. Brothers may at times choose to give more than is written in the contract, but increases or additional gifts are also likely to be agreed upon and shared. I visited one couple whose three sons had gone together to buy a new sectional couch for them. This was a gift, not something the sons were required to provide by the contract and something about which the parents boasted. The son who lives in town instigated the purchase. Gifts of this size are uncommon in the village, and I believe this son was influenced by urban views of filial piety that focus more on the quality of the relationship between the parents and children than on the need for support. Though the son in town has a higher income than his brothers in the village, each paid an equal amount for the purchase. Even where one son clearly has better means than his brothers, he does not contribute more, at least not openly.

Support by Daughters and Only Sons

The expectations of support from daughters are not written down in contracts. Some daughters, mostly those living in town, give large amounts of support while those living in the village give very little in cash but often help their parents by providing services or labor. Daughters who live in the village are more likely to give assistance of this kind than are their brothers.

Although daughters do at times provide more support financially than their brothers, it is the support of sons that can be depended upon for survival. In a typical contract, a son may be responsible for giving his parents a modest 60 yuan in cash per year plus wheat, corn, and coal. Cost for medicines can, however, far exceed these amounts. In one case, the costs for medicines ran as high as 180–90 yuan per month. More commonly people who regularly took medicines reported that they cost 10–20 yuan per month. Hospital costs can represent a huge burden to local families. Surgery for a stomach tumor cost one family 4,000 yuan. Another reported spending a total of 5,500 yuan for eye surgery on two occasions. For comparison, annual income for a household of four averaged around 10,000 yuan. Daughters are not expected to contribute to this. In one exceptional case, a daughter who lives in distant Lanzhou contributed to the 10,000 yuan fee for her 78-year-old mother's eye surgery. In another case an aged couple borrowed money from a daughter for a hospital visit since their son did not have enough money. A loan of this kind is a significant help, but sons are expected to pay for such expenses outright. As noted, however, daughters are likely to provide care and support for their sick and bedridden parents. The assistance of daughters is often preferred to that of daughters-in-law, and village elders are sometimes critical of sons who did not give them as much attention as they felt they should get. I believe this is largely what was behind the aforementioned woman's feeling that daughters would have been better than her four sons.

The aged of Lijia expect little more than that their most essential needs be met by their sons. They are delighted to show off a gift from sons, but feel that if there is something they want, they cannot ask their sons for it. Even if they feel they can ask, they are often reduced to the status of petitioners in a home that is no longer their own. By not asking much of their children, the aged may attempt to claim a moral high ground in hopes that when they fall ill their children will not begrudge them the best care they can afford. Not asking for much may also be a strategy to avoid squandering the children's resources that they hope to draw upon in time of need.

Only sons, unlike those who have siblings, do not enter into a contract since there is no brother from whom to separate. Many of the aged told me that to have more sons is better. More sons have more collective income and should be able to provide better support. In some cases they will get together and agree to buy a television or sofa, but the contract has the effect of eliminating competition between brothers. To give the amount of support agreed upon in the contract is enough. The contract justifies the amount, and even a wealthier brother is unlikely to give more for fear of creating jealousy and conflict within the family. An only son or a daughter is not limited in this way. An only son is likely to give a similar amount of support as those with brothers because this is the norm in the village. Also, even without a contract, the son is legally required to support his parents, and the village committee has on occasion persuaded a neglectful son to provide such support. As with daughters, only sons are free to give as they choose and as circumstances allow. This is not to suggest that there are no rules of exchange in these cases as well, but these rules are not written, and they are not rules that people speak of as they do of wedding, funeral, and Spring Festival gifts (Kipnis 1997; Yan 1996). The support of sons is public; that of daughters is private. The support of sons is based on a cultural norm, discussed with village leaders, written, signed, and discussed openly. The support of daughters is private. It is unspecific, poorly defined, and spoken of indirectly. The support of only sons falls between the two. It is more open to public discussion, but not contracted.

In a village where elders had little access to income, property, or other forms of power, their only recourse to obtain support from children was through legal and social means. In negotiating family division contracts, elders had little to use in the bargaining process. Socially, they also had limited tools. Demanding much from children might alienate them and also cause the parent to lose public sympathy. Expecting little, being grateful, and avoiding burdening children are, ironically, some of the most powerful tools Lijia's aged have to make sure that they receive basic support for daily needs and in times of crisis. This situation is very different from that portrayed in traditional accounts of filiality that depict children revering and pampering their parents. Given greater resources, Lijia's elders would have more power and seek independence from their children less. The interest of more affluent elders would focus less on basic support and more on the quality of affective relationships. In short, their situation would be more comparable to that of elders in wealthier villages and in China's cities. If this analysis is accurate and applicable to villages in similar economic circumstances to Lijia, it suggests that government policies that rely on families to provide social support for the aged may not be appropriate for much of rural China. In order to provide appropriate family support, it may be necessary to ensure that the aged have some ability to contribute economically to their families or to provide for themselves and have the option of living apart from their children. Such empowerment may be possible at no cost by restructuring land and housing allocation policies at the village level. Retirement and medical savings and insurance plans currently being encouraged should also help in the long run if inflation does not negate the value of the payouts. The key to successful family-based support in China is that the elders have a measure of power in their relationships with their children.

People spoke of the benefits of many sons, but those with many sons were often not convinced. Better support may be provided by having one son and several daughters than by having numerous sons. While a few people criticized their own son or someone else's as being unfilial, I never heard of talk of an unfilial daughter. There are no clear expectations for daughters to break, and since they are not the providers of essential support, their lack of gifts or a tendency to argue with their parents would not be as threatening as it would be from a son. Strong ties with married daughters were, nonetheless, of great potential benefit to the aged. In one family I visited, a married daughter was home so often it was only when she once arrived by motor scooter with her husband that I realized she actually lived in town. The visiting, gift giving, and care provided by daughters are very similar to the behavioral ideal of parent-child relationships in America, though in Lijia this behavioral repertoire has a name—filial piety—and to be filial is to be properly Chinese.

CHAPTER 3

Meal Rotation and Filial Piety

JUN JING

In this chapter, I will discuss four village-level studies of old-age support in China. My focus is the practice of meal rotation in three of these villages and the absence of meal rotation in the fourth. An explicit Chinese phrase for meal rotation is *lunliu gongyang laoren,* literally "taking turns in supporting and feeding the elderly." A popular term for it is *chi lun fan,* that is, "having meals by rotation." For brevity, "meal rotation" will be used throughout my discussion. A basic requirement of meal rotation is that married sons share and rotate the responsibility for providing regular meals to their aging or elderly parents (Fei 1939, 1986; Lin 1947). In rural China, the actual preparation of meals is usually the responsibility of daughters-in-law. Obviously, a precondition of meal rotation is that a couple have at least two married sons. Another precondition is proximity. If one son lives too far away from his parents, it is certainly difficult for him to participate in meal rotation along with his brothers. A third precondition is the dividing up of a family, mostly caused by the desire of the married sons and their wives to set up their own households. In the wake of family division and once a rotation schedule is fixed, the parents will go to have meals at the household of one son for a few days, a week, or even many weeks, before they move on to another son's household to eat. The provision of actual support is not restricted to food, as the parents may also take up residence with each of their sons and his wife during a given period of rotation (Cohen 1976; Hsieh 1985). Thus in addition to food, the other minimum needs of the parents in meal rotation include housing and help in managing the activities of daily life.

The significance of studying meal rotation is suggested by its long history in China and its social ramifications today. As one of the oldest means of caring for one's parents in advanced age, the practice of meal rotation was recorded in writing as early as the Eastern Han dynasty (A.D. 25–225). In rural China, decisions for starting meal rotation or other forms of old-age support are contingent on decisions for family division. In other words, even when a couple are not too old to work and can still adequately care for themselves, questions of how they should be supported will be raised by their children in connection with the breakup of the existing family unit that allows married sons to establish their separate households. By studying meal rotation, we also will be able to observe a rural-urban bifurcation. In the country's urban areas today, meal rotation is rare and certainly not one of the major means of old-age support. By comparison with their urban counterparts (see Davis-Friedmann 1991; Ikels 1993), the absolute majority of the elderly living in rural China have no retirement pensions to count on, and therefore they are far more dependent on their children for old-age support (see Leung 1997; Shi 1993). Moreover, meal rotation in Chinese villages is hardly a private matter confined to the domestic sphere of family life. Carried out in a fashion that begets public attention, it is bound to be a topic of public opinion. Therefore, studying meal rotation is to study public opinion on an important issue of morality, namely filial piety. I should add here that meal rotation is a routine and even favored practice in some Chinese villages, whereas it is rarely practiced and sometimes even ridiculed in other villages as if it were antifilial. I will first focus on how three Chinese social scientists have tried to explain the causes of meal rotation in the villages they studied. I will then explain why in a rural community I studied many elderly parents and middle-age villagers regard meal rotation as if it were too unfilial to practice.

The Frequency of Meal Rotation

The first set of data is from Zhuang Kongshao's *The Silver Wing* (*Yin chi*) (1996). This is a field study of Huangcun, a Fujian village featured in Lin Yaohua's (Lin Yueh-hua) *The Golden Wing* (1947). While Lin's work mentioned old-age support and meal rotation only in passing, Zhuang's discussion of the same issues is substantive. Zhuang conducted his fieldwork in Huangcun in 1989, and he carefully documented four forms of old-age support he found there (Zhuang 1996). First, seventeen villagers (including four couples) were participating in meal rotation. Second, twenty-seven villagers (including thirteen couples) were living alone and cooking for themselves while receiving some money and grain from their sons. Third, twenty-one villagers (including nine couples) lived with one of their sons and also received contributions of money and grain from their other sons. Fourth, two couples lived with and were supported by their daughters; one of these couples was sonless, and the other had four married sons (who provided their parents with material assistance but did not want to live with them). According to Zhuang, Huangcun had three elderly bachelors in 1989, and they were recipients of the government-provided "five guaranteed items" (that is, clothing, food, housing, medical care, and burial) that make up the core of the rural welfare system. If no elderly villagers in Huangcun were left out of his survey, as Zhuang says, then nearly 25 percent of this village's elderly residents were participating in meal rotation.

A more recent study of old-age support at the village level in south China was conducted in 1996 by Chen Yunpiao and two of his colleagues at Zhongshan University (Chen 1997). This study is based on a randomly selected sample of twenty-five elderly people in the village of Xilong, Guangdong Province. A tabulation of Chen's findings shows that nine of these villagers (including four couples) were participating in meal rotation, thirteen (including five couples) were living with and supported by one of their sons, and two were living alone and cooking for themselves. Both of the self-supporting elders were men. One did not have any children, and the other, who had an urban retirement pension, did not want to live with his married sons. Again, the number of people being supported by meal rotation (nine out of twenty-five elderly persons) is noteworthy, although we may want to know if the basis of Chen's sample is the village or just a segment of the village such as one neighborhood or a production team.

In a report on her 1996 fieldwork in Xiaoyangcun, a village in Hebei Province, Guo Yuhua of the Chinese Academy of Social Sciences indicates that about 10 percent of the elderly were relying on meal rotation for old-age support. The bulk of elderly residents in Xiaoyangcun, or 70 percent of the total, lived alone and cooked for themselves with some provisions of grain and money from their grown-up children. As for the remaining population of elderly villagers in Xiaoyangcun, half lived with and were supported by at least one of their sons, and the other half tried to get by on their own because their married sons or daughters-in-law refused to care for them. Guo's figures are not based on self-reports but on estimates made by village cadres (Guo 1997: 3). These estimates reveal the existence of meal rotation in Xiaoyangcun and the rather large proportion of this north China village's elderly residents who lived by themselves with no support from their children.

The fourth study I want to discuss is my own, conducted in the summer of 1999 in Dachuan Village, Gansu Province, northwest China. My study concentrated on this village's Second Production Team, and at first I relied on information provided by the village's accountant-general, the head of the Second Production Team, two teachers at a local preschool, three older women, and five elderly men. I then visited fifteen households to gather detailed information so as to better understand the figures I had collected and the descriptive information I had received from my key informants. In addition, I asked thirty villagers at two separate banquets about meal rotation. On a pilgrimage to a temple that lasted for a whole day, I broached and discussed the topic with twelve adults. In total, I talked with more than seventy villagers about meal rotation in Dachuan. About a quarter of these villagers were women. My interpretation of the data I collected in 1999 draws not only on this study but also on my previous studies in Dachuan over the past ten years.

In 1999, there were fifty-two older parents in Dachuan's Second Production Team. Of these, twenty-two (including ten couples) lived with and were supported by their only sons, eighteen (including seven couples) lived with at least one of their sons and received some money and grain as a form of shared support from the other sons they had, and eight (including three couples) lived with two to three married sons in households not yet divided. In addition, one man was supported by his nephew, and one woman lived with her daughter and her daughter's married-in husband. There were two elderly men who lived alone and cooked for themselves. One was an urban retiree who did not want to live with any of his three sons; the other was childless. This childless villager had adopted a son from his brother for old-age support, but his adopted son later refused to live with or support him.

Compared with the situations found by Zhuang, Chen, and Guo, there are two unusual findings from the Second Production Team in Dachuan. The first is the rather large number of parents who had only one son, although this does not mean that they had no daughters. The second is the absence of any formal practice of meal rotation. There were indeed a few cases of short-term arrangements in which parents moved from one to another household of their married sons to have meals on a rotating basis, but these cases were of a temporary nature and caused by extended stays that daughters-in-law had in their natal villages. My informants assured me repeatedly that even in the entire village of Dachuan I could not find a single case of meal rotation being practiced as a formal means of old-age support. In 1999, Dachuan had eight production teams, 749 households, and 4,344 registered residents. The village's accountant-general and an elderly woman did say that temporary meal rotation sometimes lasted for a long time. In one instance, it lasted for more than a year because one of the daughters-in-law of an elderly couple was so disheartened by her husband's gambling that she went back to her natal village and refused to return to Dachuan. Since this woman had lived with and cooked for her parents-in-law, her husband's brothers and their wives took care of the older couple by meal rotation. In the end, a party of five elderly villagers went to the daughter-in-law's natal village as persuasive speakers (*shuo ke*) to bring her back to Dachuan with the assurance that her husband would never gamble again.

The Reasons for Meal Rotation

To make sense of Dachuan's lack of meal rotation, in the formal sense of the term, we need to know first what justifications have been given for meal rotation in the other three village studies I have reported. In his Huangcun study, Zhuang identifies the equal distribution of a family's common property among married sons as being one of the causes of meal rotation. His explanation is that household division entails not only division of property but also a commitment on the part of the sons heading the new households to share the responsibility for taking care of their parents (Zhuang 1996). In his Xilong article, Chen (1997) offers a similar but more elaborate explanation. Meal rotation is, Chen says, a compromise between the Chinese ideal of what a family should be like and the reality of the Chinese family development cycle. So far as the ideal is concerned, the parents and their married sons, daughters-in-law, grandchildren, and perhaps even great-grandchildren would take up residence under one roof. Therefore, the parents would be well cared for by a large family unit. However, the reality is that such large multigenerational families are as rare as they are impractical. The desire of married brothers to establish their own households, the delicate relationships among their wives, and the varying ability of related individuals to make material or financial contributions to a large joint household bring too many conflicts. Thus, other means of old-age support are needed, and meal rotation is one of them. In the village of Xilong, meal rotation is regarded by the locals as more practical than fixed support, that is, the arrangement by which parents end up living with just one son while receiving additional material and financial support from the other sons (Chen 1997). In practicing meal rotation, Chen stresses, the grown-up children's equal sharing of the responsibility for the well-being of their parents is handled meticulously so as to avoid the likelihood that one son appears to contribute more than the other sons. The mere impression of unbalanced contributions is enough to cause community gossip and even public ridicule of those sons who appear to be less caring toward their parents. Meal rotation, according to Chen, serves as a leveling device and a buffer of potential conflicts among brothers (1997). (See Chapter 2 for this same argument in support of family division contracts.)

Guo's take on meal rotation is quite different, and her opinion may be a reflection of what she considers to be a collapse of filial piety, made apparent by an increasing number of elderly people who were forced to live alone and the fact that some of them had to sue their children for old-age support (Guo 1997). Guo attributes this problem to Communist attacks on Confucianism, popular religion, and lineage organization. She also mentions the lack of accumulated wealth and savings on the part of elderly villagers when they were working under the collective farming system. She argues that the lack of accumulated personal wealth and savings weakened the ability of the elderly to engage in intergenerational reciprocity. For example, a middle-aged woman in this village told Guo that the reason that she and her parents-in-law could not see eye to eye on the issue of old-age support was because the older couple believed they had done a lot for their son while she believed they had done very little. This woman mentioned in particular that the older couple failed to help her husband in meeting his marriage expenses, and therefore she and her husband should not be expected to look after his parents. Guo states that the crisis of old-age support in Xiaoyangcun also has to do with the greater participation of younger and middle-aged women in the market economy. As daughters-in-law of Xiaoyangcun are increasingly preoccupied with making money outside the agricultural sector, they find it hard to balance their double role as primary caregivers to their own children and their parents-in-law at the same time. Their first priority is their own children. Their second priority is a lucrative business: making bags, backpacks, and suitcases for export. It is against this socioeconomic background that Guo sees the practice of meal rotation in Xiaoyangcun as a disguised form of elder neglect, an excuse for doing as little as possible for the elderly.

As for my explanation as to why the formal kind of meal rotation was not found in the village of Dachuan, let me refer to the reasons given to me by my informants, and then I will offer my own observations. One of the first topics that came into the conversations I had with my informants about meal rotation was about biology, that is, some parents could produce only one son despite their wish to beget more than one. In the Second Production Team of Dachuan, ten older couples and two widowed villagers had, in each case, only one son to support them. In other words, they did not have enough male heirs for meal rotation. Yet, this demographic factor does not explain why in Dachuan meal rotation was held in disapproval.

One of the earliest interviews I conducted in Dachuan on the issue of old-age support was with three elderly men. They were among the prominent seniors of a local lineage, and their prestige in Dachuan was by and large a result of their involvement in the reorganization of a lineage-wide ceremony for ancestor worship. To practice meal rotation, I was told by these elders, there must be at least two sons heading two separate households. Meal rotation also suggests that not even one son is willing to live with his parents, thereby forcing them to walk from one household to another simply for the purpose of getting fed. "If older people are made to go around to look for food to eat, the entire village will laugh at their children. There will be absolutely no color of life on their [that is, the children's] faces," said one of these elderly informants. Even if both food and residence can be made available, it is not going to work. It is too embarrassing to let your neighbors see your parents carrying their quilts and clothes and moving from your household to your brother's, another informant observed. Mention was also made of the fact that especially if the interval of meal rotation is short, some caregivers may find it convenient to save better food to consume by themselves after the rotation period. Apparently, these informants knew what they were talking about, meaning that they were aware of how meal rotation could work against the elderly.

Then there is the related issue of parental authority and family membership. As an elderly man put it: "If elderly people agree to meal rotation, they lose their say over everything. The youngsters make all the big and small decisions. Meal-plus-residence rotation is the worst. It makes elderly people homeless." This comment reminds us of what Myron Cohen has said about the combined rotation of residence and food provision in his study of a Taiwanese village:

> In one sense, parents involved in such an arrangement can be said to be members of more than one family and household; in another sense, however, they are somewhat less than full members of any family, because this kind of collective arrangement for the father's support following [family] division means that he is no longer coparcener to any portion of the old family estate. . . . Since parents who are supported jointly by their sons in a post-division context have in fact been deprived of their family membership, I call them "collective dependents." (Cohen 1976: 74–75)

Furthermore, the issue of practicality was brought up in my Dachuan study. Older people, I was told, are not mere recipients of their children's support. "Even when we are sick and can only walk around in the courtyard, we can keep an eye on the family's property. We can look after the pigs and the sheep, so nobody dares steal them," an elderly woman said. Another older woman stated: "I take care of the grandchildren when my daughter-in-law works in the fields. My husband is 75 now and has high blood pressure. But he guards the family's watermelon plot. As soon as it is dark, he goes to the watermelon plot and sleeps in a straw hut there. We have not lost a single watermelon this year." The practicality of having older people around extends beyond work. A village cadre thus said, "I am so busy with my work. I will ask my father to go to Bami Mountain next week. He will burn incense on behalf of the whole family." The Bami Mountain he referred to has a large temple dedicated to a popular fertility deity called Mother Jinhua. Older people also make perfect family representatives at weddings, banquets, and funerary ceremonies, a phenomenon that has been observed in other parts of village China (see, for example, Watson 1987; Yan 1996).

Based on my fieldwork in Dachuan in 1992 and seven revisits thereafter, I conclude that there is a connection between the redistribution of land and the question of why people's attitude toward meal rotation in this village, especially among the elderly, was one of disapproval. In 1981, Dachuan moved from the collective farming system to making the household the primary unit of production. The breakup of the commune system provided every registered Dachuan resident above the age of twelve with an equal share of land. Even baby girls and boys under the age of twelve received half of a share. In response to demographic changes, readjustments of the land-holding system were attempted on many occasions. But widespread resistance to such re-adjustments made them unsuccessful. A result of this resistance was the transfer of land titles from the dead to the living within the extended family and from married-out daughters to the family's next generation of youngsters. As a result of farmland destruction by the building of a nearby hydroelectric dam, Dachuan had less than one *mu* (approximately one sixth of an acre) of farmland per person, an extremely limited amount to support a family. Under this circumstance, the fact that extra land means extra income is apparent to all adults and even little children.

In addition to land scarcity, a factor that makes land into a crucial issue of livelihood improvement is the village's adoption in the past seven years of greenhouse technologies for growing off-season vegetables and the establishment in the past fifteen years of more than a hundred fish ponds. These alternative land uses have produced a thriving cash economy. If Dachuan parents can keep their own land titles and those of their married-out daughters so as to benefit from the cash economy, they will have a better chance of security in old age. A consequence of recognizing the connection between land titles and old-age security is that many parents in Dachuan are reluctant to transfer the land titles under their control to their sons even after the family is divided into different households. Instead of accepting meal rotation, a common practice in Dachuan is for parents to keep their land titles firmly in their own hands and live with their youngest son before he marries. After he is married, his parents continue living with him and his wife as a stem household. The junior generation will cater to the needs of the senior generation and eventually inherit their land titles. Another preferred practice is to avoid household division as long as possible.

More important than economics perhaps is the reorganization of a local lineage. More than 85 percent of the households in Dachuan bear the surname Kong. The Kongs trace their ancestry to Kongzi (Confucius) and the origin of their local ancestry to four Kong brothers who settled in Dachuan in 1501. From the early 1950s to the late 1970s, the Kong lineage declined in terms of the kind of political power and wealth it enjoyed. But with the Kong lineage being under vigorous reorganization from the early 1980s to the early 1990s, the educated elders of the lineage, about twenty of them, took over the reconstruction of a large Confucius temple (essentially an ancestral hall) and the establishment of a preschool open to all the children of Dachuan. These Kong elders also lent logistical and moral support to a group of six elderly women in Dachuan who initiated and completed the reconstruction of four local deity temples. The active role played by at least some of Dachuan's elderly residents in some of the important communal affairs accorded these individuals great prestige. Even powerful village cadres decided to join forces with these Kong elders in managing the village-run preschool and an elaborate annual ceremony at the Confucius temple (see Jing 1996).

Some of the elderly Kongs who achieved fame and even raised their social status through the Kong lineage's reassertion in community affairs were eagerly courted to serve as arbitrators in family disputes, including disputes over the methods of caring for elderly parents. That the prominent seniors of the Kong lineage vehemently disapproved of meal rotation has had its impact on public opinion regarding the question of what forms of old-age support are suitable. Since old-age support is a widespread concern in a close-knit community like Dachuan, it is hard for decisions on caring for the old to be confined to the private sphere of family life. It is equally hard for these decisions to be made in a manner that blatantly disregards the personal opinions of certain individuals who happen to be closely associated with a lively, and one may even say inquisitive, social organization based on agnatic descent. A cornerstone of this organization is its identification with an illustrious ancestor whose teachings on filial piety must be influential in a village where most local residents claim to be his descendants.

To conclude, in Dachuan the disapproving attitude toward meal rotation arises from a cluster of complicated factors. No single factor, be it that of demographics, morality, economics, or practicality, is sufficient to account for the absence of meal rotation in this village. Having said so, not all factors of relevance are equally important, and in my view the Kong lineage's reorganization and the prestige of the lineage's prominent seniors seem to be more pivotal than the other factors in determining why meal rotation was not found in Dachuan. What can we learn from the Dachuan material? Apparently, we need to be aware of the objective conditions that motivate and inform public opinion. But we also need to know who are the agents of influence in shaping and reshaping these opinions and why. Above all, we need to know what social institutions those agents of influence represent and what impact such institutions have upon a people's ways of thinking. For these reasons I have stressed the interconnectedness between the Kong lineage, the role of the lineage's prominent seniors as respected arbitrators for solving family disputes, and the views of these particular individuals on meal rotation.

CHAPTER 4

"Living Alone" and the Rural Elderly: Strategy and Agency in Post-Mao Rural China

HONG ZHANG

For centuries, portrayals of both Chinese cultural ideals and everyday practice have focused on multigenerational households in which the older generation occupies a key role. However, it now appears that complex households have begun to "simplify." In Zhongshan, a village in Hubei Province in central China, as recently as two decades ago, for elderly parents with married sons living in the same community to live alone would have been unimaginable. Parents would have been pitied for being deserted by their own sons. Likewise, the sons would have been condemned as unfilial and shameless. Then in 1986, a father of two married sons in Zhongshan moved out of his younger son's house and started living alone. Two months later, his wife joined him. This action marked the first incidence in Zhongshan of elderly parents taking the initiative to live alone and control their own household. By 1993 and 1994, when this study was conducted, at least twenty-nine elderly parents had followed suit. At the national level, both recent ethnographic data and national surveys suggest that more and more Chinese elderly are now living apart from their grown-up children, with a range of 30 to over 50 percent living in a separate household alone or with a spouse (Chen 1998; Goldstein, Ku, and Ikels 1990; Gui 1988; Jia 1988; Shi 1994; Unger 1993). While some see in this phenomenon the collapse of the tradition of filial piety, others view it as a positive change in family relations and a move toward democratization and conjugality (Guo 1997; Xu 1996; Yan 1997). According to some studies, the economic prosperity that has resulted from recent reforms has made separate dwelling for family members more accessible, hence the increase in the number of elderly living apart from their married children (Davis 1993; Ikels 1990). The rapid increase in rural-urban migration since the reforms has also been seen as responsible for more and more rural elderly parents living alone because their sons have gone to the cities for higher paid jobs (Leung 1997; Wei 1997). Still, there are others who attribute this phenomenon to changes rooted in the political economy of socialism that for decades after the 1949 socialist revolution severely weakened parental authority and greatly enhanced the younger generation's desire for, and ability to attain, financial independence and autonomy (Greenhalgh 1994; Selden 1993).

The increase in the number of elderly parents living alone has presented a number of challenges to traditional family support for the aged in China, especially in the countryside. Unlike urban residents, who can still be economically secure after retirement since they enjoy a public pension plan and medical coverage, the rural elderly have no access to such state welfare services—their old-age support is almost entirely shouldered by the family.[1] Based on fieldwork carried out between 1993 and 1994 in Zhongshan, a rural community in Hubei Province in central China, this chapter attempts to address the following questions: Why are rural elderly increasingly living alone? What are their motivations for doing so? Are they living alone because they choose to do so or are they forced to do so? Are there any benefits to living alone for the rural elderly? How are elderly parents supported economically if they are living alone? What does this shift tell us about changed family dynamics and intergenerational relations? What are rural residents' responses and attitudes toward elderly parents living alone?

Village Setting and Data

Located about 60 kilometers north of the Zhongxiang County seat and 280 kilometers northwest of Wuhan, the capital city of Hubei Province, Zhongshan Village is mainly a farming community that grows both rice and wheat. In the late 1970s, prior to the rural economic reforms, Zhongshan Village (then known as Zhongshan Brigade) had a relatively strong collective economy. Each of the brigade's six production teams owned tractors, generators, and other farming machines and tools, as well as draft animals such as water buffalo and mules. The brigade itself ran various enterprises, such as a brick kiln, a beancurd shop, and a vegetable oil processor. Income from both grain production and the collective enterprises helped support the brigade's free primary school as well as its low-cost cooperative medical clinics. In 1983, with the rural reforms in full swing, land was returned to individual families to manage, as was collective property such as farm machines and draft animals. In the first few years of the reforms, Zhongshan's collective enterprises remained intact; in fact, one more—a winery—was added. But by the late 1980s, none of the collective enterprises survived. I never received a full explanation from the village cadres concerning why the collective enterprises collapsed, but the villagers put the blame on the cadres, saying that the enterprises failed because the cadres either put the profits into their own pockets or squandered the money entertaining higher officials in order to establish networks for themselves. Compared to a decade ago, there were some obvious signs of prosperity among the villagers though. There were more brick houses than before, electricity had become available to every household since 1986, and more than 80 percent of the households owned a black-and-white television. The local economy also appeared to be more diversified as some villagers were engaged in such nonfarming activities as fishing, carpentry, masonry, and trading local commodities. Several households also had family-run enterprises such as making liquor and beancurd, and processing oil. However, most of the villagers' economic activities were locally based, and there was not much out-migration of young and middle-aged villagers seeking jobs elsewhere. This population stability can be seen as a potential benefit for support of the elderly as it means that most parents have adult children living in the village all year round.

There is also another important feature in this local area conducive to old-age security. In Zhongshan, as well as in the surrounding area, uxorilocal marriage, in which a man marries into the woman's family, was very common both before and after 1949. Couples who had only daughters and no sons could have one of their daughters married uxorilocally and be supported by their daughter and son-in-law. Childless couples could also adopt a daughter and raise her for uxorilocal marriage. As of 1994, out of 108 elderly parents living in a three-generational household, thirty-three or 31 percent were living with a daughter's uxorilocal family. Without their daughter's uxorilocal marriage, some of these parents would either have to support themselves as long as they could, or they would have to be supported by the "five guarantees" (food, clothing, medical care, housing, and burial expenses), a welfare scheme that has been in existence since the collective period. When I visited the village in 1993–94, no elderly person was eligible. It is possible that the practice of uxorilocal marriage has reduced the number

TABLE I
Living Arrangements of Zhongshan
Elderly Parents, 1993–1994

Family Types and Support Patterns	ELDERLY PARENTS	
	No.	%
Stem family	108	60
(Living with a married son)	(75)	(69)
(Living with a married daughter)	(33)	(31)
Two-generation household	23	13
Support by turns	8	4
Living alone or with a spouse	41	23
Total	180	100

of elderly people in Zhongshan who would otherwise have had to depend on public assistance.

Although the "five-guarantees" scheme provides a form of welfare for the rural elderly, it is aimed only at an extremely small group: the childless elderly. The great majority of rural elderly depend on their families for old-age support. In Zhongshan in the 1990s, family support was becoming even more crucial since the collective economy was almost nonexistent after decollectivization. Furthermore, without the collective enterprises, the village went heavily into debt (I was given the figure of between 14,000 yuan to 30,000 yuan in 1994) in order to fund its primary school, the village clinic, and the village cadres' salaries and other expenses.

Since Zhongshan's elderly parents currently have no source of old-age support other than their own family members, their living arrangements provide a way for us to see how family support is articulated. Zhongshan Village had a population of 1,493 living in 374 households in 1993–94. There were a total of 180 people over 60 years old; their living arrangements are shown in Table 1.[2]

The greatest number of Zhongshan elderly are living in a stem family (60 percent), followed by those "living alone" (23 percent) and those in "two-generation (that is, parents and unmarried children) households" (13 percent). "Support by turns" (*lunyang*) or "meal rotation" is an arrangement in which the parents rotate among their sons for meals and sometimes for housing as well. (See Chapters 2 and 3 for further examples of this type of

arrangement.) In Zhongshan, this form of parental support was not frequently adopted, as seen in Table 1. As for those elderly parents who were living in a "two-generation household," they often still had younger unmarried
son(s) or daughter(s) while their older sons were married and had moved out
of the common household. However, what is very revealing about the
Zhongshan data is that given China's tradition of depending on sons for old-
age support, the number of elderly parents being supported by a daughter
was very high, making up almost 31 percent of the total number of stem families, and 19 percent among all types of family arrangements. Although most
of the Zhongshan parents living with an uxorilocally married daughter did
so because they did not have a son, some did have a son or sons, but they
could still claim old-age support from a daughter if she was married uxorilocally. In studies of Chinese family types, such terms as "extended family"
and "stem family" often assume that parents are living with married sons or
a married son. The percentage of parents living with a married daughter has
been found to be very low—between 2 to 8 percent in the countryside
(Goldstein, Ku, and Ikels 1990; Jia 1988). With as many as 31 percent of elderly parents in stem families living with a married daughter, Zhongshan's
data demonstrate that, owing to uxorilocal marriage, a daughter can also play
a central role in providing parental support.

If we look merely at living arrangements, the 60 percent coresidence rate is
high. If we include elderly parents living with unmarried children, the percentage is even higher—over 73 percent. This suggests that the majority of
elderly parents live with their adult children. This should not be surprising,
since by the time these rural parents had reached over 60 years of age, they
had generally retired from farming, most if not all of their children were married, and the family house and property were divided up among their married
sons if they had more than one. As mentioned earlier, there was no pension
for the rural elderly, thus they were totally dependent upon their children for
support. Thus, the question that the data in Table 1 really raises is why some
elderly parents live alone or with a spouse only. It appears that there were two
very different situations under which elderly parents in Zhongshan were living separately from their adult children. One was that their child(ren) had
moved out of the village, and the elderly parents continued to live in their old
residence. In the other situation, some Zhongshan parents were living alone
although they had married sons living in the same community (Table 2).

Of the forty-one elderly parents living alone, twelve (29 percent) did so

TABLE 2

Zhongshan Elderly Parents Living Alone
and Availability of Children

Availability of Children	ELDERLY PARENTS	
	No.	%
Children left the village	12	29
Children living in the same village	29	71
Total	41	100

because their children had moved out of the village, while twenty-nine (71 percent) did have at least one married son living in the same village. Further investigation reveals that these twenty-nine elderly parents all had lived in a stem family before they moved out and started living separately. In terms of their economic support while living separately, nine elderly parents (22 percent) reported that they solely support themselves, while the remaining thirty-two (78 percent) said their children provided them with grain (usually 600 to 700 jin of unhusked rice for each parent) and, for some, cooking oil as well, but no cash or pocket money. Most elderly parents living alone could generate some modest cash income through raising chickens and tending vegetable gardens (usually on the land surrounding their dwelling).

Motivations for "Living Alone"

In industrial countries, the decision to live alone is often viewed as "a reflection of an economic demand for privacy or autonomy," and is found to be positively correlated with income level, that is, an increase in income level is followed by an increased propensity to live alone (Becker 1981; Michael, Fuchs, and Scott 1980). Some studies in China also emphasize that more and more elderly people are economically self-sufficient, and thus have the ability to live alone. According to Aimei Jia, for example, the diversification of the rural economy since the economic reforms has allowed some elderly parents to increase their earnings: "Consequently, it is now feasible to live independently" (1988: 143). In a survey of rural Shandong, Xue Xingli, Xin Xiangmu, and Liu Guiyuan (1998) found that more than 30 percent of elderly people over 60 years of age support themselves through their own labor.

FIGURE I. Elderly parents living apart from their children occupy the older of the family residences in Zhongshan, Hubei. Photo by Hong Zhang.

Based on survey data from Wuhan in the mid-1980s, Jonathan Unger (1993) found that parents with state pensions were four times more likely to live apart from all their children than were the elderly without pensions. But if we look at the Zhongshan data, self-sufficiency was not necessarily the determining factor in elderly parents living alone, as the majority of them continued to receive their main food supply from their married sons. Thus, in Zhongshan, "living separately" does not mean "living self-sufficiently," nor does it suggest an absence of economic support from children.

Related to the issue of "self-sufficiency" is the level of prosperity or wealth. Familial interdependence and extended family living arrangements have generally been thought of as features of a subsistence, nonindustrial economy. A more developed and modern economy with goods and services readily available to anyone with cash is one in which individualism and privacy are emphasized (Becker 1981; Caldwell 1981). "Families with sufficiently high income are able to purchase the desired independence in living arrangement. Thus, economic growth in a society should reduce the need as well as the incentive for living in extended households" (Chattopadhyay and Marsh 1999: 527). Studies comparing rural and urban China on the correlation between income and living arrangements seem to support this view. Based on 1990 census data from Sichuan, Zhang Junliang found that on average the annual income of the urban elderly was almost four times higher than that of their rural counterparts—2,764 yuan for the urban elderly as opposed to only 785 yuan for the rural elderly (Zhang 1995). Higher income enjoyed by the city elderly is correlated with the high percentage of them living alone. A 1987 national survey showed that urban elderly are almost three times more likely to live alone or with a spouse than their rural counterparts (Lin 1995). An ethnographic study by Melvyn Goldstein, Yachun Ku, and Charlotte Ikels (1990) in rural Zhejiang is also a case in point. This study demonstrates that in the relatively prosperous village of Pingyuan, 50 percent of the elderly were living alone or with a spouse whereas in the poorer village of Shancun, only 26 percent did so. According to the authors, it was the greater prosperity of Pingyuan that enabled their elders to live alone. More new houses have been built in Pingyuan, and "because their sons are generally doing well economically, the elderly in Pingyuan were able to obtain financial assistance from married/separated sons in the form of regular cash payments. The elderly themselves are also doing better economically than their counterparts in Shancun in the sense of having higher income from their agricultural endeavors" (Goldstein, Ku, and Ikels 1990: 128). But if we look at the Zhongshan data, there is no clear economic pattern that determines whose parents are more likely to live alone. Some families were struggling economically according to the village's standards, and yet their parents were living alone. Likewise, some families were relatively well off, and their parents were nonetheless living in a stem-family structure.

Studies have found that in urban China age and health can be factors determining whether elders will live alone or with their married children. Based on a 1986 survey on Shanghai elderly, Unger (1993), for example, found that "as the elderly increasingly aged, they were more likely to enter the family of a married child." This survey shows that of the 835 truly aged Shanghai residents studied—those over 80 years of age—fully 80 percent "lived with married children, far greater than the 52–53 percent of Shanghai elderly sixty years old and over who were living with married children" (Unger 1993: 45). Deborah Davis's study of the elderly in urban Shanghai also leads her to comment that although "the ideal housing arrangement was an independent household for each nuclear family," the need to provide care for aged and frail parents repeatedly "overrode the desire to establish nuclear

households, and the norm was multigenerational homes and persistent complexity" (Davis 1993: 56–57). Given the lack of independent resources such
as pensions and savings that many urban elderly enjoy, it is almost imperative that truly aged rural parents live with and be supported by their married
children. However, evidence from Zhongshan shows that old age does not
necessarily guarantee a multigenerational living arrangement, as almost half
of the parents living alone were over 70 years of age, and many of them had
some health problems. Two were actually bedridden and were taken care of
solely by their respective spouses.

Why do parents move out of the stem family to live separately? What has
motivated them to do so? When asked these questions, the most frequent
answer I received was *ziyou* (freedom). According to these Zhongshan parents, life is too stressful living in a three-generation household. They have to
constantly help with household chores, from taking care of grandchildren,
to feeding the farm animals, to tending the vegetable plots. Differences in
food preferences are also frequently mentioned as a reason for separate living. Older people generally prefer to eat softer foods; and thus living together often means the elderly cannot eat what they like. Older villagers also
point out that young people are not as respectful of older people as in the
past; close contact on a daily basis often leads to more disputes and strained
family relations, which in turns adds stress to their lives. By living separately,
these parents argued, they could enjoy freedom in all aspects. They could
cook and eat whatever they liked, and whenever they wanted. They could
also control their own time and could take a nap or chat with old friends
without being constantly worried about doing household chores in their
son's family. When comparing his single-generation household life now with
his three-generation household life before, one father commented:

> I now have much more freedom (*ziyou duole*) and some cash too. I have
> some indulgences; I like to smoke and have two drinks every day. But when
> I was living with my son's family, they were very reluctant to spend money
> on me. We would quarrel over these matters endlessly, and I often ended
> up not getting my cigarettes and drinks. Now living separately from them,
> I can get some cash from the chickens I raise, and now I can smoke and
> drink whenever I want.

Disguised under the desire for more "freedom" and "convenience" are often the realities of strained intergenerational relationships. More than 80 per-

cent of the elderly parents living alone had fierce and constant quarrels with their adult children before they moved out to live separately. The fate of a 78-year-old widow provides a telling example. This woman had a married son living in the village. By all standards she should have been living with her son's family, as she was of advanced age, had bound feet, and had only one son.[3] However, there were daily arguments in the household such that living separately became the only tolerable alternative for her. She did not set up a separate dwelling but continued to live in the original family house, though she added a small kitchen space for herself. Hers is a type of living arrangement known locally as *danguo* (going it alone) or *ling kaihuo* (having a separate stove). She did not eat with her son's family and was responsible for her own daily needs including fetching drinking water, washing her own clothes, and tending to her vegetable plot.[4] However, her son was supposed to provide most of her food and cooking oil. She had lived alone for two years when I first visited her in 1993. She told me that her son had not given her any grain in the past two months, and she had to support herself by gleaning grain from the harvested fields. In tears, she said that she wished she did not have a son so that she could qualify for the "five guarantees." When I interviewed her son, one of the reasons he gave for their separation was that his mother "talked too much" and did not help him in the busy farm season as "she was busy gathering leftovers from the harvest for herself."

For some other elderly parents, one of the benefits of living separately was that it ensured their sons would contribute equally to their support. The story told by a father of two sons was a case in point. From 1983 to 1985, this man and his wife were living with their younger son's family because their older son had already set up a separate household shortly after his marriage in 1978. At that time the older son did not contribute to supporting the parents, the agreement being that since the parents were still healthy enough to bring in some extra income for the younger son's family, the latter would provide for their support. But in 1985, the father had a stroke and was partially paralyzed. For months his younger son spent both time and money to take him to different places for treatment while his elder son refused to lend a hand. When he started recovering, the father decided to leave his younger son's family to live separately. His argument was that if he and his wife started living separately from their younger son's family, both his sons would contribute equally to his old age support instead of the burden being solely on his younger son. By the time of my fieldwork in 1993–94, the father and his wife had lived by themselves for more than eight years. His two sons each were taking turns providing support, which was mainly in the form of rice, meat, and cooking oil. In return, the father and his wife also helped out their sons during busy seasons. In early 1994, his wife died, but he continued to live alone. He was satisfied with this arrangement, emphasizing that it was fair and avoided conflicts between his sons with regard to providing support. Thus, for this aging father, living alone actually became the best way of guaranteeing support from both his sons in his old age.

However, what I also found revealing from my interviews with these elderly parents was that some of them claimed that "living alone" actually made their sons more "filial," and that their relationship with their sons also started improving once they lived on their own. One couple told me that when they lived with their younger son's family, part of the agreement between their two sons was that the elder son would provide 700 jin of unhusked rice each year. However, the elder son often failed to do so on the grounds that his parents were helping with household chores in his brother's family but not his. The father had argued with his elder son many times, demanding that he fulfill his agreement, but always in vain. As a result, their relationship was severely strained. Moreover, the father also felt that his life at his younger son's household was very difficult. He was doing hard manual labor in the fields despite his age, but the younger son still complained that his father had too many "costly" indulgences and he would often deny his father's requests for drinks and cigarettes, which in turn led to fierce disputes.[5] According to the father, moving out of his younger son's family was a last resort: he had no other way to protest his sons' "unfilial" behavior. Through the mediation of the village cadres, his two sons agreed to provide their parents with 700 jin each of unhusked rice a year. The parents reciprocated by agreeing to herd their shared water buffalo, take care of the grandchildren, and cook during the busy season. When I visited the elderly couple in 1994, they had been living separately for more than two years. The father told me that in those two years, he had a better relationship with his two sons than he ever had before, and that both his sons now behaved more filially and respectfully. Here we can see how "filial piety" is redefined or compromised in contemporary rural China. Although the very act of letting one's elderly parents live alone and not providing daily care for them already violates the most basic premises of "filial piety," to this Zhongshan father his sons can still be considered filial even though they do no more than just meet their parents' basic food needs.

However, a major reason why many Zhongshan elderly consider living alone is to regain their financial autonomy and control over their own budget. For the majority of China's rural elderly, living in three-generation households means they no longer assume the role of family head and do not control the family budget. Data from Zhongshan indicate that only three older fathers out of a total of eighty-one in stem families were in charge of the common household budget. Furthermore, most elderly parents have no separate savings of their own. Many find their lives very constrained by their lack of economic power within the household. No matter whether they need some money to see relatives, to visit a village clinic, or for leisure activities, they have to ask their sons or daughters-in-law. Disputes often arise when parents' requests for pocket money are ignored or denied. By living alone, parents can manage their own budget and gain better control of their own lives. This factor becomes particularly relevant for those elderly parents who are still physically capable of light manual labor and can earn a cash income. In one case, an elderly father told me that he and his wife started living separately from their only son in order to avoid an increasingly impoverished life. According to the father, when he himself was the family head before his son was married, his household's annual income was above the average in the village. But since his son got married and started controlling the family budget in the late 1980s, his family was going downhill and had become one of the poorest in the village. Apparently, his son failed in several "business" attempts and had to borrow money to pay the land tax and fees (the father also suspected that his son had lost money gambling). Although the father might have been more capable at managing the family finances, he had little say in his son's family. He and his wife felt they had to move out in order to protect themselves against the increasing uncertainty facing their son's family. Similarly, after comparing the net income and family support in rural Zhejiang between elderly parents who lived in the "ideal" extended family and those who lived alone, Goldstein and Ku conclude that "the elderly who were living with married sons in the 'ideal' family situation had limited or no access to their household's cash income and thus generally were worse off with respect to economic independence and access to non-subsistence goods than elderly living alone or with spouses" (1993: 219).

As for their comments on their present living arrangements, Zhongshan's elderly parents all claimed that their mental state, health, and life in general had improved greatly since they started living separately. When asked if they

ever planned to move back into their sons' housholds, the answer was negative. These Zhongshan parents said that since they fared better now than in
a three-generation household, there was no point in moving back. They
cherished their newly gained freedom and were afraid that once they moved
back, they would lose it all and the same pattern of disputes and household
chores would reemerge. While most of them said they would live separately
as long as they could and then see what happened, some did mention that
when their death was imminent, they would move back so as to avoid becoming wandering ghosts. Apparently, the villagers in this Hubei community share a Chinese belief that to die at home with family members at one's
deathbed not only marks the completion of a person's life cycle but also is a
protective measure for later generations. It is believed that if one dies outside
the home, one will become a wandering ghost, which could come back to
haunt and bring ill fortune to the offspring. So it is in the interest of both
the person who dies and his or her offspring that death take place at home
and that burial be with appropriate ritual.[6] Having said this, one elderly
Zhongshan couple told me that they had lost all hope with regard to their
two sons and would never move back. They claimed that they did not care
if they became wandering ghosts since they were now no better than homeless, hungry ghosts anyway; if refusing to go home to die would bring ill fortune to their sons' families, their sons deserved it.[7]

However, elderly parents' living alone is not without controversy in
Zhongshan. The majority of the villagers still agree that the ideal living
arrangement for elderly parents is to live with and be taken care of by their
adult children. Elderly parents' living alone carries negative connotations for
both parents and their adult children. It is disgraceful for the parents, as they
would seem to be "unwanted" and abandoned by their own sons. Sons who
allow their parents to live alone would be condemned as "unfilial" for "de-
serting their own parents." These negative views are reinforced by the fact
that most of the parents moved out of their son's family as a result of ir-
reconcilable disputes. Once the elderly decided to live alone, however, they
generally won more sympathy from their fellow villagers, and it was their
sons who felt the heat of blame as "unfilial." Public sanctions against obviously "unfilial" behavior still remain strong in the community. This might
explain why some parents found their sons starting to behave more respectfully and filially after they moved out and lived alone. These sons needed to
compensate for the consequences of their "unfilial" behavior that led to their

parents living alone in the first place. In this regard, "living alone" or "living separately" has the potential to become a form of bargaining power for parents who still live in a stem family. Since "living alone" can create a public embarrassment for sons who get the reputation of being unfilial, elderly parents living in a three-generation household can force their sons to meet some of their requirements by threatening to move out and "live alone." Indeed, I know of several cases in which elderly parents had successfully used such "threats" to force their sons to perform their filial obligations. Thus, "living alone" can also become a strategy elderly parents use to renegotiate and maintain support in their old age.

Coresidence and Vulnerability of the Elderly

International discourse on the demographic transition and care for the elderly identifies what is called the "Asian care model," which is defined as family support with a high level of intergenerational coresidence. This model has often been invoked as an alternative to the government- and institution-based support found in industrial countries (Hashimoto, Kendig, and Coppard 1992; Hermalin 1997; Knodel and Debavalya 1992; Morgan and Hirosima 1983; Ogawa 1990). When examining living arrangements in six developing Asian countries between 1984 and 1991, for example, John Knodel and Nibhon Debavalya (1992) found that 66 percent to 84 percent of the elderly aged 60 and older coresided with their children, and thus they concluded that "a pervasive family system of support and care has persisted despite major social and economic change." According to Akiko Hashimoto, Hal Kendig, and Larry Coppard (1992), the relatively high incidence of extended families in such developed countries and regions as Japan and Taiwan demonstrates the strength of the cultural basis of family responsibility for the care and support of the elderly in Asian societies. Naohiro Ogawa (1990) reports that in Japan and other Asian countries, the majority of the bedridden elderly live in extended family settings and are looked after by middle-aged women who are not part of the labor force. He regards this elderly care as the standard and warns that the well-being of the elderly sick might seriously deteriorate if alternative care has to be developed as a result of more middle-aged women participating in the labor force. In some Asian countries, government policies and programs have been developed to further encourage

FIGURE 2.   Newer housing in Zhongshan is usually occupied by conjugal family units consisting of young or middle-aged couples and their children. Photo by Hong Zhang.

coresidence across generations and family-based support for the elderly. In Singapore, for example, the government provides the younger generation with numerous incentives, such as tax deductions or priority housing, if they care for or live with an elderly parent (Chan 1997).

However, some other observers claim that Asian family structures are rapidly changing, and that the role of the family in the support of the elderly is in decline due to such social changes as migration, urbanization, and increased female labor force participation (Hu 1995; Martin 1988, 1990; Mason 1992). Yow-Hwey Hu goes so far as to challenge the Asian care model as the best for the elderly in a rapidly changing social and economic environment, stating "Asian elderly are currently very vulnerable in their socially constructed total dependence on children" (Hu 1995: 199). Using the suicide rate as an indicator of the well-being of the elderly, Hu's data show that suicide among the elderly in East Asian countries is twice as high as that of their counterparts in Western countries. When comparing the suicide rates of different age groups, Hu also finds that the elderly in East Asian countries are five times more likely to kill themselves than members of the younger generations of their own societies while in Western countries, suicide rates remain more similar across all age groups. Since the elderly are more likely to live with their families in the East Asian countries, the high rate of suicide among them indicates that they do not "enjoy greater life satisfaction or a better quality of life than their western counterparts among whom independent living is preferred and direct state finance for social security and medical care are their main concern" (1995: 201). Hu argues that in rapidly industrializing and urbanizing Taiwan, the elderly living in extended families have suffered positional decline within the family and a discontinuity in social life and physical environment, making them "far more vulnerable," and putting them at high risk of suicide.

Based on her cross-cultural study of the factors affecting the well-being of older people, Jennie Keith finds that in Hong Kong, coresidence between the elderly and their adult children may not necessarily indicate a voluntary and congenial family unit, as it "may be forced by lack of economic resources and may be correlated with lower levels of well-being for the elderly people." When imposed by limited resources and a shortage of housing, coresidence may become "a setting for friction between generations estranged from each other by extreme change in both values and technology" (Keith 1992: 26; Keith, Fry, and Ikels 1990).

Most studies of the elderly in contemporary China tend to emphasize the positive aspects of coresidence: it is described as having "mutual benefits for both generations," fulfilling the "intergenerational contract, intergenerational entitlement," providing "the best and most natural care and emotional support for the elderly," and demonstrating the "long cultural tradition of caring for and respecting the aged" (Davis 1993; Davis-Friedmann 1991; Ikels 1993; Kwong and Cai 1992; Sher 1984). Given China's relative poverty, the government's lack of funds, and the huge number of rural elderly who are not supported by any state pension plan, the care of the rural elderly in the home and by family members is also the only alternative available today. Thus, the state has a strong vested interest in promoting and even regulating family support by law. The right to old-age support from one's children is stipulated in various Chinese laws such as China's constitution, the Marriage Law, and criminal law. In 1996, a new law intended solely to protect the interests and rights of the elderly was passed.[8] The second chapter of this new law is devoted to the issue of family support and care. Article 10 reads "Elderly support is mainly dependent upon family members who should show concern for and take care of their elders."

Recent increases in legal cases involving parents suing their children for failing to provide old-age support, as well as media reports of increased incidences of parental abuse and abandonment, have led to a growing public concern over whether the family is still capable or willing to take care of their elderly (Hai 1998; Xu 1996; Yao 1999). Nonetheless, there are very few studies exploring the potential negative aspects of coresidence for the elderly in today's changing Chinese society. But a family tragedy reported by Yan Yunxiang (1997) in his study of a Heilongjiang village is revealing. On a chilly winter night, a 64-year-old man ended his life by drinking a bottle of pesticide. In studying the reactions of the older villagers to this incident, to his surprise Yan found that many said that this old man's death could have been prevented if he had chosen to live alone. In other words, in many of the older villagers' minds, coresidence possibly triggered this old man's death since it had led to intensification of family conflict.

In my interviews with older villagers who live in stem families in Zhongshan, I also found a strong sense of ambiguity with regard to their living arrangements and life situation. On the one hand, they recognized that to spend their later years with their children's families was a normative way of life. On the other hand, many of them also confessed that their current living arrangements were the only ones open to them and that as a result their lives were severely constrained. Their complaints ranged from constant pressure to do too many household chores despite their frail health and old age, to distress from frequent daily disputes with their married son or daughter-in-law, inconvenience due to different lifestyles,[9] and lack of economic independence and power within the household. It seems that coresidence in the social and economic realities of the post-Mao reform era may actually make the elderly more, rather than less, vulnerable. Below I identify four new situations in the post-Mao reform period that seem to have particularly negative effects on the well-being of the rural elderly living in coresidential settings.

First, while the new reform policy, which returned land to farm families and emphasized productivity and profits, seemed to strengthen the conjugal unit, on the other hand it increased the competition among brothers to the detriment of their elderly parents. In the new freewheeling economy, brothers are now more interested in conserving and investing for the best possible return for their individual conjugal family rather than spending money and time taking care of their elderly parents. Thus brothers may find various excuses to evade their filial duty, or pass it on to others. This is especially true if their elderly parents are in bad health. According to Zhongshan villagers, agreement on old-age support was particularly hard to reach among brothers who have parents with some kind of chronic illness. If parents are in reasonably good health and can perform manual work, coresiding with their son's family often means they have to do various household chores for this son's family. It almost seems that the parents have to pay for living with their son's family. Within the household, family dynamics have also witnessed dramatic changes in recent decades. In the first three decades of Mao's socialist rule, collectivization and the state's attack on ancestor worship and parental arrangements of marriage had already weakened the traditional father-son relationship that emphasized filial piety and the absolute authority of seniority. Accompanying the decline of the father-son relationship was the rise of the conjugal-based husband-and-wife relationship. Since the post-Mao reforms, new economic opportunities seem to have reinforced the younger generation's conjugal ties and their demand for conjugal independence.[10] In stem families, this newly configured relationship often means that in family conflicts involving daughters-in-law, parents find that their son sides with his wife instead of them (Yan 1997). Many elderly parents cannot adjust to these new dynamics, and my informal interviews with older villagers reveal that they were very pessimistic about life in their son's family. In a stem family where there is close contact between the generations on a daily basis, frequent quarrels are almost unavoidable; the result can sometimes become fatal for the elderly parents. The old man's suicide in Yan's village cited above is a good example. In Zhongshan, at least nine elderly parents committed suicide between 1991 to 2000.[11] In one case, a widow with two sons lived in a household consisting of herself, her elder son and his family, and her unmarried younger son. But this widow never got along well with her elder son's wife, and relations were always tense. Thus the widow was counting on getting her younger son married and living with his family. In 1983, her younger son indeed married, and the two brothers set up separate households immediately. She moved in with her younger son's family. It turned out that as time went by, she had an even more difficult time getting along with her younger son's wife, who was notoriously sharp tongued. To make matters worse, her younger son was very quiet and had a reputation of being henpecked. In 1991, the widow got sick, and knowing that she was not going to get any treatment without causing more disputes, she took her life by hanging herself.

The second unfavorable condition for the rural elderly to be discussed here is the disintegration of the collective economy since the reforms. To some extent, the previous collective system provided a "socialist safety net" for security in old age (Lin 1995). The collective distribution system was conducive to reinforcing the senior male's role as family head, as he could still represent his household in receiving grain and cash income based on the total number of workpoints earned by family members and in that way control the family budget despite his old age (Cohen 1998; Davis-Friedmann 1991; Parish and Whyte 1978). Depending on the ratio of consumers to producers in the household, and the output of the collective economy, family income might fluctuate from year to year. Consequently, the standard of living of the elderly might rise and fall with the rest of the family members, but they were not uniquely or especially vulnerable. The collective system also guaranteed a basic livelihood for all the villagers, including even the destitute elderly who were too old or sick to work and yet who had no family to support them. The heavily subsidized medical system in the collective years also provided low-cost health service to the elderly and their family members. With the dismantling of the collective economy since the early 1980s, many of the welfare services previously provided by the collective system are no longer available. The reemergence of the family as the unit of production and management seems to give the younger generation an incentive to demand financial autonomy and conjugal independence. Their priority is their own individual conjugal unit rather than the well-being of their elderly parents. The collapse of the collective economy also means that the burden of old-age support is entirely shouldered by family members, leaving both the elderly parents and their adult children with no other alternatives. Privatization of the rural health-care system in many areas means that rural patients pay for their medical needs completely out of their own pocket. According to Gu Xinghua and his coauthors (1993), in the mid- and late 1970s, 90 percent of China's villages were covered by cooperative medical schemes that provided low-cost health services. But decollectivization has led to the collapse of many cooperative medical care schemes. "By the late 1980s, only five percent of rural residents were covered" (Gu et al., 1993: 386). Paying out of pocket has now become the main or only way for rural residents to get medical care. In Zhongshan, the village clinic, even after the reform, is still operated on a cooperative basis in the sense that the village doctors do not provide their medical service for profit but are paid a fixed salary by the village. But the cost of visiting the village clinics has gone up, as instead of paying a low flat fee as in the collective years, villagers now have to pay according to the medical service they need. Moreover, the health services available in the village exclude surgery and are restricted to treating common ailments. For more complicated medical conditions and chronic illnesses, villagers have to go to the township or county hospitals, all of which are fee-based and nonsubsidized. Taking care of elderly parents can thus become potentially costly and burdensome for rural families. I was repeatedly told that because of their lack of access both to cash and to the household budget, many elderly parents in stem families often did not get medical help when needed. In fact, many of them did not even seek medical help either because they did not want to burden their son with additional expenses or because they were afraid their son might refuse to pay. Ironically, it is those elderly who were living alone who would and did visit the village clinic as they saw fit, since they ran their own budget and controlled whatever cash income they could generate.

Third, a combination of demographic forces and changed social and economic factors also threatens the security of China's rural elderly today. As a group, the rural elderly over 60 years of age have experienced extreme vicissitudes in their lives. Most of them spent their formative years in the prerevolutionary era, their prime years in Mao's collective system, and began to enter old age just as the Mao era ended and Deng Xiaoping's reforms started. While improved health conditions and life expectancy after 1949 have enabled them to live a much longer life than most of their parents, they do not necessarily enjoy a happy and satisfactory life in their later years. They have generally been unable to take full advantage of the economic opportunities provided by the reforms, since they had already retired or were about to retire when the reforms started. On average, elderly parents in the 1990s have raised more sons than both their parents' generation and their sons' generation, the fertility of the former being curtailed by poverty and wars in the prerevolutionary period, and of the latter by the strict family-planning polices enforced since the late 1970s. However, to the dismay of many parents, having more grown-up sons in the 1990s does not necessarily guarantee them security in their old age (Yang and Chandler 1992). As their grown-up sons reached marriageable age in the late 1970s and the 1980s, these parents immediately faced the reality that more sons meant greater economic burdens and a greater drain on their limited savings, this because of the skyrocketing increase in the cost of weddings since the reforms. In

Zhongshan, the cost of a wedding during the collective years averaged around 100 to 200 yuan. But in the late 1980s and early 1990s, the average cost ran from at least 2,000 to 4,000 yuan. The end result is that if they still had a younger son or sons waiting to get married in the late 1980s and early 1990s, elderly parents had to work hard in the fields despite their failing physical strength. Once their last son is married, parents often find themselves with no cash savings and totally dependent on their sons.

Recent comparative studies have shown that the urban elderly are generally more satisfied with their lives and enjoy a better intergenerational relationship than their rural counterparts (Zhang 1995). What is different for the urban elderly is that they have access to state pensions and medical coverage after retirement, which their rural counterparts do not. Their pensions plus savings make the urban elderly more self-sufficient and less dependent economically on their families. If they are coresiding with their adult children, urban parents still have their own salary or pensions at their disposal and can set up separate living arrangements should conflicts arise. However, their rural counterparts do not have such leverage. It might well be that because of their lack of economic independence the rural elderly have to coreside with and be supported by their family members. However, as we have seen, coresidence does not necessarily guarantee that they get the care and support they need. According to one study, the rural elderly were more worried about their "lack of social support from their relatives and friends" (Liu, Liang, and Gu 1995: 1182).

The last grave problem facing the rural elderly in coresidential settings in the reform era is the lack of an effective intervention mechanism in cases of parental neglect. Although the ideology of "filial piety" played an important role in the traditional system that supported old-age security in China, it never existed in a vacuum. Before 1949, parental control of family land and property, parental authority and power within the household, and the social norms dictating behavior for the children sanctioned by the strong lineage-based local community could all serve to insure the care of aging parents. During the collective years, although the balance of power was starting to shift within the household, old-age support was not seriously undermined due to a number of reasons. First, as mentioned earlier, the collective distribution system reinforced the senior male's role as family head, which allowed him to control the family budget in his old age. Second, the collective system gave village cadres greater power in intervening in cases of parental abuse and neglect since they were in charge of distributing the grain and income for every family in the village, and could influence villagers' behavior through administrative means. With the collapse of the collective economy, however, each individual family became responsible for its own production and distribution. Consequently, cadres' ability to intervene in cases of parental abuse has been greatly reduced. Moreover, my observations in Zhongshan show that most of the current cadres were in their late 30s and 40s, and thus were themselves facing the same issue of how to balance their conjugal interest and their filial duty to support aging parents. Data from Zhongshan show that between 1993 and 1994 there were at least three cases involving village cadres' parents moving out of the stem family and starting to live alone as a result of disputes over old-age support.

Studies dealing with aging problems in developing countries, especially countries where the family plays a central role in providing old-age support, tend to emphasize that as a group the elderly are marginalized in the modernization process (Cowgill 1974; Goode 1963; Martin 1988; Mason 1992; Thornton and Fricke 1987). Industrialization and urbanization, these studies argue, erode family care, since the elderly are more likely to be separated from their family members because of the younger generation's greater participation in wage labor and rural-urban migration. The elderly are more likely to be trapped in traditional and less rewarding jobs and, lacking modern education, are also less capable of adapting to rapid socioeconomic and lifestyle changes. But recent trends in China seem to indicate that older people are by no means passive when facing a changing social landscape. In her study of elderly support in a Hunan village in 1987, Jia Aimei (1988) found that the modal preference of the elderly was "to live independently." Of the elderly she interviewed, 53 percent said they preferred to live by themselves, while only 35 percent said they would prefer to live with a son. Data from Susan Greenhalgh's three Shaanxi villages suggest that "parents were beginning to entertain doubts about the reliability of filial support. . . . Of those cared for by their sons, only two-fifths believed that such an arrangement was ideal" (Greenhalgh 1994: 54). Goldstein, Ku, and Ikels's study of two Zhejiang villages also reveals that rural elderly nowadays do not think the traditional arrangement of coresiding with at least one married son and his family is a "realistic aspiration." Changes in their sons' and daughters-in-laws' attitudes tending toward less filial piety and greater conjugal independence have made the elderly feel it is now more difficult than in the past to live an extended-family life. As a result, they generally "prefer the greater freedom and lesser conflict/stress of living alone (or with a spouse)" (1990: 127–28). Wang Yi-long's survey in another Zhejiang village in the late 1990s shows that most rural elderly think that young people nowadays are more "selfish" and "less respectful of old people" than young people in the past, and that some even prefer institutions over families to take care of their old age. Wang interviewed 15 elderly parents and asked them if they would be willing to spend their later years at the old people's home (Jing lao yuan). They all replied "very willing" (Wang 1999). Based on the national census data from several large cities, Unger (1993) found a dramatic change in parents' preference for living arrangements from 1977 to 1985. Between 1977 and 1982, about 69 percent of parents thought it best that a married child live with them. But by 1984–85, the trend reversed its course to a range of 48 to 68 percent of parents who did not want to live with any of their married children.

My interview data from Zhongshan on this issue are also revealing: most young and middle-aged villagers (in their 30s and 40s) told me that they actually preferred to have their parents live with them. The reasons given include: parents could help with childcare, do some household chores, or simply watch the house during the busy farm season. They argued that it was the old people themselves who wanted to live alone for more "freedom" and "convenience." In a way, the younger cohorts of Zhongshan villagers almost seem to put the blame on their elderly parents for choosing to live alone for the sake of their own "convenience" and "freedom." Older villagers, on the other hand, were seriously doubtful that their old-age needs were better taken care of when they were living with their children. They indeed seemed to see living alone as an opportunity to gain better control of their own lives. It is almost as if they embraced "living alone" as a way of maintaining autonomy in the face of their diminishing authority and a shift of power to the younger generation within the household. If given the opportunity, most of my older Zhongshan villagers said they would prefer to live separately from their adult children.

Conclusion

Although Zhongshan villagers may still have reservations about elderly parents living alone, doing so has not only become more acceptable, but also more and more commonplace.[12] Although in general elderly Zhongshan parents who lived alone told me that since they started living separately they were happier and healthier, they still faced real difficulties by choosing to live alone. They had to take care of their own daily needs, such as cooking, washing clothes, tending the vegetable garden, gathering wood for fuel, and fetching water in the nearby river, lake, or well. Although they might bring in some cash income for themselves by living separately from their adult children, what they could earn was very limited. Many of them told me that if they had just some minor sickness, they might visit a village clinic, but if they became very ill, they would not seek any medical help, and would just wait to die.

Moreover, even though living alone does have the advantage of allowing the elderly to control their own lives, it is not an option for many. Judging from the situation in Zhongshan, most parents over 65 years of age live with their youngest married son in a stem family arrangement. Although the Confucian ideal is to live with an elder son, many elderly parents now end up living with their youngest son because of a new form of family division that Myron Cohen refers to as "serial division" (Cohen 1992, 1998). In this form of family division, the first married son sets up a separate household soon after his marriage, leaving his parents and unmarried younger brother(s) living in the old household. This same process repeats itself when the second son marries, until the last son, who often stays with his parents in the old residence. The trend for this form of family division apparently began in the late 1960s (Cohen 1992; Parish and Whyte 1978), and it has been reported in many parts of China (Harrell 1993; Huang 1992; Selden 1993; Yan 1997). For many Zhongshan parents, to live alone thus means to build a new, separate dwelling. Not many elderly parents have the resources this requires. There is also the issue of how long they can live alone and who will look after them once they become too old to take care of themselves. Perhaps the real significance of the recent development of elderly parents living alone is that it makes the generation currently in their 40s realize that they may not be able to count on old-age support from their own children. This in turn makes them see the importance of starting to save for their later years now, while they are still in their prime of life. Indeed, Greenhalgh finds that doubt about filial support was "stronger among younger informants, who had not yet had to face the question of how they would make it through old age"; only one third of the 131 younger household heads in her survey said they considered "children the optimal means of support" (1994: 54). Since the late 1980s, the state has begun to encourage local governments to experiment with social insurance schemes for old-age security in some economically more advanced rural regions. Such schemes, however, are mostly geared toward the middle-aged, who are required to put a certain amount of monthly (or yearly) premiums aside now, and ten or twenty or thirty years later can access the money to support themselves in their old age (Cai and Zhang 2000). It is still not clear whether such social security schemes can be successfully carried out. As for those who have already entered old age, there is very little relief coming their way. For the most part, they are left to fend for themselves. One 72-year-old father of two married sons confided to me that he had accumulated almost an entire bottle of sleeping pills. When he got too sick or his relations with his sons and daughters-in-law ran too sour, he said, this bottle of sleeping pills would end it all.

CHAPTER 5

Serving the Ancestors, Serving the State: Filial Piety and Death Ritual in Contemporary Guangzhou

CHARLOTTE IKELS

The post-1949 Chinese government has viewed filial piety with ambivalence. Although in the early 1950s the state actively denounced the tyranny of the traditional family system and asked young people to draw a line between themselves and their parents of bad class background, it quickly switched directions and countered with a campaign to emphasize respect and support of parents when it found young people neglecting their elderly (Chen and Chen 1959). The 1980 Marriage Law, unlike the 1950 law that it replaced, further emphasizes the special protection of the aged (as well as of women and children) and the obligations of parents, children and, in their absence, of grandchildren to mutually support each other (Ikels 1996). State approval of filial piety has its limits, however, and nowhere is this better seen than in the case of death ritual.

Late-nineteenth- and early-twentieth-century accounts of southern Chinese mortuary rites document their importance as indicators of filial piety (De Groot 1964; Doolittle 1865; Yang 1961). During the Maoist era these same rites were condemned as wasteful and superstition-ridden, and in the urban areas cremation gradually replaced burial as the only legitimate means of body disposition. In the post-Mao era the state has held the line on cremation but has loosened up its policies with regard to other traditional practices. Here I will address the following questions: How have urban families utilized this newly opened ritual space? How have they contested state limits on the expression of filial piety? What constitutes an acceptable series of rites that will earn its sponsors recognition as filial children? Why and how do some children exceed these newly established norms?

State Models of Proper Mortuary Ritual

While the previous chapters have focused on providing care for living parents, this chapter focuses on the duties of "showing sorrow over their death," that is, providing an appropriate funeral and "sacrific[ing] to them with solemnity" through subsequent memorialization within the home and at the grave site. Precise guidelines for both of these activities could be easily found in one of the many editions of Zhu Xi's *Family Rituals* (Ebrey 1991), which since the twelfth century set the standard for filial conduct though, as Patricia Ebrey (p. xxix) points out, how people applied this liturgy to their own concrete situations no doubt varied. Indeed, Zhu Xi himself wrote as a Confucian reformer of funeral rites and explicitly denounced as unfilial the intrusion of Buddhist practices such as inviting monks to chant in order to improve the parent's postmortem circumstances because such practices impugned the parent's own virtue.

State interest in regulating mortuary ritual did not begin with the government of the People's Republic of China. The imperial state had long maintained a special interest in the conduct of mortuary ritual for at least two reasons: first, the filial piety of which it was an expression was also viewed as the basis on which loyalty to the emperor as father of the people could rest (Kutcher 1999), and second, uniformity in ritual practice was a means of promoting Confucian ideology and sentiments that could help to unify the country politically and culturally (Rawski 1988a; J. Watson 1988). Since government officials were expected to serve as models of filiality and loyalty and to promote conformity in ritual practice, they were held to the most stringent standards of mourning, for example, in the case of parental death, ideally absenting themselves from their posts for three years (understood to mean more than two years or twenty-seven months [Kutcher 1999]). Though officials and those aspiring to officialdom generally did their best to conduct mortuary rituals at least in public in conformance with state expectations, they and the bulk of the population were also influenced in their practices by Buddhism, Daoism, and local manifestations of Chinese popular religion (Cohen 1988; Kutcher 1999).

In disposing of their dead, ordinary families had three predominant concerns—all of which, from a strictly orthodox (Confucian) perspective, could be construed as unfilial. The first concern involved exposure to death pollution incurred through proximity or contact with the corpse or the site of the death (Watson 1982). Families took various precautions to mitigate their exposure to death pollution and to placate the soul of the deceased so that it would rest in peace and not come back to disturb them. Such precautions, critics argued, indicated mistrust of the good motives of the ancestors. The second concern was to assist the deceased in the transit through the underworld so that s/he would have a quick and favorable rebirth. These goals were achieved by burning paper goods and spirit money to sustain the soul on its journey and by hiring Buddhist monks to chant sutras and gain merit on its behalf. According to critics, these practices testified to doubts about the worthiness of the deceased and to a belief in a supernatural realm about which Confucianism preferred to say little. The final concern involved the ancient belief in geomancy or *fengshui* (literally, wind and water), according to which the siting of the grave could bring good fortune or disaster to its occupant's descendants. The geomantic forces flowing through the grave site were thought to be absorbed by the bones (the shared substance of the ancestors and their descendants) and conveyed thereby to succeeding generations. The unfilial aspect was the instrumental treatment of ancestral remains, regarding them as mere means to an end (Freedman 1967).

However, all of these "unfilial" concerns were masked by the elaborateness of the funeral, which in most people's eyes came to be seen as the true measure of filial piety. (See Chapter 4 for further discussion of how proper attention to parental mortuary ritual redeemed village sons who had been neglectful of still-living parents.) A handsomely made coffin, weeping and wailing descendants, chanting monks, funerary offerings, a lengthy procession to the burial site accompanied by a band playing appropriate music, an auspiciously sited grave, periodic offerings of food and paper money during the liminal period prior to rebirth (or arrival in the Western Paradise), installation of an ancestral tablet in the home of the eldest son, and annual or semiannual public "worshiping" at the gravesite were considered a parent's due, and families regularly went into debt to meet these obligations and, thereby, to maintain or enhance their local reputations. Thus, any particular set of mortuary rituals likely reflected both the social status of the deceased and/or the deceased's family and the combined influences of the orthodox Confucian model and local customs.

The reach of the state was not unlimited. During the imperial era its official authority extended directly only to the county magistrate. Below the level of the county seat, the state relied on the gentry and, particularly in the southern regions, the clan to enforce its edicts and maintain social stability (Chang 1955; Van der Sprenkel 1962). In the urban areas similar functions were carried out by guilds. Under these circumstances it behooved the magistrate to be sensitive to local practices.[1] Consequently the state did not attempt to impose complete uniformity of mortuary rituals. Rather it focused on the issue of status displays and sought to maintain clear distinctions of rank among officials and between officials as a class and commoners in death as in life (Ch'ü 1965). For example, officials were entitled to wear more funeral clothes than commoners, to have more coffin bearers and more decorations on the hearse, to employ funeral singers, to erect statuary, and to have higher mounds over their graves. Artisans and tradesmen who provided goods and services inappropriately were subject to punishment. Yet, as Ch'ü T'ung-tsu points out, sponsoring a costly funeral was regarded as a filial act and fear of punishment an inadequate deterrent, so that in effect the regulations were little more than a formality, to the extent that only the most egregious violations were likely to be pursued.

The imperial tradition of regulating mortuary ritual has been continued by the government of the People's Republic of China, though the nature of the regulations and the reasons for them are very different and have varied over time. The most stringent rules were in effect during the decade of the Cultural Revolution (1966–76) (Ikels 1996; Jankowiak 1988, 1993; Whyte 1988). The Chinese Communist Party (CCP), the architect of state policies, has three main objections to the traditional funeral and memorialization practices. First, the CCP denies the existence of any realm beyond the material one and labels a wide range of traditional beliefs and practices associated with the supernatural as "feudal superstition"—totally incompatible with a scientific viewpoint.[2] Thus, the burning of paper goods for the use of the deceased and the setting off of firecrackers to frighten away evil spirits have been officially proscribed. Second, in its efforts to promote the rational utilization of resources, the CCP has forbidden burial of the corpse and construction of elaborate tombs sited according to geomantic principles. Under the new policies, families are required to cremate the dead, reducing the body to a small heap of remains ("ashes") that can be stored in a modest container about the size and shape of a jewelry box or in a small urn. This new means of body disposition is intended to save the family money and the state valuable woodland. Furthermore, by forbidding the practice of burial in a village's communal land (or, later, in a family's private fields), precious agricultural land is retained for cultivation.[3] Third, the CCP, not wanting any organized groups capable of functioning as political rivals to local government, has sought to downplay ancestor worship, especially when it entails public assembly of a large clan or lineage.[4] Ancestral halls were converted to schools or other community uses, and during the Cultural Revolution even domestic ancestral tablets were destroyed.

The extent to which these policies were implemented in different parts of China varied according to the intensity of political campaigns, the reach of the central government, and the local availability of the necessary resources such as crematoria. To help ensure compliance, vendors of paper goods, geomancers, and spirit mediums were forced out of business, and monks were forbidden to conduct rites beyond the boundaries of their own temples or monasteries. In assessing the situation with regard to mortuary rituals in urban China during the Cultural Revolution, Martin Whyte and William Parish (1984) relied on interviews with refugees who had fled to Hong Kong. Though these refugees came from all over China, they were disproportionately from Guangdong (94 of 133), and those from Guangdong were disproportionately from Guangzhou (54 of 94), the site of my own later study (see below). Whyte and Parish found that urban households were, indeed, severely constrained in both the public and the private domains in what they were allowed to do. Publicly, all mention of the supernatural was avoided. Families were expected to hold a minimal service at the city funeral parlor attended by family, friends, neighbors, and representatives from the deceased's work unit, after which the corpse was sent immediately to the crematorium. The ashes were placed in a small container, which the mourners usually installed at an ash depository at one of Guangzhou's two cemeteries just down the road from the crematorium, though some families brought the ashes home. Traditionally, Cantonese have practiced double burial, that is, after several years when the flesh disappeared and only the bones remained, they were removed from the coffin, placed in a special container, and either temporarily buried in the hills or placed in a horseshoe-shaped grave site with favorable fengshui. In a similar fashion, the ash depository was seen as a temporary resting place; after an interval of several years the ashes were usually removed and taken elsewhere.

All of the above describes ritual activity in the public domain. But what of the private domain? Was it possible to carry out some of the nine distinct actions that James Watson (1988) found practiced during the same period by Cantonese living in the rural New Territories of Hong Kong?[5] Whyte and Parish (1984) say "No." The outlawing of the professions of ritual specialists and the absence of appropriate paper goods and other religious paraphernalia such as incense sticks made it difficult for families to carry out traditional rites at home. They also note that most deaths were occurring in hospitals, eliminating the need for people to be warned of the risk of death pollution by wailing or for families to wash the corpse themselves. Nevertheless, Whyte and Parish do acknowledge that other mortuary rites, specifically forms of ancestor memorialization, were still carried out in some urban households, even if ancestral plaques had been destroyed by Red Guards. Furthermore, dissimulation as in using mosquito coils to substitute for incense sticks and evasion by sending a dying family member back to the countryside where burial remained an option were covert forms of resistance (Scott 1985, 1990) to the state's official model.

Reform-Era Mortuary Ritual

With the opening up of China to foreign investment, trade, and tourism in the post-Mao era, the Chinese government has tried to create a more hospitable environment, especially for overseas Chinese, most of whom have their origins in Guangdong Province. With regard to mortuary ritual, the new hospitality in Guangzhou, the provincial capital, has included loosening the restrictions, or rather the enforcement of restrictions, on ritual specialists such as geomancers and spirit mediums, allowing the sale of paper goods and spirit money, restoring property to religious institutions, making it possible for overseas Chinese and their close relatives to undergo burial rather than cremation, and so on (Ikels 1996). During the 1980s, urban families, testing the limits of this hospitality, made offerings and burned paper goods not only at their residences, but also right outside the city funeral parlor. This latter practice clearly went too far and was banned in November 1990. Similarly, in the mid-1980s families began making food offerings, burning paper goods, and setting off firecrackers at the two public cemeteries during the annual grave sweeping—actually ash-box dusting—festival of Qingming. In 1993, follow-

FIGURE 3. In a town northwest of Guangzhou a seller of paper goods for the dead displays her conventional wares. Photo by Charlotte Ikels.

ing much official debate within the city government about how things were getting out of hand, setting off firecrackers—though not making offerings—at the cemetery during Qingming was banned. Basically the state took the hardest line in those instances in which it and its authority were directly involved. The funeral parlor and the cemeteries are, after all, state property. What a family did at home was less carefully supervised—the degree of supervision varying by the nature of their housing. Those living in housing provided by their work unit and surrounded by their colleagues and workmates were most subject to social pressure to refrain from "superstitious" practices, while those living away from work-unit supervision, in private housing or housing managed by the Municipal Housing Bureau, were less constrained, their deviations being less likely to come to the attention of the authorities.

To illustrate more concretely how families attempt to serve their ancestors while simultaneously serving the state, I draw on a longitudinal study that I have been carrying out in Guangzhou with 200 randomly selected households. At the beginning of the study in 1987 each of these households contained at least one member (the focal elder) 70 years of age or older. The

FIGURE 4. A few shops down the street, a competitor includes paper cell phones in his updated display of paper goods for the dead. Photo by Charlotte Ikels.

households were subsequently revisited in 1991 and 1998.[6] Over the course of the study, 133 focal elders as well as 28 of their spouses and 15 other household members have died. Extensive data on mortuary rites were obtained for nearly all senior generation deaths and include premortem preparation, body disposition, nature of the series of rites themselves, memorialization practices, and subsequent interaction with the deceased. When I was interviewing in late 1998, families indicated that regardless of what the law was, the real issue of what was done at home was whether one's neighbors were likely to report a violation. For example, despite prohibitions on Buddhist priests carrying out religious activities other than on their own temple grounds, it was possible to hire a priest to come and chant for the dead, though very few families did this. Similarly those families who felt a need to contact the deceased could visit a spirit medium. Though still officially regarded as purveyors of superstition, mediums were tolerated by local officials so long as they kept a low profile. In this accommodation to local custom, Communist cadres do not seem so very different from their imperial predecessors.

By the mid-1990s a family's options in planning a funeral for an elderly member were conditioned primarily by three factors: the place of death, the status (cadre or noncadre) of the deceased, and the degree of traditionality of the deceased, specifically, whether s/he viewed traditional ritual as desirable or essential for postmortem well-being or as mere superstition.[7]

PLACE OF DEATH

As indicated earlier, Chinese generally prefer burial of a corpse to storage or burial of ashes. The one way a person might evade cremation is to avoid dying in the city. Consequently a number of elderly in this study, such as Mrs. Jeung, whose case is discussed below, were sent or repaired to their ancestral villages when they reached advanced old age or appeared to be seriously ill and unlikely to benefit from medical treatment.

In late 1995 Mrs. Jeung, then in her late 90s, was clearly failing.[8] She had fallen six months earlier and been bedridden in her son's apartment in Guangzhou ever since. Decades earlier Mrs. Jeung, a traditionalist with regard to death ritual, had made it clear that, when the time came, she wanted to be buried in the village. Even though the Cultural Revolution was still underway at that time, the family purchased "longevity clothes," a euphemism for garments suitable for her to be buried in, as well as two large pieces of wood that were stored in the family's village house in what was then nearby Panyu County. Later, as Mrs. Jeung's health declined, the boards were made into a coffin that was oiled and kept in readiness for her. Two weeks before her death Mrs. Jeung was brought back to the village and looked after by her son, daughter-in-law, and a hired attendant. Because of her great age her funeral was considered a "happy" event and a lucky one for those who participated. Instead of fearing death pollution, attendees thought that association with her corpse, her clothing, and the dwelling in which she had died would bring longevity. Mrs. Jeung's life force was believed to be so potent that women who had had difficulty conceiving brought the bowls from which they had eaten home from the funeral meal and placed them under their pillows in the hope of becoming pregnant.[9] The family's guests filled eight to ten tables at every memorial meal—the funeral meal itself and those marking the second and third "sevens" (see below), the hundredth day anniversary, and the one year anniversary. Mrs. Jeung's 70-year-old son spoke with pride of how they had had to schedule most of these meals on a Saturday so that everyone who wanted could attend.

But retreating to a village did not work for everyone. When 87-year-old Mr. Lo, a childless widower, returned to the countryside shortly before his death in 1988, he had no close relatives in his ancestral village. Instead he went to a neighboring village where he had a nephew who had been reared by a foster mother. When Mr. Lo died, the villagers refused to allot the nephew a piece of land for his burial, insisting that he hire a tractor to haul the body to a crematorium. The nephew, as heir to a very modest savings account, apologized to Mr. Lo's neighbors for having failed to secure him a burial.[10]

An even larger number of elders who wanted to return to the countryside were persuaded or required by their families to remain in the city on the grounds that they were too ill to travel or that there was no one in the village to look after them now or later, that is, no one would be there to make offerings on the anniversaries of their deaths. Furthermore, the option of flight to the countryside is rapidly disappearing as the province has, since 1998, built forty-three new funeral parlors (including cremation facilities) and constructed more ash depositories (Zheng and Zhou 2001).[11]

For elderly remaining in Guangzhou, the central issue was whether death occurred in the home or the hospital. Deaths were almost equally divided between these two sites, and in both cases representatives of the state become involved immediately. In at-home death, a family member must notify its residents committee (in the past one would have notified the tutelary deity). A member of the committee comes to the home to certify the death as a nonsuspicious one and gives the family member a certificate to take to the local police station. The police then call the funeral parlor to send a vehicle to remove the corpse. While waiting for the funeral vehicle, the family might or might not wash and dress the corpse in garments kept in preparation for this eventuality. After removing the corpse, the attendants from the funeral parlor spray the room where the death occurred with some kind of poison, regardless of the cause of death, "to remove the dirt." People were evasive on this topic, but the dirt almost certainly refers to the death pollution described by Watson (1982). For example, in the case of Mr. Lo described above, a neighbor was charged with removing his belongings from his room in Guangzhou. She offered them to various people, carefully explaining that nothing was dirty (C. *laahttaat*)[12] because Mr. Lo had not died in the room. This spraying of the premises by attendants from the funeral parlor appears to be one of the few areas where the state has made concessions to popular concerns. (The main other concession is facilitation of the celebration of Qingming, when vendors of paper goods are permitted to line the street between the two public cemeteries and police are provided to direct traffic.) Ostensibly the spraying is done for hygienic purposes, but it occurs regardless of the cause of death.

If the death occurs in the hospital, the corpse is sent directly to the funeral parlor. A surprising number of people suffering from chronic illness and reported as dying in the hospital in fact died en route to the hospital and were reported as dead-on-arrival. The haste and desperation with which some of these people were moved out of the dwelling (along with remarks others made) suggested that their families or, more likely, their co-tenants greatly feared having a death occur at home because it was unlucky, that is, they feared the death pollution.

CADRE VERSUS NONCADRE STATUS

What is publicly appropriate for a cadre funeral is prescribed. Whereas during the imperial era, state officials were allowed the most sumptuous funerals, under the Communists the situation is reversed. Cadres will have the minimal service as described by Whyte and Parish (1984) at the funeral parlor and little or no additional ritual at the home. The higher the rank, the higher the likely number of attendees and commemorative wreaths and the more exclusive the location of the ash box. The cadre cemetery has two ash depositories with one reserved for the highest cadres, but otherwise the service is indistinguishable from that provided for ordinary citizens. If the deceased was not a cadre or a Party member but some of the chief mourners are, the situation is a little more complicated and necessitates some careful negotiations. William Jankowiak (1988) describes such a case in Huhhot that ended with the siblings barely on speaking terms at the postfuneral meal.

Noncadre families normally hold a range of rituals at the home beginning the night of the deceased's death whether the body is still present or not and regardless of whether the death occurred at the home or in the hospital. A shrine to the deceased is prepared in the main room of the dwelling where the mourners might or might not sleep until they disperse after the funeral. Incense is burned at the entry to the dwelling, and the door might be kept open to facilitate the comings and goings of the spirit of the deceased and of those making condolence calls. During these condolence calls, the visitors normally present the chief mourner or a representative with a sum of money in a white envelope. The mourners are told that the money should be used to buy a (paper) floral wreath in the name of the donor, but the money can be used to defray any of the funeral expenses.

On the day of the funeral the mourners dress in dark suits or dresses or in dark lower garments and white shirts or blouses and pin a black armband or a small black swatch to their clothing. The use of black to indicate mourning is a complete reversal of the traditional use of white. On arrival at the funeral parlor the guests sign their names and are presented a small packet containing a tiny white towel to which is attached a black swatch that they pin to their clothes, a sweet wrapped in cellophane, and a coin or (real) paper currency. The towel wipes away tears, the sweet takes away the bitterness of the event, and the coin is said to be a token of appreciation. If the packet contains paper currency, the note(s) may be fastened with a needle pulling a red thread. The words for piercing (C. *gat*) and sharp (C. *leih*)—attributes of the needle—are homonyms for "luck is coming," and the color red symbolizes happiness; thus, the presentation is another means of fending off the bad luck associated with attending a funeral. Most of these items should be disposed of before one returns home.

Once home, noncadre families usually burn offerings for the deceased, including paper garments, paper money, and in some cases even the deceased's real clothing. This ritual is followed by a meal involving two or more tables at a restaurant. Most noncadre families will then carry out a Buddhist rite seven days after the death, at which time they remove the deceased's picture from a low table where it had been receiving offerings to a shelf high on the wall, indicating that the deceased has completed the journey through the underworld. This is a very accelerated and abbreviated version of the traditional rite, which involved chanting and making offerings every seven days up until the forty-ninth day following the death and is referred to as "doing the sevens." A substantial number of families, including, as we saw, the Jeungs, carry out three of the "sevens."

Most families, including cadre families, have some form of commemoration of the dead in their home: a picture on a high shelf (indicating that they performed at least one of the "sevens"), on a god shelf at a more accessible level, or perhaps on a dresser. Instead of or along with a picture a tablet with the ancestor's name might be displayed. Depending on the family, incense is burned for the deceased twice a day, only on the first and fifteenth of the lunar month, or only on holidays and the birth and death anniversaries of the

FIGURE 5. The Buddhist Guangxiao (Glorious Filial Piety) Temple in Guangzhou serves as a depository for ancestral tablets of many local residents. Photo by Charlotte Ikels.

deceased. In the mid-1990s, a new option became popular in one of the neighborhoods where I worked. This neighborhood abutted the fortuitously named Temple of Glorious Filial Piety, and it had become possible to purchase a soul tablet and install it in one of two large halls on the temple grounds. One could then go to the temple to burn incense and make offerings. In 1998 these tablets came in two versions and sold for either 5,000 or 10,000 yuan plus a small amount for the inscription. Other Buddhist temples offered the same option.

Most families leave the ashes of the newly dead at a depository at the cemetery for several years and pay their respects annually at Qingming. When the initial contract expires, families may choose from among several options: renewing the contract; installing the ashes in a permanent location at a special facility on the city's outskirts; bringing the ashes back to the deceased's village and burying them or bringing them back to their own dwelling, scattering them as was done for Zhou Enlai; or, reflecting a new sensitivity to environmental concerns, using them to plant a tree.[13] As indicated earlier, the practice of renegotiating the location of the ashes is, of course, reminiscent of the traditional practice of double burial.

Although I have been emphasizing the official restraint of cadre death ritual, it should be noted that at times the very fact of cadre status can allow the highly motivated filial son to circumvent or ignore official regulations. For example, the older son of Mr. Choi was a high-ranking cadre with a politically powerful state unit. When he reported that he had arranged to have his father, who died in late 1991, buried, I sought clarification.

CI: You mean you buried the ashes?
MR. CHOI: No, it was a burial.
CI: But isn't cremation required?
MR. CHOI: Yes, but I arranged with the people at the crematorium to carry out only a 70 percent cremation.

He then explained that the people in charge of carrying out cremations know exactly how long the process takes and the state of the body at each point along the way. At a certain point after the flesh has been consumed, the bones have been transformed but are still hard, dark, and intact. At that point Mr. Choi's younger brother and a cousin collected the bones and put them in a special large container. From the hand motions that he made to indicate the shape of the container, it was clear that it resembled the traditional one used in double burial when, five to seven years after the first burial, the bones are exhumed and reburied in a new location. Mr. Choi had, indeed, managed to execute a traditional burial, compressing the time required for the removal of the flesh down to an hour or so. The only explanation he offered for this surely risky activity was that he thought it was a way of showing respect for his father. That he did not do the same for his mother who predeceased the father by two years leads one to speculate that more than respect was at issue: the bones of male but not of female ascendants are of geomantic importance.

The state, however, has moved to foreclose opportunities for this kind of manipulation. After more than five years of construction, Guangzhou's new state-of-the-art funeral parlor (and crematorium) opened in September 2000 on a large tract of land adjacent to the sites of the old crematorium and the two public cemeteries/ash depositories. The new facility is more than double the size of the old one and able to handle 40,000 cremations a year compared to the latter's 7,000. Most significantly, the new facility obviates the six-kilometer journey from the old funeral parlor to the old crematorium, a journey that was not only inconvenient but also an opportune time for the commission of irregularities, such as the removal of the corpse. To avoid further irregularities the whole staging of the funeral and cremation is done with minimal human involvement: following the funeral service the section of the floor on which the coffin has rested sinks down to the next floor, and the corpse is placed on a conveyor belt and sent directly to be cremated (*Guangzhou ribao* 1998a; *Yangcheng wanbao* 2000). Guangzhou's interest in increasing the cremation rate can no doubt be traced to the provincial government's decision to make it one of the most important standards for assessing the performance of municipal governments. Now an unacceptably low rate means a stalled career for those in charge (*China Daily* 1998).

TRADITIONALITY OF THE DECEASED

Among both cadre and noncadre families the traditionality (or religiosity) of the deceased and his or her kin also plays a role in how elaborate the various mortuary rituals are likely to be. Some elderly are secular materialists and insist that they want absolutely nothing beyond the minimal prescribed ceremony. Some are Christian and expect a Christian service. Most would like something approaching a traditional set of rites that will neither bankrupt the family nor get them into trouble with the authorities. For descendants, meeting filial obligations to deceased parents is important for several reasons: (1) family reputation, (2) personal regard for the deceased, (3) the example it sets for one's own descendants, and, for some, (4) the assurance that the deceased rests in peace and does not cause problems for the family. Meeting these goals is made difficult by the fact that the current generation of urban adults with elderly parents has lived most of its life under socialism and is relatively ignorant of how to conduct the rituals. Families are unsure of how much the state will allow. Specialists remain in short supply, and people must depend on the advice of older, often rural, relatives who themselves may not be too clear about why or when something should or should not be done and have unrealistic expectations of what is allowable in the city. Consequently it is easy for family members to feel, should misfortune subsequently strike, that perhaps they did not carry out a ritual properly and have somehow angered the deceased.

The first line of defense in avoiding such an outcome is to do as much as one thinks one can get away with. For example, in the late 1980s, before transport of a corpse by anyone other than those sent by the funeral parlor was absolutely prohibited, one family in my study successfully smuggled the body out of the house and into the hills for burial.

The second line of defense is to make sure that whatever one does, one does it correctly. One man essentially shadowed the funeral attendants when they came to remove his parent's corpse from their dwelling. He wanted to be sure that the corpse exited the door feet first. Another man was disappointed by what he regarded as the perfunctory spraying of the room in which his mother-in-law had died and insisted that the family decontaminate the room themselves. One family found that every time they went to the cemetery at Qingming they encountered bad luck, such as a car accident, so they decided, against the advice of some relatives, to bring the ashes back to their home to avoid future bad luck. Not long thereafter, however, the middle-aged son who had brought the deceased's ashes back died. Relatives could only shake their heads. All of which leads to the third line of defense.

The third line of defense is to recognize when one has done the wrong thing and make amends as quickly as possible. In the course of one of my visits, the middle-aged third son of one of my deceased informants suddenly turned to me and asked whether I was superstitious (*mixin*). In response to my noncommittal answer, he went on to say that he and his brothers had never been superstitious, but following the death of their mother, they had been forced to rethink their position. To make a long story short, their mother's spirit made her continued presence in the dwelling known almost from the day of her death. The very first night she rang the doorbell trying to get in. At first doubtful that this could possibly be the case they had set up a watch to see who could be teasing the family by ringing the bell. But they never saw anyone and finally decided to leave the door open so that her spirit could come and go freely. After seven days, the out-of-town mourners had all gone home, but the spirit continued to visit the dwelling, turning on the lights and the air-conditioning in the middle of the night. After two or three months of this they were truly anxious and consulted a spirit medium (C. *sahnpoh*) who contacted the deceased. The deceased reported that she came back to look for things. Then everyone immediately understood what was disturbing her. They had burned only incense and had not sent any clothes or other useful items to her. The second daughter-in-law, in fact, had simply thrown the deceased's old clothes into the trash along with the guest book of people who had attended the funeral. The family immediately apologized and "sent" her clothes by burning them.

The most elaborate memorialization I encountered was on behalf of Mr. Jau, who had died of a stroke at the age of 89 about eight months earlier. In addition to the usual death-related activities, Mr. Jau's family had done three of the "sevens" and then installed his picture in a specially built piece of furniture six feet high for which they had paid 2,400 yuan. His daughter-in-law burns incense in front of his picture three times a day and also presents daily offerings of fruit and other foods to him. Next to his picture are his ID card and a set of house keys so that he can come and go as he wishes. On the table a tape recorder plays Buddhist chants day and night so that "he will not feel lonely." I began to understand the reasons for this unusual attentiveness when Mrs. Jau revealed that not long after her husband's death, their 37-year-old son developed a kidney ailment and has been on sick leave ever since. The family wondered whether the illness was a sign that Mr. Jau was in distress and arranged to contact him. He assured them that everything was fine, but clearly they have chosen to be on the safe side by providing him with food and "company"—the tape recording—and making him feel welcome by providing the set of keys. These behaviors are made more comprehensible by considering the circumstances of Mr. Jau's death. Although he died in the hospital, he suffered a stroke at home. His wife and son lifted him from the floor where he had collapsed into a sitting position and put him on the bed. At the time Mr. Jau was unable to move and barely able to speak, yet the family did not send him to the hospital until the next day because they were very "busy." He died just a few days later. In terms of filial piety this family did not fail in the performance of death ritual but in their initial response to Mr. Jau's collapse, the seriousness of which they probably realized too late.

Conclusion

This chapter has addressed the following questions: How have urban families utilized the ritual space newly opened in the post-Mao era? How have they contested state limits on the expression of filial piety? What constitutes an acceptable series of rites that will earn its sponsors recognition as filial children? And why and how do some children exceed these newly established norms? We have seen that in organizing parental funerals the middle-aged generation has tried to walk a fine line between serving the ancestors and serving the state. Public conformance is matched by private resistance as descendants attempt to accommodate the more traditional expectations of their elders or rural relatives. Every legitimate (and some illegitimate) means to avoid cremation has been considered: sending an expiring parent back to the ancestral village, smuggling the corpse out of the house rather than relinquishing it to the official funeral attendants, and even stopping the cremation 70 percent of the way through. But the state is determined to promote cremation as the only acceptable form of body disposition. It has fought back with ever more restrictive regulations on who may have access to a corpse and has greatly increased the number and availability of funeral parlors and crematoria. Similarly, when families attempted to set off firecrackers and burn clothing and other items at the funeral parlor, the state intervened and prohibited such practices.

However, the state cannot afford to alienate the population entirely. It allows offerings and the burning of paper goods at public cemeteries during Qingming as well as the sale of paper goods throughout the year. Privately, families can and do utilize these materials as well as the illegal services of ritual specialists to meet their parents' needs and to demonstrate their own filial piety. Urban dwellers are frequently caught between the restrictions of the state and the expectations of their relatives. No matter what they do, they risk offending someone—the state, their relatives, or the deceased. Death, the last transition, is inherently stressful for all concerned; ritual performance paradoxically adds to that stress at the same time that it attempts to reduce it.

CHAPTER 6

Filial Obligations in Chinese Families: Paradoxes of Modernization

MARTIN KING WHYTE

In imperial China filial piety was a central value of family life, and the centrality of family life in Confucian statecraft made filial piety a lynchpin for the entire social order. Down through the centuries parents constantly stressed to their children that the way they treated their elders was a central measure of their moral worth. Obligations to defer to parental wishes, tend to parental needs, and provide attentive support in old age trumped children's personal desires and preferences. Socialization of children in filial piety was reinforced by the larger culture and the state. Examples of such official reinforcement include the "twenty-four tales of filial piety" that honored extreme examples of sacrifice by grown children in the service of parental needs and whims, and the severe penalties that could be imposed on an unfilial child.[1] As in other agrarian societies, grown children provided the only source of support for most aging parents. Filial obligations extended even beyond the grave, with careful tending to the needs of deceased parents and earlier kin through ancestor worship seen as essential to the fates of surviving family members.

Available ethnographic evidence from nineteenth- and early-twentieth-century Chinese communities indicates that these filial obligations were widely honored. The great majority of aging Chinese lived with one or more married child, and given the patrilineal nature of the kinship system, in most cases this meant living with a married son or sons. Sons, daughters-in-law, and grandchildren provided the physical, emotional, and financial support that parents needed to face old age on at least tolerable terms. Daughters provided such support as well until they married, but after that their primary support obligations were transferred to their husbands' parents. Even grown children who lived elsewhere (sons as well as unmarried daughters) shared in these obligations, with cash remittances from earnings, holi-day visits, and other filial acts expected.[2] For most Chinese the main threat to security in old age came not from unfilial grown children, but from high mortality rates that left some of the elderly without any grown sons to pro-vide old-age support.

The PRC and Taiwan: Two Contrasting Development Paths

What has happened to this system of familial support for the elderly in the wake of the tumultuous changes of the twentieth century? How did obliga-tions of grown children toward their aging parents survive the collapse of the imperial system, the chaos of the warlord period, the attacks against Confu-cianism of the May Fourth movement, World War II and the Civil War, and the political lurches and rapid pace of economic change after 1949? Since 1949 China has been divided into two antagonistic political regimes: the People's Republic of China (hereinafter PRC) on the mainland, and the Re-public of China on Taiwan (hereinafter Taiwan). In which Chinese setting has the traditional system of filial support for the elderly been eroded, or al-tered, the most? In this chapter we present comparative survey data from ur-ban areas in the PRC and Taiwan in an effort to answer these questions.

These two political systems have pursued modernization in quite differ-ent ways. Broadly speaking, Taiwan pursued development in a market-based capitalist framework throughout, with close cultural and economic integra-tion into the global system dominated by Western societies. Until the 1980s, Taiwan's economy grew much more rapidly than the PRC's, and today the island still has a much higher level of development (industrialization, ur-banization, universalization of education, and so on) than does the main-land.[3] But in certain respects Taiwan's development took on a "traditional" cast, as in the ROC portraying itself as a defender of Chinese traditional val-ues and Confucianism, and in the dominance of family-run enterprises in the island's economy.[4]

In contrast, the PRC largely closed itself off from economic and cultural involvement with the outside world until the end of the 1970s, and its lead-ers regularly denounced traditional values, and Confucianism in particular, as "feudal" remnants that should be eliminated. In addition, the commit-ment of Mao Zedong and his colleagues to socialism led to a socialist transformation campaign in the mid-1950s that eliminated private property and family businesses and made all citizens of the PRC dependent on work and other organizations controlled by the state. Furthermore, although the ruling parties of both the PRC and the ROC shared similar, Leninist origins, by the final decades of the twentieth century they operated in quite different ways, with the Chinese Communist Party under Mao imposing totalitarian controls on society in the mainland, while the Guomindang on Taiwan had evolved into a more conventional authoritarian party.[5]

The implications of these contrasting development paths for family change in the two Chinese societies are not entirely clear. The classic theoretical treatment of how modernization affects family life is William J. Goode's book, *World Revolution and Family Patterns* (1963).[6] According to Goode, modernization leads to a shift away from vertical family and extended kinship obligations, and toward the priority of the conjugal bond between husbands and wives. The stress on the conjugal bond and the nuclear family has a large number of consequences in Goode's theory, including a weakening of the patrilineal nature of kinship ties and obligations in favor of an increasingly bilateral emphasis on kin ties on both sides of the family. As a consequence of this weakening of the patrilineal principle, sons and daughters would increasingly be treated equally and seen as of equal value to the family.

Given these expectations, an initial prediction might be that, since Taiwan is much more modernized than the PRC and has been more deeply affected by Western cultural influences (including the Western idealization of conjugal families), families on that island should exhibit more weakening of traditional filial obligations than families in the PRC, and more of a shift toward an equal role of daughters and sons in meeting any remaining filial obligations. However, the state championing of Confucianism and other traditional values and the continued primacy of family firms and property on Taiwan may have offset these forces for change and helped preserve the traditional system of filial support for the elderly.

For urban areas of the PRC there also are contradictory influences at work. On the one hand, the PRC's denunciation of Confucianism and other elements of traditional culture, totalitarian imposition of a modern doctrine (Marxism-Leninism), and elimination of family firms and assets might be expected to erode filial obligations. However, the substantially lower levels of modernization achieved and the near total exclusion of Western cultural influence until recently might have retarded such changes. Given these contradictory forces in each case, it is no longer clear whether we should expect the filial support system to be more eroded or altered in Taiwan than in the PRC.

Survey Data from Two Chinese Societies

In the following pages we seek to answer the question of which set of conditions produced the greatest erosion of the traditional Chinese filial support system by examining survey data from both the PRC and Taiwan. The strategy followed here will be to examine first a range of data from a survey of family patterns and intergenerational relations conducted in Baoding, Hebei, in 1994. That survey resulted from a collaboration between the Department of Sociology at the University of Michigan, the Department of Sociology at Beijing University, and the China Research Center on Aging.[7] The Baoding parent sample consisted of a probability sample of 1,002 individuals over age 50 living in the three main urban districts of that city. We also included a grown child survey, which involved randomly selecting one adult child living in Baoding for each parent interviewed. The resulting child sample consisted of 753 grown children.

After this initial consideration of the Baoding results, we will then present selected comparisons with data derived from two surveys conducted in Taiwan, in 1989 and 1993. Those surveys were jointly sponsored by the Population Studies Center and the Institute of Gerontology at the University of Michigan and the Taiwan Provincial Institute of Family Planning. The 1989 survey involved a probability sample of 4,049 individuals over age 60 living in Taiwan. In the 1993 survey 3,155 of those respondents were reinterviewed, and then all children of a randomly chosen one fourth of the 1993 parents were interviewed, yielding a child sample of 662. Although the 1994 Baoding survey was not a full replication of the Taiwan surveys, an overlap in researchers in both survey projects led to the inclusion in the Baoding questionnaire of exact or close replications of selected questions used in the Taiwan surveys.[8] This overlap in researchers and questions makes possible a rare comparison of data on family changes in the PRC and Taiwan.

Given differences in the sampling plan in the two projects, it is necessary to make some adjustments before comparing the results from these two survey projects. Primarily this means only using parents over age 60 in Baoding, to conform to the age limits of the 1989 Taiwan survey, and only using parents residing in the five large cities in Taiwan (Taipei, Keelung, Taichung, Tainan, Kaohsiung), in order to make comparisons with urban Baoding. So when we shift later in this chapter to an examination of comparative results, the resulting sample sizes will be 509 parents in Baoding and 1,149 in urban Taiwan, and 731 grown children in Baoding and 662 grown children in Taiwan.

Family Patterns and Filial Support of Baoding Parents

In examining the situation of our sample of Baoding parents, the first feature to note is that a high proportion (81 percent of those over age 60; two thirds of those over age 70) are still married. This relatively high percentage means that for most Baoding elderly there is a spouse available to provide emotional, and sometimes financial, support, perhaps making the need to rely on grown children less than if widowhood were the norm.

Another characteristic of the Baoding sample is that most have several grown children available to potentially provide old-age support. Although many commentators are worried about the implications for old-age support of China's "one child policy," most Baoding parents we interviewed had completed their families before that policy went into effect (in 1979). In fact the average number of grown children per Baoding parent is 3.2. Perhaps even more important in terms of the potential impact on filial support is that a very high percentage (about 90 percent) of all grown children we interviewed still live in Baoding. As a consequence, the average parent we interviewed has about three grown children living in the same city and thus potentially available to provide support on a regular basis.

This relative geographic immobility of grown children is largely a legacy of the bureaucratic job assignment system and lack of labor and other markets in China's form of socialism. Specifically, in the Mao era the urban young were assigned to jobs by the state, and it was very difficult to change jobs or residences on their own volition. Except for special circumstances (for instance, for graduates of keypoint universities), such assignments were almost always local.[9] Indeed, during the 1970s and well into the 1980s, a bureaucratic procedure was followed that allowed a parent to retire early from a job in a state enterprise in order for his or her child to be assigned a job in that same enterprise. Under this procedure (termed the *dingti* system), adult children ended up not simply living in the same city, but working and usually living in the same work-unit complex with their parents. In sum, despite the anti-Confucian rhetoric of the Chinese Communist Party during the Mao era, the workings of Chinese socialism and the absence of a labor market actually kept most grown children tied closely to their aging parents. The economic reforms launched in China after 1978 had not altered this immobility very much as of the time of our Baoding survey in 1994.

When it comes to the household arrangements of Baoding parents, however, things look decidedly less traditional. It is true that about 64 percent of Baoding parents live with one or more grown child. However, a substantial proportion of this coresidence involves relatively young parents living with an unmarried child or children. (The reader should keep in mind that our Baoding parent sample included individuals as young as 50.) Only about 35 percent of Baoding parents were living in extended families with one or more *married* child. Even of those over age 60, less than 40 percent live in such extended families. The predominant family form of the Baoding elderly is thus nuclear—residence either only with a spouse, or with a spouse and one or more unmarried children. In other words, it is not obligatory, and furthermore it is not even the most common situation, for an older Baoding parent to reside in an extended family with a married child. While we will examine the comparison with Taiwan later, it appears that the Baoding situation in 1994 represents a substantial decrease in extended family living for the elderly compared to the past (and to the situation in contemporary rural China).[10]

When they do live in an extended family unit, it is almost always a stem family structure with only one married child, rather than the traditionally favored joint family involving two or more married children and their families. In such stem families in Baoding it is still much more common to live with a married son, rather than with a married daughter. Specifically, it is about three times as common to live with a married son as with a married daughter. The departure from traditional arrangements revealed in our Baoding data involves the propensity of elderly Baoding residents to live separately from all of their married children in a nuclear family, rather than any tendency to coreside with a married daughter instead of a son.

It should be emphasized once again that Baoding parents do not end up in nuclear family structures because there are no grown children available to live with. As noted earlier, most have several children available, and for the older parents in our sample, most of those grown children are married. But coresidence with a married child does not seem to be necessary, and it may not even be preferred. (See Chapters 1 and 4 for discussion of the preferences of rural elderly for living arrangements.) While an interpretation of this pattern must await the presentation of data on other aspects of intergenerational relations, the figures just presented seem to point to an increasing acceptance of a new pattern some have termed "networked families" (*wangluo jiating*), with parents living near several grown children who cooperate in providing support and assistance, but without the need to coreside with any one such child in order to find old-age security.[11]

Financial security is a concern of the aged in any society, and in agrarian societies that security comes from having grown children to support you. In China in the past it was said that one had sons to guard against old age, and that the more sons one had, the more prosperous one would become (and presumably remain as one became elderly). What is the situation in contemporary Baoding? The first point to stress is that most of the Baoding parents we interviewed had earnings of their own and did not have to face total dependency on their children. Overall, about 85 percent had some earnings, with 25 percent having wage income only, 51 percent having pension income only, and 9 percent enjoying both pensions and wages. Men are favored over women in this realm, both in terms of continuing to work and receive wages until a more advanced age, and also by being more likely to have met the qualifications for pensions from their work units.[12] However, given the low figures on widowhood presented earlier, most parents who do not have any income of their own (primarily mothers) often have a spouse who does. In other words, for the great majority of Baoding parents, there is no need to rely totally on support from grown children to obtain financial security. For most Baoding elderly, financial contributions from children are supplementary, rather than primary and essential.[13]

To what extent do grown children provide financial support to their parents, even if such support is not essential? We inquired about such financial support in two forms—both cash assistance and the provision of food, clothing, and other material goods. Overall, only about one fourth of Baoding parents were receiving cash assistance from their children, while a little over one third were receiving material goods, with the proportions increasing with the age of the parent. We had expected that at least token cash or other material assistance would be given by most children, but that turns out not to be the case. Most parents in the sample were not receiving financial assistance from their children, and the provision of such assistance reflects parental needs more than simply customary expectations. As noted above, most Baoding parents do not have strong financial needs, and quite a few (about 19 percent) even follow the more modern pattern of providing cash regularly to one or more grown child.[14] Furthermore, very few Baoding parents (less than 3 percent) reported that they needed financial assistance but were not receiving it, or needed more than they were receiving. In other words, the relatively low proportions of grown children who are providing regular financial support to their parents is not a testimony to growing neglect of parents and decreased filial sentiments, but rather to the supplementary and nonessential nature of child financial assistance for most parents.

What is the state of relations between aging parents and their grown children in other realms besides finances? In our Baoding survey we included questions for both parents and children about many aspects of intergenerational relationships. The picture provided by these questions is quite consistent and positive. In general, parents and their grown children are embedded in a rich variety of mutual exchanges and frequent interactions. For example, while only 42 percent of our child respondents were living with a parent, another 30 percent claimed they were in daily contact with their parents, and many of the remaining 28 percent of grown children were in only slightly less frequent contact. Very few parents (only about 4 percent) were receiving physical help from any of their children with activities such as going to the bathroom or getting dressed, but about one third were receiving some regular assistance with household chores. As with finances, very few parents reported that they needed assistance in these realms but were not receiving it from their children. And by percentages ranging from 75 percent to 95 percent, parents reported that their grown children listened to their advice, treated them with respect, and were filial or very filial toward them. More than 95 percent of parents reported they were satisfied or very satisfied with the emotional support they were receiving from their own children. (However, 60–65 percent of both parents and children we interviewed claimed that in Chinese society in general, respect for elders had suffered a decline.) (See Chapter 8 for a similar disparity between personal performance and perception of others' in Korea.) Even discounting these figures somewhat for any tendency of respondents to put the best public face on family relationships for our interviewers, there are no signs in our data of any serious erosion of filial obligations and how the elderly are treated.

Even if the net flow of intergenerational exchanges is upward, from adult children to parents, this is by no means a relationship only of benefit to the elderly. Parents have in the past provided assistance in multiple ways to their growing and adult children—in such realms as helping them get into good schools or acquire a favorable job, financing their weddings, and providing housing in a scarce market. For many grown children the assistance from parents continues in multiple ways as well—through providing childcare assistance in particular, but also (as noted earlier) in some cases by providing financial assistance, help with shopping and household chores, and through advice and the mobilization of personal contacts (from the parents' *guanxi* network) to help solve particular life problems. In a social order that until recently was not designed to stress services and convenience for consumers, and in which full-time jobs for both husbands and wives are the rule among young couples, it has been very difficult to cope with the demands of daily life without the extra assistance that parents and other kin can provide.

We had expected, nonetheless, to find signs of generational conflict in the attitudes and values of the parents and grown children that we interviewed. The popular literature on Chinese social trends stresses that the rapidity of social and cultural change as well as China's tumultuous political shifts have produced marked contrasts between the life experiences and views of young people today and earlier generations. Indeed, when we examined a range of social and political attitudes of Baoding parents and their grown children, we found consistent differences. In general, the parents expressed more support for both traditional socialist and age-old Chinese values than did their grown children, who voiced somewhat more support for individualistic views.[15] In tastes for music, films, television shows, and reading matter, there are also clear signs of a generation gap, with parents again more likely to favor traditional forms (for example, traditional Chinese opera) and socialist genres (for example, films about revolutionary battles) than their children, who tend to favor music, films, and other cultural products with a contemporary popular or international flavor.

However, when it comes to attitudes about family obligations and filial support, there is no sign of any such generational conflict in our Baoding data. Indeed, where there are differences, it is generally the case that grown children feel that they should make more sacrifices to serve the needs of their parents than their parents feel they should. Similarly, it turns out that both parents and grown children tend to see the advantages of coresidence between the generations as outweighing the disadvantages, and both generations rank specific advantages and disadvantages in very similar ways. Furthermore, when asked to provide an overall assessment of the benefits and problems of coresidence between aging parents and their grown children, 92 percent of the Baoding adult children cited the benefits, compared to 82 percent of the Baoding parents we interviewed.[16] Once again we may wonder whether an ethic of "family altruism" leads both parents and children to report levels of intergenerational amity that are somewhat higher than the reality.[17] However, the data reviewed earlier suggest that there is something lying behind these kinds of results beyond simply a desire to portray family relations positively to the outside world. The multiple forms of assistance and support given by both parents and grown children to each other provide firm structural support for continued cooperation and obligation even when parents and grown children do not see eye to eye on many "outside" issues.

What interpretation can we give to the results we have reviewed thus far, in terms of our research question concerning the relative weakening and/or alteration of the pattern of filial support for the urban elderly? The absence of comparable data from Baoding in the past, or for that matter from other Chinese settings, makes it difficult to speak definitively about whether filial obligations have weakened over time or not. What seems clear, at least, is that there is little sign in our Baoding survey data that Baoding parents feel that their needs are being neglected, or that their own children are lacking a strong sense of filial obligation. There are no signs of a "crisis" of filial support for the Baoding elderly in our data.

When it comes to the question of whether the form in which such support is provided has altered, however, we see many signs of change, rather than simply continuity. Already we have noted several significant changes in comparison with the past. Most aging parents in Baoding in 1994 had some income of their own as well as other resources (for instance, subsidized public housing, medical insurance coverage), making reliance on their grown children in most cases supplementary, rather than essential. As a consequence, the proportion of Baoding parents who are regularly receiving financial, household chore, and other assistance from their grown children is less than 50 percent for each kind of assistance we inquired about.[18] We also have noted that only a minority of aging Baoding parents live in an extended family with one or more married children, a situation that suggests a substantial reduction in such intergenerational coresidence in comparison with the past.

In addition to these departures from the patterns of the past, we discovered that for most of the kinds of assistance to parents we inquired about, adult children who do not coreside provide their parents with about as much regular assistance overall as do coresiding children. To be specific, not surprisingly, coresident children provide their parents with significantly more help with household chores than do children who live elsewhere. However, for physical care (help with going to the bathroom, getting dressed, and so on), financial assistance, and the provision of regular gifts of food and clothing, children who live elsewhere provide somewhat more assistance than do those who live with the parents (although these latter differences are not statistically significant). In sum, the pattern of relations we referred to earlier as a "networked family" (wangluo jiating), involving aging parents living on their own, but with several nearby grown children providing assistance as needed, seems to have increasingly replaced the traditional pattern of parents binding at least one married son to them in a coresidential arrangement in order to obtain old-age security.

Has the nature of the network aging parents rely on also changed? Have grown and married daughters increased their role in supporting their own parents, as well as the parents of their husbands? Our Baoding data yield multiple signs that the traditional patrilineal basis of filial support for the elderly has broken down. In response to questions about filial attitudes, married daughters voice as much support for filial obligations (toward their own parents) as do married sons. Among married children who do not coreside with their parents, daughters visit their parents just as often as do sons. In terms of the kinds of support given to aging parents included in our Baoding survey (physical care, help with domestic chores, financial assistance, and the provision of material goods), on balance married daughters do as much or even slightly more than do their brothers.[19] Although the interpretation of this shift toward equal reliance on daughters as well as sons will be deferred until the conclusion, these findings are particularly striking. Although Baoding parents generally report that they are being well cared for by quite filial children, the specific ways in which their support needs are being met have altered quite dramatically in comparison with the past. Filial daughters, even after they marry, are now just as important as filial sons in providing support.

Filial Support in Chinese Societies: Baoding and Urban Taiwan Compared

As noted earlier, by restricting our Baoding sample to parents aged 60 and above, and the Taiwan survey data to parents living in the five largest cities on that island, we are in a position to make selective comparisons of the patterning of filial support in urban areas of Taiwan and Baoding. We are presuming that in at least a rough way, Baoding can represent the situation in medium- and large-scale cities in the PRC generally. We begin our review by comparing and contrasting key features of the situation of the parents in these two distinctive Chinese societies.

To begin with, fewer urban parents in the 1989 Taiwan survey were still married, in comparison with the situation in Baoding (61 percent versus 81 percent of those over age 60). The Taiwan urban parents had a somewhat higher number of living children than their Baoding counterparts (4.3 versus 3.7), but fewer of them currently lived nearby (70 percent versus roughly 84 percent). The net result is that the Taiwan and Baoding parents have about the same number of adult children living nearby (3.0 versus 3.1).[20] Parents in Taiwan's five largest cities were substantially less likely to live on their own or with a spouse only than their counterparts in Baoding (19 percent versus 47 percent), and substantially more likely to live in a stem family with a married child (50 percent versus 38 percent).[21] If we exclude the demographically unusual Mainlanders from the Taiwan sample and focus only on the Taiwanese, then the contrast in family structure is much greater—only 13 percent of the Taiwanese live on their own or with a spouse only, while 63 percent live with a married child.[22] Here we see one intriguing hint of greater family traditionalism in urban Taiwan than in Baoding.

Slightly more of those over age 60 in urban Taiwan than in Baoding were still employed (25 percent versus 20 percent). However, those who have retired are much less likely to receive pensions in urban Taiwan than in Baoding (27 percent versus 77 percent). If we again exclude the Mainlanders, who are the ones most likely to benefit from continued state employment into old age and from pensions when they retire, we see that for urban Taiwanese the comparison with Baoding is even more dramatic. Overall 21 percent of urban Taiwanese over age 60 were still employed, but only 13 percent were receiving pensions. Here we see another indication that Taiwan, despite its higher level of economic development than the PRC, is not a more modern society in all respects.[23] It is entirely likely that the urban elderly on Taiwan have more need to rely on their grown children or other family sources for old-age financial support than do their Baoding counterparts.

The data we collected on four key types of support from grown children in Baoding (physical care, household chore assistance, financial support, and the provision of material goods) are exactly comparable to data in the Taiwan surveys, and a comparison of the figures yields somewhat mixed results. Urban elderly in Taiwan were substantially more likely to be receiving financial assistance than their Baoding counterparts (69 percent versus 32 percent), and they were also much more likely to be receiving assistance with household chores (65 percent versus 38 percent). However, they were slightly less likely to be receiving physical care (4 percent versus 7 percent) and also to be receiving material goods (30 percent versus 45 percent). Across all types of assistance, Taiwanese are more likely than Mainlanders on Taiwan to be receiving assistance. Specifically, the proportion of urban Taiwanese receiving assistance was 77 percent for finances, 69 percent for household chores, 5 percent for physical care, and 41 percent for material goods (versus 48 percent, 57 percent, 3 percent, and 20 percent for Mainlanders). If we take into account the fact that for most parents, financial and chore assistance are more important than physical care and material goods, and also focus on the demographically more "normal" Taiwanese, on balance we conclude that regular assistance from grown children is more frequent and important in urban Taiwan than in Baoding.

There are also important differences in who is providing the various kinds of assistance that parents receive. The clearest contrasts are visible in a comparison of the *main providers* of physical care and household chore assistance, as displayed in Table 3. If we focus on the contrast between Baoding and urban Taiwanese, we see that in regard to physical care Baoding spouses are most often reported to be the main providers, much more often than spouses are mentioned in this context by the Taiwanese. The person next most likely to be named as the main provider of physical care is the daughter in Baoding, and she is twice as likely to be portrayed in this role as a daughter-in-law. Among the urban Taiwanese, in contrast, daughters-in-law are equally as likely as daughters to be reported in this role. The contrast is even more marked in the case of household chore assistance. Again the spouse is most often reported as the main provider of chore assistance in Baoding, while the spouse only takes second place among urban Taiwanese.

TABLE 3

Percent Distribution of Main Provider for Physical Care and Household Assistance in Baoding and Urban Taiwan

		Physical Care		
	BAODING	URBAN TAIWAN		
		Taiwanese	*Mainlander*	*Total*
% Receiving Support*	6.7	5.0	2.9	4.2
Distribution of Main Provider				
Spouse	41.2	16.2	66.7	28.6
Son	17.6	13.5	0.0	10.2
Daughter	23.5	21.6	0.0	16.3
Daughter-in-law	11.8	21.6	0.0	16.3
Other relative	2.9	5.4	0.0	4.1
Combination**	0.0	10.8	0.0	8.2
Non-relative	2.9	2.7	8.3	4.1
Formal/government	0.0	8.1	25.0	12.2
N*	34	37	12	49

		Household Assistance		
	BAODING	URBAN TAIWAN		
		Taiwanese	*Mainlander*	*Total*
% Receiving Support*	35.8	66.9	54.0	62.3
Distribution of Main Provider				
Spouse	35.7	30.1	71.0	42.7
Son	23.1	4.4	2.3	3.8
Daughter	23.1	6.5	1.8	5.0
Daughter-in-law	11.5	48.7	14.9	38.2
Other relative	6.6	2.6	1.8	2.3
Combination**	0.0	5.3	2.3	4.5
Non-relative	0.0	0.0	2.8	0.8
Formal/government	0.0	2.2	3.2	2.4
N*	182	495	221	716

* Represents number receiving support and identifying main provider.
** Represents combination of two or more relatives of different type (e.g., daughter and son-in-law). Those responding "sons" or "daughters" without specifying a specific child were included with the category named.

The person most often reported as the main provider of chore assistance among urban Taiwanese is the daughter-in-law, who is far more likely to be in this role than either sons or daughters. In contrast, Baoding parents rate sons and daughters equally as the next most important in providing chore assistance after the spouse, with both nominated about twice as often as daughters-in-law as main providers of chore assistance.[24] The contrasts between Baoding and Taiwan in the patterns of main providers of financial and material goods assistance are not as striking (details not shown here), but in both realms daughters play a more prominent role in providing support in Baoding than in Taiwan.

We presume that a major contributor to these contrasts between the role of daughters versus daughters-in-law in providing support for the elderly (particularly in the realm of household chores) is the much higher levels of urban full-time employment of young wives in the PRC than in Taiwan (roughly on the order of 90+ percent versus 40 percent). In Baoding, daughters-in-law, like daughters, are almost all working in full-time jobs in bureaucratic organizations, and when they have any free time to provide such assistance, they direct their support primarily to their own parents. In fact, in regard to household chores the direction of assistance is sometimes downward, from retired parents to their busy adult children. In Taiwan, in contrast, many more households of the elderly contain a daughter-in-law, and a much higher proportion of those daughters-in-laws are either not employed full time, or are working in the family's own business, where they may more readily also help out in other realms. Here we see another indicator of greater traditionalism in urban Taiwan than in Baoding.

We conclude this selected comparison by examining some family attitude questions that were asked in comparable or similar forms in the two Chinese settings. We collected data from both the grown children and their parents, and the results were broadly similar. We present only the parent data here. In Table 4 we show the responses parents gave to four such questions in Baoding and urban Taiwan (with the results of a fifth question asked only in Taiwan also displayed). What do these figures indicate?

Although the somewhat different wording of the initial question shown in Table 4 complicates the comparison, it appears that Baoding parents voice substantially more support in general (70 percent versus 38 percent) for old people living on their own. This contrast is not all that surprising, in view of the greater actual propensity of the Baoding elderly to live independently in

TABLE 4

Comparison of Attitudes of Taiwan Elderly and Baoding Elderly

ATTITUDES	QUESTIONS AND ANSWERS	
	Taiwanese	*Baoding*
Living Arrangements	Do you think an elderly couple is better off living with a married son or daughter or living alone? Or do you think there is another better arrangement?	As long as health permits, an older person should live independently and not depend on (his/her) children.
	Married Child = 62.5% On own/other = 37.5% (N = 809)	Disagree = 30.0% Agree = 70.0% (N = 509)
	If an older person is widowed, do you think he/she is better off living with a married child, living alone, or living in another arrangement?	An older person who is widowed should not live alone.
	Married Child = 67.0% On own/other = 33.0% (N = 801)	Agree = 72.7% Disagree = 27.3% (N = 487)
	If a couple has no sons, do you think they are best off to go live with a married daughter, live on their own, or move to a senior citizens' home? How is it best arranged?	N/A
	Married Daughter = 31.8% On own/other = 68.2% (N = 803)	
Widow Remarriage	If an older woman has been widowed for some time, do you think that it is appropriate for her to remarry?	If an older woman has been widowed for a period of time, it is all right for her to remarry.
	No = 61.2% Yes/depends = 38.9% (N = 803)	Disagree = 7.6% Agree = 92.4% (N = 503)
Inheritance and Respect	Do you think it is important for old people to keep property to make sure that their family treats them with respect?	Do you think it is important for old people to keep property to make sure their family members treat them with respect?
	Yes = 77.9% No/depends = 22.2% (N = 790)	Yes, important = 41.4% No, unimportant = 58.6% (N = 490)

a nuclear family unit, as described earlier. However, in the case of a widowed older person, we find that a high proportion of parents in both societies prefer living with a grown child, with Baoding parents even slightly more likely than their Taiwan counterparts to express this view (by 73 percent versus 67 percent). The next panel in Table 4 shows that Taiwan parents have a sufficient aversion to living with a married daughter that they would prefer to live on their own if no son is available (by 68 percent to 32 percent). Unfortunately we did not ask this question in our Baoding survey.

The remaining figures in Table 4 show contrasts that are much more dramatic, based upon question wording that is identical or very nearly so. In China in imperial times a wife whose husband died was expected and pressured not to remarry, and in some instances memorial arches and other symbols were erected to honor particular examples of "chaste widows." In the PRC, the 1950 Marriage Law contained a provision denouncing this custom, and prohibiting interference with the remarriage of widows. Contemporary attitudes on this question in these two Chinese societies are strikingly different. Among the elderly in Taiwan 61 percent disapprove of the remarriage of widows, while 92 percent of the elderly in Baoding voice *approval*. Finally, we see from the bottom of Table 4 that a much higher percentage of the elderly in Taiwan (78 percent versus 41 percent) feel that they have to maintain control over some important property in order to induce their families (presumably their grown children in particular, as the expectant heirs) to treat them well in their old age. Where there are differences, the figures in Table 4 indicate that some familial attitudes are strikingly more traditional in urban Taiwan than in Baoding.

Conclusions

A number of important conclusions emerge from our comparative consideration of survey data on filial support for the elderly in Baoding and in urban Taiwan. Overall, as of the mid-1990s, there was little sign of any crisis or sharp erosion of filial sentiments in either setting. Aging parents in both Baoding and in urban Taiwan generally expressed satisfaction with the support they were receiving from their grown children, and with the strength of filial obligations that those children expressed. Thus, at the most global level our data lead us to conclude that filial support obligations have survived quite well despite the hectic pace (and contrasting paths) of social change in these two Chinese societies.

When we look at the patterning of the filial support system in the mid-1990s, however, we see some marked differences between Baoding and urban Taiwan. These differences fit a predictable pattern in which urban Taiwan looks more traditional, while Baoding looks more modern. To be specific, we have seen evidence that:

—Baoding elderly are more likely to live in nuclear families; urban Taiwanese elderly are more likely to live in extended families with a married son.
—Baoding elderly are more likely to retain earnings of their own, with many depending upon pensions; urban Taiwanese less often have pensions or other sources of income, making them more dependent upon money provided by their children.
—Baoding parents are less likely to receive financial and chore assistance from their grown children; urban Taiwanese are more dependent upon these kinds of assistance.
—Intergenerational exchanges are more balanced in Baoding; in Taiwan they are more likely to involve a predominant flow of assistance upward from adult children to aging parents.
—Coresidence with a married child is of relatively little importance in shaping support for the elderly in Baoding; coresidence with a married child (usually a son) continues to provide an important structural basis for support of the elderly in urban Taiwan.
—Daughters and spouses play very central roles in the provision of support for the elderly in Baoding, with the structuring of support increasingly bilateral; daughters-in-law and sons remain more central to the provision of support for the elderly in urban Taiwan, reflecting the continuing centrality of patrilineal kinship in the filial support system on the island.
—Family attitudes in Baoding are more modern in realms such as the desirability of independent living for the elderly, widow remarriage, and the lack of a need to use family property to insure filiality; in urban Taiwan family attitudes in these realms are more traditional.

At first sight it seems paradoxical that the filial support system in urban Taiwan, a much richer and more highly developed society than the PRC, should be more traditional. How can we explain this paradox? In order to answer this question, we need to decompose the notion of modernization.

This is a global term that encompasses many different aspects and changes—rising income per capita, expanding educational attainment, industrialization, urbanization, secularization, and many other things. A central component of modernization is the decline in the family as a production unit, and the rise of employment in nonkin-based bureaucratic firms and agencies. Similarly, modernization generally involves the decline in the family's ability and/or desire to command resources to supply its own needs and reduced salience of family property and inheritance as a basis for the social placement of children. Wages, benefits, and resources supplied by employers or made available through markets or by state benefit programs increasingly replace family-controlled resources.

In Taiwan these aspects of modernization have been "held back" by the continuing centrality of family-run firms and assets and the resulting reliance on family employment and resources (but more so for the Taiwanese than the Mainlanders on the island). In Baoding and other cities in the PRC, in contrast, these aspects of modernization were substantially "accelerated" by the socialist transformation of the mid-1950s. That major change eliminated the family as a production unit, made family property ownership and inheritance inconsequential, made social mobility dependent upon education and bureaucratic allocation to jobs, provided secure wages and a range of fringe benefits (including pensions) for most urbanites, and made cramped public housing available at nominal cost through bureaucratic allocation. Other aspects of the socialist system made full-time employment of urban women between the ages of 20 and 50 almost as common as for men, at well over 90 percent. In other words, a detailed examination of these "microinstitutional" features of Chinese socialism versus Taiwanese capitalism leads us to reverse our initial conclusion. In these particular respects, it is Baoding and not urban Taiwan that is the more modern social order.

However, the microinstitutions of urban China after the 1950s also contained certain features that supported filial support of the elderly. In particular, the extreme shortages of urban housing in the PRC made at least temporary coresidence of married children with their parents very common. Furthermore, the lack of a labor market and the system of state allocation of jobs kept a higher percentage of grown children close at hand than was the case in urban Taiwan. The sustained high fertility of the 1950s and 1960s combined with the "iron rice bowl" of secure jobs and benefits enjoyed by

parents also made the burden on any particular grown child of providing filial support in the 1990s fairly bearable in most cases.

As a result of all of these contrasts, Baoding families differed from their
Taiwan counterparts in multiple ways despite their common cultural roots.
Baoding parents were much less likely to have family businesses or other
property available to structure the patterns of family relations. Instead,
Baoding families were much purer versions of the "consumption units" that
Talcott Parsons (1971) and others tell us are typical of modern societies, in
which families pool and manage the wages and benefits available to various
members in order to meet their needs. The absence of family businesses and
property to inherit helped to undermine the patrilineal structure of family
relations, as did the high external employment rates and secure incomes of
unmarried and married daughters. The failure of the socialist system to provide substantial public or commercial services to meet family needs for
childcare, laundry, food preparation, or other needs reinforced the tendency
of hard-pressed urban families in the PRC to draw on the assistance of other
members of their family network in order to cope with the pressures of daily
life. For adult children, intergenerational relations were much more a mutually beneficial exchange, rather than primarily a one-sided return by children of the assistance provided by parents in the past. In sum, the complex
set of institutions and practices developed in the PRC after the 1950s helped
to preserve strong filial obligations and intergenerational exchanges even as
it altered the patterning of these exchanges into more modern forms. Taiwan, despite being a richer society, retained family-based microinstitutions
that tended to pattern intergenerational exchanges along more traditional
lines emphasizing patrilineal kinship and coresidence.

At this point the reader may find it puzzling that the discussion has
stressed the impact of Chinese socialism after the 1950s. China launched its
market reform programs in 1978, and it might seem that by the time our
Baoding survey was conducted sixteen years later, in 1994, that set of socialist practices would have substantially eroded in favor of market-based practices shared with capitalist societies like Taiwan. Such a supposition would
be incorrect. As of 1994 Baoding and most other cities in the PRC had been
transformed in some ways by the reforms, but in other realms relatively little change had occurred. The microinstitutional features that we have focused on in explaining the Baoding–urban Taiwan contrasts in this chapter,

in particular, had not yet been much altered. For example, very few of the Baoding parents or grown children we interviewed in 1994 worked in private enterprises, none acknowledged owning or running a private business, and relatively few rented privately owned housing from others.[25] The great majority were still working in or retired from socialist state or collective enterprises and living in "unreformed" public housing that was cramped but cost very little; pensions were being paid; medical insurance coverage was still intact; and few had lost their jobs.

It was only in the late 1990s, in fact, that a new state reform effort designed to eliminate the "iron rice bowl" of socialist job and benefit security was launched, coinciding with efforts to create commercial markets in housing, labor, medical care, and other realms. So in some sense we were observing in 1994 the family consequences of institutional practices that were set in place during the 1950s, but whose days appear to be numbered.

The generally optimistic cast of our findings must therefore be qualified. We have stressed the generally positive features of the lives of the Baoding elderly in 1994. Most of the aging parents we interviewed felt quite secure and satisfied with their lives. Such feelings were a product of two main features of the social order: the socialist practices built during the 1950s that provided them with substantial security and made them less than totally dependent upon their grown children, combined with other practices that kept most of their grown children nearby and ready and willing to provide supplementary support as needed. Since 1994 both of these key sources of a sense of old-age security have been threatened.

To begin with, the dramatic reduction of urban fertility rates since 1970, and even more so the imposition of the one child policy after 1979, mean that most future elderly will have only one, rather than three or even more, grown children available to provide support. Also, the dismantling of the bureaucratic system of allocation of youths to jobs and the rising importance of labor, housing, and other markets means that it is not so certain that most grown children will remain close at hand where they can provide regular assistance. At the same time, young and old urbanites are being confronted with multiple threats to the security that they formerly enjoyed from work units and the state. Some state work units are going bankrupt, while many others are laying off substantial portions of their employees and failing to pay promised pensions to former employees. Medical insurance coverage and benefits are being cut back in favor of co-payment and deductible schemes, while public housing is being privatized, making housing costs a much more substantial factor in family budgets. Market-based reforms are making family-run and other private firms more common and increasing the possibility of family asset accumulation, although for most urbanites family property inheritance is not yet a major consideration. We do not yet have a clear picture of the varied ways in which urban families have adapted to these post-1994 changes.

To sum up, we have seen that in Baoding in 1994 a set of institutional practices fostered a high level of security for most elderly persons and a rich web of intergenerational exchanges that produced satisfaction for both parents and grown children. We also have learned that the patterning of the filial support system in Baoding was in many ways more modern than existed roughly contemporaneously in urban Taiwan. The contemporary strength of this filial support system cannot be attributed simply to China's ancient traditions of filial piety and strong family obligations. Rather, in key ways the filial support system owed its vitality and shape to the socialist institutions and practices created in the PRC in the 1950s. Those institutions are now being threatened or dismantled, with uncertain consequences for the filial support system that we have described. Filial obligations of grown children to their aging parents have survived multiple waves of social change in China (and in Taiwan) in the past. We will have to await the results of future research to learn whether or how well the filial system of support for the elderly survives this latest assault.

CHAPTER 7

The Transformation of Filial Piety in Contemporary South Korea

ROGER L. JANELLI AND DAWNHEE YIM

A small group of middle-aged and older male villagers were quietly conversing near the center of the village of Naeari (pseudonym). As Roger Janelli approached them, one of the men asked him, "In the United States, people go to old-age homes (*yangnowŏn*) when they get old, don't they?" All the men looked to see as well as hear the response, their faces showing a measure of apprehension. Evidently the question was of concern to the entire group, perhaps arising out of a conversation the men had been having among themselves.

After replying "Some elderly go to old-age homes but others don't," the ethnographer saw the men's facial expressions had remained unchanged, and, thinking that perhaps they wanted more information, he elaborated. Sharing some of his own personal perceptions and experiences, he added that elderly people in the United States faced many difficulties, illustrating the point by relating an almost daily experience that the authors had had in Philadelphia while walking from their apartment to campus during the years immediately preceding their fieldwork in Naeari. As they passed in front of an apartment building where a number of elderly residents regularly gathered, one of the group would ask, "Do you have the time?" This question seemed motivated not from a need to know the time of day but from a desire to initiate social interaction and relieve the group's loneliness and feeling of isolation. The men of Naeari received these comments with silence and still unchanged facial expressions, and Roger Janelli wondered if his Korean language skills were inadequate to convey his intended meaning. More than two decades later, he would learn that his words had been all too well understood.

*

In this chapter, we explore the continuities and transformations of perceptions, understandings, and practices relating to filial piety in South Korea during the past few decades. For a close-up view of the meanings of this moral norm, we focus on Naeari, where we have been conducting recurrent fieldwork over the past few decades, but we also look to the broader national and international discourses and political economies with which the village's residents have become increasingly engaged. A better comprehension of changes in filial piety is afforded by combining microscopic and macroscopic perspectives.

Our initial and most recent fieldwork in Naeari spans more than twenty-six years. From 1973 to 1974, and again in 1978, we spent a total of about eighteen months in the village. Popular religious practices and ideas relating to the ancestor rites comprised one of our main interests (Janelli and Janelli 1982). In the fall of 1993 and in the spring of 1999, two decades after our earlier visits, we returned to the village to conduct further fieldwork over several months, living a few days a week in the village and spending the remainder of our time in Seoul. During the intervening years South Korea underwent extreme political and economic transformations, and Naeari, located not far from Seoul, could not avoid being involved—perhaps more than most other rural communities.

A Tale of Two Villages

Naeari resembled many other South Korean farming villages when we first took up residence there in 1973. Surrounded by agricultural fields and woodlands were clusters of wattle-and-daub houses, most of them roofed with thatch. Only a few were roofed with corrugated metal or other material, though the South Korean state, through its New Village movement, was pressuring local villages to replace their thatch with other roofing material. The steel frame of the first factory in the vicinity of the village had been erected, but the structure was not yet completed and the factory did not begin operating until after we had left the following year. Neither the roads to the village nor its internal lanes were paved, there was no bus service to the village, telephone service was unavailable, and the village's only commercial enterprises were a cigarette concession and a rice mill.

By the 1990s, Naeari had become a very different community, looking more like a suburb of Seoul than a rural village. About two dozen factories surrounded the settlement on all but its southern side, and nearly all of the roads and lanes to and within the village had been paved. Four minisupermarkets, a few restaurants, a stationery store, a barbershop, a video rental store, a karaoke hall, and a video game parlor had opened, though the rice mill had closed and the cigarette concession was gone. Many households had acquired their own small-sized rice mills, and cigarettes could be purchased at the supermarkets. Most of the houses had been modified or completely rebuilt to accommodate various modern conveniences, such as indoor plumbing and central heating, and a few small apartment buildings containing about twenty new residential units had been added. Two five-story apartment buildings, including a total of about 170 dwelling units, had been constructed in a neighboring village located only a few hundred yards away, just across a small patch of rice paddies and dry fields located on the southern side of Naeari. By the very end of the decade, very few wattle-and-daub houses were left in the village, even more commercial establishments had been added, and two large apartment buildings had been built within its own boundaries.

As these changes in appearance suggest, Naeari had been transformed from an agricultural to an industrial community. In 1973, nearly all the residents had depended primarily on farming for their livelihood. Twenty-six years later, several families still cultivated small plots of land on which they produced vegetables for their own consumption or to give to their children residing in cities, but only five or six families earned most of their income from farming. Instead, most of the community's adult residents worked in nearby factories or obtained their livelihood from construction work or various enterprises located nearby. This major shift from primary to secondary and tertiary industries was largely the result of the South Korean state's export-led industrialization policies, but more specific state actions also affected Naeari. For example, the state built South Korea's first major superhighway in the early 1970s, placing one of its exits within a few miles of Naeari. In addition, the state declared large portions of farmland and wooded areas near the village suitable for industrial use, thereby enabling villagers to sell varying portions of their farmland to entrepreneurs who sought it for factory sites or other business purposes.

Related changes could be seen in the composition of the village's residents. In 1973, thirty-three of the village's fifty-six families comprised a local lineage of Chinhae Kim (pseudonym), a nationwide patrilineal descent group that claims several hundred thousand members. Seven more village families were headed by "sons-in-law," men of other kin groups who had married daughters of the lineage and settled in Naeari during the preceding few decades. Most of the remaining sixteen families, which belonged to a variety of different kin groups, had moved to the village within the preceding decade to sell their labor to families of the Chinhae Kim. Nearly all were unrelated by kinship to the local lineage. By virtue of their poverty, small number, employment status, recency of arrival, and lack of political connections, members of these unrelated families occupied a politically and economically disadvantaged position compared with that of lineage members. Dominated numerically and politically by one kin group, Naeari comprised what Korean anthropologists and rural sociologists often called a "single-surname village" (*tongsŏng purak*) or a "lineage village" (*chongjok maŭl, tongjok purak, ssijok purak*).

In 1993, by contrast, about 180 families lived in the village, and the number of Chinhae Kim families had shrunk from thirty-three to twenty-eight. A few more families of daughters and sons-in-law had been added, but nearly all of the other new residents had moved to the village in order to obtain employment in the nearby factories and were unrelated by kinship to the principal lineage. These unrelated families rarely worked for lineage members. Comprising the overwhelming majority of residents with sources of income independent of the local Chinhae Kim, the unrelated families had ostensibly far more equal relationships with lineage members than in the past. Political and economic disparities between individual families of the lineage appeared to be just as great as those between lineage and non-lineage members, but relations between the older and newer residents were sometimes strained. Village activities typically drew nearly all of their support from the original residents, and several organized friendship groups within the village were composed almost entirely of the more-long-term residents, including some of those who had emigrated but returned to the village for the meetings of organized social groups to which they belonged.

The erection of several factories and the arrival of many new residents not only brought social changes within the village but also represented some of the ways in which the village was increasingly integrated with the world beyond. Most social life in the 1970s took place within Naeari itself. Villagers referred to themselves and each other as "persons of our village" (*uri maŭl saram*) and as "country persons" (*sigol saram*), the latter term contrasting with "Seoul person" (*Seoul saram*). What had been South Korea's main road prior to the opening of a superhighway was only about a half mile from the center of the village, and public buses ran there about every ten or fifteen minutes. The road itself connected Seoul and Pusan, South Korea's two largest cities. But villagers did not often leave the village, except on periodic market days, which occurred every fifth day. Few residents knew enough Chinese characters to read newspapers, and acquiring a newspaper would have required walking, riding a bicycle, or taking a bus to a nearby town. Most village homes had radios but only six had televisions, recently acquired. Though younger children left the village daily to attend nearby primary or middle school, only older children rode the bus to attend high school. The village had produced at least a few college graduates, but nearly all of them lived in Seoul and seldom returned to the village. A number of sons and daughters migrated from the village to work in Seoul or other urban centers, but they too seldom returned, except for major holidays or important social events of their families or close kin in the village. Contrary to our expectations, no one expressed resentment of the absence of eldest sons, nor did anyone represent separate residences as marking a permanent division of a family. In the early 1980s, for example, one villager told us that his eldest son's home in Seoul had no shrines for household deities because it was but an extension of his own house in the village.

The villagers' relations to the outside world had changed significantly by the 1990s. Every household had acquired a television, several owning more than one. Not only did households have telephones, but many residents carried cell phones. One villager in 1999 urged us to obtain a cell phone too, pointing out that a regular phone was fine if we were at home, but it did not allow others to reach us whenever we went out. Several families had also acquired automobiles, and so many children had left the village (and so dramatically had birth rates dropped) that the average size of the Chinhae Kim households had shrunk from 5.9 in 1973 to about 3.6 in 1999.[1] Residents' activities far more frequently extended beyond the village, to recently burgeoned nearby cities that had formerly been small towns, to the county seat, to what is now called the Seoul Metropolitan Region, and to foreign nations. We no longer heard the terms "persons of our village" or "country persons" used to refer to those who lived in Naeari. Instead, people spoke of *purak chumin* (village residents), long-time inhabitants using the term *wŏnjumin* (original residents) to distinguish themselves from those who had moved in within the past few decades. Moreover, the South Korean government had abolished the township to which the village formerly belonged, as the entire county of which it was a part was declared a city. One family had a son who pursued a professional career in the southwestern United States; another had a cousin living in Hawai'i, who happened to call while we were visiting in order to arrange a bank transfer as a wedding gift for a daughter who was about to be wed. Other residents had visited Japan, the Middle East, China, or the United States. A number of former residents maintained their ties to the village, returning sometimes to their otherwise vacant homes in the village, to attend major social events nearly every weekend, and, especially on weekends in the spring and summer months, to engage in small-scale weekend farming on land they still owned in or near the village. Others, including daughters, came to visit parents or siblings and to help with weekend or full-time farmwork. Village residents reciprocated by attending a variety of events outside the village, especially on Sundays, when many stores and offices were closed and their employees freed from work. Indeed, Sunday had become the busiest day of the week for most residents. Instances of having to attend multiple social events outside the village on Sundays were not uncommon, especially among the more prosperous households.

Filial Piety in the 1970s

During our 1970s fieldwork in Naeari, we could not have avoided hearing about filial piety. One villager told us of an official award he had received from the township office for his demonstration of this virtue. A text recited at death day rites for ancestors proclaimed that "an offspring's indebtedness to parents is as limitless as the sky." A well-known funeral chant that had been sung when a deceased person was carried from the village to her or his gravesite reminded all of the obligations that offspring incurred from the pains that parents had taken to raise them. Performing the chant in Naeari had ceased just a few years before our fieldwork because the professional singer who had been hired to sing it had died, but villagers remembered portions of its text and one sang it himself to lead the tramping of the earth above a new grave after the coffin had been placed inside. The man recited the song for our tape recorder (Janelli and Janelli 1982: 66–69), a few segments of which are:

When my parents raised me
What efforts they made.
Parents lie in a wet place
To lay their baby in a dry place.
With food as well, they first taste it,
Eating the bitter themselves
And feeding the sweet to their baby.
On the hot days of May and June
They worry of mosquitoes and bedbugs [biting their baby];
Though tired they cannot sleep.
With both hands they hold a fan
And chase away all kinds of worries.
They carry me on their backs
And spare no effort.
[They think:] Silver baby, golden baby,
Treasure baby from the deepest mountains,
    . . .
Could we buy you even with gold?
Could we buy you even with silver?
The boundless love we feel for you
How can we express?
When one thinks of one's indebtedness to one's parents,
Isn't it bigger than the greatest mountain?
Who would deny this?

Filial piety entailed more than obligations to repay forebears, however. It also testified to a person's— and by extension his or her lineage's and village's—moral worth; and publicly acknowledged moral worth was a form of symbolic capital that enhanced social standing and political influence among local communities. Our particular interest in the village's ancestor rites, another form of filial piety, probably eased our initial acceptance by Naeari residents.

The significance attached to filial piety in the 1970s was also conspicuous in an ongoing debate that surrounded the possible construction of a new ancestral hall. Until that time, the local lineage of Chinhae Kim in Naeari offered rites every fall at the graves of each of its ancestors beyond four generations, walking from grave to grave until all the rites were completed. Since many of the graves were located on mountains and hillsides some distance from the village, performing all the rituals took four days. In 1973, a closely related lineage of Chinhae Kim who had also followed this practice built an ancestral hall in its village and commemorated there in a few hours all its own ancestors beyond four generations. Members of that lineage pointed out that their new form of commemoration not only saved time and money but also relieved the kin group from having to provide another ritual estate to finance yet another rite every time a pair of ancestors passed beyond four generations and became eligible for commemoration by the entire lineage.

In Naeari, the creation of an ancestral hall for collective rites was viewed as a simplification of ritual practices and, by implication, a curtailment of filial piety. This implicit understanding was voiced by some elders during a lineage meeting at which the creation of a new hall was discussed. Arguing against the creation of the hall, one elder proclaimed that ancestor rites were a form of filial piety. Those favoring the hall did not challenge this moral norm but chose instead to define it more broadly. They pointed out that by creating the hall, the lineage would no longer need the extensive land holdings that were used to finance all the separate rites at gravesites. Some of these ritual estates could then be sold to provide funds for the education of promising descendants, which would also be a form of filial piety, they maintained. Their strategy drew on the understandings that social status was popularly assumed to be hereditary and that the success of offspring benefited an ancestor's reputation not only because of this assumption but also because prosperous descendants could bring more public attention to the merits of their ancestors.

The ancestral hall was ultimately built in the early 1980s. By that time, many of the elders who had opposed its construction had died or retired from active social life. The lineage did establish a scholarship fund that granted a small monetary award to any son or daughter who gained admission to a two-year or four-year college. By 1999, however, so many descendants had gained admission to college that the lineage leadership decided to limit the number of awards by granting them only to those who had gained admission to four-year tertiary institutions.

During the 1970s, cultural understandings of filial piety were also implied in a variety of comments given to us regarding the care of elderly parents. Adult villagers frankly acknowledged that caring for elderly parents was onerous. One villager told us he would dance happily when his father died. One of Korea's best-known legends, the Koryŏjang story, tells of an alleged former custom whereby an elderly parent was carted off to some distant place by a son and left there to die. Yet no one denied that offspring owed heavy obligations to parents, and versions of the Koryŏjang story always included the son's recognizing the error of this custom and carrying the parent back home. Moreover, while elderly parents were portrayed as cantankerous and demanding, an open dispute between elderly parents and adult offspring was usually blamed on the younger generation.

Despite adult offspring representing their filial obligations as onerous, elderly parents were often at the mercy of their offspring. As Vincent Brandt (1971) and Kyung-soo Chun (1984) have both observed, age entitled a person to respect but not real power. Parents gradually transferred the management of household affairs to the succeeding generation, ultimately yielding occupancy of the main room and moving to another room of their home, usually sometime in their sixties. Parents typically surrendered management of the household somewhat earlier than usual if a spouse died, for that event deprived the survivor of a partner with whom to manage the house's affairs. An elderly woman who had died some weeks before we first entered Naeari was even said to have been driven to suicide by the harsh treatment received from her daughter-in-law. The daughter-in-law's daughter soon suffered a serious accident, and most villagers readily attributed this misfortune to the wrath of the deceased grandmother.

As we have argued elsewhere, filial piety obligated offspring primarily to *repay* rather than *obey* their parents (Janelli and Janelli 1997). Offspring were expected to take the initiative in caring for their parents rather than wait to be told what to do. This allowed an offspring to use his or her own judgment as to what was in the parents' best interests. Parents and offspring did not always agree on what was best for the parents. Our best example is the story provided by a then-elderly man who told of temporarily abandoning his father years earlier, allegedly for the latter's own good.

Because the father seemed very lonely after his wife died, his sons found another woman to provide him with companionship in his old age. Unfortunately the woman turned out to be a schemer with whom their father became helplessly infatuated. She soon began to persuade him to transfer all the property of his household to her name. When he finally consented, our informant moved out of the house and refused to return until his father had rid himself of the woman. The old man eventually yielded, for he knew he could not live without the help of his eldest son. (Janelli and Janelli 1982: 49)

The various narratives, comments, and discussions we heard in the 1970s also implied that filial piety was primarily an obligation imposed on sons. Women were not expected to be actively involved in the care of their own parents and, with the exception of some of those whose husbands were resident sons-in-law, few were. Nor was a woman expected later to bow, offer wine, or assume any of the ritual roles in ancestor rites after the termination of the mourning period, for her own or her husband's parents, though married women were present at the rites for their parents-in-law and prepared the necessary food offerings. Though the same moral injunctions were imposed on girls and young women regarding their own parents, a woman's separation from her natal home and village at marriage usually made it difficult for her to make many efforts on behalf of her parents. A young upper-class wife in a focus-group interview nicely captures the frustration that many women in rural Korea probably felt:

> Before marriage I didn't prefer a son. Now, however, I prefer a son to a daughter. As a daughter myself, I think about the things I might do for my own parents, but I have to direct all my efforts only toward my parents-in-law. Because of these traditional customs, in fact, I'm not able to do anything for my own parents. I often wish I were a son myself. (Kim 1994: 28)

Both JaHyun Kim Haboush (1995) and Clark Sorensen (1988b) have noted the contradiction between enjoining women to repay parents for the gift of life and the efforts made in raising them but then removing them from their natal homes and thereby preventing their fulfillment of this obligation. Perhaps this is why a woman's filial piety is a frequent theme in Korean oral literature. Both authors have pointed to a well-known Korean myth, Pari Kongju, that tells of a filial daughter (Haboush 1995; Sorensen 1988b); and the story of Sim Ch'ǒng, one of Korea's most popular epics, tells of a daughter who was willing to sacrifice her own life for the sake of her blind father (Pihl 1994; Haboush 1995). In elite Korean discourse, women were supposed to transfer to their parents-in-law the filial obligations owed their parents (Haboush 1995), but this hardly resolved the contradiction: a woman did not receive from her parents-in-law the gift of life or nurturant care in her early years. At any rate, this elite idea does not seem to have taken hold throughout the general population, and we encountered no evidence of it in Naeari. An elderly woman lived with her even older mother-in-law, caring for her needs, and though the two women appeared to have an amiable relationship, no one ever represented the daughter-in-law's behavior as filial piety. Indeed, some measure of conflict between a woman and her daughter-in-law was not regarded as particularly unusual or as stigmatizing as conflict between a son and his parent, especially a father. In our view, sons often had a more difficult relationship with their fathers than daughters had with either parent-in-law precisely because the norm of filial piety rendered it socially more embarrassing for a son to express whatever hostility he may have felt (Janelli and Janelli 1982).

Sons also had graded degrees of responsibility for the care of parents, and this gradation was usually invoked to explain the uneven shares of inheritance allotted to male siblings. (Daughters received only a dowry at marriage.) Because an eldest son had the primary obligation to care for parents and offer ancestor rites, villagers explained, he was given a larger share than any of his male siblings, whose obligations were secondary and, at most, contingent upon the elder brother's failure or inability to care for parents or perform ancestor rites.

State Interventions

The most critical political and economic event that affected social life in Naeari was arguably the Park Chung Hee government's decision to adopt a policy of export-oriented industrialization. By granting low-interest loans, special licenses, and a host of other privileges to entrepreneurs who built large-scale production facilities that took advantage of economies of scale and South Korea's low wages, the state fostered urban-centered economic development and a highly concentrated industrial economy that drew many young adults from the countryside to South Korea's burgeoning cities in search of employment.[2] As a result, more and more older couples were left alone in the countryside, no longer receiving the daily care and shelter that adult sons had been obligated to provide in the past. Some sons sent cash to their parents (see, for example, Sorensen 1988a), though in Naeari we heard more often of grain and produce that offspring received from their parents' small farms. Farming itself had become increasingly mechanized, owing in part to another state intervention, and the cost of buying or renting special machines required to transplant, harvest, thresh, and bag rice made small farms less efficient and less economically rewarding.[3]

The state's policy of promoting industrial development and higher standards of living primarily in cities did more than motivate young adults to move to urban areas for economic gain or the supposed attractions of city life. It also legitimated moves that might be made for other reasons. The eldest son of one Naeari family obtained employment in a factory that was only about a hundred feet from his natal home, but the son and his wife moved out of the village after living there for a few years following their marriage. The son told us that they had chosen to live in a nearby city because it offered better educational opportunities for their child, but his mother observed that her daughter-in-law had never done any farm work and surmised that the young woman felt uncomfortable living in their rural home, which lacked such amenities as indoor plumbing.

Yet another state intervention was the creation of a transportation and communication infrastructure to promote capitalist industrialization. Telephones came to the village in the 1980s, and local bus service to Neari started in the 1990s. These developments added to the acquisition of televisions, newspapers, and other means of connecting the village with the outside world. As better means of transportation strengthened these linkages, ties within the village were perhaps weakened, but more frequent contact between urban-dwelling offspring and rural-dwelling parents became possible.

The state's intervention went beyond altering the material conditions under which Naeari residents and other South Korean citizens led their lives. Another state initiative aimed at promoting economic development was the adoption of a very active family planning program from the 1960s until the late 1980s. Examining consequences of declining birth rates, Yun-Shik Chang (1989) points to a transition from filial piety to "love of children." As he notes, families were urged to have no more than two children through a variety of means, including tax incentives and other economic benefits, such as preferential status for acquiring less expensive housing. In addition, the state employed various forms of propaganda, particularly stressing that a family could not adequately care for a large number of children. Moreover, separation from grandparents and other kin who would have formerly assisted in child-care duties increased the efforts needed by parents themselves to properly fulfill their role. In addition, large families were disadvantaged by the rising costs of raising children, in part due to longer years of formal education and competitive university entrance examinations that privileged students who received extra educational training. So prevalent had the expectation of a two-child family become that two Korean sociologists observed in the mid-1990s that "those who gave birth to a third child feel the burden of needing to make an explanation" (Yi and Han 1995: 146). By the late 1980s, South Korea's birth rate dropped to the point where the maintenance of the current population level was threatened, which prompted the state to withdraw its incentives for family planning.

Yet another change that may have impinged upon filial piety was the greater involvement of young people in the selection of their own spouses. In the early 1970s, many people in their forties had told us with a chuckle that their wedding day was the first occasion on which they saw their spouse's face, whereas most young couples at that time were already finding their own partners. Perhaps a greater degree of affection toward spouses in early years of marriage undermined parental authority and left parents more vulnerable. According to a recent survey, when asked if it would be better for parents to live with their offspring, the implication being that they would reside with a son's family, 80.1 percent of husbands but only 50.1 percent of wives (*chubu*) agreed (Kwŏn 2000). With the rise in wage employment, farm women too have gained more control over the management of the household budget, thus leaving parents of a virilocally married son more dependent on their daughter-in-law.

Re-Gendering Filial Piety

As elsewhere in the world, the capitalist industrialization promoted by the state and the consequent urbanization in South Korea sharply transformed cultural expectations regarding household responsibilities. By separating workplace from home, the economic contribution of married women to their households was obscured. When farming prevailed, women were usually in charge of the planting, cultivation, harvesting, and even marketing of dry field crops. These dry fields, moreover, averaged more than a quarter of a South Korean's agricultural lands, although the value of their crops was lower than that of the paddy field, cultivated primarily by men (Ministry of

Agriculture and Fisheries 1977). A large portion of South Korea's early industrialization was also made possible through the labor of women, but these women were usually unmarried and lived separately from their families, even though significant portions of their wages were contributed to their natal households (Kim 1997). Urban married women, by contrast, had lower rates of employment, and became almost exclusively charged with childrearing, household maintenance, purchasing, home decoration, fashion tracking, maintaining the family's social relations, selection of gifts, other status-production work (Papanek 1989), and much else.

Increasing industrialization and urbanization thus promoted a new gendered division of labor for married couples, with long hours for men at their workplaces and heavier responsibilities for household management for women. In addition to taking charge of nearly all matters related to household management, many women engaged in informal economic activities, such as rotating credit societies, informal investment activities, real estate investment, and, later, investing in the stock market. Sometimes these activities were hidden from husbands, however, in order that the women involved could have an autonomous operating fund of their own. As one Seoul woman told us, men could not be trusted with household funds, for they tended to spend them carousing with friends or on other frivolous activities. Many husbands, by contrast, complained of the tight control maintained by their wives over their households' finances and kept secret funds of their own.

The new gendered ideology that emerged thus charged men ostensibly with earning household income and women with almost all work related to "the home," though many of their expected labors, such as paying taxes, negotiating with the neighborhood government office, and informal economic activities were extra-domestic. With increasing levels of education needed to obtain employment, moreover, women took on added tasks related to managing their children's education. This involved not only helping with homework, but gift giving to teachers, participation in PTA activities, finding the best preschool and extra-school training, and hiring effective tutors to give their children a competitive edge (or at least minimize any competitive disadvantages) in highly selective college-entrance examinations. Because most of the women's efforts were not commoditized, their monetary value was not readily calculable and the value of their labor to their households' economy became obscured.

In the context of this new gendered division of labor, few of the elderly have chosen to live with their daughters. A recent study found that 50.2 percent of those over the age of 60 lived with a son and only 5.9 percent lived with a daughter (Yi et al., 1994 cited in Cho 1997: 109). In part, this may be due to the perpetuation of older assumptions, but we suspect it is also the result of the new definitions of family roles. Because a husband has become the only apparent contributor to a household's economy, living with a married daughter and her husband is perceived as living off a son-in-law's charity. Living with a son, on the other hand, gives the appearance of enjoying an entitlement. The individual cases familiar to us of elderly parents who reside with an adult daughter have all occurred in households in which the daughter was either single, widowed, or earned her own income through career employment.

This gendered asymmetry in intergenerational living arrangements persisted despite a major revision of inheritance laws in the early 1990s. The new law entitled all children to equal shares of their parents' property; formerly, an eldest son was entitled to two shares, younger sons one share, unmarried daughters one-half of a share, and married daughters only one-quarter of a share. This legal change would probably not have had a major impact on actual inheritance practices if parents continued to distribute before their deaths portions of their property to a younger son when he and his wife established a separate residence, but this former premortem distribution of property has been rapidly disappearing. Urban-resident children have little use for farmland, except to sell it, and many parents are now reluctant to surrender their assets during their lifetimes, knowing that relying on offspring for their care in old age entails a substantial risk. The cultural understanding that differential inheritance is linked to the care of elderly parents has not disappeared, however. A 1998 decision by the Seoul family court ordered an extra half share of inheritance be given a married daughter because she had returned to her natal home to take care of her sick father for several years (Int'ŏnet han'gyŏre, Sept. 29, 1998).

The advisability of parents holding on to their property is evident in other activities as well. A recent survey reported that only 27 percent of parents received their living expenses from an eldest son in 1998, a drop from 33.1 percent four years earlier (Kwŏn 2000: 3). Tellingly, the same survey also reported that 50 percent of the elderly who became lost at expressway service areas suspected that the children who support them deliberately caused them to be lost (Kwŏn 2000: 3).

Easier means of transportation and a rising proportion of nuclear households potentially enabled married women to give more attention to their natal parents, including those parents still residing in rural areas. The greater affordability of automobiles, for example, has made it easier for many women to travel from city to country in order to visit their natal families. Women also contribute more to the care of elderly parents, although they seldom assume primary responsibility unless they regard their brother's treatment of their parents as inadequate and have the means to provide better care themselves. Because married women's new responsibilities included maintaining the social relations of the family, moreover, many of these women have chosen to maintain relationships not only with their husband's natal kin but also with their own. With the massive migration of younger men and women to major cities, moreover, a young couple may live closer to the wife's than the husband's kin, resulting in the family's choosing to spend all or a portion of their holidays with the former (see, for example, Kendall 1996). When asked whom they would most like to see on Ch'usŏk, one of South Korea's two major holidays, 56.9 percent of housewives surveyed chose their natal parents. Only 6.4 percent chose their husband's parents (Kwŏn 2000: 2). Another survey, conducted in 1998, found 34.7 percent of elderly women who lived separately from any of their children identified their eldest daughter as the relative with whom they had the most frequent contact, whereas only 20.9 percent identified their eldest son (Kwŏn 2000: 5).

A National Debate

The South Korean state of the 1960s and 1970s sought to promote filial piety, much as did the Chosŏn dynasty, as a model of loyalty to the state. Evidence of that state policy could be seen in the case of the Naeari villager who received an award for filial piety from the township office. Other organizations have also attempted to employ filial piety to strengthen control. In the offices of a major company that we studied in the 1980s, for example, the owners and senior managers attempted to evoke this moral norm in their efforts to legitimize what lower-ranking white-collar workers often regarded as a distasteful authoritarian system of control (Janelli with Yim 1993). The following text, allegedly contributed by a female worker, appeared in the March 1987 issue of the conglomerate's magazine:

> We tend to let ourselves feel that relationships between superiors and subordinates are very self-interested and difficult. How about looking at them from a different perspective, however: as relationships between parents and children?
>
> Parents never feign ignorance of their children's talents and abilities. [Instead,] they cultivate their children's abilities and strive to acknowledge their talents. The children too have complete trust and faith in their parents and a respectful attitude toward them. . . .
>
> Let's try grafting this atmosphere onto the office. The managers have warm human affection, like a parent's devotion, toward the employees [sawŏn], cultivate the knowledge and abilities of each individual, and guide their talents and ability to evaluate [their own] work. The employees too, like sons and daughters toward parents, have faith in and respect for them. (Janelli with Yim 1993: 119)

Such uses, or perhaps "abuses," of filial piety have prompted some intellectuals to condemn the concept as harmful. An activist involved in the movement to form a South Korean teacher's union, for example, has written: "A number of anti-democratic traditions in South Korean society remain, including the Confucian concepts of loyalty and filial piety" (Yu 1997: 77).

Yet filial piety continues to have its supporters. Newspapers, magazines, and more recently websites devote pages of commentary to relations between parents and offspring, and "problems of the aged" (noin munje) has recently become a popular phrase in media and sociological writings. Various enterprises have announced plans to build "silver towns," residential communities aimed at the needs of the elderly. A synopsis of reports on relations between the elderly and their succeeding generation was published in December of 2000 by the Wŏlgan Chosŏn, one of South Korea's most popular monthly magazines (Kwŏn 2000). It cited results from no less than sixteen surveys by various media, research institutes, marketing companies, governmental agencies, and nongovernmental organizations.

Some organizations are actively engaged in the promotion of filial piety. The Filial Piety Cultural Center, located in the city of Suwŏn, created a website that advertises its intention to institute a program to promote filial piety and spread this ideology to the rest of the world, including a world expo in 2003 (www.hyoexpo.com). Another institution, the Sŏngsan University Graduate School of Filial Piety, with programs leading to M.A. and Ph.D. degrees, recently opened its doors. When its website is accessed, an animated banner reads "The nation lives only if filial piety lives" (hyoga saraya naraga samnida) (www.hyo.ac.kr).

A number of religious organizations are also visibly engaged in movements to halt a perceived decline in filial piety. Implicit, and sometimes explicit, in their pronouncements is the perception that filial morality is declining and, according to some sources, is threatened by South Korea's industrialization and the importation of Western culture. A web page of the Ch'ŏnt'ae (Tiantai) sect of Buddhism, for example, states:

> In modern society, first of all, the moral relationship between parents and offspring is collapsing and we should shore it up. One can see that parents still sacrifice and make great efforts for their offspring, but offspring forget the benefits they received from their parents. And while parents are important and the benefits received from them are enormous and sacred, offspring fail to realize this and commonly cause their parents pain. (Editing Department 2000)

In like vein, the Pure Evangelical Church, a well-known Christian denomination, proclaimed in an editorial entitled "Let's Direct Our Effort toward Policies for the Aged":

> It is a fact that our people's ideology of filial piety shone as it came down to us over the ages.
> However, since the importation of new cultures and the introduction of Western ideology, our family system became nuclear before we knew it. With a tendency toward slackening respect for elders, the beautiful customs of etiquette have grown dim. Moreover, society is becoming more scientific, medicine is better, life has been extended, and society is aging. The average life expectancy has increased to 70, and the problems of the aged have become truly conspicuous. (*Sunbogŭm sinmun* 2000)

These reports of declining filial piety, however, omit mention of alternative means of repaying parents. Many of those who do not dwell with elderly parents in the same household have opted for separate residences that nevertheless allow them to attend to parents' needs. A survey of current social changes authored by two South Korean sociologists reports the emergence of "creative living arrangements" whereby parents and the families of their offspring are often located nearby, sometimes in the same apartment complex, and that many offspring are actively engaged in visiting parents, bringing them meals, lending them moral and economic support, and providing other forms of care (Yi and Han 1995). In a similar vein, anthropologist Kwang-kyu Lee (1997) observes that the Korean family has become geographically "extended": though not sharing a common residence, family members continue to cultivate close ties. Yet there are some ambiguities in these new family arrangements. Pak Pujin, for example, found that mothers-in-law, when enumerating the members of their families, tended to include their married sons and daughters-in-law even if the younger couple resided elsewhere; but their non-coresident daughters-in-law were not inclined to share that conceptualization of family membership (Pak 1994).

Back in the Village

We seldom heard the phrase "filial piety" in the 1990s. The lineage hall had been built and simpler rites were offered there every fall rather than at gravesites. No longer recited was the phrase "an offspring's indebtedness to parents is as limitless as the sky," for by then the Chinese character texts that had contained those words were no longer heard at deathday rites. Those who knew how to intone these texts properly had all passed away. And the funeral chant was no longer sung to accompany the tramping of earth over new graves, as such work was done with mechanical rather than human labor.

But cultural understanding of indebtedness to parents had not disappeared. Rather, filial piety was often implicit in many discussions we had with elderly parents regarding their relationships with their offspring. Inheritance practices, for example, had changed but were still linked with the care of elderly parents. In the case of one elderly couple whose married daughter had become deeply involved in their care, the daughter was entrusted with the proceeds from the sale of the family's last piece of farmland to take care of the parents, and upon their deaths decided how it was distributed among the siblings. When we asked another elderly Naeari couple how they planned to distribute their property to their married offspring, all of whom had left the village, the husband replied they he thought his sons should get more. His wife quickly interjected, "Why should they get more? They don't take care of us."

Not surprisingly, the eldest sons of some of the largest farming and wealthiest households continued to live with their parents after marriage, but many other sons had left the village to live elsewhere. Sometimes elderly parents ultimately joined them, but several others, including a number of widows and widowers, lived by themselves in the village, receiving widely varying degrees of care and attention from their absent offspring. Some reported that they had been invited to join their offspring in cities or apartment complexes outside the village but were reluctant to leave their own homes. A move late in life would place them in an unfamiliar environment and without close social ties to others of their own age cohort, whereas in the village they were among people whom they had known for decades. Some were openly apprehensive about the sincerity of the invitations or the quality of life they would have living in an offspring's home. As one villager had told us in the early 1980s, if you visit a son's family for three days, you get a three-day treatment; if you visit for seven days, you get a seven-day treatment. His wife spoke of their eldest son's radically different lifestyle in the city, noting that his family often ate breakfast as late as nine o'clock in the morning.

Evidence of creative living arrangements was sometimes apparent in Naeari in the 1990s. An elderly widow who lived alone told us that her daughter-in-law, who lived in a nearby village, brought her two meals a day. Another elderly widow was cared for by her married daughter and her husband for several years in return for free housing, although the daughter and her husband ultimately moved to an apartment complex outside the village. An elderly widower lived with his middle-aged unmarried daughter until his death. Another elderly widower received various forms of economic support from the son of a deceased brother, whom the widower had raised since childhood after the brother's death.

Because employment in nearby cities often did not require an offspring's move from the village, many parents offered various economic inducements to keep one of their sons and his family living with them. A major means was to provide them with free housing, though this strategy sometimes backfired. While living rent-free with parents, some young couples quietly accumulated their earnings until they had saved enough money to acquire a home of their own outside the village. Other parents considered arranging the inheritance of their property to induce one of their sons to remain at home after marriage. One elderly man had told us in the 1980s, for example, that he was thinking of leaving his land to the youngest of his three sons, because that son was the most likely to stay in the village. Other parents openly offered inheritance of their house site and farmland, which had become very valuable real estate. An older brother of an elderly widower tried to persuade one of the widower's sons and his wife to remain in the village, pointing to the substantial inheritance they would receive in return, but the wife replied, "We don't need money." One particularly dramatic case involved a couple who had three sons and three daughters, all of whom had emigrated from the village. The elderly wife suffered a series of strokes and became too ill to cook, and her husband was ill equipped to assume this responsibility. Villagers surmised that the couple was forced to live mostly on instant noodles. One of the daughters became actively involved in the care of this couple because one of the sons and his family lived with them, moved out, and then returned during their final days. Disputes over the care of the parents and entitlement to the last portion of their property seriously strained, if not ruptured entirely, relations between some of the siblings.

One 60-year-old resident whom we had first known as a young man later came to live alone with his wife, all of his children having left to live elsewhere. He related nonchalantly that he and his wife intended to live by themselves rather than with any of their offspring. "When we get really old and can no longer manage on our own," he said flatly, "we'll go to an old-age home."

Even those elderly who managed to live in the village with an offspring were not entirely enviable. According to village gossip, one elderly man had been starved to death by his offspring. One elderly woman and her husband lived with a married son who disliked farm labor and contributed little to the welfare of their household. Though her industrious daughter-in-law seemed to have assumed most of the housework in their home, the elderly woman nevertheless told us "it makes no difference whether one has children or not."

A number of women in their seventies and eighties, some of whom lived alone and some with married sons, told us of the difficulties they faced. One complained bitterly of the onerous chores her son asked her to perform. At one of their frequent gatherings at the home of an elderly widow who lived alone while her son lived in a nearby city, this group of women contrasted the past with the present by referring to *nunch'i pap*, a term used to designate food eaten while having to watch and gauge other's people's feelings about the amount one consumed. Formerly the phrase could be used as a figure of speech to characterize the difficult and vulnerable position of a new daughter-in-law in her husband's household, but the women implicitly contrasted the past and present as they lamented "These days it's the mother-in-law who eats nunch'i pap."

Their use of this trope, however, overlooked the sufferings of the elderly at the hands of their offspring in the past as well, but this oversight is not difficult to comprehend. Though now very advanced in years, these women were younger and not dependent on their offspring two decades ago. Thus they did not personally experience the plight of the elderly. It was their own age cohort whose children first started leaving the village in large numbers but who did not initially seem to mind their next generation's absence, although they had started to become apprehensive by the late 1970s.

Villagers' disparagement of present intergenerational relations is also partly due to the shaping of their perceptions by the media. Not only does every house now have at least one television, several residents read newspapers and magazines, and many work outside the village. A few decades ago, we watched in Seoul a fictional television program that told of offspring who took their parents on a holiday trip to Cheju Island, a popular resort located off the peninsula's southern coast, and abandoned them there. Village residents came to know similar stories as well. One elder reported it as an actual occurrence. "It's the new form of Koryŏjang," he related, though we know of no documented instances or archaeological evidence to indicate that children ever carried off and then abandoned their parents, either in the past or the present.

Conclusion

Several discourses regarding obligations to parents appear to focus on whether filial piety is, ought to be, or ought not to be disappearing, but this issue seems ultimately unresolvable. Its resolution would depend on how this moral norm is defined, not only in past but also in present contexts. A few decades ago, obligations to parents were assumed to be repaid primarily by an eldest son and his family, who continued to live in the son's natal home, who provided parents with food, clothing, shelter, and other forms of support, who refrained from acting in ways that were injurious to their interests, and whose adult males offered ancestor rites for them and the earlier generations of ancestors to which the parents had been obliged. Assuming these burdens justified the larger share of farmland inherited by an eldest son. Judged by those former standards, appropriate to a primarily agricultural way of life, filial piety is less evident today.

Though the abstract standards of filial piety may have been unchallenged under past circumstances, how those norms ought to be applied in specific cases was often contested. One disagreement was expressly verbalized in the debate over offering rites at each grave or establishing a scholarship fund. Other disagreements arose regarding the extent to which a younger son was obligated to perform ancestor rites if the eldest son's family was unwilling to perform them, sometimes because of conversion to Christianity. And the narrative of the man who openly defied his father by moving out of his father's house, allegedly for the father's own good, could be interpreted as either filial or unfilial.

Rather than pose the unanswerable question of whether or not filial piety has declined, it seems more fruitful to look for modern practices that exhibit a continuing sense of obligation toward parents. A number of elderly parents still live with one of their offspring in Naeari or elsewhere in South Korea, especially in their very final years, when they are in greatest need of care and support. Daughters now contribute more actively to the care of elderly parents. Differential shares of inheritance are still linked conceptually with assuming greater responsibilities for parents, even if that responsibility is not assumed by an eldest son and his wife. And the various national campaigns to revitalize filial piety as a moral code indicate a continuing awareness of this obligation.

The representations of elderly Naeari residents imply that they no longer receive as much care and attention as parents did in the past. A few decades ago, elderly villagers were almost assured of support from their eldest son and senior daughter-in-law, or in their absence a second son and his wife, to care for them in their later years. Witnessing or experiencing the withdrawal of that security generated anxieties about what their final years would be like. Contemporary elderly residents now retain control of their household assets rather than surrender them to nonresident offspring, and the value of those assets has increased many times during the past few decades, giving many elderly a measure of economic autonomy that few enjoyed more than two-and-a-half decades ago. Yet that greater material wealth is not seen as a replacement for the assured care and protection that has been lost.

Though the conditions of the elderly have also been alleviated by the increasing involvement of daughters in their care, no one in Naeari represented this as a trend. Instead, only individual cases were reported matter-of-factly. Evidently this is because contemporary conditions also hinder married daughters from becoming ostensibly the primary caregivers of their parents, except under certain limited circumstances. The former contradictions resulting from residence patterns that separated married women from their natal parents have been replaced by the rearrangement of household roles brought about by capitalist industrialization. In the past, sonless couples had the option of bringing in a son-in-law and giving him all or a portion of their land in return for their daughter's and his care, thereby avoiding an obvious dependence on his charity. In the 1990s, however, living with a son-in-law who is regarded as his family's "breadwinner" is a demeaning arrangement for the elderly.

Local perceptions of intergenerational relationships have been shaped not only by contrasting past experiences with those of today, but also by an increasing awareness of discourses that prevail beyond the village. Contemporary residents of Naeari are familiar with the concomitants of an industrialized way of life alleged by modernization theory. American movies with Korean subtitles or soundtracks that are regularly received by their televisions do not emphasize neighborhood communities or the care of elderly parents. Naeari residents have come to speak of a decline in community spirit, neighborliness, and human feelings. In the 1970s we heard that the village was one in which people were kind-hearted (*insimi chot'a*); but by the late 1990s, we often heard instead about the self-centeredness (*chagi chungsim*) and heartlessness (*kakpakhada*) that had arisen over the past few decades. Their awareness of the alleged "new Koryŏjang" custom, which none of them ever experienced, testifies to the effects of extravillage discourse on their understandings of current relations between adult offspring and senior parents.

Finally, we too, albeit unwittingly, contributed to perceptions of relations between elderly parents and their adult offspring in an industrialized society by conveying our own impressions of the United States, which many villagers represented as a prototype of an industrialized nation. During our fieldwork in 1999, we talked with a man in his seventies, in whose home we had rented a room twenty-six years earlier. His wife had left him about twenty years ago, and the youngest coresident married son and his family had moved out. As a result, he lived alone, renting unneeded rooms of his house to families of workers employed in factories that had been constructed next to the village. Commenting on his living arrangements, he lamented, "Now we've become just like the United States." Then he mimicked Roger Janelli's mimicking of the lonely elderly in the United States who asked passersby for the time of day.

CHAPTER 8

Filial Piety in Contemporary Urban Southeast Korea: Practices and Discourses

CLARK SORENSEN AND SUNG-CHUL KIM

On April 5, 2001, a headline in the *Chosun Daily* announced, "Garnishment of subsistence funds of children who don't support their parents." The article went on to explain:

> From children who are capable of supporting their parents but do not do so the regional authorities having jurisdiction plan to seize the subsistence fee that the government paid in the children's stead. It was revealed today that the city of P'yŏngt'aek in Kyŏnggi Province reported according to the Basic Living Preservation Law implemented in October of last year that it intends to extract two months of subsistence paid to parents by the state in place of nineteen children. This month again, P'yŏngt'aek City plans to garnishee from fifteen among the nineteen the third month's subsistence stipend given by the state, excluding four who have promised to provide subsistence to their parents. Anyang in Kyŏnggi Province, too, has decided to garnishee the parental subsistence fee from four or five persons.

In a country that has traditionally set filial piety, the obligation to take care of parents in their old age, at the center of its ethical universe—and even into its legal code—this report could not be anything but shocking.[1] Moreover, it follows other, occasional accounts in the media of neglect of parents. Has urban, industrial Korea lost its ethical core? There may be reasons to believe so. After all, the transformation of Korea from an underdeveloped periphery of the Japanese empire at liberation in 1945 to a wealthy, industrialized, urban, and modern society today is one of the most rapid and thorough cases of social change known to history.

When the Republic of Korea was founded in 1948 it was a Confucian-Buddhist country of twenty million with little industry and one or two cities barely worthy of the name. It occupied less than half the historic territory of the Korean nation and its population was 80 percent rural and largely illiterate. Devastated by an internationalized civil war from 1950 to 1953, the country by 1960 had barely regained the living standard of 1940, much less achieved prosperity. Yet forty years later the country has become highly industrialized, is some 85 percent urban, and has been flirting with high-income status.[2] Illiteracy was virtually eliminated by the 1960s, and by 1995 68 percent of the population above the age of six had graduated from the twelfth grade (Korea National Statistical Office 1999).[3] Today, more than a third of the population continues on to postsecondary education, giving South Korea one of the highest postsecondary enrollment rates in the world. Whereas in 1960 most of the population considered themselves Confucian, Buddhist, or Ch'ŏndogyo, and only 6.4 percent reported themselves Christian (Korea National Commission 1960: 347, 351), today Christians (about four fifths of whom are Protestant) now slightly surpass in number the quarter or so of the population who report themselves Buddhist (Korea National Statistical Office 1995).[4]

The changes South Koreans have experienced in the past two generations cover all the most important areas of social life. The former predominant occupation of subsistence farmer or landlord has changed to factory worker, clerk, technician, or businessman. A nation that used to live primarily in single-family homes in villages tightly structured by family and kinship ties now typically lives (in order of preference) in anonymous urban high-rise apartments, mid-rise "villa apartments," row houses, or the neighborhoods of small, tightly packed houses. Education that used to emphasize Confucian moralism now favors "modernity, rationality and science" (Sorensen 1994).

Rapid rural-to-urban migration has changed the family. The traditional rural family had been a patrilocal stem family in which daughters married out and the parents arranged for a daughter-in-law to be brought in as wife of the eldest son. The oldest son (known as *maji*) and senior daughter-in-law (known as *k'ŭn myŏnŭri*, or "big daughter-in-law") were supposed to reside in the "big house" (*k'ŭn chip*) all their lives caring for the husband's parents. Younger sons and daughters-in-law would coreside for only a short time (if at all) after marriage, and then partition to form branch houses (known as *chagŭn chip*, or "little houses"). Elderly parents expected to live out their lives in stem families, cared for by their senior daughter-in-law, but few families had more than one coresident daughter-in-law at a time. Thus, although the Chinese ideal of all sons under one roof was never sought, up through the 1960s roughly a quarter of Korean families were three-generation stem households (Yi 1983). Rapid industrialization has led both younger and eldest sons to move to town, however, often leaving their aged parents alone in the village. Some well-established children have been able to bring their parents to live with them in the city, but spacious apartments are expensive and today's urban wives of love matches frequently do not feel obliged to care for their parents-in-law the way daughters-in-law of arranged marriages used to.

These lifestyle and cultural changes have been accompanied by demographic changes. Couples that at mid-century usually married in their late teens or early twenties and had half-a-dozen children now marry in their late twenties or early thirties and bear only one or two children. With improved health and nutrition, life expectancies have also increased. Whereas people tended to die between 55 and 65 at mid-century, today they typically die between the ages of 65 and 75, and many live well into their 80s—even 90s. As in other developed countries, the phenomenon of aged retirees taking care of their still-more-aged parents is not unusual. In fact a television documentary on this phenomenon was widely broadcast. Nationally, only 11.2 percent of the population lived in stem families in 1995 (Korea National Statistical Office 1999), however. This tends to suggest the nuclearization of the family consequent to industrialization and urbanization as predicted by William Goode and others (Goode 1963; Ember and Ember 1983).[5] Under such circumstances, the survival of the traditional value of filial piety (*hyo*) that seems contingent on complex family organization might well be questioned.

Filial Piety in Korea

Filial piety has long been fundamental to Korean ethics. During the Buddhist Koryŏ dynasty (918–1392), the Sutra of Parental Grace (*Pumo ŭnjung kyŏng*) was popular, but it was the Confucianizing reforms introduced at the beginning of the Chosŏn dynasty (1392–1910) that made Confucian family ethics central to Korean elite culture. Not only did the Chosŏn state banish Buddhism from the capital and establish Confucian examinations as the basis for recruitment into the state bureaucracy, but in 1419 it made the Confucian family ritual as outlined in Zhu Xi's *Family Rituals* compulsory for the ruling elite (Yi 1978). From this time until the introduction of modern education in the late nineteenth century, education in Korea consisted of memorization of snippets of edifying Chinese-language texts as collected in such works such as *Precious Mirror for Enlightening the Mind* (*Myŏngsim pogam*) followed by study of such standard Confucian texts as the *Great Learning*. Because of the way these Chinese-derived norms were promulgated in Korea—as state-led top-down reforms for elites that only gradually spread to the rest of the population (Yi 1978; Deuchler 1992)—they acquired a status-marking flavor in Korea they may have lacked in China. The *yangban*, or notability (Lee 1996), from which holders of central state office were recruited, maintained their status partly through Chinese-language education and properly Confucian lifestyles. Well-established farmers eventually emulated the notability, though this probably did not become widespread until the seventeenth or eighteenth century. Lesser folk such as tenant farmers, unable to get a permanent foothold in villages, as well as fisher folk, artisans, entertainers, butchers, and slaves were not in a position to dispute hegemonic state Confucian ideology, but the degree to which they adhered to, or even believed in, Confucian norms in all respects is an open question.

During the colonial period (1910–45) under the Japanese, the Confucian norms of loyalty and filial piety continued to be taught in schools. Members of the Confucian notability were to the extent possible co-opted by government-controlled institutions, such as the revived Sŏnggyun'gwan Confucian Academy, and the norms of the patriarchal stem family with a male house head were written into the Civil Code. Household registration records used to enforce these norms also served to aid the colonial authorities in social control. After liberation, some Koreans reacted to this co-optation by rejecting Confucianism as both antinational and antimodern. Filial piety, however, continued to be taught in ethics education classes that reached virtually the entire population with the expansion of public education that followed liberation, and has not been seriously challenged.

Korean academic writing on filial piety has almost uniformly concentrated on the explication and analysis of classical texts. Most important is the *Classic of Filial Piety* (*Hyo kyŏng*), which lists five behaviors necessary to perform filial piety: obey one's parents, care for them in old age, give them a good funeral, practice ancestor worship, and have descendants to continue the family line. This kind of filial piety would lead, of course, to a family emphasis on the ties between the generations—especially between father and son—as opposed to conjugal ties.

Filial piety as a folk concept, however, and the relationship of filial piety to everyday concerns has seldom been the object of empirical study, even though the ethnography of Korea is filled with informants' references to filial sons and daughters (Janelli and Janelli 1982; Kendall 1985; Kim 1988; Kim 1997). Korean folklore, too, is full of references to filial piety. The legend of Koryŏjang, in which ancient Koreans are supposed to have taken elderly parents up into the mountains to die until changing their ways after observing their own children planning to do the same to them, is known to every child and frequently comes up in interviews on filial piety. The famous folktales of Princess Pari, the Cast Out Daughter, and of Sim Ch'ŏng are both panegyrics on filial daughters, or *hyonyŏ* (Haboush 1995; Sorensen 1988b; Walraven 1994). As these tales focus on daughters, however, the folk emphasis in Korea may be quite different from that on the father-son tie in classical texts.

It is not only folkloric material that gives one a view of filial piety that differs from classical texts. One can also find in the ethnography evidence of interaction between the concept of filial piety and pragmatic adaptation. For example, Sorensen has noted that the Korean stem-family cycle legitimized by filial piety provides maximal continuity in the family labor supply and an efficient mechanism for the support of the aged. He also has demonstrated that modernization up into the early 1980s in South Korea, at least, had not destroyed the rural stem family system (Sorensen 1986, 1988a). Interviewing in periurban villages in South Kyŏngsang and South Ch'ungch'ŏng provinces in 1986, however, he found that although filial piety remained a cherished value, the old pragmatics were no longer pertinent (Sorensen 1990). Use of machinery, hired labor, and commercial cropping had changed the nature of the family farm and the need for family labor. Most young men and women had moved to town for factory and other work.

Nevertheless, he was still able to collect tales of filial piety and found in one village that an exemplary filial son (*hyoja*) and filial daughter-in-law (*hyobu*) had both received "filial piety prizes" (*hyosang*) from the county. He found that among these rural people the conceptual center of filial piety was located in care for parents in their old age and "setting their minds at rest." Most people, moreover, viewed filial piety more as a natural human response to parents' loving care than a specifically Confucian ethical norm. Though filial piety as a value remained, the rural people interviewed in the late 1980s had already begun to adapt their notions of filial piety to the new situation. Most—but not all—thought children could be filial even though they no longer lived with their parents. There was discursive disagreement, however, about the role of material support. Those with traditional education, who generally had higher status, seemed to emphasize filial piety primarily as an ethical norm, while poorer people seemed inclined to see it as equivalent to any kind of material support for parents.

Whether these findings would be relevant for an urban sample, however, could be questioned. Although many current city dwellers have roots in the countryside, the majority these days are urban-born, and even many of the rural-born migrated to the city at an early age. Contemporary Korean city dwellers have high levels of formal education and extensive exposure to print and broadcast media that make them more inclined to think of alternatives to filial piety as an ethical norm. Some have political experience and think in terms of government policy. Urban people clearly differ in lifestyle from rural people, moreover, because of the need to operate in a money economy with a competitive labor market.

In 1992 Sŏng Kyut'ak (1995) undertook one of the few empirical studies of the motivations of Koreans for upholding filial piety. In a questionnaire administered to 1,250 students and adults selected from various parts of Seoul, he found that love for parents, repayment of parental grace (ŭn), maintenance of family harmony, respect for parents, sense of responsibility or duty, and sacrifice for the sake of parents were the most popular motivations (in that order). Questions of inheritance and face were the least popular motivations. He found no particular gender differences, but found that sacrifice, responsibility, and repayment of parental grace were positively (though weakly) correlated with income. A subset of the sample, winners of the Samsung Prize for Filial Piety, tended to emphasize duty and respect for parents rather than the more popular love. Factor analysis revealed three semantic clusters: (1) ideological reasons—sacrifice for parents, responsibility, repayment of parental grace, (2) emotional reasons—love, respect, and family harmony, and (3) social reasons—maintenance of family continuity and preservation of family reputation.

Pragmatic Adaptation and Cultural Change

In his study, Sŏng did not ask *whether* people maintained filial piety, but only *why* they did, on the apparent assumption that all do, in fact, favor continuing filial piety. Our own experience led us to believe that he was not mistaken in this. Sŏng, however, did not inquire into standards of performance or whether these have changed. To investigate these questions, the coauthors devised a questionnaire about filial piety to administer to a sample of residents of southeast urban Korea in the summer of 2000. We took Sŏng's findings into account in formulating our questionnaire, but we used semistructured interviewing techniques that encouraged informants to formulate answers in their own way, and thus got fewer formulaic answers expressed in terms of traditional Confucian ideology of parental grace, filial obligation, and social order. Since we were interested in the question of maintenance of filial piety, we asked directly and indirectly not only about our informants' personal feelings about maintenance of filial piety, but also their opinions about filial piety in Korean society in general. We also asked about personal and community standards of performance of filial piety so as to uncover interaction between pragmatic concerns and the construction of the meaning of filial piety.

Social change in Korea, as elsewhere, works most obviously on the behavioral level as people make pragmatic adaptations to urban life. Even a highly idealized and hegemonic value such as filial piety allows some flexibility in its standards of performance. The ability to create and make use of this flexibility allows people to pragmatically adapt their standards of performance to new situations. As society itself is constituted through concrete activity, this brings about social change. Pragmatic adaptation, however, is never *just* pragmatic. Since each adaptation is made by a specific person in possession of concrete amounts of economic, cultural, and social capital, that person's adaptations soon take on social meaning. People are labeled as good or bad, high class or low class, modern or traditional, cosmopolitan or parochial, progressive or conservative, and so forth. These labels then become available for the social placement of people and contribute to the structuration of society.

The way in which a family does or does not maintain filial piety, thus, is not a simple issue of maintenance of social norms: it is one of the ways through which a family constitutes its social personality in terms of respectability, modernity, access to social and cultural capital, and thus class. Old behaviors may be dropped as maladaptive, but they also take on new significance as people reinterpret them in light of the new situation. New behaviors appear, but they always do so among specific people with specific social characteristics. If the traditional patriarchal stem families that used to produce high status are reinterpreted as backward and repressive, then the nuclear families of husband, wife, and children that used to be seen as "selfish" might come to seem modern, middle class, and progressive. This is especially likely if the new, modern families still retain considerable social capital.

To the extent that people compete for access to pecuniary, social, and cultural capital, one expects that they also will compete over the meaning of behavior, because this meaning will affect their access to social and cultural capital. Contestation over meaning—a discursive struggle—thus will complement the adaptive struggle. While it is conceivable that an old value might simply be discarded if it no longer fits well with social reality, a fundamental value may be hegemonic to the extent that people are unable to easily conceive of alternatives. As we expected this to be the case for filial piety, we proceeded in two fashions in designing this research. On the one hand, we wanted to document the changes in family behavior—the pragmatic adjustments—that have followed urbanization and industrialization. We looked particularly at those aspects of family behavior that have traditionally been interpreted as expressions of filial piety. On the other hand, we also wanted to judge the extent and parameters of any discursive struggle that may revolve around filial piety. We thus also directly interviewed people about whether they feel filial piety is still maintained in Korea, and what their personal feelings about filial piety are, both in terms of the importance (or lack thereof) of its maintenance, and in terms of their views on what concrete behavior is necessary to its maintenance. Since, as explained above, maintenance of Confucian norms such as filial piety in Korea are redolent of tradition and have class implications, we also directly asked informants about their views on the relationship of class to filial piety both in behavioral and conceptual terms.

South Kyŏngsang Province

Interviews were conducted in the Pusan-Kimhae metropolitan area and the Masan-Ch'angwŏn area in the summer of 2000. Our decision to concentrate on these cities in South Kyŏngsang Province in the southeast corner of the Republic of Korea was partly for convenience's sake,[6] but because South Kyŏngsang Province is the most urbanized and industrialized part of South

Korea outside the capital region of Seoul and its surrounding areas, it also seemed a good place to look for changes in social values. Being far from Seoul, the main center of intellectual production and foreign contact, and thus the main area described in scholarly research (Mun ed. 1992; Kendall 1996; Lett 1998; Nelson 2000), the area has yet been little studied. (See, however, Kang 1990; and Kim 1997.) The province in 1995 had a population of 3.8 million, 63.4 percent of whom resided in cities of 100,000 residents or more. It surrounds the separately administered Metropolitan City of Pusan—Korea's premier seaport and a city of 3.84 million—and has ten other cities of 100,000 residents or more including the provincial capital of Masan, the industrial city of Ch'angwŏn, and the bedroom community of Kimhae, the three cities in which interviews were done.[7]

The concentration of industry in South Kyŏngsang Province is a reflection of geographical and strategic as well as political advantages the region has recently enjoyed. Pusan, a remote and backward village until late in the nineteenth century, began to develop as Korea's premier port because of its superb deepwater anchorage close to shore, its moderate tidal range, and its convenience for communication with Japan and the rest of the world. Masan enjoyed similar advantages, and both port cities were provided with convenient rail connections inland and to Seoul during the colonial period (1910–45). During the Korean War, Pusan and Masan—being both distant from North Korea and easily supplied by sea—were two of the few large cities that escaped occupation by the North Koreans in the summer of 1950. Pusan, in fact, became the wartime capital of the Republic of Korea, and many refugees from North Korea eventually settled there.

Thus when President Park Chung Hee—a native of neighboring North Kyŏngsang Province—threw the government behind massive industrialization in the mid-1960s, South Kyŏngsang Province was one of the main beneficiaries. South Korea's first Foreign Export Zone was set up in Masan in 1962, and Pusan and Masan began at that time prospering on light industry—particularly athletic footwear, textiles and garments, and electronics. Masan doubled in size between 1965 and 1975, and Pusan gained about 1,000,000 residents during the same period.[8] Both cities prospered until political and economic changes in the late 1980s and early 1990s made Korean labor relatively expensive so that labor-intensive light industry began migrating to cheaper countries, such as China and Indonesia. Masan suffered a more than 10 percent loss of population in the early 1990s.

During the Heavy and Chemical Industrialization Program of the 1970s that followed the light industrialization of the 1960s much defense-related heavy industry was also located in the politically well-connected North and South Kyŏngsang provinces, which were also most safe from North Korean attack. Ulsan, site of Hyundai Heavy Industries (steel, cars, shipbuilding), and Ch'angwŏn, a new city set up for the machine tool industry in 1976, were two of the main beneficiaries. Just across Masan Bay from Masan itself, Ch'angwŏn went from a small town of 43,000 in 1975 to a city of 384,000 by 1990. Today Ch'angwŏn is larger than the older city of Masan, which now seems almost like a bedroom community for prospering Ch'angwŏn.

Kimhae, located across the Naktong River from Pusan, was once the capital city of the ancient Kaya kingdom. Long a provincial town (ŭp), it was upgraded to provincial city (si) in 1985 when Pusan could no longer contain its sprawling growth within the city limits. Kimhae did its part to attract people from Pusan and other parts of South Kyŏngsang Province by accommodating an industrial zone for small- and medium-size industries, constructing roads and building apartments, and serving as the site of Pusan's international airport. By the time of the interviews, Kimhae had become a city of 264,000 people.

Most of the residents of Kimhae are so-called ttŭnaegi (literally "itinerants," but locally used to denote short-term residents who lack a feeling of belonging to the local community) from Pusan, including young white-collar workers who seek inexpensive housing. In fact, Pusan and Kimhae can be called one commuting community since downtown Pusan is no farther away from Kimhae than it is from some districts of Pusan proper. In addition to the ttŭnaegi are Kimhae natives, who mainly run truck farms for the metropolis. Unlike village farmers in the interior who tend to be poor, peri-urban truck farmers can often make an excellent living. Most of the residents of Ch'angwŏn-Masan have white- and blue-collar occupations in the plants and branch offices of the chaebŏl corporations as well as local subcontracting firms.

Rural migrants streamed into the cities of South Kyŏngsang Province most rapidly in the 1970s and 1980s, and as a result slightly more than half of our informants over the age of 30 had rural origins. On the other hand, all but two (11.8 percent) of our informants in their twenties were urban-born. Although the residents of Pusan and the cities of South Kyŏngsang Province come from all over Korea following their jobs, 85 percent of the urban

FIGURE 6. The rural-to-urban transition in Kimhae is clearly visible from the vegetable garden in the foreground and the dozens of thirty-story apartment buildings in the center. Photo by Sung-chul Kim.

dwellers of South Kyŏngsang Province are from South or North Kyŏngsang Provinces, or from Pusan. This was also true of our sample. Though South Kyŏngsang Province is fully as urban as Kyŏnggi Province surrounding Seoul, it is often regarded as socially conservative. Possible evidence for this proposition lies in the fact that in 1995 Protestant Christians, at 9 percent of the population, constituted a smaller proportion of the population than in any other mainland province of Korea. This proportion was less than half that of the nation as a whole, and about one third the level of Seoul's 26 percent (*Wŏlgan Chosŏn* 2001: 524).

The Interview Process

The interview sample of forty-seven informants was selected on the basis of age, residence, and income standing to investigate the views on filial piety of the so-called urban middle class (*chungsanch'ŭng*).[9] We strove to get a distribution of middle-aged informants so as to investigate attitudes and practices for those actively facing problems of care of their parents, and informants in their twenties so as to be able to test for secular changes. The interviewees were almost evenly mixed between males (46.8 percent) and females (53.2 percent), and ranged in age from 21 to 52. We were able to get a fairly even age balance: 36.1 percent in their 20s, 27.7 percent in their 30s, 31.9 percent in their 40s, and 4.2 percent in their 50s. Almost 75 percent of the interviewees classified themselves as middle or upper-middle class, with 10.6 percent upper class and 12.8 percent lower class (one informant could not be classified). All but the three who were in agriculture and the three who were in service industries would be considered educated white collar.[10] Two thirds were urban-born, and all but one are current residents of Pusan, Kimhae, Masan, Ch'angwŏn, or other nearby cities.

Informants were introduced to the interviewers by colleagues, students who had lived in the region for more than five years, and sometimes by the interviewees themselves. To secure the reliability of the data, such items on the questionnaire as occupation and economic standing were confirmed with those who had introduced the interviewee. When an interviewee was contacted, he or she was invited out to a local coffee shop or cafeteria of his or her preference. Interviews were intentionally conducted outside the interviewee's residence and away from his or her neighborhood. This was to provide a more anonymous and comfortable atmosphere to discuss something that might be delicate on one hand, and to avoid the unnecessary influence of someone who might be present during the course of the interview on the other.

The interviews were conducted by Dr. Kim and by an assistant, Ryung-yŏng Lee, a graduating student in social welfare.[11] Each interview lasted about two hours as the interviewer established rapport and explained the purpose of the interview and the questions that would be asked. The questionnaire formulated by the coauthors was divided into three sections. The first introduced informants to the subject of filial piety through questions about a well-known television show on "the aged caring for the aged" and questions about family ceremonies. The second section asked informants to talk about the maintenance of filial piety in Korea, and informants' personal attitudes toward, and performance of, filial piety. The third section asked about changes in filial piety and the reasons for them.

Interviews were not recorded. The interviewer wrote answers on the questionnaire during the interview, and this material was subsequently typed up. Quotations are thus reconstructed from field notes. Most of the interviewees did not seem to be uncomfortable even when asked about their economic standing: they would just smile and say things like, "Just write lower-middle," or "I think I am lower-middle, but everybody will say I am upper-middle." This lack of discomfort is partly because they seemed to understand how the interview should proceed, and partly because the issues brought up might be familiar ones they themselves had chatted about with their friends or relatives. With few exceptions, questions were open-ended, and the interviewees normally were allowed to say whatever they wanted to say unless they deviated too far from the issues under discussion.

Contemporary Performance of Filial Piety

Our questions about informants' behavior focused on what has traditionally been interpreted as expressions of filial piety (Sŏng 1995): (1) obedience to parents—particularly in choice of marriage partner and place of residence, (2) care for parents in their old age through coresidence, personal service, and financial support—particularly by the eldest son and senior daughter-in-law, but also by other children, (3) observance of relevant family ceremonies, such as sixtieth-birthday celebrations, funerals, and ancestor worship, and (4) continuing the family line through procreation. Since we were interested in the degree to which the traditional patrilocal stem family based on the eldest son has been preserved, we asked specifically about sibling birth order and whether filial obligations fall mostly on the eldest son.

OBEDIENCE TO PARENTS AND PLACE OF RESIDENCE

Traditionally, children were expected to obey parents. The supreme test of obedience was accepting the parents' choice of spouse. The vast majority of matches in South Korea today are love matches or "half-love, half-arranged" matches chosen by the children and sanctioned by the parents (Kendall 1996). Marriages arranged through go-betweens are not uncommon when considerations of status and education are paramount, or when children have trouble finding a partner, but even here children can veto any prospect they dislike. Until the 1989 revisions of the Civil Code, male house heads (*hoju*) had the legal right to determine the place of residence of all family members, including adult sons and their wives and children. Although younger sons usually partitioned from the main house, acquiring property and authority as heads of their own, separate families, eldest sons were not legally allowed to do this, so the eldest son and his family remained under patriarchal authority until his father's death. Although this authority was occasionally exercised in preceding decades, the rapid rural-to-urban migration beginning in the 1960s made it moot by the time it was abolished in 1989. When asked about obedience, therefore, some informants made remarks such as, "When you have differences with your parents, you don't follow them blindly." Surprisingly, however, 17 percent of our informants listed obedience to parents as one of the ways they perform filial piety today. Typically, however, such informants qualified their remarks, as did a 36-year-old female informant who said, "We do practically everything our parents-in-law say. Well, rather than obey we more or less act like we're not going against them."

CARE FOR PARENTS IN THEIR OLD AGE

This is the core of filial piety. At first glance, since 80.9 percent of our informants were members of nuclear families of parents and unmarried children, and only 19.1 percent of stem families, one might suppose stem families to be disappearing. Most Koreans have this impression, too. A 43-year-old daughter-in-law who was coresiding with her parents-in-law told us that such coresidence is uncommon. However, a closer look at the data shows that a significant portion of the population live in stem families. The low proportion of stem families in the entire sample comes in part from the fact that only half the sample consisted of families of eldest sons that traditionally would form stem families. Of those families headed by eldest sons with living parents ("big houses"), fully half were in stem form—a surprisingly high number for an urban sample.[12] We asked our informants whether they had living parents and, if so, where their parents now live.[13] Four replied ambiguously, but 17 percent replied their parents lived with the eldest son (whether themselves or a sibling), and another 17 percent replied that their parents lived with a child who is not the eldest son (most often with a younger son, but occasionally a daughter). Nineteen percent responded that their parents lived alone in rural villages, and 15 percent that they lived alone in urban settings. Most people explained such arrangements were what their parents wanted.

Mother [71 years old] is still able to live in the countryside. It's what she still wants. It could be that she's used to country life and wouldn't adjust to the city. I meet her face-to-face once a month to check on how she's doing. My native village is a clan village and it has a strong sense of solidarity. When I was little, if you didn't greet the elders properly you would be punished.

Another informant, whose mother lives in an urban neighborhood, told us, "Although I want my [widowed] mother to live with us, she doesn't want to because friends live near her and she is still able to get about. The decision of a conference was that I listened to her friends." A small number of parents lived in institutions (6.4 percent), an arrangement available only to the better-off informants.[14] Almost all informants (93.7 percent) said they gave their parents financial support.

Although a third of our informants were rural born, we could detect little difference in attitude or behavior between this group and those of urban origin, perhaps because most of the former had migrated to town in their late teens, before their attitudes were fully formed. We also found little difference between age cohorts in the frequency of stem family formation, suggesting attitudes toward stem families are not changing quickly. Several student informants in their 20s not only were living in a stem family at the time of the interview, but also expressed strong support for the efficacy of stem family organization for inculcating filial piety. One thoughtful young woman remarked, "When I look at my friends—those who live far from their grandparents—their attitude and respect for their grandparents is different from that of those who live together with them. Those who live separately have less respect. So when I get old, in order to teach filial piety to my children, naturally I will have to live with them."

On the other hand, we did find strong class patterning in the incidence of stem family formation. None of the upper-class families were stem families, yet fully one third of the upper-middle-class families were. Stem families were found in numbers comparable to their national incidence in 1995 of 11.2 percent among both the lower-middle- and lower-class informants.[15] The upper-class attitude was well expressed by one informant: "As long as both parents are alive it is desirable to live separately from them . . . but, of course, in some cases the parents may not have the financial means to do so, and so the eldest son must take responsibility for them." A lower-class informant, on the other hand, expressed the hope that he would be able to better his economic circumstances so that he could bring his parents from the countryside to co-reside with him, and thus allow them to retire from farming. Many middle-class informants mentioned that a "silver town" (silbŏ t'aun)—a specialized re-tirement community—is the most desirable residence for the elderly. Most people are familiar with the idea from the media, but it remains a dream rather than reality for most Koreans. None of our informants had a parent in a silver town. One informant had had a maternal grandmother who had lived in a silver town, but this had only been possible because she had been able to sell her farmland to urban developers. (She also did not get along with her daughter-in-law.) "Throwing your parents out into an institution" (pumonim ŭl kigwan e naebŏrinŭn kŏt) tended to be condemned by middle- and lower-class informants as trying to "purchase" what should be done personally. As we shall see below, this issue is an important discursive focus.

Even most of the relatively large number of informants in our sample who coresided with their parents did not live in stem families formed ac-cording to rural traditions. Only seven informants (14.9 percent) reported continuous coresidence of parents and married eldest son from the time of his marriage as tradition would require, and about half of these were from families that hailed from the countryside or were engaged in periurban truck farming.[16] The other half of the informants who maintained continuous coresidence since marriage were from upper-middle-class white-collar fami-lies. Most informants, even eldest sons, in our sample partitioned from their birth family either at the time of marriage or after a short period of co-residence. (See Chapter 1 for a Chinese example of the "ritualization" of a brief period of coresidence at marriage.) Two thirds of the eldest sons who partitioned, however, expected to take their parents in when they became widowed or no longer able to care for themselves economically or physically. Sometimes informants were rather blunt about the short-term nature of this commitment, saying, for example, "My husband wants to live with his par-ents while they are dying."

DAUGHTER-IN-LAW VERSUS HOUSE MISTRESS

In stem families, the burden for care of the eldest son's parents falls, of course, not on the eldest son, but on his wife, the senior daughter-in-law (k'ŭn myŏnŭri or man myŏnŭri). Unmarried children of both sexes living in stem families often spoke sympathetically about their mothers' heavy burden of domestic labor. Middle-aged married men, on the other hand, could be matter-of-fact. One 48-year-old man remarked casually, for example, that "filial piety, of course, depends upon the daughter-in-law, that is, the house mistress (*chubu*). Many of the most difficult aspects are the daughter-in-law's. In passing down filial piety, the position of the wife (*anae*) is most important."[17]

Because daughters-in-law in stem families have to endure day-to-day supervision by mothers-in-law, or even fathers-in-law, however, stem family formation goes beyond domestic labor to encompass power. Although some daughters-in-law in stem families were philosophical about the effort it takes to live in a large family, one informant expressed bitterness about patriarchal control, saying,

> You have to live picking up after them every day, and when something bad happens, everybody just has to bear it. Even though you want to dress comfortably, you can't for fear of father-in-law. And even though you want to buy and prepare tasty treats for your children, you get to worrying about what father-in-law would think. Occasionally you don't want to cook and would like to just have a simple meal, but because of father-in-law you can't do that either.

Power was occasionally an issue for men as well, and they sometimes frankly noted the desire of parents to retain power within the family, or control money, saying such things as, "Until her seventies my mother still tried to grab leadership. . . . I want to have my mother live with us, but she is still too active," or "Right now my parents say they want to hold onto their money until they die, because your children ignore you if you don't have money." Most conflict, however, involves the mother-in-law and daughter-in-law rather than the son. Such conflict is common enough to have its own name, *kobu kaldŭng*. In Korea, mother-in-law/daughter-in-law conflict rarely reaches the dire levels sometimes reported for China (Wolf 1975), but nonetheless it often leads to partition, and sometimes to divorce. One of our informants, a married younger son coresiding with his parents, commented, "I wouldn't live with my parents if they had continued to live with my older brother, but my sister-in-law and my mother were in constant conflict. I did a lot from below, but my parents were never satisfied with her. The two kept on having spats and this led to conflict."

Thus although the daughter-in-law brought into a stem family at the beginning of her marriage can easily become oppressed, in most instances women who have had the experience of running their own households as chubu, or house mistress, clearly acquire veto power over coresidence with their parents-in-law. This is in spite of the patriarchal attitudes of many Korean men. The married younger son mentioned above who was coresiding with his parents, for example, claimed in discussing the reasons for his elder brother's partition, "The man must draw the line, and make objective valuations," but ruefully noted, "If my older brother took my parents' side various problems would only get worse," tacitly admitting the limits to a husband's patriarchal authority. A 43-year-old eldest son, who twenty-five years before as an unmarried young man had moved to town from a poor village where his 73-year-old father still lives, expressed his limited power this way: "Father came and said he wanted to live [in the apartment] with us, but I think this would have caused resentment (tchajŭngi issŭl kŏt katta). I think my wife would have different feelings toward me. You know, because we would keep bumping into each other. You would think it would be natural [for him to live with us], but there could be clashes." When asked between whom the clashes would be, he replied, "Husband and wife." These household dynamics were widely recognized by our informants to the extent that even unmarried young men were aware of them, noting in several cases that their parents' desire for coresidence will most likely have to yield to their future wife's expected desire for a separate household.[18]

To those who theorize women's power to be closely correlated to their role in productive labor (Sanday 1974), this enhanced power might seem paradoxical. The high-status ideal for Korean upper- and middle-class urban married women is that they be "full-time housewives" (chŏnŏp chubu) who do not participate in formal-sector employment.[19] In our sample, all of the married upper-class women and two thirds of the married upper-middle-class women were full-time housewives. The majority of women in other classes worked, but limited hiring opportunities and considerations of status tend to limit middle-class women to the education sector or self-employment. Service-sector employment for women, found among several informants, is by definition lower class in Korea.[20] Because Korean families have a clear division of labor between the man's "outside labor" (pakkannil) and the woman's "inside labor" (annil) (Sorensen 1983), however, husbands, as a rule, do not interfere with the female domain. In the urban context, this means the housewife of a nuclear family has full control over running the house—not simply managing housework, child care, and consumption, but also managing public relations with (husband's) kin, neighborhood organizations, and local government, and total responsibility for managing the family income and usually its capital assets, as well. Women typically need wide-ranging contacts to manage family capital, investing it frequently as "key money" (*chŏnse*) for their dwelling, in revolving credit clubs (*kye*) among their network of friends and relatives, or these days in a variety of financial instruments (Mun 1992; Nelson 2000). Housewives, though engaged in what is culturally defined as "inside labor," clearly are not confined simply to the "domestic sphere" as defined by Michelle Rosaldo (1974; see also Mun 1992). This may be the reason that in urban Korea, just as Carol Rogers (1975) has argued for France, control of the household can itself be a source of female power.

FAMILY CEREMONIES

The family ceremonies traditionally performed as an expression of filial piety include sixtieth birthday celebrations (*hoegap* or *hwan'gap*), funerals (including mourning), and ancestor worship. For the farming population, old age and retirement were thought to begin at the age of 60. In well-established rural families, attainment of this ripe old age was celebrated in an elaborate ceremony at which descendents bowed to the celebrant in a "living ancestor worship ceremony" (Janelli and Janelli 1982), followed by a banquet for friends and neighbors. Since people's health and longevity have improved, and as the burden of heavy labor has been lightened, however, people now consider old age to begin later than sixty. Only two informants mentioned sixty as the contemporary age of retirement (sixty-five is the standard retirement age for civil servants and employees of large concerns); more than 60 percent cited the age of seventy or above, adding the remark that people do not turn "idle" (*soilgŏri*) and become economically dependent until that time. Because of the "aging of old age," many informants remarked that "Nowadays seventieth and eightieth birthday parties are more common than hoegap," or, "My mother didn't want me to arrange a hoegap because she didn't want to be treated like a senior citizen." Nevertheless, thirty-four of our informants (72.3 percent) reported celebrating hoegap, while only a third reported attending or planning seventieth birthday parties (*ch'ilsun*) and fewer yet eightieth birthday parties (*p'alsun*).

Half of the people who described banquets and celebrations for parents and grandparents to us reported small-scale get-togethers at home with family. Christians sometimes reported inviting their pastor to a home dinner. The fashion for better-off people, however, is to hold such events at restaurants and "buffets" (*pwip'e*, sometimes located in wedding halls). Those of upper-class status chose the more expensive option of hotels. These ceremonies provide a good occasion for status-enhancing display, and some informants gave us surprisingly precise particulars about the number of guests invited, costs, gifts, and counter-gifts. A woman whom we judged to be our most affluent informant reported:

> We didn't have a hoegap for my birth parents because my grandparents were still alive at that time, but we had a seventieth birthday party for my parents last year at Kimhae Tourist Hotel. About 600 people came and the price of the food was 30,000 wŏn per person.[21] We gave return gifts to the guests [who would have brought envelopes with monetary contributions to the celebration] of a golden spoon and chopstick set for each family. You see, after the youngest of my siblings got married, the seven houses gathered money through a revolving credit club to pay the costs. The oldest son and oldest daughter [our informant] contributed more as individuals. We sent our parents on a trip to Southeast Asia.

Funerals have been subject to much more dramatic change than hoegap. Country funerals were once elaborate three-day affairs put on by the whole village. The chief mourners personally prepared the body, and the funeral was followed with daily ancestor worship at mourning shrines (*sangch'ŏng*) and annual tombside rites during the three-year mourning period (Janelli and Janelli 1982). Although half of our informants mentioned traditional funerals as a way they had practiced filial piety, the full traditional funeral is no longer observed in urban areas. Most hospitals today have rooms that can be used for funerals, and funeral parlors take care of most of the arrangements. Many families no longer set up mourning shrines (some informants did not even know what they are), and the end of mourning (*t'alsang*) comes after three days, five days, or at most forty-nine days (the number of days Buddhists believe it takes for the soul to pass through the Seven Hells to the Western Pure Land). Informants who said they had given their parents "traditional" funerals meant that they engaged in mourning followed by burial (rather than cremation). No one reported observing the full three years mourning, though one older informant had a cousin who had done so.[22] The remoteness of traditional funerals to most urbanites' lived experience came home to us when an informant remarked, "It is a rare thing for traditional funerals to happen the way they are shown on television."

Observation of ancestor worship and traditional holiday banquets that include ancestor worship, such as the Harvest Moon Festival (*ch'usŏk*) and Lunar New Year (*sŏl*), was almost universal, being reported by 93.6 percent of our informants. As one informant told us, "Filial piety is the vein that connects us, so all Koreans engage in ancestor worship." The ancestor worship practices reported, however, varied greatly (see also Lee 1989). Some families hold relatively traditional ceremonies, such as the one described by an informant who claimed, "On holidays we'll observe long, old-fashioned ceremonies (*chesa*) together with lots of food, and with the men sharing conviviality. We'll put about twelve bowls of rice [for various ancestors] on the altar. In addition to this, we observe seven ceremonies (chesa) [on the death days of individual ancestors]." But many informants noted that ceremonies have been adjusted to new circumstances, particularly in changing the hour the ceremony begins from the traditional hour of midnight to a more convenient time. Frequently informants mentioned reducing the number of ancestors worshiped. Traditional household worship, especially among the notability, was supposed to extend to the great-great-grandparents, but one informant remarked, "It's senseless to observe chesa for third or fourth generation great-grandparents whose face you never knew." Several other informants noted telescoping the generations, such as holding chesa for one's own parents on their individual death days, but worshipping higher generations as a group on *ku-il* (ninth day of the ninth lunar month), an auspicious day traditionally thought appropriate for religious ritual.

Although we did not specifically ask our informants about religion, a number of them spontaneously informed us of their Christian faith and explained that Christians may hold ancestor worship ceremonies (chesa), but do not bow in front of the altar.[23] Some Christians refer to these rites as "memorial services" (*ch'umo yebae*) rather than chesa, remarking, "Cherishing the memory of the ancestors is good, but the form of chesa is not." Since ancestor worship was traditionally an obligation the eldest son in the senior line undertook for the entire lineage, Christian conversion of an eldest son can cause significant turmoil among agnates. One eldest son reported,

My parents and relatives expect me to hold ancestor worship ceremonies, but I have a [Christian] memorial service, instead. Because we are members of the Kim clan of Andong there was strong opposition, but now there is no discord. At older sister's marriage in 1984 there was absolutely no talk of going to church among the relatives. But later on I converted and refused to hold the traditional ancestor worship ceremonies. After we argued until two in the morning, we finally did it my way.

CONTINUING THE FAMILY LINE

Three quarters of our informants listed having children as a practice for maintaining filial piety. The few who talked about the issue mostly did so in natural terms, such as the informant who said, "Because parents have lived for the sake of their children, children also live for the sake of their own children. Without filial piety one can't love those who follow after [in the family line]." This issue did not stimulate much discussion, however.

INNOVATIONS

We left space in our interviews for our informants to volunteer examples of filial behavior that we had not thought of. Most frequently mentioned was *hyodo kwan'gwang,* or "filial piety tourism." This is an innovation found in some of the more affluent middle-class families in our sample, and was almost universal among the upper- and upper-middle-class families. "Filial piety tourism" is the practice of children either collecting money to send their parents on a holiday, or personally taking their parents on a holiday. For the most affluent, such as the family mentioned above who celebrated their parents' seventieth birthday in a fancy tourist hotel, the trips are to destinations abroad, but more common are trips to Cheju Island and other scenic spots in Korea. Several of our informants made a point of mentioning that they did not just "throw their parents out" on a trip, but took them personally. One informant mentioned that each sibling in turn accompanied his parents on a trip.

Pragmatic Adaptations, Contending Discourses

As mentioned above, we expected filial piety to be hegemonic to the extent that few people were willing to oppose its continuance, or even imagine its rejection. It continues to receive emphasis in the moral education (*todŏk kyuyuk*) given in schools. Local urban governments, like their rural counterparts, still give prizes to citizens for exemplary filial piety. One of our informants, in fact, received such a prize for taking care of her invalid parents-in-law for more than a decade. Many of our informants clearly could not imagine a moral order not based on filial piety. We were told both that "Buddhism is no problem because it makes filial piety a fundamental principle" and that "Filial piety is a foundation of Christianity."[24] When asked whether maintaining filial piety was personally important to them, three informants (6.4 percent of our sample) were willing to venture that other things might be more important in today's society, but none was willing to reject filial piety. Forty-three informants said that maintaining filial piety was somewhat or very important to them, and one did not answer this question.

At first glance, then, this would seem to show that Koreans have maintained the value of filial piety by reinterpreting it for modern society and by pragmatically adjusting performance standards to new circumstances. Most of our informants, in fact, consider filial piety to be a natural reaction to parental love and take it as natural that children will marry and continue the family line. While middle-class urban dwellers in southeast Korea have given up blind obedience to parents and such inconvenient customs as three-day funerals and three-year mourning, the overwhelming majority continue to care for their parents in old age—whether directly at home or by giving them money—and to maintain family ceremonies such as hoegap that honor the aged. They have, however, modified the content of these customs to conform to modern lifestyles or the Christianity to which some of them have converted. In addition, they have enriched and elaborated new life-cycle ceremonies for the aged such as seventieth birthday parties, and developed such innovations as "filial piety tourism." More than 57 percent of our informants, thus, felt either that most people perform filial piety or at least tend to.

When asked about which groups perform filial piety most ardently there was substantial agreement among almost all our informants. The middle-aged, of course, were considered most filial. Our informants who expanded on this notion, however, did not for the most part see this as a sign of secular change. Though many informants mentioned cultural change when asked the reasons some people might not perform filial piety, the most popular explanation for lack of filial piety (mentioned by 19 percent of our informants) was lack of love. One informant sounded eerily like a newspaper advice columnist in saying, "It's the fault of the environment in which they grew up. They weren't loved by their parents, because there's the saying that people who have been loved know how to give."

People explained differences between the generations in terms of life cycle. Informants told us that people in their 50s are those directly caring for their parents, so of course they are filial, but the young, as one informant explained, "sometimes can't perform filial piety because youth is the time for getting a job. But for individuals to confirm their position in life and develop themselves is nothing less than developing the country."

This may require them to move out of the house and do other things that might be considered unfilial, but informants saw this as a temporary necessity, rather than a sign of secular change.

The general effectiveness of the pragmatic behavior indulged in by our informants, however, did not shield filial piety from discursive challenges. While claiming to be filial themselves, almost a third of our informants were willing to think the worst of their fellow Koreans and say either that most did not maintain filial piety, or that there is a tendency not to maintain filial piety in Korea today. Thirty-eight percent felt that lack of filial piety is a social problem, most typically because they believed its absence leads to social or familial disorder. How could it be that more than 90 percent of our informants could report performing filial piety, and yet almost two fifths of them feel that lack of filial piety is leading to disorder?

One cynical informant pointed us in an intriguing direction, commenting, "From the point of view of the son, if the parents have no money they don't maintain filial piety. Absolute, traditional piety has died out. It's relative. Anyway, olden times were just like today, weren't they?" It seemed significant to us that this informant is upper class, for when asked about class (or wealth) and filial piety, informants of all backgrounds agreed that the middle classes are most diligent about performing filial piety, while the rich are less so. Some thought the poor have a hard time performing filial piety for economic reasons, but still outperform the rich. Most thought industrial workers also do a good job. A few suspected that highly educated white-collar workers are too involved in their careers to maintain filial piety. When we asked about their reasoning on this question, informants revealed contending discourses about the relationship of wealth and consumption to filial piety.

Three attitudes appeared among our informants about the relationship between wealth, inheritance, and consumption and the performance of filial piety: (1) that wealth facilitates the performance of filial piety, (2) that too much wealth hinders the performance of filial piety, and (3) that there is no relationship between wealth and the performance of filial piety. Our cynical informant illustrated the first attitude, the attitude that was dominant among the upper class, and found among some in the lower-middle class, that wealth or inheritance facilitates the performance of filial piety. Some informants noted that a certain level of income is necessary for people to help their parents and hold family ceremonies, or noted other practical financial concerns that affect performance of filial piety such as competition between the needs of children and those of parents:

> It's a problem of practicality. Nowadays practical problems are economic. You have economic problems about children. Cram schools come first; parents come afterwards. The children have to come first. People cast their parents off to the old people's home beneath the mountain fortress or to Haeundae [a Pusan seaside resort] during the summer hot season. There are awful cases in which parents themselves tell the children to do it. To what extent are you going to place value on the parents? Nowadays, unlike the villages, cities are a problem for parents.

However, as with our cynical informant, most people who connected wealth with the performance of filial piety tended to formulate the relationship in the syllogism "only when there is inheritance will people be filial." More than 80 percent of these informants, while professing to value filial piety themselves, were likely to think that others do not preserve filial piety well. Since they assume inheritance is a necessary motivation and they know many people inherit little from their parents, they seemed to reason that many ought therefore to be unfilial. Our cynical informant displayed knowledge of inheritance law that most informants would be embarrassed to reveal when she noted, "The recent revisions of family law are proof that children who live with the parents receive more."[25] One informant, however, also cited expectation of inheritance as one of her reasons for coresiding with her husband's parents.

The second attitude—that too much wealth hinders the performance of filial piety—however, was the dominant attitude: it was expressed by twice as many of our informants as the first or third attitude. None of our upper-class informants expressed this opinion, but it was the dominant one among our upper-middle and lower-class informants and tied with "no relation" among our lower-middle-class informants. We collected many remarks from our informants illustrating this attitude, such as the following:

> The rich are too concerned with property, and for that reason they can't be truly filial.
>   The rich and the middle classes on the outside are similar, but for the rich [filial piety] is a formality while for the middle classes it's an attitude.
>   For the rich, filial piety is something that has to do with money rather than something to do with your attitude.
>   The people who best perform filial piety are those who grew up in poor families where parents made special sacrifices.
>   Those strata without much money do it better than rich people. There are many cases where the relationship between father and son has been shattered because of money.
>   The upper stratum fights more than it does filial piety. The plutocrats (*chaebŏl*) are more material than spiritual.

The people who expressed these opinions were divided about whether other Koreans preserve filial piety today or do not. Half expressed the opinion that filial piety is not well-preserved in Korea, while the other half said that it is. Since less than a third of our informants as a whole thought filial piety is not well preserved by others, however, this group expressed more pessimism than our informants as a whole.

The third attitude, that there is no relationship between performance of filial piety and class, property, or inheritance, was found almost exclusively among lower-middle-class informants. These informants tended to see filial piety as a matter of attitude and emotion that emerges naturally from growing up and thought that it is unrelated to economic considerations. A typical informant in this group told us: "Filial piety is important. It's natural for me to respect my parents who gave me life. It's not a fierce desire to pay back my parents, but just a natural thing toward those who gave me birth and taught me. There is absolutely no relationship to inheritance." Another said, "I'd say that if you overemphasize the material side your emotions dry up. Filial piety is not an economic thing, and it has no relation to religion (including Christianity), either." Almost all the people in this group thought that filial piety is quite well maintained in today's South Korea, but few thought of it as a specifically Confucian value.

This patterning of attitudes about the relationship of wealth and inheritance to filial piety among our informants seems to reflect typical South Korean ambivalence and worry about overconsumption (see, for example, Nelson 2000). The Confucian virtue of frugality and avoidance of material show has long been emphasized in Korea, and as late as the 1970s the government of Park Chung Hee issued sumptuary regulations for civil servants and simplified standard family ceremonies (*kajŏng ŭirye chunch'ik*) for all to discourage wasteful material display. In accordance with this ambivalence about consumption, the majority of our informants found the core of filial piety to lie in personal attendance on parents, even suffering for their sake.[26] (We had, in fact, deliberately used the term *subarhada*—to wait on, or provide personal attendance close to the body—in asking about care for the parents.) Most thus saw filial piety as both natural and as a matter of attitude, education, and ethics.

Although those who were actively dealing with aged parents were aware that filial piety has an economic component, these informants typically denied that economic support is simply a matter of consumption of the proper services. A typical comment was, "People find it hard to make a living, and they are busy—but true filial piety is not simply a material thing." It was not unusual, in fact, for informants to express disapproval of excessively elaborate life-cycle celebrations for the aged. One informant, for example, replied pointedly to one of our questions about family ceremonies,

> These days [family ceremonies] seem like carrying your parents piggyback, and then doing business. It isn't really a banquet for the sake of your mother and father. In olden days you directly prepared the food and held a banquet, but the great majority these days are busy and say it's irksome, so they do it at buffets or restaurants. And so I think they are most concerned with the celebration's cost.

A subset of our more affluent informants, however, was quite willing to discharge their filial obligations through consumption practices. These informants emphasized the comfort and importance of independent living for both parents and children. They neither wanted nor expected parents to require personal assistance in their old age. Their parents were capable of living off their own assets with no help from their children. If their parents became unable to care for themselves, they were willing and able to make use of hired nurses, hospitals, or silver towns to care for them. The core of filial piety for these informants tended to lie in elaborate status-enhancing life-cycle ceremonies, with frequent phone contact substituting for personal vis-

its. A few less affluent informants who lacked the wealth necessary to purchase the services of filial piety sometimes also showed consumerist attitudes
when they complained about the lack of government support for old-age
"facilities" (*sisŏl*), but the notion of commodified old-age care that this expresses was only common among the affluent.

The reason that almost all our informants claimed to personally value and
perform filial piety while at the same time a significant number of them suspected filial piety to not be maintained in Korea, then, seems to lie in attitudes toward commodity culture. And these attitudes tie into discourse about
class. Those affluent informants who linked performance of filial piety to
inheritance tended to be cynical, seeing material gain as the basic motivation
for filial piety, and thus much reason for backsliding. The majority who
denied the validity of commodified filial piety, on the other hand, were optimistic about the performance of filial piety in Korea and questioned only
whether the over educated and affluent lack the true spirit of filial piety
and thus perform it, if at all, only pro forma through consumption practices
rather than personal service.

Conclusion

Have urbanization and development led to a crisis in filial piety in Korea today? If one means by this question to suggest that Korean parents are not
adequately cared for by their children, our data for middle-class southeast
Korea point to a negative answer. The evidence of this study shows that
most families in each of the classes in our study seemed willing (though not
always cheerfully) to care for their parents through coresidence or by giving
them allowances. And almost everybody continues to maintain life-cycle rituals that express honor and respect for the aged. There were cases of parental
neglect mentioned to us by our informants, but almost all of these cases
came from the media rather than personal experience. On a national level,
the April 5, 2001, article in the *Chosun Daily* cited above mentions only 207
cases out of a population of 44 million of children capable of supporting
their parents whose wages were being garnisheed by the government. This
suggests that whatever problems of filial performance there are in Korea,
they are of manageable proportions.

But there *is* a discursive crisis over the relationship of consumption to filial piety. The majority of our informants saw filial piety as weakly linked to material consumption and necessarily involving personal care of parents. An affluent subset, however, thought that modernity and prosperity have legitimately provided opportunities for liberation of the nuclear family from stem family complications through the purchase of services for the aged that make coresidence and other forms of personal care old-fashioned and unnecessary. Yet even these informants take the occasion of life-cycle rituals to consume lavish status-enhancing rituals of filial devotion. The link of filial piety performance to social status is not actually new for Korean society. The old yangban notability based their social position partly on the moral superiority created by their relatively lavish and properly Confucian family rituals. However, this had traditionally been accomplished through kinship and patronage networks rather than material affluence per se. What is new is the ability of families to purchase services such as fancy banquets, filial piety tourism, and old-age care as a commodity. It is these families who consider purchased commodities an adequate means of performing filial piety—the affluent and educated—who are suspected of insincerity and shallowness in their performance of filial piety.

CHAPTER 9

Culture, Power, and the Discourse of Filial Piety in Japan: The Disempowerment of Youth and Its Social Consequences

AKIKO HASHIMOTO

Filial piety in East Asia today is at once a family practice, an ideology, and a system of regulating power relations. As practiced in the family, filial piety defines a hierarchical relationship between generations, particularly that of the parent and the child. In this ordered space, filial piety prescribes the ideology of devotion by the grateful child to the parent, and also places debt and obligation at the heart of the discourse on parent-child relationships. Contemporary filial piety is in this sense not merely a vestige of a past family custom, but an ongoing practice of surveillance and control that unleashes considerable disciplinary power. Using the discourse of gratitude and indebtedness, a hierarchy of power is reproduced in everyday life, privileging the old over the young and the parent over the child.

In the several decades since the patriarchal stem family *ie* and primogeniture systems were formally abolished, the Japanese family has, without a doubt, experienced major changes. The changes brought about particularly by the Family Law of 1947, enacted during the American Occupation in the wake of defeat in World War II, had considerable social consequences. To use the common refrain, as Japan ushered in the new postwar era, the Japanese family discarded its old garb—the ie and primogeniture systems—and effectively remade itself in a new image, an image modeled largely on the "Western" ideal of the nuclear family. This was a radical makeover: the "new" postwar family was represented in the language of equality, individual rights, freedom of choice, and voluntary unions—civic principles derived from a Euramerican paradigm that was entirely distinct from the preceding Confucian patriarchy. The prewar authoritarian way of life, the "feudal"

(*hōkenteki*) way of life, was now seemingly cast aside, discredited, and con-
signed to history (Smith 1996). The new family promised to turn a new leaf
and promote family relations based on democratic and individualistic rules
of engagement (Kawashima 1950).

Following these fundamental legal changes, the demographic profile of
the Japanese family was transformed dramatically in the course of the past
decades. Postwar Japan has seen an upsurge of nuclear families, freer patterns of marriage, geographic mobility, urban housing, and so on, all of
which are more common today. Innumerable changes have also taken place
in the life course of the family, ranging from rising ages of marriage and
childbirth, to higher divorce rates, lower birth rates, and longer life expectancy (Yuzawa 1995).

As the legal framework and the demographic profile of the Japanese family changed, so did the discourse on the ideal family. Patriarchal authority
was apparently displaced as the locus of absolute power in the family. This
displacement has seemingly reached such a stage that today's children, when
asked about their ideal image of parents, overwhelmingly say that they want
their parents to be "like friends" (*tomodachi no yōna oya*) (White 1993).
These sentiments expressed by Japanese children surely attest to their desire
for nonauthoritarian parenting, a finding consistent with most other youth
surveys. Yet, this desire to have the parents act like their peers also points to
an unarticulated ideal about parenting, with a somewhat indeterminate view
of what specifically the parents can do for the children.

By contrast, cultural ideals about specific behavior of children, that is,
what the children might do for their parents, have met fewer serious challenges in the course of those postwar decades (Isono and Isono 1958;
Kawashima 1957). The very ideal of piety—expressed as *oyakōkō* especially in
the postwar version—has for the most part remained relatively unscathed
even as families began to shrink in size and move with some frequency from
one urban location to another. Even though the postwar expression of piety
shifted in emphasis from the child's obligation to serve the parents to the
child's gratitude to the parents (Lanham 1979), the discourse of oyakōkō itself continued to command cultural legitimacy. This robustness of the piety
discourse is evident especially in the care of the elderly as a prescription to
privilege parents' needs, especially in old age, over those of the adult children (Hashimoto 1996; Long 2000; Traphagan 2000b). Thus, in many
ways, the generational dynamics of the postwar family, while ostensibly

transformed by the demise of the ie system, is embedded in the sentiment of piety discourses from the past.

In this chapter, I inquire into the dynamics of the Japanese family today by focusing on the discourse on filial piety (oyakōkō). I approach this topic by addressing the Japanese family as a web of power relations, rather than a web of emotional attachments or a series of kinship ties that are more customary in most family studies. My focus is the piety discourse as an articulation of power in intergenerational family relations and its cultural reproduction across generations. I will explore how the piety ideology recycles in today's society both as an indisputable cultural tool that legitimates the hierarchy of social difference, and an indispensable narrative discourse that safeguards a sense of ontological security. I will then turn to the significant social consequences of the piety ideology today, especially among Japan's youth. I suggest that the piety discourse engenders a disempowerment of youth, and explore its impact on current endemic issues such as social withdrawal, school absenteeism, classroom anarchy, teen prostitution, and juvenile homicide. I identify these youth "problems" as forms of response to social disempowerment and as modes of passive resistance to a generational power hierarchy rooted in a world of social obligations.

The Cultural Reproduction of the Filial Child

The social reforms introduced by the American Occupation in the wake of defeat in 1945 wrought a momentous formal rupture with past traditions in Japanese society. The continuities between prewar and postwar family are due therefore in no small measure to intangible and tangible reinforcements in social practice, especially in emotional and moral socialization (Isono and Isono 1958; Sekiguchi et al. 2000). The values of obedience and deference toward parents central to kōkō (filial piety) have been subjected effectively to this method of transmission, especially as long-standing virtues deeply rooted in the Confucian moral education of Tokugawa Japan (1603–1868) and the nationalist education of late Meiji (1868–1912) through early Showa Japan (1926–89) (Collcutt 1991; Dore 1984; Gluck 1985; Rozman 1991a). The power of these once-state-sponsored values in the postwar era is apparent by recalling that state promulgations expressing the ideology of sacrifice for the family and nation were being issued as late as 1942 and 1943 (Sekiguchi et al.

2000).[1] The making of the filial child in contemporary practice draws on these cultural resources for emotional socialization, adapted to the realities of the new nuclear family (Hara and Minagawa 1996).

This theme of early emotional socialization as a key ingredient of social continuity in the Japanese family finds resonance in studies of child-rearing practices, early child development, socialization, and the nature of parent-child relations, focused especially on the quality of obedience as the ideal of the "good" Japanese child (Kumagai and Kumagai 1986; Masataka 1999; Shwalb and Shwalb 1996; White and LeVine 1986). As Thomas Rohlen (1989) remarks, these studies show how Japanese families frequently place high, positive value on qualities of obedience and cooperation (*sunao*) in the upbringing of children, traits commonly prized as an expression of their innate goodness. The high level of compliance with adult authority is achieved often primarily through the close emotional attachment of the mother-child relationship. Mothers regularly use the close bond as a means to control the child's behavior and to *thwart* the child's will to separate, and so through a strong identification with the mother and a potent fear of losing the maternal bond, the child comes to understand quickly what is required of her/him. In this sense, the making of the good child (*iiko*) points to the desirability of qualities of agreeableness, congeniality, and good-naturedness, which are fostered by a kind of anticipatory discipline that thwarts less desirable outcomes.

Outside of the home, preschool socialization also plays a significant role in the making of the filial child (Peak 1989; Tobin, Wu, and Davidson 1989). Observers have illustrated the everyday routines in the preschool that instill discipline, some of which bear directly on the socialization of piety. Learning to recognize the age and gender hierarchy of family members, for example, may be accomplished in the course of learning to articulate deferential language; teaching the discipline of gratitude may be achieved by requiring children daily to verbalize their gratefulness to their mothers and fathers for giving them lunch. Learning to integrate with peers at preschool, therefore, goes hand in hand with learning to distinguish those peer relations from hierarchical relations.

Moreover, preschool teachers are known to thwart disobedience by artfully outmaneuvering the children under their charge (Peak 1989). By systematically refusing to take the role of authority, they can deprive the child of an opponent against whom to rebel, effectively undermining the child's disobedience. Teachers may therefore co-opt the child—without force—to the point that the child comes to understand that rebellion is useless, that it results in defeat, and that she/he is powerless to do otherwise than acquiesce.

With routine exposure to the piety socialization and discourse, it is reasonable to suppose that many children come to learn the behavioral rules *and* internalize the sentiment of piety. They learn what Arlie Hochschild (1979) calls the "feeling rules" that define what they are supposed to feel in daily life. They learn to develop and adopt normative feelings—in this case, gratitude, indebtedness, and obligation—as they know that those are what they should be feeling to be accepted in their rank-ordered world. Our understanding of the workings of feeling rules and normative feelings thus helps us see the subtleties of subverting children's resistance to filial piety. Children learn what they should, should not, and "must" be feeling, according to such rules that are unwritten and unarticulated but ubiquitous in everyday life. In this sense, the making of the filial child hinges on the adoption of the sentiment of piety to feel normal. This sentiment directed through piety, then, expresses the love for, and the desire to be loved by, the parent in the most socially sanctioned way (Isono and Isono 1958; Kawashima 1957).

As the iiko grows older, the parental image of the filial child may extend further to school performance, often expressed in the ideal of the diligent, high-achieving child (*seiseki ga iiko*) (Kawai 1997b; Kawakami 1999; Serizawa 2000). The measure of iiko here is not goodness per se, but achievement and success, represented in the willingness to work hard to get good grades, pass exams, and get into good schools. Given the prevailing gender hierarchy, these expectations for performance are more consequential for boys, while those for girls might be better captured in the quality of likability and cuteness (*kawaiiko*) (Kinsella 1995). At the same time, disciplinary power itself is exercised more oppressively over girls, inducing the level of obedience and subordination required to reproduce that gender hierarchy.

Having adopted what is expected of them to feel and think, the children's emotional experience of the world is far less democratic and individualistic than the ideals described in the postwar Family Law. Many have internalized the reality of power hierarchy in the family and society in meeting the behavioral expectation of the good child. The filial child knows that despite the outward trappings of the "democratic" family, age hierarchy is nonnegotiable in the reality that they live in. The kōkō discourse and practice help to keep this nonegalitarian hierarchy in place, refocused on gratitude and indebtedness, and assiduously rewarding obedient attitudes and behavior.

That those children with abundant qualities of "goodness"—obedient, polite, and clean high achievers—are today joining the ranks of "problem children" in Japanese society, however, is not altogether surprising considering the often oppressive and conflicting nature of demands placed by the kōkō imperatives. Clearly, not every child can achieve good grades and good manners, and, for that matter, not every child has parents and a family worthy of compliance. That those who become violent at home (*kateinai bōryoku*), refuse to go to school (*tōkōkyohi*), or semi-prostitute themselves in the public market (*enjo kōsai*) have "all the appearances of ordinary children" attests to the pervasiveness of compliance that was exacted of them until then, the powerful pressure they experienced to conform, and the limited means through which they may legitimately protest the pressure (Kawai 1986, 1997a; Kiire 1999; Saitō 1998; Serizawa 2000). The social pathology that relates to the piety discourse will be discussed in more detail in a later section after I examine the broader spectrum of the filial discourse.

The Discourse of Disciplinary Power

Writing at the dawn of the postwar Family Law, Kawashima Takeyoshi (1950) declared that absolute authority in the Japanese family is experienced not as a direct violation of being, but it is mediated by the sentiment of piety. Thus, he suggested, piety as a culturally encoded sentiment buffers the experience of subordination and obedience. To wield wide disciplinary power, then, filial piety requires key discursive narratives that can effectively elicit this sentiment. Below I identify three narratives that are critical today to legitimating the sentiment of the piety discourse: the sacrificial mother, the industrious father, and the pervasive, gazing ancestor.

That filial piety is an instrument of dominance founded on the gendered ideology of the mother's sacrifice for the family has often been pointed out as part of Japan's psychosocial dynamics (De Vos 1980; Slote 1998). Japanese mothers are certainly not alone in their penchant for fostering their power base through self-portrayals of suffering, but the Confucian piety code further legitimates their hold over their children by prescribing the return of the sacrifice as the culturally appropriate response. The piety imperative is to match the parents' sacrifice with the child's sacrifice—an interchange of sacrifices—so that the obligation of the "indebted" young generation can be articulated unambiguously. As many observers have noted, the strength of the mother-child tie is the key to reproducing obedience and subordination (Rozman 1991b; Schooler 1996).

The industrious, hardworking father, on the other hand, is less easily and overtly articulated as a narrative that elicits the piety sentiment because fathers/husbands have for the most part been absent from the home in postwar Japan. Nonetheless, incalculable debt (*on*) is owed to the provider—the father who diligently strives to provide for his dependent family—who would be otherwise mostly unavailable for family matters. His power base—control of livelihood—induces indebtedness as well as fear of reprisal. As the "modernizing" postwar nuclear family has tended to shift the locus of patriarchal authority from the father to the husband (Ueno 1994), it has also conveniently eclipsed and obscured the locus of disciplinary power, leaving children without a clear authority against which to direct their resistance. This condition of "fatherlessness," then, leaves children under surveillance but without a primary relationship and without a model to outgrow in the process of maturation (Mitscherlich 1969; Nishiyama 1999). Indeed, the piety discourse then requires double duty, as the filial child is called upon by the mother to replace the absent father.

But the ultimate strength of Japan's patriarchal power derives from the fact that it emanates not from the personal power of individuals or of individual parents per se, but from the lineage that links them to higher moral authority. Patriarchal power derives its ultimate legitimacy from upstream lineage, the lineal connection to the family's predecessors. Without the existence of those predecessors, the present successors would not exist, and in this sense, today's family totally owes its existence to them. Ancestors are such predecessors in generic terms and are the vital source of one's existence and one's ultimate defense against existential uncertainties. The discourse of gratitude and indebtedness in filial piety alluding to ancestry and heritage, then, offers a sense of ontological security as part of a sacred mission (Arichi 1977; Lock 1993).

This imagined connection to ancestors—especially identifiable ancestors—has profound implications for parent-child relations in the Confucian cognitive understanding. It means that the filial tie is in effect prolonged beyond death, and that the parent-child tie never ceases. Therefore, the relation of domination never ceases and as a result the status differentials are permanent (Yim 1998). Thus when predecessors are invested with imagined moral authority, they can ultimately unleash a supremely effective surveillance system that regulates the behavior of the successive, subordinate generations. Our behavior can therefore be "seen" everywhere by ancestors who are at once the lineage and the imagined transcendental power: the ancestors' gaze is omnipresent, even if they are invisible to us. They can protect us, and they can also punish us. We can make our ancestors proud with our good behavior (*gosenzo sama ga yorokobu*), and we can also bring them shame with our bad behavior that calls for remorse (*gosenzo sama ni mōshiwake nai*). There is no cultural contradiction in invoking the dead as moral authority any more than there is in invoking any other supernatural being (Arichi 1977; Smith 1974).

Foucault (1980) famously likened this type of social control to a panopticon, a surveillance system that wields immense disciplinary power over subordinates under constant, unceasing supervision wherever they are, at all times. The surveillance is relentless not only because the disciplinary "gaze" is ubiquitous, but also because the gaze is immutable. When the locus of authority—the eye of the power—is not readily visible, the subordinate is rendered powerless by not knowing where to direct resistance. It stands to reason that generalized obedience and conformity should become one of the most salient lines of self-protection and defense against this form of discipline. The ancestors' gaze fused with that of the parent and that of the community both buffers us from existential uncertainties and wields disciplinary power over us. Along these lines, new religious sects like Agonshū go so far as to invest ultimate power in the gazing ancestors as the direct source of good fortune and misfortune and as the ultimate arbiter of reward and punishment of descendants (Reader 1991).

Criticism of Authority

For a youth movement to successfully challenge a social order, as S. N. Eisenstadt (1956) observed, it often requires a purposeful attempt to disconnect young people from their families in order to intensify conflict between generations and consolidate the new social order. This link between public defiance and rejection of family makes sense in that overturning a social hierarchy may conflict with family attachments and entanglements, and more to the point, attacking the legitimacy of traditional obligations at the level of society opens the door to the questioning of all obligations (Hunt 1988).

In a surveillance society under the gaze of ancestors, criticizing and attacking the legitimacy of traditional authority is especially difficult because family authority is totally embedded in an absolute hierarchy of the social system. This has been the case in Japan even more so than in China, where the purge of traditional authority figures and anti-filial-piety movements have been historically more prevalent under conditions of radical social transformation (Hsu 1998; Rozman 1991b). Observations on how radical students in Japanese revolutionary movements in the twentieth century have related to their own families shed light on this difficulty of defying at once the social and the family order. For the most part, these radical students are characteristically seen to have congenial family relations, especially relations with the mother. For example, activists imprisoned during wartime for their subversive communist activities are reported to have had respectful relations with their parents; and imbued with a sense of indebtedness, it was ostensibly out of sympathy for their parents that many of them eventually recanted their commitment to communism (*tenkō*). Similarly, radical students of the violent social movements of the 1960s and 1970s are also reported to have had rather positive, cordial relations with their parents. Even these extreme examples point to the potency of the need for family protection and lineage while trying to defy the outer social hierarchy and control (Doi 1971; Isono and Isono 1958; Krauss 1974; Lifton 1970; Pharr 1980; Smith 1972; Steinhoff 1984, 1991; Tsurumi 1991).

Comparisons of the nature of filial piety (*kō*) and loyalty (*chū*) between Japanese and Chinese Confucianism also shed light on the variation in the legitimacy of criticizing authority in the two societies. Eisenstadt (1996) refers to three important features of Chinese Confucian orthodoxy that Japan does not share, pertaining to the legitimacy of *criticizing* absolute authority and *inheriting* absolute authority. Chinese Confucianism condoned moral criticism of rulers in the political practice of the literati; it required subordinates to admonish, however humbly, a master who deviates from appropriate action; and it placed the status of emperors under the mandate of heaven. Such elements of the orthodoxy could lend legitimacy to anti-filial-piety movements in China, while Japan had no such legitimacy at its disposal.

By contrast, the Confucian and neo-Confucian ideology that evolved in Japan has been characterized by a greater tendency to condone absolute power and unilateral duties in the prescription of loyalty and piety (Isono and Isono 1958; Maruyama 1992; Rozman 1991b; Tu 1996). Because moral authority was inherited rather than achieved, it was also omnipotent; such a system of moral authority contributed to a more stable and rigid class hierarchy and greater intergenerational continuity, while thwarting the development of a critical tradition toward authority. As a system of absolute authority, no legitimate venue existed for the subordinate to question the ruler's fitness to rule, and by the same token, for the child to question the parents' fitness to rule, even when they ruled badly. The obligation of the subordinate to serve was accordingly fixed and nonnegotiable. Indeed, the ultimate legitimacy of authority was such that even malignant parents at the turn of the twentieth century could not be held accountable for instigating a child to murder them (Arichi 1977; Isono and Isono 1958; Kawashima 1950).

The psychological dynamics of Confucian authority-subordination relations are especially relevant to the question of critical disobedience. Referring to the extraordinary hold of familial authority in Confucianism compared to Christianity, Robert Bellah (1991) has observed that the capacity to ask questions of the ultimate requires shifting the focus of ultimacy from the natural social order to a transcendent reference point. Hence, when there is no such external power that transcends social power, criticism and challenge of authority is unjustifiable. Disobedience and rebellion against authority without a transcendent, absolute referent point outside the family to legitimate the disobedience is, in his view, psychologically impossible. The Confucian framework of father-son relationships, in other words, blocks any outcome of ambivalence except submission to a pattern of personal relationships that is held to have ultimate validity.

George De Vos (1980), in a more explicitly Freudian framework, makes a similar comparative observation regarding the importance of psychological leverage for questioning and criticizing authority in the Christian tradition compared to the Confucian. He maintains that this lack of leverage significantly impedes the filial child who tries to reject or overcome the parent. Taking this point further, he suggests that Japan is inhospitable to Freudian psychoanalytic theory precisely because these theories are essentially anti-family. Quite the contrary, Japanese psychotherapy like *naikan* indeed emphasizes renewing one's sense of gratitude to one's parents. Some new religions such as Kurozumikyō likewise reinforce the practice of expressing gratitude to parents as an important avenue for seeing oneself out of one's problems (Hardacre 1986). In the final analysis, then, one's ontological security must be found in family and group continuity.

Resistance to Authority

Relations of unequal power provide the subordinate with some degree of control over the other in defining the conditions of reproducing power through the very act of participating in that relationship (Giddens 1984). It follows, then, that there is always to some degree resistance wherever power is exercised (Foucault 1980). In the dialectic of power in Japanese filial relations, this resistance often takes the form of passive noncompliance, nonconfrontational strategies that camouflage the subordinate's intent. The two sons introduced by John Traphagan in the next chapter illustrate these passive strategies at work. Mr. Fujiwara, the schoolteacher who is caught between obligations to two sets of elderly parents, resists his father's request to live with him with inaction—that is, staying put, and doing nothing to realize his father's wishes. This inaction is noncompliant, but he actually does nothing *against* his father's wishes, while also framing the reasons for what he does within the respectable piety discourse (his wife's obligation to her elderly parents). Mr. Matsumoto, the electronics engineer who was unable to reject his parents' demand to live with them in Mizusawa, ultimately accomplished his act of noncompliance (moving back to Yokohama), but only by deploying a proxy, prevailing on his wife to do the filial act in his place. This latter case also speaks to the extent to which the reproduction of filial piety continues to depend on the exploitation of women's acquiescence and labor.

These cases are examples of common strategies of resistance in key Japanese domination-subordination relations. Margaret Lock (1993) identifies two common styles of passive resistance—retreatism and ritualism—by building on Kazuko Tsurumi's typology. Retreatism refers to the voluntary withdrawal or separation of the subordinate from the realm of conflict, that is, deploying resistance by opting out of the relationship of domination. The second style of resistance, ritualism, refers to a form of internal nonconformity that gives the external appearance of conformity, that is, a ritualistic conformity (Lock 1993; Tsurumi 1970). Takie Lebra (1984b) also points out

nonconfrontational strategies of resistance as modes of conflict management, including anticipatory management, negative communication, situa-
tional code switching, triadic management, displacement, self-aggression,
and acceptance (see also Ishida 1984).

In offices, schools, and other contemporary Japanese institutions, examples of passive disobedience and noncompliance are commonplace. They are
subtle, nonconfrontational, and often also undetectable. For example, female subordinates may deploy ambiguous tactics of resistance against brow-
beating male superiors in the workplace, deliberately committing errors of
omission. At school, students may render inconspicuous their rebellion
against demanding upper class students (*senpai*) by silently sabotaging the
required menial work. In nursing homes, elderly residents are known to resist management demands in many covert ways (Bethel 1992; Ogasawara
1998; White 1993).

The weakness of these tactics of avoidance, withdrawal, and sabotage is evident as they fail to bring about any effective change in the behavior of the
dominant. Retreatism enforces a certain kind of self-destructiveness in the
subordinate, and ritualism may result in a kind of self-alienation rooted in
the contradiction between the internal and external sides of conformity.
These forms of resistance come at a higher price to the subordinate than to
the dominant, as to some degree they induce isolation and alienation. Yet,
this disengaged approach is often perceived to be the only recourse of dis-
empowered youth against oppression. Recognizing the meaning of these often inarticulated acts of resistance therefore helps to shed light on the widely
discussed adolescent "pathologies" today. Problems of growing pains notwithstanding, I suggest that conspicuous social withdrawal—such as withdrawal
from family and social life (*hikikomori*), withdrawal from school life (*tōkōkyohi*), or withdrawal from adult life (*adaruto chirudoren*)—comprises a pattern
of resistance against the oppressive discourse of the "good" child.

The Disempowerment of Youth and Its Social Consequences

Filial piety is ultimately a discourse that diminishes the power of the young
successively in the interest of safeguarding the hierarchy of social difference
(Hashimoto 1996). It effectively regulates the interests of the younger generation by assigning obligations and debt to them. These basic premises and

ground rules are not written in any legal document or book of moral instructions in Japan today, but they comprise a powerful force of normative regulation that controls intergenerational interests. The ground rules of this discourse that privileges the old at the expense of the young constitute the backbone of the patriarchal template in Japan.

This considerable strength of the kōkō discourse fifty years after the abolishment of the ie family system also signals a continuing unwillingness in Japan to respect the power of its youth. Being unwilling and unable to alter the power dynamics between generations, Japan is locked in a deep social contradiction between attempting to move forward, while, at the same time, holding back the creative power of the young that is so indispensable to that very same process. It is characteristic of this stalemate that Japanese youth today are reported to have some of the lowest levels of entrepreneurial interest among youth in postindustrial societies.[2]

Japanese youth have responded to this predicament variously with compliance, muted anger, and withdrawal, which have also contributed to their increasing alienation, apathy, disorientation, and rage. The list of youth "problems" has grown exponentially in the past decade, coinciding, not incidentally, with the long economic and social stagnation that Japan has experienced. To be sure, juvenile crime rates remain relatively low by international standards, notwithstanding the extraordinary cases of serial murders of children by children that have received wide attention (Keisatsuchō 1999; Yoneyama 1999). Yet qualitatively, behavior deemed "deviant" has diversified more widely from staple bullying (*ijime*) and refusal to go to school, to classroom disruption (*gakkyū hōkai*), teen semi-prostitution, lethal family violence, social withdrawal, and a generalized experience of social suffocation (*heisoku*) (Hayami 1997; Kawai 1997a, 1997b; Kawakami 1999; Kiire 1999; Kishida 2000; Murakami 1997; Nishiyama 1999; Saito 1998; Serizawa 2000; Takahashi 1998).

In assessing the causes and possible solutions for these increasingly visible "disorders," however, commentators in the Japanese public media today have directed curiously little attention to issues of power per se in parent-child relations (Kawai 1997c). Although they seem ready enough to assign blame to the ills of modernity, erosion of traditional values, pressures of school entrance examinations, and isolation of the nuclear family and the like, the oyakōkō discourse itself seems to remain almost as sacred as a taboo that cannot be touched, even in discussions of family violence of or by children. As a result, few observations seem to be directed to parental abuses of power, except in extreme murder cases (Kishida 2000; Noda 1999). Oyakōkō is clearly bracketed out of this discourse on social remedies, as is the premise of disempowering the young.

These problems of alienation are as conspicuous in what children do as much as what they do not do. Compared to Korean, American, and German children, Japanese children are least likely (22 percent) to intercede in school bullying (39 percent, 48 percent, and 53 percent respectively for Korea, the U.S., and Germany). They are also most likely to have never tried to stop friends from fighting (30 percent), compared to those in the same three countries (Korea 9 percent, U.S. 16 percent, and Germany 14 percent) (Kodomo no taiken katsudō kenkyū kai 2000). What emerges from such accounts is a picture of a profoundly disengaged, apathetic, and indifferent youth.

This apathy of children (*shiran puri*, literally a sense of nonchalance, looking the other way, pretending not to know or see) also seems to be learned by emulating adults at home and in the school (Masataka 1999; Yoneyama 1999). Compared to parents in Korea, the United States, and Germany, Japanese parents offer their children the least amount of instruction. A very large proportion of Japanese youth report, for example, that they were never taught by their father or mother to be truthful (never taught by father 71 percent; by mother 60 percent). The disengagement of Japanese parents from their children far exceeds that of Korea (never taught by father 27 percent; by mother 22 percent), the United States (never taught by father 22 percent; by mother 21 percent), and Germany (never taught by father 42 percent; by mother 38 percent) (Kodomo no taiken katsudō kenkyū kai 2000). Japanese children learn far less from parents, siblings, and teachers compared to American children. The percentage of those who report they have nobody to talk to about values is consistently much greater in Japan than in the United States (Sengoku 1998). While some of these comparative differences may arguably come from the Japanese practice of privileging learning over teaching (Masataka 1999), the reality of parent-child estrangement is undeniable.

The oyakōkō discourse in effect camouflages this estrangement, reproduced further by parental indifference, incompetence, and neglect, as well as by the retreatism of children themselves. In many cases, parents seem to pretend not to recognize a problem, take no responsibility for solving the problem, and may be actually incompetent to offer instruction, so that the net result is more child disempowerment. In this way, the piety discourse effectively allows parents to become bystanders in the lives of their own children (Noda 1999); by modeling, they also promote further apathy in their children, who, in turn, become bystanders themselves in their school, workplace, and family. The disempowering consequences of filial piety in Japan today must be recognized if any remedy is to be found to alleviate the social suffocation that Japanese children experience routinely (Nakanishi 2000).

Conclusion

Undoubtedly, the discourse of filial piety has played a significant role in Japanese society for a long time as a means to safeguard its social hierarchy and ontological security. The piety discourse has served those goals effectively, both as a system of surveillance that reproduces obedience, and as a system of beliefs that offers a narrative that accounts for our ultimate existence. The potency of filial piety in both prewar and postwar Japan is unmistakable, and so are its social consequences. I have argued that the kōkō discourse has always derived its strength at the expense of the young through the practice of disempowerment and has exacted a high price from the new generations of Japan. The alienation, apathy, disorientation, and muted anger of Japanese youth manifest in their "problems" today stem in part from a continuing unwillingness in Japan to empower and respect its youth so that they may give priority to their own lives above those of their parents.

Today, more than fifty years after the dismantling of the ie system, which itself formally existed also for approximately fifty years, the Japanese family is at a significant crossroads. While today's children can obviously see that there is no real payoff for the self-sacrifice that is being preached to them, there is nothing that readily replaces the ideology of kōkō for them. Filial children's interest in consenting to the continuity of intergenerational hierarchy for a promise of return on their investment has diminished, as the prospect of inheriting the political, cultural, and symbolic power in their turn seems too far away, too uncertain, and too exacting (Hashimoto 1996). As a resilient teenager in the enjo kōsai market remarked, no adult seems to care what they do as long as they don't get caught; and at the same time, she just wonders about that gaze of her grandfather as she flirts with older men on the street (Kawai 1997a). The surveillance system remains effective; but she just might have a better chance at fulfillment if she could empower herself and direct her disobedience in a constructive, rather than destructive, direction.

CHAPTER 10

Curse of the Successor: Filial Piety vs. Marriage Among Rural Japanese

JOHN W. TRAPHAGAN

I was sitting in a family restaurant one evening, sipping coffee and comparing notes on the trials and tribulations of being an only child or eldest son
in Japan and the United States with one of my informants, Ichiro-san.[1] After a while, I noticed that most of the people surrounding us at neighboring
tables appeared to be couples. Many of them were in their early twenties,
with hair dyed orange, as has become ubiquitous among younger and increasingly middle-aged Japanese. At the time, Ichiro-san was in his late thirties and had been married for several years; I thought about the courting
couples around us and asked him, "Being the eldest, did you have any troubles with getting married?" Ichiro-san rolled his eyes and laughed:

> I had a lot of trouble with finding a wife. For example, one evening I was
> out on a date with a woman, and we got to talking about family. I
> mentioned that I was the eldest, and the woman just said, "eeeeehhhh?"
> Other women found less overt ways of showing their disapproval with the
> situation, but it was obvious that most of the women I dated didn't like the
> idea of wasting their time on me because I was *chōnan* (the eldest son), and
> they had no intention of marrying one. A lot of women think, "marrying a
> chōnan is awful." So once they knew I was one, well, that was the end of
> the relationship.

Being born first, particularly if one is male, has taken on something of
the character of a curse in contemporary Japan. In many families, the eldest
is expected to care for, and, perhaps more significantly, live with his or her
parents as they grow old—a situation that many younger Japanese men and
women find an unattractive characteristic for a spouse, at best. In this chapter, I explore the effects of the Japanese concept of filial piety on the life ex-

periences of eldest children and their spouses. In particular, I consider the expression of filial piety through coresidence, which is one of the central symbols used to represent an individual's concern for and willingness to carry out responsibilities to his or her parents. I will use two case studies and data from other ethnographic interviews to discuss the difficulties successor children face in finding a spouse and to explore the reasons why many women, in particular, are unwilling to marry a successor son. The central point of the chapter is that, for many, filial responsibilities and expectations are in direct conflict with nuptial responsibilities and expectations.

The fact that eldest sons are generally expected to provide care for their parents in old age is not simply a matter of the dyadic parent-child relationship, but involves a matrix of family members and potential family members who surround him (or another child who anticipates providing parental support and possibly health care). Although diminished in comparison to the past, parents in Japan often have considerable power over their children in shaping decisions about living arrangements and marriage partners (see Traphagan 2000a). Parental participation and influence over mate choice is particularly intense in the case of an eldest son or other child who is destined to become the household head (Takeji 1999). However, the fact that others are involved means that the expression of filial relationships and the nature of filial piety in a given family involve negotiation between and among those who are affected by the parent-child bond.

Fieldwork in Northern Japan

The northernmost end of Japan's main island of Honshū, where I have conducted fieldwork in four trips since 1995, is a mix of villages and small to medium-sized cities—the larger cities such as Morioka and Akita being around 230,000 and 315,000 people, respectively. Although rice paddies form much of the scenery and agricultural production is an important part of life, the economy of the region has diversified considerably over the past twenty-five years. Ski resorts and hot springs have emerged as important draws for tourists to the region's mountains, and industrial parks have become a common feature of the landscape.

From 1995 to 1996, I conducted fieldwork in a hamlet known as Jōnai, which consists of about 400 people living in 120 households. Jōnai is situated in the town of Kanegasaki, which is in an area that exemplifies this diversity. The town is largely devoted to agricultural production—primarily rice paddies and dairy farms—but also has several major factories for products such as automobiles, computers, and pharmaceuticals that are situated in a large industrial park nestled in the rural hills. Due to heavy truck traffic and a shift to an automobile-centered lifestyle, bypass highways have been built to divert traffic away from the old town centers. Along these bypasses one can find an array of bookstores, convenience stores, shopping malls, home centers, and supermarkets, most of which are parts of national or regional chains, as well as restaurants such as McDonald's, Kentucky Fried Chicken, and Sushi Gourmet.

The growth of tourism and industrial production in the region has meant that, as compared to the past, younger people are considerably less dependent upon the family farm or business as a means of support in adulthood. However, although job opportunities for younger people exist in the newer companies, most of the work for local residents is on the production lines; management positions are generally held by people who have been relocated, often temporarily, from other parts of Japan. Those who seek other types of corporate positions normally must leave; out-migration of younger people is a common feature of life both within small towns like Kanegasaki and for the prefectures of the Tōhoku region.[2] Migratory destinations include nearby cities such as Mizusawa and Kitakami, the prefectural capital of Morioka about 60 kilometers to the north, and the regional center of Sendai, which is about 160 kilometers south of Kanegasaki. However, the most common destination is Tokyo, which forms the focal point for education, industry, and government for the entire country. During the mid-1980s, the drain from rural areas like Tōhoku into Tokyo was quite pronounced: in 1986–87, Tōhoku as a whole was losing more than 60,000 people annually due to out-migration, most of which was centered on Tokyo (Statistics Bureau, Management and Coordination Agency 1994). This pattern has changed significantly, such that there developed a relative balance of in-migrants and out-migrants to the Tōhoku region by the late 1990s. Nonetheless, thousands of younger people annually migrate to Tokyo and other large cities, which leaves a significant geographical distance between these children and their parents.

In 1998, I spent six months in the city of Mizusawa living in a neighborhood in which few of the residents have any connection to agricultural production; most either work in local industries or in government. In the summer of 2000, I conducted further fieldwork in Akita Prefecture, which neighbors Iwate Prefecture, but faces the Japan Sea side of Honshū. This research was conducted in a town of approximately 8,000 people that is almost entirely devoted to agricultural production. Again, this research provided an opportunity to develop a comparative data set, by focusing on a region of Japan that has been frequently cited in the news as having serious social problems associated with an aging population, including the nation's highest suicide rate among the elderly (Asahi shinbun 2000).

Data collection during each field trip centered around a combination of semi-structured interviews with individuals I met via participation in local organizations and institutions related to the elderly, such as senior citizens clubs and senior centers, and participation in neighborhood activities such as picnics, athletic meets, and other outings. In general, my starting contact person for interviews that involved entire households was an elder member of the household; however, in a few cases my initial contact person was a younger member of the household. Although in each of the three fieldwork projects the focus was on older people, interviews were conducted with individuals of a variety of ages ranging from 23 to 95.

Population Aging in Tōhoku

Population aging and declining population have been central features of the demographic landscape in the Tōhoku region for several years. It is clear by looking at population distributions for Japan that agricultural areas generally have higher proportions of people over the age of 60 than large urban areas. Figure 7 shows the population distribution for Akita, Iwate, and Miyagi Prefectures, based on the 2000 census. I have included Miyagi because it is the prefecture in which Sendai, a city of approximately one million people, is located. Sendai serves as a regional magnet for younger people in search of a college education and is home to the offices of many large corporations. Immediately evident in Figure 7 is the top-heavy orientation of Akita and Iwate prefectures as compared to Miyagi. From the age of 50, the percentage of population in the older age ranges is considerably higher for the more rural prefectures than for Miyagi. By contrast, the age ranges from 20 to 40 show higher proportions of people for Miyagi, suggesting the

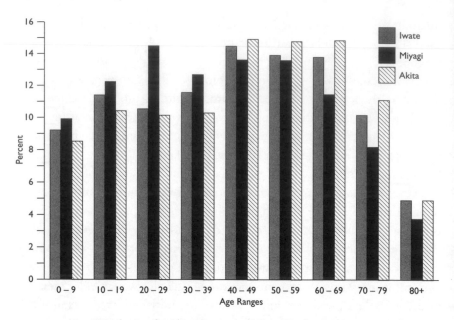

FIGURE 7. Age Distribution for Akita, Iwate, and Miyagi Prefectures (2000 census).
Source: Japan Statistical Yearbook 2002, Statistics Bureau/Statistical Research and Training Institute, Ministry of Public Management, Home Affairs, Posts and Telecommunications.

influence of out-migration of younger people from rural areas on the population distributions in the region.[3]

Figure 8 compares the age distributions for the Tōhoku region as a whole with all of Japan using figures from the 2000 census. Again, we see a comparatively high proportion of people over the age of 65 living in Tōhoku; in Japan as a whole those 65 and older represented slightly more than 19 percent of the population, but within Tōhoku, they represented approximately 20.5 percent.

Considered at a more micro level, the magnitude of demographic change is striking. For example, a small town in Akita Prefecture has been experiencing a steady population decline since the 1950s. From 1975 until 1995, the population dropped from 10,158 to 8,885, while over the same period there was a rapid increase in the proportion of the elderly (defined as those over age 65). In 1975, 10 percent of the population was older than 65; by 1995 this had increased to 21 percent, and by the year 2020 it is expected to rise to 37 percent. Another small town in the prefecture is expected to experience a rise in the elderly population from 26 percent in 1995 to more than 47 percent by 2020 (Akita-ken 1999: 5). These numbers are indicative of expected

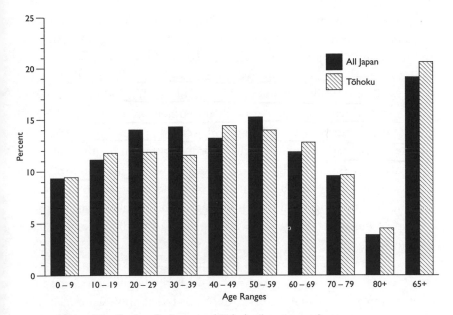

FIGURE 8. Age Distribution for Japan and Tōhoku (2000 census).
Source: Japan Statistical Yearbook 2002, Statistics Bureau/Statistical Research and Training Institute, Ministry of Public Management, Home Affairs, Posts and Telecommunications.

population change in predominantly agricultural areas throughout Japan and are the result of a combination of low fertility, increased longevity, and out-migration of young people to the cities (Traphagan 2000a, 2003).

The Family in Agricultural Japan

Tōhoku is often characterized in the Japanese media as the most traditional part of Japan, meaning that it is viewed as adhering most closely to what Japanese perceive as the traditional family structure and familial values associated with agricultural life. This family structure and value set, represented through the concept of the *ie* (household, family house), has been widely discussed and debated in Japanese anthropology and sociology, hence it does not need to be explored in detail here (see, for example, Brown 1966; Long 1987; Nakane 1967; Traphagan 2000a, b). However, for the purposes of this chapter, it is important to identify a key attribute of the ie that is central for understanding the notion of filial piety as it is experienced and expressed in Japan.

Japanese Confucianism prior to the Second World War was tightly integrated into the institution of the ie such that, as Takie Lebra points out, "one was inconceivable without the other" (Lebra 1998: 211; see also Hardacre 1989). One of the central features of the ie is a gender ideology that defines offices within the family and household, each of which is endowed with symbolic capital, which is the ability to influence others on the basis of the position one holds, rather than on the basis of accrued power related to personal successes (social capital) (see Bourdieu 1990). Central among these offices is that of the successor to the household headship, which, from an ideological perspective, should be passed from eldest son to eldest son, or, in cases where no competent consanguineal male is willing or able to take the headship, to an adopted husband (*mukoyōshi*) who marries into the family and, usually, takes his wife's name.[4]

This pattern is an outgrowth of the samurai family system that, via the Meiji Civil Code of 1898, was extended to the entire population. As a system of succession and inheritance this pattern was based upon Confucian concepts that emphasized patrilineal succession through eldest sons. The eldest received all of the property unless an arrangement was made to split some of the property off to another son, in which case a branch family (*bunke*) was sometimes formed. In addition to receiving the property, he also would succeed to the headship of the household and take on the corresponding position as head of the family farm or business. In practice, other sons have often taken on the position of successor, and, as noted above, in households with no available male, descent would be carried through a daughter, while an adoptive husband would become successor to the household headship.

Regardless of who occupied the position, succession to the headship of the household did not come without a price. In return for receiving the bulk of inheritance and the office of household head, the successor was expected to coreside with his parents in his natal house and provide social support and whatever health care might be needed as they grew older. Furthermore, he was expected to be the primary keeper of the family altar, make daily offerings and prayers to the family's ancestors, and take care of the family grave site in which the ashes of the ancestors are collectively stored.

Although the Civil Code of 1947 outlawed this inheritance pattern, it persists into the present in terms of the actual practice of household succession and the passing on of family fortunes. It is common for the eldest son, another son, or, where no son is available, the eldest or another daughter to receive the land and house in which the parents reside, in return for which the successor is expected to coreside with the parents and care for them in later life. Although there is a preference for having the oldest male carry out this responsibility, any child, regardless of birth order, who does so is considered to be *oyakōkō*, a concept that connotes respect and caring for one's parents and a willingness to carry out one's duties to them—filial piety.

It is not unusual for an eldest son to defer inheritance to a sibling who is willing to take on the responsibility to care for the parents, and conflict sometimes occurs over who will actually carry out the responsibility (Hamabata 1990). For instance, in a case from Akita Prefecture, refusal to accept responsibility to care for the family altar and gravesite led to serious conflict. Because of his job, the eldest son moved to Yokohama. The parents gave a plot of land to the third son, with the expectation that he would care for the family property and grave. Much to the surprise of the other family members, the third son indicated that he was unwilling to take care of either the family property or the grave. His father became so angry about this that he told the other children he was considering donating all of the remaining property to the town. The father's concern over the future of the family grave has been so severe that he has told his family that he is afraid to die until the issue of who will care for the ancestors (including himself) has been resolved.[5]

Because the Japanese notion of filial piety is closely tied to the concept of the ie, and because the ancestors are viewed as part of the ie, carrying out one's filial duties as successor inherently involves caring for the ancestors (see Smith 1974). Other children share some responsibility for caring for the ancestors, but the majority falls on the coresiding successor. Within the main (successor) household (*honke*), ancestor veneration typically involves daily prayer and offerings before the family altar. It also means being the primary focal point for larger ancestor-related celebrations and rituals such as funerals, care of the family grave, and the summer festival of the dead (*obon*). This can entail considerable financial outlay for large events such as funerals, and also regular money offerings to the local temple priest when he comes to pray for one's ancestors or when one goes to the temple. In a case from Akita, the main household spent more than the equivalent of $10,000 to repair the room in which the family altar is kept. The wife of the successor complained that they had received no financial assistance from other parts of the family connected to the stem family, most of whom live in the immediate neighborhood.

In short, coresidence with one's parents is actually a matter of coresidence with one's parents and ancestors, and successorship involves, among many other things, caring for one's parents in old age and taking on primary responsibility for familial religious activities (Plath 1964). Provision of care for parents and ancestors, coupled with coresidence, indexes a child who is appropriately and dutifully carrying out his or her filial responsibilities. At the same time, particularly for men, from the perspective of one's spouse, it can also index a child who is not sufficiently carrying out his responsibility to his own nuclear household.[6]

According to most people with whom I spoke, emphasis on coresidence is a major contributor to the difficulties successor children encounter when seeking a spouse. Demographic data tend to support this observation. For example, the Japanese census indicates that for several years in Iwate Prefecture there has been a steady increase in the proportion of men who are unmarried after the age of 30. In 1975, 5 percent of men from 35 to 39 (inclusive) were unmarried. By 1995 this number had risen to 23.5 percent. For less densely populated areas, the number went from 4.1 percent in 1975 to 26.9 percent in 1995. Women, by comparison have shown a considerably smaller rise, from 7.4 percent in 1975 to 12.6 percent in 1995 for more densely populated areas and from 2.6 percent in 1975 to 4.5 percent in 1995 in less densely populated areas.

When considered on the basis of occupation, it is evident that men engaged in farming and fishing have particularly pronounced delays in marriage. Data for Iwate Prefecture show that between the ages of 30 and 34 (inclusive) for 1990, 37.3 percent of the men engaged in these occupations were unmarried; by 1995 this had risen to 47 percent. For the age range of 35 to 39, the numbers were 25 percent and 34.7 percent, respectively. By comparison, 28.2 percent (1990) and 32.6 percent (1995) of men between the ages of 30 and 34 living in Iwate who were engaged in office work were unmarried, and for the ages of 35 to 39, these numbers had dropped to 11.7 percent (1990) and 15.5 (1995) percent, respectively.

The shortage of potential mates for eldest sons has led to the recruitment of foreign brides, largely from the Philippines and China, who are coupled with Japanese men, often with the aid of local Japanese government offices. Government sources show that as of 1998 there were 24 people from the Philippines living in Mizusawa, of whom 22 were women. Although precise data are not available, it is reasonable to assume that most, and perhaps all, of these women came to Mizusawa as brides for local men. Concerns over the difficulties these women experience in Japan and with their new families has led some prefectures to establish government programs to help foreign brides with adjusting to daily living, learning the language, and coping with problems such as interacting with local schools (Kasuga 1993).

Where Do We Go From Here?

The family across the street from my apartment in Mizusawa in 1998 presented one of the most poignant examples of the conflicts related to filial piety and coresidence that can arise within a family. Over the course of about a month, I interviewed all members of the Fujiwara family independently to discuss issues related to succession and coresidence. Here, I will focus primarily on an interview with the eldest son, who described his situation in great detail and pointed out the serious conflict that had arisen with his father concerning where he and his wife will reside in the future. This will be supplemented by a portion of the interview with his father.

Fujiwara-san is an elementary school teacher who lives in Kitakami, about 15 kilometers from the school where he teaches, which is in a town that neighbors on Mizusawa and which is about a ten-minute drive from his parents' house and about fifteen minutes from his in-laws, who also live in Mizusawa. Fujiwara-san's wife is also an elementary school teacher, at a school in Kitakami. Thus, they live closer to her work, and he commutes. At the time of our interview, he was 35, had been married for about two years, and did not have any children (see Traphagan 2003: 203).

> JWT: Since you work in a school close to your parents' and in-laws' houses, why don't you live with either of them?
>
> FUJIWARA-SAN: Well, there is a connection to my wife. When I got married, I had the intention of moving back to live in my natal home in Mizusawa. However, my wife is the eldest daughter, and there was a sense at that house that she wasn't a *yome* [a term for wife that implies having married out of one's natal family and into one's husband's family].[7] My in-laws also live in Mizusawa, but in a part of town about 8 kilometers from where my parents live. We don't live with them, either, although it is still closer than Kitakami.
>
> JWT: Are there any males among your wife's siblings?

FUJIWARA-SAN: No, that family has only two girls. And it is a household with
                a long history. So, if possible, they wanted to get a
                mukoyōshi to continue the ie. But in this sort of strict envi-
                ronment, getting an adoptive husband is very difficult. So
                they gave up on that idea. The younger daughter was living
                there, but she has now married out as yome, so they have no
                hope of getting an adoptive husband into the household.
                There is no way I can go to their ie as an adoptive husband
                because of my responsibilities in my natal household.

JWT: Marriage between an eldest son and eldest daughter is diffi-
                cult, isn't it?

FUJIWARA-SAN: Well, yes it is, indeed. And for that reason there are a lot of
                people who decide not to get married because of this con-
                flict. And there are a lot of couples who are stressed about
                what to do.

JWT: So what do you and your wife plan to do?

FUJIWARA-SAN: Well, since both households are in Mizusawa, we are think-
                ing that we will build a separate house somewhere between
                the two and take care of both sets of parents. Then we can
                handle both sides. But we can't really go to either house to
                live with our parents. We will probably buy some land and
                build a house.

At this point, Fujiwara-san hesitated and then began to sip some of the
tea sitting on the table. After a fairly long pause, I began to ask questions
based upon my experience interviewing his father, who told a rather different story about the future plans of his son. In the natal household, his father
(66), mother (63), and younger sister (33) live together. His father had indicated that they had already made plans to build a multi-generation house, in
which the parents would live on the first floor and the younger generations
would live on the second floor. The plan was to tear down the current family house in Mizusawa and build a new one in the same lot. During that previous interview, I had asked Fujiwara-san's father what he plans to do if he
needs some form of care in the future. He replied:

FUJIWARA-SAN (SENIOR):   Our son and daughter-in-law have offered to build
                         us a new house and this is the cornerstone of our
                         plans for the future. The timing has yet to be de-
                         cided, but we plan to build a multi-generation
                         house. Although the living facilities will be sepa-

rate, there will be only one TV in the house. We do
not yet have grandchildren, but the idea of only
one TV, which was my son's idea, is that we do not
want to have completely separate lives. If we have
only one TV, then the entire family will gather
around that TV in the evening and that way there
will be a good opportunity for the family to communicate and spend time together. We want to live
in a house in which the generations interact and
can communicate.[8]

By comparing the two interviews, it is immediately evident that the perspectives of father and son are very different concerning where the son and
his family will live in the future, as well as whose idea it was to build a multi-
generation house. Although, as will become clear below, the son and father
did, indeed, discuss and begin plans for a multi-generation house to replace
the current family house, contrary to the senior Fujiwara's expectations,
the issue of coresidence has by no means been resolved. Based upon my
interview with his father, which occurred about a month prior to the interview with the son, I asked Fujiwara-san about the idea of building a multi-
generation house.

FUJIWARA-SAN (JUNIOR):   We were thinking about doing that at first. I consulted with my father, and we decided that we
would build a multi-generation house. My parents'
house is now quite old and is in need of some repair,
so we thought that would be a good way to go. At
that time, we thought it was a good idea. This occurred before we got married and I spoke with my
wife at that time about it and she said it was OK. I
explained that we would live in the same building
but would have completely separate living spaces
and separate kitchens, etc. I had absolutely no hesi-
tation about this and was thinking that we would be
living with my parents. We had gone as far as to begin designing the house, but, well, we got opposition from the other side [meaning his in-laws].

This has truly turned into a major problem for
us. My father, because I am the eldest son, is totally
convinced that we are coming to live with them.

He still thinks this, even though I've talked to him about the problem quite a bit. But, you know, people from the old days don't see things the same way. It was expected that the eldest son would come to live with them and there wasn't any question about this. But times have changed. There aren't as many children these days, and so my sort of eldest son / eldest daughter marriage creates a situation such that it is a major point of uncertainty as to what one should do. The same is true of my in-laws in terms of their wanting an adoptive husband to live with them.

JWT: What do you think will happen if you do not return to your natal household?

FUJIWARA-SAN: My father will be disappointed unless we return and live with them. We already have had one big fight over this, between my father and me. He said, "We already have the land and we can just replace the existing house. Why do you want to build another house in a separate place?" We can't really talk about this at this point because it turns into a fight. I don't know how this will work out. My father is very stubborn. I really want him to come to understand what I am saying and why this is a problem, but he doesn't understand. It would be very helpful if he would come to understand a little. I think it will take more time. Maybe if we talk more it may get better. We will continue living in our apartment in Kitakami and as the time goes on, perhaps he will change. It is a waste of money to live in an apartment, and we have thought of buying some land, but we are really unable to do anything right now until this is resolved.

The Missing Husband

Matsumoto-san is in her mid-forties and lives in a large house, which is part of a compound of buildings on land that belongs to her in-laws and that sits amid rice paddies in Mizusawa. Her house is built completely in a Western style, lacking tatami mats and other features typically associated with traditional Japanese architecture. The house sits directly in front of the house in which her in-laws live, and in which her husband grew up. She has two sons, the younger of whom is 9 and the older 11. Matsumoto-san's husband works for a large electronics company and lives in Yokohama, several hundred kilometers to the south and about three hours away via bullet train, where they originally met, occasionally coming back to visit, a point that will be explained in detail below. Although Matsumoto-san is originally from the town of Kanegasaki, just north of Mizusawa, she lived for several years in Tokyo and Yokohama and prefers living in a large city.[9]

MATSUMOTO-SAN: I took care of my father-in-law when he became ill, both at home and while he was in the hospital. I would go to the hospital and take care of him during the day and come home and make food for the family in the evening.[10] I also was expected to bring food to him. This situation of caring for and feeding my father-in-law went on for about two years. Fortunately, I didn't have to do it every day, but was able to share the work with other relatives.

JWT: When you married your husband, did you know that he would become the successor in the household and return to live in Mizusawa?

MATSUMOTO-SAN: No, I didn't know [laughs]. I never expected it. My husband is the third son, but his elder brothers have both married and live in Tokyo. They both married women who are only children, so there is no chance that they will return—nor do they want to return. This situation has left it on my husband to be the successor. If I had known that he was going to become the successor and we would have to live with his parents, I don't think I would have married him.

JWT: What prompted your husband's decision to return?

MATSUMOTO-SAN: My husband's parents kept demanding that we return. They were getting old, but were not sick, but they had been bugging us to come back all along, constantly asking when we would come back and telling us to come back. I thought they were very irritating and nagging. I didn't like it at all. Whenever we got a telephone call from my father-in-law, he would say, "When are you going to return?" or something like that. My in-laws always stated the return as either an order or saying, "when are you returning?" But never asking *if* we would return. It was constant.

When my husband decided to return, I couldn't understand. We liked living in Yokohama, and he found his work very interesting. So I just couldn't understand why he felt we had to return, and he had said he didn't want to return.

JWT: Then why did he decide to return?

MATSUMOTO-SAN: My husband, well, his parents were getting old, and he said he wanted to be a filial child one time before they died. What was really bad was that as soon as my father-in-law died, my husband got himself transferred back to Yokohama. I thought this was very unfair. He went back and left us here to take care of his mother. I would like to go back. My husband has said that he will remain in Yokohama until retirement. He has no intention of returning. He has not told his mother this and, in fact, has lied to her that he will return at some point in the future.

JWT: Why doesn't the whole family go?

MATSUMOTO-SAN: Well, my husband's mother is living alone, so I was left to take care of her. We asked her if she would be willing to move to Yokohama and she said no. She said that she will not move and that she wants to live here to the end.

JWT: What were things like at the time your husband moved back to Yokohama?

MATSUMOTO-SAN: We fought a great deal, and I was very troubled. We had also had fights about returning to live with his parents when we were in Yokohama together. I said to my husband, "You're more concerned about the lives of your parents than you are of your own family." I thought at the time about not coming back at all and divorcing him because of his behavior.

JWT: Why did you build a separate house when your in-laws have such a large house?

MATSUMOTO-SAN: It was one of the conditions of moving back. I told my husband that I would not return unless we built a separate house to live in. My in-laws did not oppose the idea of building a separate house, which was good. They under-

stood that we would not return unless the separate house
was built.

JWT: Why was it important to have a separate house?

MATSUMOTO-SAN: I was concerned about a variety of things and wanted privacy. I felt that there would be a great deal of conflict between myself and my mother-in-law if we lived in the same house. A lot of old people badmouth their daughter-in-law (yome). The grandmothers want the yome to go out and do some sort of work at a job while grandma takes care of the children. If the yome doesn't want to do this, then there is conflict because the grandmother thinks the yome should be bringing in income. I think this is related to concerns older people have about the values of younger people. The grandmothers try to take control over the grandchildren in order to raise them to behave and think in a way they consider to be oyakōkō. It is a power struggle over the raising of the children, and to some extent the grandmother has the upper hand because it is her family and the yome is essentially an outsider. All of the younger yome around here want to raise their own children, but the grandmothers are strong on trying to get the yome to go out and leave the children to them. This creates a lot of stress between the yome and grandmother. It seems as though grandmothers want to take away the grandchildren from the yome. The younger women around here say that they might as well go off and get their own apartment because they have no role in raising their children. And the husband won't say anything; if the yome complains, the husband just defends the ie and his parents. It is very hard to live together.

Discussion

These two case studies reveal some of the complexity, conflict, and feelings of ambiguity that can arise over carrying out the responsibilities associated with filial piety. In both cases, it is clear that the execution of filial responsibilities exists in relation to, and often in conflict with, the execution of nuptial responsibilities. In the case of the Fujiwaras, because they are both eldest, there is a direct conflict over issues of coresidence and care of parents. Fujiwara-san intended to coreside with his father when he married, but this was vetoed by his wife's parents, who had wanted an adoptive husband to come into the family and live with them. Although both have sisters who could conceivably bring in an adoptive husband, in Fujiwara-san's wife's case this is no longer possible, as her sister has married out of the family. In his own sister's case, it remains a possibility, but, according to his sister, marriage itself, due to her age, has become difficult, and she does not have a strong desire to marry in any case.

Although the possibility of Fujiwara-san's sister bringing in an adoptive husband remains, since she is neither male nor the eldest, she does not carry a heavy responsibility to solve the problem of succession and coresidence. The pressure to coreside and to take his role as successor rests squarely on Fujiwara-san. The inability to resolve the conflict has placed the Fujiwaras into a liminal state (Kawano 1995; Traphagan 2000a; Turner 1977), in some ways trapped, unable to move forward toward buying separate property located between both parents and prevented from moving in with either set of parents because of the emotions and expectations both parents have expressed. They are resigned to remaining in an apartment in Kitakami until some resolution arises, while hoping that Fujiwara-san's father will eventually accept the difficult situation of his son and daughter-in-law in terms of their responsibilities to both sets of parents. The Fujiwaras' case underscores the power of parents in determining the residential situations of children, as well as the limits on that power (Traphagan 2000a). While the Fujiwaras are able to refuse to live with either set of parents, they are not able to move forward to correct the problem in the way they have deemed best. Concern over angering both sides limits their ability to act, placing them into a liminal condition of nondecision, blocking them from living with either set of parents or building a separate house of their own.

The conflict also highlights the centrality of filial obligation in the framework of familial relationships. While the Fujiwaras are contesting coresidence, they are not contesting their basic responsibility to care for their parents. As eldest and successor children, they both feel a keen obligation to organize their lives in a way that satisfies the needs and expectations of their parents. And yet, the probable ultimate solution, to build a separate house situated between both parental couples, is likely to leave both sets of parents disappointed.

Matsumoto-san's situation emphasizes, perhaps in a somewhat extreme way, the reasons why so many eldest sons in particular have difficulty finding a wife. Matsumoto-san clearly sees the responsibilities of her husband toward his parents as being in direct conflict with his responsibilities to his wife and children. From her perspective, the decision to return to Mizusawa and his concern about carrying out his filial responsibilities was made without consideration for the needs of his nuclear family. It is clear by his move back to Yokohama that her own fate was calculated into the carrying out of filial responsibilities. Having returned to his old job and lifestyle, he has left his wife and children behind to care for his mother should the need arise. In each step along the way, Matsumoto-san has contested both her husband's privileging of his responsibility to his natal family over the responsibility to his nuclear family and her own role as yome, requiring that she care for her in-laws as they grow older.

Again, while the Matsumotos' situation may be somewhat unusual, it falls within the expected pattern of the successor having carried out his filial obligations, because it is the daughter-in-law on whom the vast majority of provision of health care will fall. This is why many women are unwilling to marry an eldest son, as noted in Ichiro-san's comment at the beginning of the chapter. In Japan, women represent the vast majority (approximately 90 percent) of those providing health care to family members (Campbell 1992: 221; Jenike 1997). Although increasingly daughters are filling that role, traditionally it has been the daughter-in-law married to the successor son who carries out the work of providing health care to her in-laws (see Harris and Long 1993; Harris, Long, and Fujii 1998). This can mean an extended period of caring for a convalescent person about whom, as is the case with Matsumoto-san, one may in fact have ambivalent feelings, at best. This strain may be compounded by situations in which mother-in-law and daughter-in-law are in direct conflict over issues such as proper child-rearing practices, which can generate animosity in the relationship. This issue was sufficiently important to Matsumoto-san that, in order to control this situation, she negotiated the building of a separate house prior to returning to Mizusawa, thus effectively removing her in-laws from the context of daily presence in and control over her life and that of her children.

By examining these two case studies, we are able to get a glimpse into some of the complexities in carrying out one's filial responsibilities as a successor child or the spouse of a successor child. In both cases, the idea of filial responsibility and the importance of filial piety (oyakōkō) was not disputed, although in Matsumoto-san's case, her husband's own expression of this ideal via coresidence came only after his elder brothers made it clear that they were unable or unwilling to carry out the responsibility. It is important to stress that the manner in which this ideal is being carried out in both cases is negotiated. In other words, there is not a simple acceptance of the idea that a successor child will coreside and care for the parents. Instead, there is a complex of relationships between successor and parent, successor and spouse, successor and children, and among siblings, that contributes to a negotiated conclusion to the ways in which filial obligations will be executed and expressed. Indeed, in the case of Ichiro-san, it is clear that the negotiation process even involves potential family members—potential spouses who may decide to end a relationship out of an unwillingness to be part of that web of filial obligations.

In contemporary Japan, the ideal of coresidence remains a central index that points to a child who is expressing and carrying out his or her filial responsibilities. In practice, limited mate choice, creating more couples who are both successors, and the unwillingness of many women (and men) to coreside with in-laws has had a significant effect on the ability to express filial piety in that way and has forced children to come up with alternatives. The notion of filial piety remains a key factor in shaping the parent-child relationship and is a central feature of the ie, understood as a conceptual framework in which people think about familial relationships. But in actual practice the content of that ideal is negotiated within a complex of relationships in which love, animosity, resentment, ambivalence, and resignation shape the specific expression in each family.

CHAPTER 11

Alone in the Family: Great-grandparenthood in Urban Japan

BRENDA ROBB JENIKE

I met Mrs. Sakai at the House of Warm Contact (Fureai no ie)—which, despite its euphemistic name, is not a house at all but an adult day care center in the western Tokyo ward of Suginami.[1] With stiffness and troublesome spasms in her legs, Mrs. Sakai needed a walker to get around the center. Aside from her legs, however, she was healthy, sharp-witted, and energetic at 87. A widow for more than a decade, this great-grandmother, the former matriarch of her family, lived in the midst of a large, four-generation household. Surrounded by her eldest son and his wife, her grandson and his wife, and her great-grandchildren, Mrs. Sakai, with her health and attentive family, was leading an ideal old age by Japanese cultural standards. So why, then, when five of the elderly women at the day care center were chatting over tea, did she offer the opinion that no one needed to live past 85? And why did the others, also all great-grandmothers living with their adult children, readily agree?

It is widely believed in Japan that the elderly are happiest residing within a family. Coresidence with one's children in old age, traditionally (and still most typically) with one's eldest son and his wife, is a fundamental social expectation, signifying the successful maintenance of primary relationships over the life course. A person living alone in Japan, especially an elderly person, no matter how active, content, or self-sufficient, is thought of as "lonely" (Hashimoto 1996: 9) or, worse, abandoned. The majority of the oldest-old (those 85 and over) in Japan currently do live in an extended family household, and have typically lived within a family their entire lives.[2] Because of dramatically increased longevity in the last few decades, the current generation of the oldest-old in Japan is the first cohort to experience an extended period of not only grandparenthood in their household, but also great-grandparenthood. Japanese cultural and societal expectations for the elderly have not, however, caught up with the realities of this extended longevity. The unfortunate result is that Japanese of all generations seem unprepared to handle the additional years of advanced old age.

Drawing from extended participant observation as a volunteer in a public adult day care center in Tokyo in 1996–97 and informal interviews with attending seniors and their family members, I illustrate in this chapter how formerly productive and socially active elderly residents of Tokyo can experience a severe role loss upon becoming a great-grandparent. This loss cannot be attributed to decline in function alone. Rather, public and private assumptions of decline in function and dependency in later life play a greater role in limiting activities of oldest-old elders. These assumptions, rooted in the cultural ideal of filial piety (expected coresidence, intergenerational obligations, indulgence and encouraged dependency), combined with the succession of kinship roles in the Japanese family, work to limit meaningful social participation and sense of purpose for the very old. While the family and the wider society provide specific sociocultural roles for grandparents, the great-grandparent fills only a symbolic role. With no duties to perform within the household, a great-grandparent can be left lonely and isolated even in the midst of a large, bustling extended family.

Filial Care and Other Tales of an Aging Society

The life course of Japanese has lengthened considerably in only a few decades. Until quite recently, extreme old age—that is, not one, but two or three decades of life post-retirement—was not a consideration for the average citizen and his or her family. Up until the end of World War II, average life expectancy for Japanese males and females was around age 50 (Kōseishō 1996). Just half a century later, males can expect to live an average of 77.2 years, and females 84 years. This is not only the highest longevity in the world, but it also exceeds prior United Nations' predictions of maximum life expectancies in human populations (Horiuchi 2000). Thus, today living into grand old age has become a normative part of the life course for Japanese citizens.

Moreover, the proportion of the population aged 80 and over within the total senior population during this same time span has steadily increased. Just 9 percent of seniors in Japan were 80 and older in 1950; by 1970, this figure had only modestly increased to just under 13 percent. However, by

1995, 21.25 percent of the senior population was 80 or over (national census in *Asahi Shinbun Japan Almanac 1999*). The Health and Welfare Ministry of Japan estimates that by 2020 half of the senior population will be aged 75 and over (Kōsishō 2000: 7). Further, there are now fifty-nine times the number of centenarians in Japan than there were in 1960, with 8,491 persons aged 100 years or older in 1997 (*Asahi Shinbun Japan Almanac 1999*).

How, then, is this newfound extended old age viewed in Japanese society? As the rapid aging of Japan's population rose to the forefront of public consciousness, the status of the elderly in Japanese society, their well-being and entitlements, have proved to be a source of both public and private angst and ambivalence. Emerging discourses in the late 1970s and early 1980s ranged from dire predictions of an impending social and economic "crisis," to moral messages in the mid- to late-1980s on adult children failing to fulfill their filial obligations (Campbell 1992; Jenike 1997; Lock 1993; Plath 1983). An example in English of this rather overt moral tone can be seen in NHK's documentary *Aging in Japan: When Traditional Mechanisms Vanish* (Films for the Humanities 1990). Aired in Japan in the late 1980s, the film looks at how some elderly in a Nagoya suburb, unwanted and not in control of their own lives, are left by their daughters-in-law or sons to aimlessly pass their time in a bathhouse. The blame is squarely on their adult children, who are portrayed as cold or selfish.

In the 1990s, this moral finger pointing was toned down by a more realistic feminist call to action regarding family caregiver burden and burnout. As social welfare services for seniors continue to expand nationwide, the professional voice of physicians and social workers regarding proper care of the aged has begun to supersede that of family experiential knowledge (Jenike 2002). Chronic conditions of old age such as senility (*boke*) that were previously viewed as a natural or expected part of old age are becoming medicalized as Alzheimer's disease (*arutsuhaimā*) or dementia (*chihō*), conditions to actively manage (Traphagan 2000b). Currently, discussion regarding care of seniors tends to promote community involvement for all ages and tout benefits of service usage for family and elderly parents alike (Jenike 2003). Throughout these multiple discourses, however, the place of the very old in society and their well-being have remained firmly centered in the context of the Japanese family, rather than in the context of the individual elder. In Japan, in the minds of the current cohort of oldest-old elders and their (aging) adult children, the physical, emotional, and social support of the very old (who are not childless) are still the responsibility of the child with whom they reside.

This unwavering expectation among the oldest-old cohort is in accordance with the norms of filial piety (*oyakōkō*) upon which they were raised. According to Confucian thought, the tie between parent and child is one of the five primary human relationships, calling for the benevolent leadership of the parent and willing obedience of the child. As anthropologist David Plath explains, "devotion to one's parents in particular is the root of all virtue and the model for all human propriety" (Plath 1988: 507). To learn to honor a parent was to learn to respect one's rulers, resulting in harmony for society as a whole. During the Meiji Restoration, at the end of the nineteenth century, Confucian concepts, *bushidō* (the ethical code of the former ruling samurai class), and emperor worship were combined to create a new national ideology (*kokutai*). Codified in the Meiji Civil Code, this ideology was propagated by the state in ethics classes in public schools until the end of World War II. The current cohort of oldest-old elders in Japan, having completed their education in the Taishō period (1912–25), is well versed in the Confucian ethic of filial piety and the virtues of repaying one's obligations (*on*) to parents for their years of hard work and sacrifices for their children (Benedict 1946; Bethel 1992; Lanham 1979). Indeed, attendees at the adult day care center where I worked in 1997 could still recite from memory the Confucian and nationalistic passages on morality from a Taishō-period schoolbook that a staff member brought in to view. One woman, Mrs. Mita (age 85), explained how she had had to memorize and formally recite these passages in order to graduate from grade school, bowing her head at appropriate times as she pledged her love and obedience to her mother and emperor alike.

Much like behavior accorded to young children in what Ruth Benedict (1946: 279) referred to as the "second privileged period," cultural ideals for old age in Japan call for loving indulgence by family members and an accepted dependence on the part of elderly parents. This pattern is best understood in the context of the Japanese kinship system, which is still based on the principles of the traditional *ie* stem family prominent in prewar Japan. The ie is "a vertical lineage consisting of member families, living and dead, which are all related by blood, lineally and collaterally" (Takeda 1976: 474). Within the structure of the prewar patrilineal, patriarchal, and virilocal ie, the preference was for the family line (and thus any business or trade) to be continued through the eldest son in each successive generation.[3]

In this preferred pattern of primogeniture, as written into article 970 of the Meiji Civil Code of 1898, the elderly parents, the eldest son, his wife (known as the junior wife or *yome*), and their children would reside in one household. Daughters married out. Younger sons either formed branch families or married out as well. Upon the retirement or illness of the older couple, the eldest son would inherit all family property and succeed to the position of master of the house. The yome would become the senior wife. The aged parents continued to live in the household, but often took up residence in smaller retirement quarters, known as the *inkyo*. The eldest son and his wife were responsible for the elder couple's care until their deaths. Even after their deaths, when the parents join the family ancestors, the yome was still responsible for their well-being in the form of proper care of the memorial tablets (*ihai*) and Buddhist altar (Bethel 1992; Lebra 1984a; Plath 1964). Thus, continuation of the ie ensured not only the preservation of the family enterprise, but also the welfare of the senior couple in old age, the proper care of their departed spirits, and the continued care of all ancestors in the family line.

Although the ie system was abolished as law during the Occupation in favor of an inheritance system built on the American model (all offspring having an equal claim to inheritance), much of the patriarchal nature of the ie system has survived to the present. Among the current oldest-old cohort, succession, inheritance practices, and expectations for care still largely follow the prewar pattern. Further, the patrilineal stem family pattern has continued on in postwar Japan as a residential unit, now referred to as a household (*katei*) or three-generation family (*sansedai kazoku*), as opposed to a nuclear family (*kakukazoku*) (Kelly 1993). Other patterns include extended residence with a younger son or a married or single daughter.

Rather than all generations residing in one common living space, however, remodeling or tearing down and rebuilding a home to incorporate two separate residences on the same property has become a popular option over the last decade. For apartment or condominium dwellers, elderly parents might take up residence in an adjacent or nearby residence (Jenike 1997). The pattern of lifelong intergenerational coresidence practiced by today's oldest-old cohort is thus being replaced with delayed coresidence among younger cohorts of elderly (Hashimoto 1993); that is, the junior couple moves in with parents or vice versa according to financial or care needs only during the parents' later years. (See Chapter 10 for Traphagan's discussion of the delicate "negotiations" this transition involves.)

Whether or not a family continues to follow the inheritance and residence patterns of the patrilineal stem family system, the intergenerational care contract fundamental to this system has endured. Cultural norms dictate that the designated family successor is still responsible for the *total* care of aged parents. Plath (1972: 149) describes how, in Japan's collectivist society, "attachments within a small web of a 'personal community' of a few others" are critical to the stability of a Japanese self. Disengagement from such relationships can be emotionally devastating. For the current cohort of oldest-old elders, coresidence and care in later life symbolize the successful maintenance of these relationships. As stated above, expectations for care include not only functional support, but also economic, emotional, and social support. So pervasive is the belief in the family as responsible for the welfare of the elderly that the Japanese public, including social workers, gerontologists, and policy makers, assumes the social and emotional support of elderly residing with family members to be adequate due to coresidence alone, rather than considering the frequency and quality of interactions between generations, or the level of social participation outside the home (see Koyano et al. 1994 for this criticism of social gerontology in Japan). Furthermore, within Japanese families, social support is conceptualized as "listening to" the elderly, but not necessarily including them as equally valued members of the household, with responsibility and authority. Social support for the elderly thus becomes unidirectional, like a parent comforting a child.

A key characteristic of this filial care is *amae* dependency (Doi 1973; Johnson 1993), which has been termed "permissive dependency" (Vogel and Vogel 1968), "indulgent dependency" (Lebra 1976), or, more recently, "legitimized dependency" (Hashimoto 1996). While the term *amae* is most often applied to the relationship of a dependent young child on its mother, an aging parent will likewise in turn begin to seek the indulgence and support of his or her adult child. Like a mother understanding the needs of her child, an attentive adult child (or daughter-in-law) should understand and attend to an aged parent's needs without the parent having to ask for assistance. This parent-child role set thus "encourages passive helplessness" by one partner and "active nurturing" by the other (Kiefer 1987: 104). In my previous research, my caregiver respondents described this relationship, based on the feelings of oyakōkō, as a natural desire to care for one's parent, rather than a duty (*gimu*) (Jenike 1997). In Japan, an aged parent deserves support as part of a lifelong reciprocal relationship, in which the parent has accumulated social capital through contributions to the household and sacrifices for his or her child and grandchildren (Hashimoto 1996).

As David Plath (1972, 1983), Christie Kiefer (1990), and Wataru Koyano (1989) among others have pointed out, these cultural ideals of filial piety in Japan should not be confused with actual practices. Plath (1972: 135) writes, "The vision of old age as a time of honored, privileged, accepted dependency has high prescriptive value, but its descriptive value is far from high, for there is strong evidence to the contrary." While dependency of aged parents on the younger generations is expected and encouraged, becoming an undue burden (*meiwaku*) on family members by outliving and exhausting the social capital accrued through reciprocal intergenerational relationships over the life course breaches the intergenerational contract, and should be avoided (Hashimoto 1996; Lebra 1984a; Traphagan 1998a; Young and Ikeuchi 1997). John Traphagan (1998a: 336) explains how "a tension arises when the dependent relationship is perceived as becoming burdensome; a situation that is seen as developing in conjunction with the onset of physical and mental decline." By becoming bedridden or senile (*boke*) in one's later years, an elderly parent forces his or her child into a long-term unilateral relationship of giving (Hashimoto 1996; Traphagan 2000b). The existence of numerous *pokkuri* ("swift" death) temples frequented by elderly Japanese who pray for a peaceful and timely death, receive counseling on family matters, and buy amulets for the prevention of senility and other disabling conditions of old age attests to the strong desire among elderly to avoid falling into this unilateral relationship of dependency (Plath 1983; Wöss 1993; Young and Ikeuchi 1997). In addition, the suicide rate for Japanese aged 65 and over (32.4 per 100,000 persons for 1997) continues to be the highest for any age group and is high when compared to that for elderly in other industrialized nations (*Asahi Shinbun Japan Almanac 1999*). These two phenomena point not only to the increased awareness among Japanese seniors of the consequences of long-term chronic illnesses in old age, but also to the long-held cultural belief that an individual has an obligation to leave this world if he or she has become burdensome (Plath 1983).

These dual themes of filial obligation and meiwaku avoidance for the very old abound in Japanese popular culture. Perhaps the most influential of this genre has been Sawako Ariyoshi's 1972 novel *Kōkutsu no hito* (The Twilight Years), about a daughter-in-law's exasperating but eventually spiritually uplifting experiences caring for an elderly father-in-law as he progresses into advanced senility. Also making a lasting impact was Niwa Fumio's earlier and less sympathetic short story "Iyagarase no nenrei" (The hateful age). In biting terms, Niwa depicts an unlovable octogenarian widow as an example of an elderly parent who is "the scourge of relatives and a burden to society" (Niwa 1962: 340). The most enduring reference among Japanese when speaking of the tension between ideals of filial piety and the realities of frail old age—and a figurative reference to alternatives of family care such as nursing homes or retirement communities (Bethel 1992)—is the legend of Obasuteyama ("Throw-Out-Granny Mountain"). For more than a thousand years, this tale, which Plath (1988: 510) has aptly described as "the site of the peak cultural nightmare of filial rejection," has been told and retold in literary and popular forms throughout Japan.

According to the legend, eldest sons in parts of ancient Japan had to carry their elderly parents up to a mountaintop and leave them to die from exposure when the parents reached a certain age. A recent revival of this legend is Imamura Shōhei's award-winning 1983 movie *The Ballad of Narayama* (*Narayamabushikō*), a film based on the popular 1956 story and song of the same title by Fukuzawa Shichirō. This film provides a particularly brutal rendition of the Obasuteyama legend, complete with a craggy mountaintop littered with gruesome, gray-haired skeletal remains of countless elders. Relying on an ecological model for gerontocide, the story is set only one hundred years ago in a tiny mountain village in rural northern Japan's snow country. Life is exceedingly harsh, with the villagers barely living at subsistence level.

The Ballad of Narayama is not, however, a dialog on the ethics of gerontocide in the face of starvation. Rather, it is a tale of the virtues of old Orin, who, robust at 69, nonetheless insists on being taken to Narayama (Oak Mountain) to "go to the gods" a year early for the sake of her family's well-being. The fourth generation is on the way, and there will be too many mouths to feed. Despite Orin's continued productivity and immense contributions to her family—she weaves, fishes, prepares meals, cares for her baby grandchild, gathers foodstuffs—she is respected and admired for her insistence on the timely succession of the generations. Orin's noble behavior, an example of *shikkari shiteiru*, or "persever[ing] against adversity with silent strength and courage" (Bethel 1992: 127), is in stark contrast with that of Mata, a seemingly senile old father who tries to steal food from his children. Kept tied up by his son, Mata is taken to Narayama by force. He yells and struggles to survive as his son pushes him off a cliff. Orin, on the other hand, is lovingly carried by her eldest son to the mountaintop, where she sits silently praying on her mat. She is rewarded with the first snowfall, a sign of a "truly good pilgrimage" (Plath 1972: 139).

While myth rather than historical fact (Cornell 1991), Obasuteyama remains in the Japanese consciousness as a powerful message regarding old age for two reasons. First, even though positive versions do exist, in which the son changes his mind or the old mother proves her usefulness through her wisdom and the law is changed, Obasuteyama lingers as a disturbing symbol of abandonment of the elderly by the very family member supposed to care for them. It is also, however, a tale of meiwaku avoidance. The old people of the community, even if healthy, are still taken to the mountain to "go to the gods" so they do not burden their families. The timely succession of the generations is thus enforced, with the preservation of the family as a structural unit more important than the needs of its individual members.

Anthropologists have noted that, for older Japanese, continuity of the family line is more of a concern than the idea of personal death (Bethel 1992; Plath 1988), for the ie family line is believed to exist "above and beyond all members of a family of each generation" (Takeda 1976: 474). Examining kinship and aging cross-culturally, Meyer Fortes (1984: 104) theorized that, "The succession of the generations . . . is the essence . . . of the reproductive process, first for the physical replacement of each generation but second and more fundamentally for its social and cultural replacement by the next generation." Extended old age has indeed delayed physical replacement of each generation within the Japanese family. Social and cultural replacement, however, still seem to proceed according to an earlier, shorter life cycle.

Transitions in the Domestic Cycle

Why, one may ask, would an individual living in an extended family need a meaningful role as great-grandparent if he or she is still a parent and a grandparent? Japan, both urban and rural, is still an age-based society (Brinton 1992; Hashimoto 1996; Lebra 1984a; Traphagan 1998a), in which "age remains a legitimate criterion for differentiating social participation" (Hashimoto 1996: 40). Rather than multiple domestic roles for each member, there is a succession of kinship roles in the domestic cycle of the Japanese family. Plath, who has written extensively upon the life course in Japan, notes that there are "key transition points along the domestic cycle" such as marriage, childbirth, and marriage of one's children (Plath 1980: 89). As an individual makes these transitions, he or she enters into a new set of sociocultural roles, expectations, and obligations both in the domestic sphere and in the public sphere, and is no longer responsible for those of the former phase.

Sociologist Mary Brinton describes the timing of life-course transitions in Japan as "more irreversible than temporary," exhibiting "little variance or spread across individuals" and very little overlap of statuses (Brinton 1992: 83). For a female, these phases include daughter, young wife (yome), mother, and grandmother (mother-in-law). For a male, he is first a son, then a husband and father, then grandfather. These kinship roles are mirrored in societal roles and dictate appropriate social participation. For example, a woman who is married and in her late 20s to early 30s is no longer addressed in public as *ojōsan* (young lady) or *musume* (daughter), but as *okusan* (wife), *okāsan* (mother), or *obasan* (aunt), and, by the time she reaches her 60s, as *obāchan* (granny). Margaret Lock (1993) has demonstrated through the narratives of middle-aged women who did not conform to this ideal life course pattern— single, divorced, widowed, or professional career women—how structurally difficult it is to challenge these kinship-based gendered and generational stereotypes in Japanese society. Even the types of social participation, interests and hobbies, and hairstyle and dress of one age group are generally deemed not appropriate for that of another.

Each kinship role within the Japanese family—daughter, young wife and mother, grandmother—has clearly defined expectations and obligations. As a young wife and then a mother, a Japanese woman must care for her family and household. A grandmother in Japan has traditionally been responsible for care of her grandchildren, and for helping to run the household, which includes cooking, shopping, and cleaning. Women in middle and late-middle age will also often hold part-time jobs or participate in clubs, classes, and other social activities. Quite a few Japanese women in their 60s have commented to me that this period in their lives, if they are not caring for an ailing parent or spouse, is the most enjoyable time for them (also noted in Lebra 1984a and Lock 1996). They have the authority, health, and freedom to do as they please.

This busy and authoritative role as a grandmother and mother-in-law does not, however, extend through advanced old age. When a woman's grandchildren grow up, and her daughter-in-law or daughter, whomever she resides with, becomes a mother-in-law and grandmother herself, the older woman becomes a great-grandmother (*hī-bāsan* or *sōsobo*) and is no longer responsible for her former duties of childcare, cooking, and housework. Note, though, that although the role changes to great-grandmother, the term of address remains obāchan (granny). This causes some confusion for great-grandchildren, with two obāchan in one household.[4]

The same progression is true for men, who tend to experience role loss earlier than women, usually at the time of retirement from paid employment. Social participation outside the home also declines with advancing age, primarily due to lack of mobility and a dwindling of one's social network.[5] Role loss is logical when the elderly grandparent suffers from physical or cognitive decline and can no longer perform former household chores without risk to his or her own personal safety. I found among my respondents in Tokyo, however, that elders were not limited as much by physical or cognitive impairment as they were by their family members' assumptions that advanced old age is a period of decline and dependency, suitable only for rest and quiet, simple activities.

Public Programs and Policies for the Very Old

Most Japanese continue to embrace an image of the elderly as frail and dependent even though demographic data on the senior population attest otherwise (Koyano 1989, 1997). According to the Ministry of Health and Welfare, in 1996 a quarter of seniors aged 85 and older needed "intensive caregiving" (functional assistance). These seniors were either bedridden (20.5 percent of seniors 85 and over) or suffering from dementia alone (3.5 percent) (Kōseishō 1996: 117). The majority of very old elders, then, does not require intensive assistance for the activities of daily living, and does not fit the public image of a helpless, frail, and dependent great-grandparent.

The image of frailty is perpetuated in part by frequent media images of caregiving for bedridden or demented elderly, as well as the publicizing of predictions for skyrocketing rates of both these conditions in the near future. Overstated predictions helped to garner public support for increased social welfare expenditures and the implementation of the national long-term care insurance system. Compared to other nations, rates for bedridden elderly in Japan are indeed high, but this is in part a statistical artifact from the lack of distinction in Japan between chair-bound and bedfast conditions, both referred to under the umbrella term *netakiri*. It also reflects previous policies at hospitals that routinely kept elderly patients overmedicated and immobile in beds for extended stays. With Japan's high rate of strokes, the unavailability of rehabilitative therapy and the reluctance of family members to force their parents into painful rehabilitation contributed to permanent loss of mobility (Jenike 1997; Kiefer 1987). Government officials called attention to the high rates of bedridden elderly in part to push for the implementation and use of rehabilitation services offered under the new social welfare program.

The expectation that the elderly will be frail is also a basic component of the intergenerational contract in Japan. Akiko Hashimoto (1996) describes the Japanese intergenerational contract for care of elderly parents as "will need," meaning that Japanese assume an elderly parent will need care in old age, and prepare accordingly through early consensus on who the family caregiver will be and plans for future coresidence. She contrasts this with the American attitude of "might need," in which Americans assume self-sufficiency for the elderly parent until a health crisis signals otherwise. For Japanese, helplessness is not the state of needing help, but the "state of not having help" (Hashimoto 1996: 175). Social welfare policies for the very old in Japan are a product of this assumption of functional decline and need for instrumental assistance in old age. The majority of programs begun with the Gold Plan of 1989 (a ten-year strategic social welfare plan for seniors) and now part of the national long-term care insurance system (implemented in April of 2000) are designed specifically to support home care for disabled elderly. Home helpers, visiting nurses, adult day care, short-stay service, bathing services, meal delivery, and nursing home placement all serve the dual purpose of respite for family caregivers and instrumental care for disabled elderly.

Measures specifically designed for social support, that is, programs to increase the social participation of seniors in the community, known as *ikigai* (purpose of life) policies, are not inclusive of the special needs of the very old. For example, Silver Human Resource Centers, job placement agencies run by the Japanese government, assist the newly retired in finding part-time paid or volunteer work, as Japanese seniors, especially men, consistently rank work as their greatest source of ikigai (Suginami-ku 1996; Thang 1997; Tokyo Metropolitan Government 1993: 25). Another vehicle for encouraging greater social participation for elderly are senior citizens clubs (*rōjin kurabu* or *rōjinkai*). These community organizations for senior citizens are supported by national and local governments, but run by the seniors themselves. There are more than 133,000 senior clubs nationwide, with just under nine million members (Okamoto 1996). Open to all community residents aged 60 and over, clubs hold monthly meetings where members can exchange news, chat over tea, and participate in organized group singing. Clubs also sponsor "gateball" (see Traphagan 1998b, 2000b) and sports teams, and take day excursions or travel together, such as to *onsen* (hot springs) or to temples on pilgrimages. Community centers and senior centers (*keirō kaikan*) as well may offer classes in traditional arts and crafts, sponsor choral, dance, or sports groups, hold lectures, or simply provide a bathing facility and gathering space for elderly residents. Although the very old are in theory included in club and community center activities, in practice, these activities are geared to the young-old and middle-old. Oldest participating members are typically in their mid-80s.

This bias towards the young-old and middle-old can be seen in the text of the 1989 Gold Plan, which states:

> It is necessary not only to change the awareness and sense of value of
> the people, but also to adjust and reform the entire economic and social
> system to make it appropriate for 80-year life. . . . Opportunities will
> be provided and an environment will be developed so that the aged can
> make social participation [*sic*] as social members contributing to the
> society, taking advantage of their rich life experiences and knowledge
> and skills, instead of just being recipients of protection and assistance.
> (Kōseishō 1989: 22)

For those past the age of 80 living at home, there is day care service offered once to twice a week by municipalities.

Although a handful of adult day care centers existed in Japan as early as 1979 (Anbäcken 1997), the program was not widely available nationwide until after the 1989 Gold Plan made day care one of the three pillars of the new social welfare system for the elderly (home helper and short-stay services were the other two). Whereas there were only 1,080 day service centers nationwide in 1989, by 1998 there were 11,458 (Kōseishō 1995, 2000: 168). I therefore found that in 1997, day care programs in Tokyo were still only a few years old in most communities. The first center in Suginami Ward, for

FIGURE 9. Group exercises at a day care center for the elderly in Tokyo. Photo by Brenda Robb Jenike.

example, opened in 1992. To try to keep pace with demand, new day care centers are scheduled to open every year (projections are for a total of 17,250 centers nationwide).

Demand for day care is high, and waiting lists are long. To accommodate a greater number of participants, national guidelines call for small groups of seniors (five to fifteen, depending on level of care) to attend on alternate days for a maximum of two days per week for each group. Meant as both respite for families and as social support and rehabilitation for homebound elderly, day service is reserved for disabled elderly residents who are unable to participate in the community on their own, who are living alone, or whose family has difficulty caring for them during the day.[6] The daily program includes lunch and a snack, a simple health check, and a day of planned group activities such as singing, exercise, crafts, and games. Bathing service is included in dementia day care.

Day care programs are run year round, from June through the following May. The cost can vary depending on the municipality, but ranges from free to minimal, with a small charge for meals. Every April, elderly attendees and their families are reevaluated for admission to the program. According to both demand for the service and the health of the elderly applicant, applicants may be rejected, transferred to a more care-intensive center, recommended for other services, or allowed to continue on at the same center. Personnel may also be shuffled between facilities yearly. This constant shuffling and reassignment is characteristic of Japanese bureaucratic institutions, but is also intentionally done to discourage personal attachments between staff and day care attendees.

The great distinction between day care and either rōjinkai or senior centers is not one of content, but of environment and access. Whereas elderly have to transport themselves to a club meeting or senior center, day care attendees are escorted to and from the day care center in a specially equipped van (sōgei basu). At day care, the rooms are warm, and there are places to lie down and rest. Large toilet stalls accommodate wheelchairs or walkers, hallways have handrails, and there are elevators rather than stairways, with attentive staff always lending a helping hand. Facilities for rōjinkai vary, but, like the club I attended in northwestern Tokyo, may be in an older building, with steep, narrow staircases, drafty, dark, and cramped rooms, only one narrow toilet, and other problems that exacerbate the health conditions of the very old or completely preclude their participation. Senior centers are often in newer and better-suited facilities, but elderly who frequent these centers cannot rely on receiving transportation or much assistance from staff. For the very old, then, who are healthy and mobile but reluctant or unable to venture out into the community without some assistance, the assumption is that, if they are living with their children, their needs are adequately met within the family setting. This assumption can unfortunately be far from the truth.

Voices from Day Care

Toshi oite
ikiru chikara
o furishibori

[Growing old, striving to the utmost to live]

—Haiku composition by a female day care attendee, age 88[7]

Suginami Ward is a large, primarily suburban district in western Tokyo, with a population of more than half a million and a high population density of 14,910 persons per square kilometer (average for a Tokyo ward). Located conveniently close to Shinjuku, Tokyo's western business hub, and with a reputation among young people as a fashionable place to live, Suginami has become increasingly expensive. Neighborhoods consist mainly of small and narrow single-family homes, tucked in tightly together without space for yards. Unlike the sprawling suburban cities to the west, Suginami was a developed urban area prior to World War II. Some elderly residents have lived in Suginami since prewar days, and quite a few of the homes there are owned by the elderly. Younger generations are willing to move in with their aged parents primarily to live in this much desired location. The reverse pattern is true for other elderly residents, who moved into the ward later in life from outlying prefectures in order to live with their urban offspring.

Long known for its lively and bustling marketplace of small shops and stalls, the part of Suginami in which I worked was brightly lit and teeming with life. Streets and sidewalks were crowded and narrow, proving difficult for seniors to navigate. In the 1990s, this increasingly white-collar area had also become a favorite haunt of artists, musicians, and college students due to its numerous offbeat bars and cafes. The neighborhoods in Suginami, then, seemed to be in transition from the former modest *shitamachi* (downtown, working-class) atmosphere to that of a fashionable and more upscale white-collar community.

On a par with the rest of Tokyo's wards, 13.8 percent of Suginami's residents are aged 65 and over (Takahashi et al. 1994). In 1997 there were thirty-nine senior centers, four gateball parks, and one hundred senior clubs in Suginami. Ten adult day care facilities were up and running, with two additional centers set to open the following year. The adult day care center where I volunteered accommodates forty-five elderly residents in groups of fifteen for day care twice a week. The purpose of this "light care" facility is to provide recreation, exercise, a meal, and an opportunity to socialize for elderly residents who are otherwise housebound due to physical limitations, or whose families need respite. Opened in 1993, it is in high demand, with a waiting list of twenty.

For nine months, as part of my fieldwork on caregiving for the elderly, I worked as a staff helper with the Monday-Thursday group. My primary objective at the day care center was to understand the views of the elderly participating in community care. Through various outings we had for seniors and their families, I was also fortunately able to meet and talk with most of the day care participants' primary family caregivers. The Monday-Thursday group whom I came to know well was comprised of thirteen women and two men, whose ages ranged from the mid-80s through the early 90s. None had known each other prior to attending day care. All were widowed and lived with at least one family member. Three lived with single daughters, one lived with her niece and nephew, and the rest lived with an eldest son and daughter-in-law. Former occupations were primarily middle-class urban professions, such as a tailor, a physical education instructor, shopkeepers and clerks, and housewives. A few had moved from outlying prefectures, where they had at one time farmed or fished. Their sons and daughters were mainly in or retired from white-collar, middle-class occupations, reflecting the change in the community in the last few decades to an increasingly up-scale bedroom community of white-collar corporate commuters.

Despite advanced age, the attendees were generally healthy and both physically and mentally capable of participating in center activities such as cooking, complex card and board games, traditional arts, and modified physical exercises. Chronic health problems were relatively minor, such as arthritic hands or legs, fatigue due to high blood pressure, or minor loss of hearing or eyesight. I am purposely presenting cases of the most healthy and energetic elderly at the center rather than those with more debilitating health conditions in order to emphasize my thesis that advanced age alone, not functional decline, limits Japanese elders' social roles and participation.

Mrs. Kawatani at age 91 was the oldest female attendee and had been coming to day care for three years. With her shortly cropped white hair always neatly combed back, she walked with a steady shuffle and slight hunch, often relying on her cane for support. Although she moved cautiously, she was fully mobile, mentally alert, energetic, and enthusiastic in her participation at the center. Mrs. Kawatani resides in a four-generation household, living on the first floor of her home with her eldest son and his wife. Her son's daughter and her husband live with their children in a separate residence on the upper floors. Mrs. Kawatani has always lived within a family—first with her natal family until marriage, then with her husband's parents after marriage, and now, a widow for more than twenty years, with her son's family. She says she cannot imagine living alone, for she feels that living with her family is "safe and secure" (*anzen*) and "sets her mind at ease" (*anshin*). She takes pride in how her family, her four children, eleven grand-children and seven great-grandchildren, gathered at her house to honor her, the symbolic matriarch of the family, on her ninetieth birthday. She is well taken care of by her family, and by Japanese cultural standards is leading an ideal old age.

Yet, when I would inquire periodically about her daily life, she revealed that she does not leave the house except to come to day care. She spends her days at home resting, watching television, reading, or listening to music. Although she was active in community activities and hobbies as well as in her own household until her early 80s, her family members now prefer for her own safety that she stay inside the house. She cherishes her opportunity to come to day care and is anxious each year that she will be invited back.

Mrs. Sakai (age 87), whom I previously introduced, lives in a four-generation household similar to that of Mrs. Kawatani. Having converted her home into separate residences for each generation, Mrs. Sakai occupies the first floor by herself. She was involved in numerous neighborhood activities through her 70s. That came to an end, she says, when her legs weakened. Now that she needs a walker, she can no longer leave her home on her own. The main obstacle is actually her *genkan* (entrance hall). Slippery polished wood and a steep step down to the front door, as well as two additional steps outside, make it impossible for her to exit or enter her home without assistance. With the rest of the family away at work or at school during the day, Mrs. Sakai is left to herself. Intelligent and thoughtful, with a cheerful demeanor and gentle manner, Mrs. Sakai is well liked by the staff and seniors alike. She is, however, often reluctant to return home at the end of the center's day, wishing she could stay and talk with her friends longer.

Also excited to come to the center and reluctant to leave is Mrs. Endō (age 88). A former athletic instructor, Mrs. Endō, unlike the more delicate Mrs. Sakai, still has a strong, broad physique. The great conversationalist of the center, Mrs. Endō possesses an unbridled curiosity, and, sharp-witted, she often amused me with her humorous stories. Despite some arthritis in her hands, she keeps busy at home by sewing purses and eyeglass cases from kimono remnants. Unfortunately, at the center, she is often visibly saddened by her home life, particularly lamenting the loss of her former authority in her household. Her daughter-in-law is now the main power, and they do not get along. Except for short walks in her neighborhood, Mrs. Endō is also at home all day and is not allowed to do any housework. With little control over her own life, she was bitterly disappointed when her daughter-in-law and son took her to stay with her daughter for the weekend but then failed to pick her up in time to attend a special event at the center that she had looked forward to for weeks. Mrs. Endō, Mrs. Sakai, and Mrs. Kawatani were all jubilant during the occasional day care field trips, when we rode in buses to view cherry trees, eat at a new restaurant, or go shopping. It was their only chance in recent years to venture outside their own neighborhoods. All of the seniors, in fact, were visibly amazed to see how areas of Tokyo just outside of Suginami Ward had changed.

I wondered why, when they are able to get around with only minor assistance, these seniors had become so isolated. As stated above, all day care members resided with family members, either with an eldest son and his family or a daughter. With only one exception, these adult "children" are in their 60s. In Japan as a whole, half of all family caregivers to the disabled elderly are age 60 or older (Kōseishō 1996). A television commercial for the New Reform Party (Shinshintō) that aired during the 1996 fall elections commented on this very situation. A hand is shown reaching down to adjust the blanket of an elderly man in a wheelchair. As the camera pans back, we see the hand belonging to a gray-haired woman, with the superimposed words "Those caring for the elderly are elderly themselves." For someone in his or her 60s, care of an aged parent is difficult and tiring. Assisting an elderly parent to venture outside the home or allowing her to work inside the home is more trouble than just having the parent home and idle. Family members tend to worry that an elderly parent risks falling or other injury if let out of the home or could become overly tired or stimulated by an excursion. Staff at the day care center thought families tended to overestimate the frailty of their elderly parents, and therefore invited family members on center outings and to seasonal parties at the center in order to "impress upon them" the image of their parents as active.

To most Japanese, coresidence implies inclusion in family life. In my informal and formal interviews with day care attendees, other elderly in my community, and their children and grandchildren, I came to realize that coresidence does not necessarily mean daily interaction between the generations. Mrs. Sakai, for example, lived in her own separate residence in the household, with her own entrance, kitchen, and bath. She did not see her other family members unless they chose to come down to visit her. Meals were not shared. Daughter-in-law and daughter caregivers have told me in interviews that preparing meals for a multigeneration family is too much work, for each generation prefers to eat different types of food.

Further, elderly and their family members alike were acutely aware that the pace of their lives differed greatly. In an extended family I interviewed in northern Tokyo who does share living space in an older, traditional Japanese home, the younger generations felt overly limited by their grandmother, who, upon going to bed at seven each night, demanded that the family not watch television or speak loudly. Due to these inconveniences for all generations concerned, there has been a move toward close but completely separate living residences for the older and younger generations. This type of household, while more comfortable, does indeed limit interaction between family members. The situation of one of my neighbors during my fieldwork is typical of life in this modern extended family household. Living with her 90-year-old mother and her 72-year-old husband, Mrs. Akiyama (64) does not visit with her son and his wife and their two children more than once every two weeks, even though they live just upstairs. She does not even know if her daughter-in-law currently works, or where she goes during the day. Mrs. Akiyama says she tries to give them their privacy so they will want to continue to live with them. (See Miller's observations in Chapter 2 and Zhang's in Chapter 4 of similar strategies employed by rural Chinese elderly to keep on good terms with their descendants.) More the rule than the exception, the Akiyama family's coresidence arrangement does not carry the expectation of emotional intimacy or daily social interaction.

In multigeneration families as well, there exists a noticeable cultural generation gap between the prewar generations of elders and their postwar children, grandchildren, and great-grandchildren, due largely to sweeping social, educational, and economic changes over the last century. Heavily influenced by the prewar family and educational system, as well as wartime experiences, today's elders have witnessed drastic changes in almost every aspect of their society. For example, elderly women and men, forced to leave school at a young age to help support their families, have typically had no formal education past grade or middle school. Their children, however, have finished high school, and their grandchildren are highly educated. Elders in such households are often characterized by the middle and young generations as *ganko* (stubborn) or simply *furui* (old-fashioned). For their part, elderly can be critical of the moral laxity they see in younger Japanese. Women in adult day care frequently voiced their opinion that young mothers were too self-centered (*wagamama*) and tended to cater to their children's needs rather than respect the authority of their husbands. They saw this erosion of patriarchal order, something they had been socialized to accept and had strictly adhered to in their own lives, as the root cause of current societal ills such as divorce and delinquent children. Furthermore, in the past, a yome, weighed down by labor-intensive housework and restricted by family and society alike, worked in the home. Today, daughters-in-law, daughters, and grand-children go off to work or school every day, leaving elderly parents to fend for themselves until the evening. For single daughter caregivers, leaving the home each day to work is a necessity. Mr. Marushima's unmarried daughter, for example, must leave her 85-year-old father home alone in order to support them both. She worries about his well-being, but has no alternative, since day care is only offered a maximum of two days per week, and, still independent, he does not qualify for subsidized home helper service.

Mrs. Endō once commented to me that she is the first in her family to live into her 80s. Her elder sister and brother both died in their 60s. Another female attendee, Mrs. Hayase (age 88), added that, likewise, all of her family had died in their 70s or younger. Mrs. Sakai is also the first to live so long. The women seemed at a loss as to what their extended old age meant, view-ing it as "new territory" and acutely aware that they had "lived too long." They all agreed that 85 would have been the right time to die. They "didn't need" the years after that. No longer able or allowed to venture out on their own and lacking authority at home, they now felt overly dependent. There was a general consensus among the staff at the day care center that the el-derly attendees were limited more from psychological problems than from physical ones, the root of which were poor family relations. It was reasoned that if the families were more attentive, then the elderly parent would not need day care. From my own observations, and from my observations at other day care centers, some level of depression, or at least boredom, among attendees was pervasive.

Although I encountered one case of elder abuse during my fieldwork, which was eventually remedied by the intervention of social workers, the families of the adult day care attendees in Suginami Ward are not neglectful, but typical of the more than fifty families I met during my research. No one would consider them selfish or cruel in leaving their elderly parent idle. Family members, the elderly parents themselves, and the wider society hold no social or cultural expectations for meaningful domestic or social partici-pation for the very old. Families were meeting their obligations by attending to their elderly members' physical needs and allowing them to lead a leisurely life. All purposeful roles in the family (breadwinner, caregiver to children, homemaker, and so on) are filled by other members. Neither the elderly parent nor their family members expected them to live into grand old age, and no one knows what to do with this extended time. Coresident family members either fail to recognize the onset of depression in their elderly parent or have no idea how to address it.

Discussion: A Need for Greater Social Participation by the Oldest-old

The tendency of Japanese to reside with and provide family support for elderly parents does not stem from greater compassion, but from structural obligations reinforced by social pressure and institutionalized in the social welfare system (Hashimoto 1996). The lack of meaningful participation for the oldest-old in Tokyo in both private and public spheres is, of course, exacerbated by functional decline, but it exists even when there are no health problems. Age alone—and lack of consideration for special needs of the aged in the urban environment—precludes participation. Living within a family, with their physical needs provided for, is thought of as adequate. Nothing further is expected. A busy household, however, can be a lonely place for a member who can no longer make a contribution, or worse, for one who feels he or she has become a burden. This idea of a physically and mentally able older person being isolated and depressed *within a family* is not widely recognized.

To begin to address this problem, the notion of well-being for elders needs to be expanded from simply coresidence alone to the level of meaningful participation in family and community activities. Although I do of course attribute agency to elders, cultural assumptions and beliefs held by the oldest-old elders themselves limit their ability to solve their problems of social isolation on their own. For example, elders of the prewar Meiji and Taishō generations do not consider visiting friends in the private family home to be proper etiquette. Informal socializing with the opposite gender is also thought of as improper, thus limiting friendships to the same gender. Uncomfortable with activities that lack the hierarchical structures to which they are accustomed, elders with differing career experiences (an agricultural work history versus urban) or educational attainment (either more than the norm or less) may shun or halt their participation with the undifferentiated groups of seniors in day care or senior clubs. In Tokyo, many elders also have a disrupted social network stemming from radical changes in their communities during the postwar period, or from moving into Tokyo late in their adult lives. Such elders have few longtime friends in their own neighborhood. Furthermore, the frantic pace of life in Tokyo, including racing cars, people, and bicycles, and wide use of stairs instead of escalators or elevators, serves as a serious obstacle for elders who wish to venture outside their homes.

Perhaps, then, as the physical care of elders is increasingly shifting from the family alone to the community, the emotional care of elders can also begin to be addressed though community services and programs. A move to building community centers in more accessible facilities or the implementation of a local shuttle service for seniors and the disabled would greatly increase the participation of the very old. Established public day care programs, although far from perfect, do work to facilitate social participation for shut-in older residents.[8] This service should be expanded to accommodate healthy elderly as well as those with functional decline. Such inclusion could prevent the unfortunate situation like that of my neighbor Mrs. Akiyama's mother, Miyo, who, robust at ninety, was allowed to attend day care in our community for one year owing to her advanced age and slight stiffness in one knee. She enjoyed her days at day care immensely, making friends, improving her calligraphy, learning new crafts, and feeling worthwhile assisting other attendees who were not as agile as she. Still lovely, with a charming smile, smooth skin, and long hair worn in a bun, she even became a model for the brochures of the city social welfare office.

Unfortunately, the following year when demand for day care increased, city officials deemed Miyo "too healthy" to participate. With that decision, Miyo suddenly found herself socially excluded, at home every day with nothing to do, while all of her friends continued to go to day care. She tried to compensate by attending tai chi in the park, but the ten-block walk each way through traffic was too challenging. She did attend senior club meetings as their oldest member, but that was only once a month. Within a few weeks of being denied day care, the formerly active and cheery Miyo no longer wanted to get up in the morning and would spend the day sitting quietly in her room. Her daughter worried about her mother's gloomy state, but, with an ailing husband and a household to look after, had neither the time nor the energy to assist her mother through a day of activities. Miyo's growing inactivity stemmed both from her depression at being shut out of day care, and her inability to independently participate in any comparable activities elsewhere. She had also, however, purposely become less active so that her legs would weaken and she could again qualify for day care. The following year her legs had indeed gotten worse, and she was invited back. The unfortunate message for Miyo was that, in her community, being disabled means social participation, whereas being healthy in advanced old age only leads to isolation.

Summary: Life After Eighty-five

Ashi omoku
jiyū ni naranu
kono tsurasa

[Loss of freedom from heavy legs, the bitter sorrow]

—Haiku composition by Mrs. Sakai, age 87

Drawing upon social and symbolic capital accumulated over the life course (Hashimoto 1996; Traphagan 1998a), elderly Japanese are allowed to enter a second childhood in which they are free from helping out in the household, and deserving of support and care from their offspring. The problem with this traditional pattern for old age, as I have pointed out, is that the life course has greatly lengthened, increasing the likelihood that an individual will live for one to two decades in this final dependent phase. The result is loss of purpose, isolation, and depression in one's final years.

I have perhaps overly discounted the health limitations and frailties of the elders I worked with in day care during my field research. The difficulties in coping with and compensating for a weak heart, stiff joints, failing eyesight, or other chronic conditions are not as noticeable to an observer as they are to the person experiencing such decline. The greatest limiting factor for the social participation of elders in their advanced years is of course declining health resulting in chronic physical and mental impairments. The greater an elder's impairments, the more assistance he or she requires in order to continue participating both within family and community settings. Social isolation and the lack of a meaningful role within one's family are also not the only factors involved in depression among the elderly. Decline in function and associated pain, or the death of a spouse or close friend may trigger depression, with social isolation, real or perceived, being a symptom rather than the root cause. Furthermore, a caregiving daughter-in-law, son, or daughter can find it difficult to force an elderly parent to participate in a new activity and enter an entirely new social setting if he or she refuses to do so. My point is, however, that even if we assume functional decline and the need for assistance among the very old, oldest-old elders in Japan are able to do more, and more importantly, desire to do more than they are currently allowed or encouraged to do.

To summarize, I have argued that the norms of filial piety have made the family unit responsible for the total care of aged parents. Instrumental care (assistance with activities of daily living) of Japanese elders is now supported and provided by a range of subsidized senior services that started with the Gold Plan of 1989 and are now part of the newly established long-term care insurance program. Seniors as a group are being increasingly encouraged by the media and government organizations to remain socially active through continued work, travel, club participation, or hobbies. Yet society, caregiving family members, and the elderly themselves hold no such expectations for the very old. In other words, as the responsibility for the physical care of the elderly in Japan has moved from the family alone to that of the family and the community, the basic responsibility for the emotional and social support of oldest-old elders still lies firmly with the family.

Unfortunately, the structure of the Japanese family as it now exists does not allow for the oldest members to participate in a meaningful way in family life. The succession of clearly defined roles and obligations for members from childhood through grandparenthood, combined with the cultural norms of filial piety that call for deserved dependence and indulgence for aged parents, result in great-grandparents being left without authority or purpose in their own extended families. Organized social activities for the very old are available in day care services nationwide, but these programs are meant only for the disabled and dependent elderly. In fact, the norms of filial piety, still upheld by the oldest cohorts, work to discourage such participation in favor of increased dependence on the family.

The obstacles to overcoming these minimal expectations for the very old include general inexperience with oldest-old elders and widespread public assumptions of ill health, frailty, and dementia for the oldest cohort. Elders and family members alike have no role models on which to base appropriate behavior and expectations, for their own parents and grandparents died at younger ages. As long as coresidence alone is thought of as a sufficient measure of the well-being of an elderly person, the quality of life within that household will not be considered. Quality of life within a family context can lack meaningful interaction due to multiple factors. A poor or weak relationship between a parent and child (especially between in-laws) cannot be easily remedied in the last years of the parent's life, when he or she is in need of care. There is also a perceptible generation gap between family members raised and educated in prewar Japan and those raised in postwar prosperity and a reformed educational system. In addition, the changing structure and needs of modern family life have increasingly led to all members but the elderly parent being absent from the home most of the day.

Just as the lives and needs of the young-old and middle-old seniors in Japan have been addressed in the last decade, it is time to consider the desires for continued meaningful participation of very old elders as well. Until the wider society in urban Japan catches up with the demographic reality of a large, healthy cohort of elders over 85, and makes adjustments in assumptions regarding the aged, the environment, and community services, Japanese great-grandparents will continue to be left alone in the family.

Reference Matter

Glossary

Chinese

chi lun fan	吃輪飯	eat in rotation (among one's sons)
danguo	單過	"go it alone" or live separately
dingti	頂替	to substitute; replace parent at work
fengshui	風水	geomancy ("wind and water")
fu	福	good fortune
gat (C.), ji (M.)	吉	luck
guanxi	關係	social relationships
jin	斤	unit of weight equal to 1/2 kilogram
Jing lao yuan	敬老院	old people's home
laahttaat (C.)	辣㿺	dirty
lao	老	old; aged
Laotian	老天	Heavenly God
leih (C.), li (M.)	利	sharp (edged)
ling kaihuo	另開火	have a separate stove; cook separately
lunliu gongyang / lunyang	輪流供養、輪養	rotate among one's sons for support
mixin	迷信	superstitious
mu	畝	a unit of measure (approx. 1/6 of an acre)
sahnpoh (C.), shenpo (M.)	神婆	female spirit medium
shuo ke	說客	mediator ("persuasive speaker")
wangluo jiating	網絡家庭	networked families
xian zhi	縣誌	county annals (gazetteer)
xiao	孝	filial piety

xiaojing	孝敬	filial respect
xiaoshun	孝順	filial submission
zi	子	son
ziyou	自由	freedom
ziyou duole	自由多了	(have) "more freedom"

Japanese

adaruto chirudoren	アダルトチルドレン	"adult children"
Agonshū	阿含宗	a "new" Japanese religion
amae	甘え	indulgence; invited dependence
anshin	安心	feel relieved; rest assured
anzen	安全	safe; secure
arutsuhaimā	アルツハイマー	Alzheimer's disease
boke	ぼけ	senility
bunke	分家	a branch or secondary family
chihō	痴呆	dementia
chōnan	長男	eldest son
chū	忠	loyalty
enjo kōsai	援助交際	teen semi-prostitution ("assisted companionship")
fureai	触れ合い、ふれあい	emotionally warm contact or encounter
furui	古い	old; old-fashioned; dated
gakkyū hōkai	学級崩壊	classroom disruption
ganko	頑固	stubbornness; obstinacy; headstrong
gimu	義務	a duty
gosenzosama ga yorokobu	ご先祖様が喜ぶ	ancestors are happy/proud
gosenzosama ni mōshiwake nai	ご先祖様に申し訳ない	showing remorse to ancestors
heisoku	閉塞	social suffocation
hī-bāsan	ひいばあさん	great-grandmother
hikikomori	引きこもり	social withdrawal
hōkenteki	封建的	feudal
honke	本家	main or head family in the stem family system
ie	家	house; home; family line

ihai	位牌	Buddhist memorial (mortuary) tablets
iiko	いい子	good child
ijime	いじめ	bullying
ikigai	生きがい	a sense of purpose in life; something to live for
inkyo	隠居	traditional quarters for retired senior couple of ie household; retirement; a retired person
kakukazoku	核家族	nuclear family
katei	家庭	household
kateinai bōryoku	家庭内暴力	violence at home
kawaiiko	可愛い子	cute child
keirō kaikan	敬老会館	senior center ("Respect-for-the-aged hall")
kōkō, kō	孝行、孝	filial piety
kokutai	国体	national polity; 1930s wartime ideology of nation as an extended family with emperor as supreme head
Kurozumikyō	黒住教	a "new" Japanese religion
meiwaku	迷惑	a burden; trouble; annoyance; inconvenience
mukoyōshi	婿養子	a son-in-law adopted into his wife's family
musume	娘	daughter
naikan	内観	a Japanese therapy
netakiri	寝たきり	bedridden (immobile)
obāchan	おばあちゃん	grandma or granny
obasan	おばさん	aunt
Obasuteyama	おば捨て山	"Throw-out-granny mountain" folktale
ojōsan	お嬢さん	young lady (polite; can connote privileged status)
okāsan	お母さん	mother
okusan	奥さん	wife
on	恩	an obligation; a sense of moral indebtedness
oyakōkō	親孝行	filial piety

pokkuri	ぽっくり	suddenly (used in reference to a sudden death from acute causes versus one from prolonged illness)
rōjin kurabu, rōjin kai	老人クラブ、老人会	senior citizen club or association
sansedai kazoku	三世代家族	three-generation family
seiseki ga iiko	成績がいい子	high-achieving child
senpai	先輩	upper-class students
shikkari shiteiru	確りしている	silent perseverance against adversity (admirable)
shiran puri	知らんぷり	apathy
shitamachi	下町	downtown; working-class
sōgei basu	送迎バス	shuttle bus or van for senior care facilities ("welcome and send-off bus")
sōsobo	曽祖母	great-grandmother
sunao	素直	obedient
tenkō	転向	abandoning communism
tōkōkyohi	登校拒否	refusal to go to school
tomodachi no yōna oya	友達のような親	parents who are like friends
wagamama	我がまま	selfishness; self-centered
yome	嫁	daughter-in-law

Korean

anae	아내	wife (native Korean word)
annil	안일	housework ("inside labor")
chaebŏl	材閥	business conglomerate
chagi chungsim	自己中心	self-centered
chagŭn chip	작은 집	branch families ("little houses")
chesa	祭祀	ancestor worship ceremonies
ch'ilsun	七旬	seventieth birthday
Ch'ŏndogyo	天道教	a Korean syncretistic religion
chongjok maŭl	宗族 마을	lineage village
Ch'ŏnjugyo	天主教	Roman Catholicism
chŏnŏp chubu	專業主婦	full-time housewife
chŏnse	傳貰	key money
Ch'ŏnt'ae	天台	Tiantai (a sect of Buddhism)
Chosŏn Ilbo	朝鮮日報	*The Chosun Daily*

chubu	主婦	house mistress, wife
Chubu saenghwal	主婦生活	*House Mistress's Life*
ch'umo yebae	追慕禮拜	memorial service
chungsanch'ŭng	中産層	middle class
chungsanch'ŭng chubu	中産層 主婦	middle-class housewife
ch'usŏk	秋夕	Harvest Moon Festival
hoegap	回甲	sixtieth birthday
hoju	戶主	legal head of household
hwan'gap	還甲	sixtieth birthday
hyo	孝	filial piety
hyobu	孝婦	a filial wife (daughter-in-law)
hyodo kwan'gwang	孝道觀光	filial piety tourism
Hyo kyŏng	孝經	*Classic of Filial Piety*
hyoga saraya naraga samnida	孝가살아야 나라가 삽니다	The nation lives only if filial piety lives
hyoja	孝子	a filial son
hyonyŏ	孝女	a filial daughter
hyosang	孝償	a filial piety prize
insimi chot'a	人心이 좋다	good natured
Kaesin'gyo	改新敎	Protestantism (lit., "reformed")
kajŏng ŭirye chunch'ik	家庭儀禮準則	standard family ceremonies
kakpakhada	刻薄하다	to be heartless
Kidokkyo	基督敎	Christianity (Protestantism)
kobu kaltŭng	姑婦葛藤	mother-in-law/daughter-in-law conflict
Koryŏjang	高麗葬	abandoning the elderly
ku-il	九日	ninth day of the ninth lunar month
k'ŭn chip	큰 집	main family ("big house")
k'ŭn myŏnŭri	큰 며느리	senior daughter-in-law
kwangyŏk si	廣域市	Metropolitan City
kye	契	revolving credit club
maji	맏이	eldest son
man myŏnŭri	맏며느리	senior daughter-in-law
Myŏngsim pogam	明心寶鑑	*Precious Mirror for Enlightening the Mind*
noin munje	老人問題	problems of the aged
nunch'i pap	눈치밥	food eaten nervously while watched
pakkannil	바깥일	outside labor

p'alsun	八旬	eightieth birthday
Pari Kongju	바리 公主	Princess Pari
pumonim ŭl kigwan e naebŏrinŭn kŏt	부모님을 기관에 내버리는 것	throwing one's parents out into an institution
Pumo ŭnjung kyŏng	父母恩重經	Sutra of Parental Grace
purak chumin	部落 住民	village residents
pwip'e	뷔페	buffet
sangch'ŏng	喪廳	mourning shrine
sawŏn	社員	employee
Seoul saram	서울 사람	Seoul person
si	市	city (provincial level)
sigol saram	시골 사람	country person
silbŏ t'aun	실버타운	"silver town"
Sim Ch'ŏng	沈淸	[name of Korean epic heroine]
sisŏl	施設	a facility
soilgŏri	소일거리	idleness
sŏl	설	lunar new year
ssijok purak	氏族 部落	lineage village
subarhada	수발하다	to wait on
taesang	大祥	second anniversary ancestor worship
t'alsang	脫喪	ending of mourning
todŏk kyoyuk	道德敎育	moral education
tongjok purak	同族部落	lineage village
tongsŏng purak	同性部落	lineage village
t'ŭkpyŏl si	特別市	"special city" (Seoul only)
ttŭnaegi	뜨내기	itinerants; short-term residents
ŭmbok	飮福	meal following ancestor worship
ŭn	恩	parental grace
up	邑	urban township; county seat
uri maŭl saram	마을 사람	person(s) of our village
Wŏlgan Chosŏn	月刊朝鮮	*Monthly Korea*
wŏnjumin	原住民	native inhabitants
yangban	兩班	traditional officialdom; the notability
yangnowŏn	養老院	home for the aged

Notes

Chapter 1

1. Under the custom of patrilocal residence, couples in rural China today normally marry in the husband's village. Unless otherwise noted, in this chapter "parental household" refers to the household of the husband's parents; "parent" refers to the husband's parent.

2. The three rules of obedience refer to the social expectation that a woman be obedient to her father before marriage, to her husband after marriage, and to her sons in widowhood. The four virtues refer to a woman's fidelity, appearance, propriety, and needlework.

3. Individuals, especially those who were subordinates, had subcultures and family aspirations different from those acclaimed by mainstream culture. In Stone Mill, the daughter-in-law's hope was to have a household of her own, in which she was independent and in control; this was also the case for women in other areas (see, for example, Wolf 1972). An old folk saying features not only a woman's aspiration for her own household but also a militant sentiment against the repression of daughters-in-law exerted by the complex household:

> Standing by my stove,
> Getting hold of my cooking scoop,
> Even if I am poor, and even if I have to drink cold water, I still feel good.

The aspiration for one's own household is symbolized here by owning a stove and expressed by the willingness to give up a wealthier life in the parental household. Women's aspirations for households of their own, as shown later in the chapter, were finally achieved in the late twentieth century.

4. According to the state, the feudal marriage system was characterized by arranged marriage, bride purchases, concubinage, polygamy, and child brides. The patriarchal marriage–family system, which empowered men (over women) and the old (over the young), was feudal, backward, and oppressive, especially with regard

to women. A modern civilized marriage should be based on monogamous love, free choice in marriage partners, and the right to divorce. The Marriage Law (1950, 1980) outlawed traditional practices and established the individual's right (rather than the parents' right) to choose his/her spouse and to share in family property. See Meijer (1971) for the marriage laws (or regulations) of the PRC and the earlier Chinese Soviet Republic, as well as the official interpretations of and elaboration on the marriage laws and the feudal marriage–family system.

5. Many studies have been conducted on changes in the Chinese family during the socialist period and the postsocialist period (especially during the 1980s). For a comprehensive view of aspects of change in the Chinese family during the socialist period, see Parish and Whyte (1978); for changes during the postsocialist period, see a collection of papers in Davis and Harrell (1993), and papers in Rural Economic Reforms and Chinese Family Patterns (A Symposium on Rural Family Change), a special issue of *China Quarterly* (no. 130, 1992).

6. Indeed, in order to compensate for the lack of a rural welfare system, the state made great efforts to enhance, legally as well as ideologically, care of elderly by their families. However, because of the proximity of houses in Chinese villages, care of elderly people does not require coresidence. Moreover, the custom of an elderly parent coresiding with a son or rotating residence among his/her sons has ensured that the elderly are taken care of in their later years.

7. Villagers' views on intergenerational relationships were collected from interviews, as well as from their answers to open-ended survey questions: "How should children/parents treat parents/children?" "Do you agree with the popular saying that 'children will always be children before their parents?'" and "What does a good happy life (*fu*) mean to you?"

Chapter 2

This chapter is based upon research funded by the Wenner-Gren Foundation for Anthropological Research, Gr. 6170. I am deeply indebted to the hospitable people of Lijia who opened their lives to me, and to Qi Li for her assistance in deciphering the handwritten and poorly photocopied division contracts.

1. Recognizing the importance of sons to support in old age, the government in many rural areas allows people who have a daughter a second chance to have a son. Two only-children who marry will also be allowed to have two children.

2. Lijia is a pseudonym.

3. Cohen also discusses the significance of the fact that the father typically does not sign the contract along with the sons and refers to it as a succession rather than an inheritance (1998: 116ff.).

4. This means the parents will rotate between the sons' homes.

Chapter 4

Research for this chapter was first carried out during my fieldwork in China in 1993–94, and subsequently in the summer of 2002. My research was supported by a Dissertation Fieldwork Grant from the Wenner-Gren Foundation for Anthropological Research, and by a Colby College Humanities Grant in 2002. I would like to thank Charlotte Ikels, David Nugent, and Constantine Hriskos for comments on earlier drafts. The editorial help of my colleague Kim Besio is also greatly appreciated.

1. During the prereform era and the initial years of the reforms, urban workers, especially those in the state sector, enjoyed a free health care system based on the workplace. However, since the 1990s, when marketization of state enterprises went into full swing, China's health care system has undergone some fundamental changes. As a result, a new contribution-based system administered by local governments has come into being. Under this new system, employees (including retirees) contribute a certain percentage (4–8 percent) of their salary or pension to a medical insurance plan. When seeking medical help, they also have to pay a certain percentage of the total cost, the exact amount varying from work unit to work unit and from region to region (Gu 2001; Ikels 1996; Saunders and Shang 2001; White 1998). While more recent reports and studies show that urban retirees are increasingly paying more out of pocket, especially if their original work units have gone bankrupt or ceased to exist (Li 1999; Wang, Bai, and Jia 1997; Zhang 2001), their lot is still much better than that of their rural counterparts, who are not entitled to any medical coverage at all.

2. The data were obtained in two steps. The initial data about villagers older than 60 were gathered from the village's household registration book. Then, with the help of both the village cadres and Zhongshan informants, I conducted a survey of living arrangements. My survey reveals that most of the elderly parents who were currently living separately from their adult children were actually listed in a stem household structure (that is, under either their son's or daughter's household) in the household registration book. This indicates that information on family composition and living arrangements gathered from household registrations can be misleading. The data in Table 1 represent the actual living arrangements of Zhongshan's elderly, not arrangements according to the village's household registration book.

3. The widow has a uxorilocally married daughter in the village too. However, the daughter was not obligated to support her mother since parental support was divided between her and her brother so that she only supported her father while her brother was supposed to do the same for the mother.

4. Interestingly, the same term, *danguo,* is also used for what Cohen describes as now almost a standard procedure preceding family division in Chinese rural

households. According to Cohen, danguo "involves separation in eating and economic life, but it is not the same as family division or *fenjia* . . . [which is] the settlement once and for all of the distribution of family assets and obligations" (Cohen 1998: 110–11). However, the danguo arrangement discussed by Cohen usually refers to the situation in which a married son splits from his parents. In Zhongshan, when an elderly parent or parents move out of the stem family and start living separately, they are also said to danguo. These parents must take care of their own daily needs but they are still entitled to support from their children. In other words, the economic tie is not completely cut in this separate living arrangement.

5. This is the same father I quoted above who claimed that living separately from his son had given him much more freedom (*ziyou duole*).

6. While there seems to be a general decline of filial practices in the care of the elderly, some ritual manifestations of filial piety with regard to proper funerals and burials remain strong. In fact, because of recent economic prosperity and a more liberal social environment, funeral ceremonies for parents have become much more elaborate and expensive. The irony lies in that the children seemed to be more willing to spend the money on and invest the effort in funeral rituals than seeking medical help and providing care for their parents when they were still alive. There are several possible reasons for this. But I think it certainly has a lot to do with regaining or maintaining the reputation of the family in the community. Funerals of parents are very much public events, and an elaborate and expensive funeral is often seen as an act of filial behavior. Even though the children may not have acted filially when their parents were alive, if they gave their deceased parents a decent and proper funeral, they would "be forgiven" by the community, for at least they did something acceptable and appropriate in the eyes of their fellow villagers and relatives.

7. Four months after I interviewed this couple in early 1994, the husband died in the small hut where he and his wife had been living. He was already bedridden and had a lung disease when I interviewed him. He never got any medical treatment as he had no money for a doctor and his sons refused to pay.

8. The Standing Committee of the People's Congress passed the Law Regarding the Rights and Security of the Elderly in the PRC (Zhonghua renmin gongheguo laonianren quanyi baozhang fa).

9. The most common complaint in this respect is that old people have different food requirements and that they cannot eat what they like. There are also differences due to education and modern ways of life.

10. For an excellent discussion of the transformation of family relations from the vertical father-son axis to the conjugal husband-wife tie in contemporary rural China, see Yan (1997).

11. I obtained this figure in a trip to China in the summer of 2000. Suicide among the rural elderly is a subject that needs further study. My guess is that the situation is very serious. There is yet not much research on this issue. Data may also be difficult to obtain since no autopsy is performed if the deceased is elderly, and facts may be covered up since parental suicide causes great controversy and embarrassment for the family and the local community. In a report published by *Legal Daily* (*Fazhi ribao*), parental abuse and neglect were blamed for the deaths of at least 187 elderly residents of rural Zhejiang between 1989 and 1990 (cited in Ikels 1993).

12. In my most recent follow-up research in the summer of 2002, the number of elderly parents living alone was even higher; out of the 144 elderly over 60 years of age in Zhongshan, seventy-eight or 54 percent were living separately from their adult children, compared to 23 percent in 1994.

Chapter 5

1. Van der Sprenkel (1962: 150) provides extracts from the *Zuozhi yaoyan* or Precepts for Local Administrative Officials by Wang Huizu, which was first printed in 1785. Wang, who served as a legal secretary for sixteen different magistrates, based the Precepts on his own experience. He advised respecting local customs.

> The primary study for a legal secretary is to know the code, but skill in its application depends still more on being in sympathy with the ways of the people. Now as customs vary from place to place, it is essential to find out all about them, without preconceptions, and make it your chief concern to abide by them. If you never act on a penal law or an edict without first seeing that it does not conflict with what local custom values, then there will be harmony between yamen and people . . . whereas applying the law rigidly on every occasion would probably give rise to much dissatisfaction and complaint.

2. The Chinese government's position on religious practice is complex. Religious organizations formally associated with Buddhism, Daoism, Islam, and Christianity are required to register and may own property, run schools, and hold services, including funeral services. More religiously or spiritually eclectic organizations, Falun Gong being a conspicuous example, are viewed with suspicion, denied registration, and forbidden to conduct services. Chinese popular religion is largely a set of local beliefs and practices derived from Buddhism and Daoism as well as containing an admixture of officially disfavored beliefs and practices, such as spirit possession (shamanism), that are labeled "feudal superstition."

3. According to an article in *China Daily* (Zheng and Zhou 2001), Guangdong Province at the end of 2000 had a cremation rate of 80 percent—40 percentage points higher than the national average. As a result, from 1998 to 2000 the

province saved more than 580 hectares of farmland and more than 170,000 cubic meters of timber, and the families of the deceased saved more than 5.9 billion yuan (US$714.5 million) in funeral expenses over the same period.

4. How the dead and their graves could be utilized by families and lineages for political purposes is illustrated in Rubie Watson (1988).

5. Described in J. Watson (1988). Based on historical studies and his own field-work in Hong Kong's rural New Territories in the 1970s and early 1980s, Watson discerned nine distinct actions associated with the funeral rite itself (not including additional actions associated with body disposition and memorialization). In a vil-lage in which people mostly died at home, these nine actions were: (1) public noti-fication of death by wailing; (2) donning of white clothes by mourners; (3) ritual-ized bathing of the corpse; (4) transfer of food, money, and goods to the deceased; (5) preparation and installation of a soul tablet; (6) ritualized use of money and the employment of professionals; (7) music to accompany and calm the spirit of the deceased; (8) sealing the corpse in an airtight container; and (9) expulsion of the coffin from the community (pp. 12–15).

6. I am grateful to the Committee for Scholarly Communication with China for funding to carry out the 1991 and 1998 research and to the Armington Profes-sorship at Case Western Reserve University for additional support for the 1998 research.

7. The term "cadre" designates a government (local, provincial, or national level) official or, more broadly, a government employee (civil servant). A cadre is not necessarily a Communist Party member, though the higher a cadre's rank the greater the probability of Party membership and the more stringently s/he will be required to follow state policies. I am using the term "cadre" to refer to a govern-ment official.

8. All names are pseudonyms.

9. Mrs. Jeung's son and daughter-in-law, both older than 60 themselves, pro-vided many examples of people who wanted to touch the corpse and wear the clothes of the deceased for their longevity-begetting qualities, but lamented the fact that people brought up in the city and even young people in the village today no longer share these ideas.

10. See Ahern (1973) for a discussion of the linkage between inheritance and responsibility for mortuary rites and memorialization.

11. Also in 1998 Guangdong issued new regulations mandating cremation in all jurisdictions under the city, not only the official urban districts but also the "county level cities," that is, whole counties that had newly been promoted to city status, such as Panyu, where Mrs. Jeung had been buried. See *Guangzhou ribao* (1998b).

12. Here and elsewhere "C." stands for "Cantonese term." Cantonese terms are

used when no equivalent standard (Mandarin) Chinese term is available or when a play on words in Cantonese is not meaningful in standard Chinese as the words are no longer homonyms.

13. The permanent ash storage facility represented one of Guangzhou's first joint ventures with foreign investors involving services related to body disposition. The facility was funded by a company from Taiwan around 1993–94. Demand was so high that people bought multiple spaces and treated them as real estate investments. The city government was completely taken aback and closed the facility. However, there are people in Guangzhou who believe that just as other fields, such as manufacturing, hotels, and restaurants, have been opened to investors, so should the funeral industry. See Fan (2000).

Chapter 6

This chapter is drawn from a larger, collaborative survey project and from the volume that reports many of the principal findings of that project: Martin K. Whyte, ed., *China's Revolutions and Intergenerational Relations* (Ann Arbor: University of Michigan Center for Chinese Studies, 2003). An earlier version of this chapter appeared in a Chinese journal. See Whyte (2001).

1. The twenty-four examples include a 70-year-old filial son who dressed and played as a child in order to amuse his even more elderly parents and another son who threw himself against an attacking tiger in order to save his parents. See the translation by Ivan Chen (1910). That volume also includes a translation of the *Classic of Filial Piety* (*Xiaojing*), one of the thirteen "sacred books" of Confucianism. In the Chinese legal system of late imperial times, it was permissible to sell or even kill a disobedient child, while striking a parent was a capital offense.

2. See, for example, the case of successful Chinese restaurateurs in London who remained obedient and filial toward their (often much poorer) parents living in New Territories villages in Hong Kong, as described in Watson (1975).

3. For example, in 1995 Taiwan was estimated to have a GNP per capita of U.S.$12,396, in contrast to the PRC's estimated U.S.$620. Similarly, in that same year 87 percent of the youths of suitable age in Taiwan were enrolled in secondary schools, and 26 percent in tertiary schools, in contrast to 55 percent and 4 percent estimated for the PRC. Figures for Taiwan from Council for Economic Planning and Development, ROC (1997) (for GNP per capita) and Directorate-General of Budgets, Accounting, and Statistics, ROC (1996) (for school enrollments). Figures for the PRC are from World Bank (1997).

4. Authorities have estimated that through the 1980s at least, something like 80–95 percent of all firms on Taiwan were family-run, with no clear signs of decline in their importance. (However, given the small size of such family firms, they

accounted for a considerably smaller proportion of total economic output on the island.) See Greenhalgh (1988).

5. See Dickson (1997). In the mid-1980s the ROC instituted further political reforms and became a democratic regime, while on the mainland the political liberalization launched by Deng Xiaoping after 1978 pushed that regime in a direction away from totalitarianism and toward authoritarianism.

6. In subsequent pages, the terms "modern" and "traditional" will follow the usage of Goode's version of the then-fashionable modernization theory, rather than an interpretation derived from postmodernism or other more recently fashionable theoretical schemes.

7. Primary support for the survey project came from a grant from the Luce Foundation to the University of Michigan, where the author was teaching at the time. In the 1990 census Baoding had a population in its urban districts of about 600,000, making it a middle-sized city. We cannot claim that any one city, and Baoding in particular, is representative of all urban areas in the PRC. However, at the same time the very ordinariness of Baoding probably makes it more representative of urban China generally than the large cities that have more often been studied—for instance Beijing, Shanghai, or Guangzhou.

8. Specifically, I am greatly indebted to my former colleague, Albert Hermalin, who was the principal investigator for the Taiwan surveys and also a member of the research team for the Baoding survey. Many of the specific results from the Taiwan surveys that I draw on in later portions of this chapter come from papers and reports authored by Hermalin and his Taiwan project collaborators.

9. One major exception to this generalization occurred during the Cultural Revolution decade (1966–76). Millions of urban secondary school graduates were mobilized to settle in the countryside and become farmers. However, after Mao's death and the launching of China's economic reforms in 1978, almost all of these "sent-down intellectual youths" were allowed to return to their cities of origin. So even in this case the end result, for most youths raised in Baoding, was an eventual job in that same city.

10. One compilation of estimates provided figures of 56–71 percent of parents over age 60 on Taiwan living with a married child, and 38–52 percent for parents over age 60 in urban areas of the PRC. See Logan, Bian, and Bian (unpublished: table 1). Figures on extended family residence of the elderly in rural China are generally even higher. For example, an ethnographic study of a village in Heilongjiang shows that 64 percent of those over age 60 were living with a married child in the mid-1990s. Figures computed from Yan (2003: chap. 7). Note also the figure of 60 percent of elderly parents in a Hubei village living in stem families, noted by Zhang in Chapter 4, Table 1.

11. See the discussion of the growing acceptance of "networked families" in urban China in Unger (1993).

12. For example, of the respondents between ages 50 and 59, 82 percent of the men were still employed, but only 30 percent of the women. At the other end of the age scale, 96 percent of the men over age 70 were receiving pensions, but only 29 percent of the women. These disparities stem from various features of the employment system of socialist China, including the adoption of Soviet-style earlier retirement ages for women and having more women either not regularly employed or working in small collective, rather than state, enterprises—that is, firms that did not provide pensions.

13. Only about 3 percent of our Baoding parent respondents had no income of their own and no spouse with earnings.

14. One generalization from gerontological research around the world is that in developing countries the flow of assistance between generations tends to move upward from grown children to parents, while in developed countries it more often flows downward, from aging parents to grown children. This developmental shift is the central focus of John Caldwell's theory of the demographic transition. See Caldwell (1982).

15. See Whyte (1997: esp. table 3). To cite some specific examples, parents more than their adult children agreed with the view that public property is superior to private and that comradeship is a higher form of relationship than friendship, but at the same time they were also more likely to agree with a statement that there would be chaos unless society is ruled by single set of common values and that the family is happiest when the man works and the wife takes care of the family. Adult children not only spoke more in favor of private property and friendship, but also were more likely than their parents to say that either a man or a woman could have a happy life without marrying.

16. For further details see ibid. Note the paradoxical fact that Zhang's essay in the present volume (Chapter 4), based upon fieldwork in a village in Hubei, reports less general support for stem family living by both the young and the old than we found in Baoding. Perhaps the more crucial nature of support from grown children in rural China produces more conflicts and anxieties than in urban China when the generations do coreside.

17. Research on intergenerational relations in the United States has also found a similar tendency for each generation to stress their obligations more than their needs in relation to the other generation. See Logan and Spitze (1995).

18. To be sure, if we cumulate these various forms of assistance, then more than 50 percent of Baoding parents are receiving at least one kind of specific assistance from their parents—to be specific, about two thirds. But still that leaves a

substantial minority of parents—the remaining one third—who do not report receiving any regular support from their grown children of the types we inquired about.

19. Before controlling for other variables, it initially looks as if married sons are more likely to provide cash assistance to parents than married daughters, and that they give somewhat larger amounts of cash when they do. However, when one controls for other variables (and particularly for the fact that males have higher incomes than females and sons are more likely to coreside with parents than daughters), it turns out that the net effect of being a daughter on financial assistance is negligible and not statistically significant. On the other hand, married daughters are more likely to provide material goods (for example, food and clothing) to their own parents, and this is still the case even after statistical controls have been applied. For more details on the comparison of support from sons and daughters, see Whyte and Xu (2003). In some areas of rural China it is common for young brides to return often to their natal families in the early years of their marriages and to continue to provide some help and assistance (see Judd 1989). However, unless the stem family is uxorilocal, the long-term dependence of rural parents is on their married sons, not their married daughters. See, for example, the discussions in Chapters 2 and 4 in the current volume.

20. The reader should bear in mind that the figures provided for Baoding in this section differ somewhat from those presented earlier, since now we are restricting our attention to only those parents aged 60 and over, not the full sample of parents above age 50.

21. The remainder of the cases involve living with unmarried children (23 percent in Taiwan; 13 percent in Baoding) and in some other arrangement (8 percent in Taiwan, 2 percent in Baoding).

22. Mainlanders, originally primarily the predominantly male migrants who fled to the island with Chiang Kai-shek in 1949, tend to have a less traditional family profile due at least in part to their unusual demographic features. For example, more of the older Mainlanders than Taiwanese are males, and an unusually high proportion of them are unmarried (if we discount wives left behind in China) or married to much younger women. See the discussion in Thornton and Lin (1994).

23. To be sure, if we had data on the rural elderly in the PRC we would find that very few of them are receiving pensions. Still, these data for Taiwan provide a striking indication that much employment even in *urban* Taiwan does not take the form of bureaucratic corporations and public agencies that provide retirement pensions and other modern fringe benefits.

24. The Mainlanders show an even more prominent role of the spouse than do

Baoding parents, but a much less prominent role of the daughter (as well as the daughter-in-law), in comparison to the Taiwanese.

25. To be specific, only 2 percent of parents and 3 percent of adult children were either self-employed or working (or had worked, in the case of retired parents) in a private firm. Similarly, only 1 percent of parents and 5 percent of children were renting privately owned housing from others.

Chapter 7

1. Average household size was more difficult to calculate in 1999 as some persons shared our own peripatetic lifestyle, living part-time in the village and part-time elsewhere.

2. For a study of this massive rural exodus, see Koo (1990). In 1960, 58 percent of the South Korean population lived in farm households; by 1995, less than 11 percent did (Korea National Statistical Office 1961: 18, 83; 1998: 114).

3. Another of the state's interventions was ordering the rearrangement of rice paddies, consolidating each household's often scattered and irregularly defined plots into a larger rectangular plot suitable for mechanical plowing, transplanting, and harvesting.

Chapter 8

1. The obligation to support one's parents is found in the family law section of the Civil Code, and has been there since the founding of the Republic of Korea.

2. The World Bank classifies countries as low income, lower middle income, higher middle income, and high income. The nominal per capita income benchmark for high income is around $10,000 per year. South Korea had long been the most affluent of the upper middle income countries and before the 1997 currency crisis had joined the Organization for Economic Cooperation and Development and been classified as high income. The fall in income measured in dollars consequent to the 1997 currency crisis has knocked South Korea out of the high income category for the time being, but it is likely that it will regain momentum as it addresses its economic and structural problems.

3. In 1995, 26.1 percent of the population over age 6 were in school, 65.3 percent were graduated from school, and 2.1 percent were dropouts (mostly from high school or college). Only 6.5 percent had no schooling, and most of these were females over 60.

4. Ch'ŏndogyo, or Religion of the Heavenly Way, founded in the late nineteenth century, syncretizes indigenous folk religion, Chinese philosophy, and Christianity. It was important to the nationalist movement during the colonial period (1910–45), and the period immediately after liberation. In 1960, 1.5 percent of

the population reported themselves to be Catholic, 4.9 percent Protestant, and 5.3 percent Ch'ŏndogyo. As lay Buddhism was not yet well developed, equivalent figures are not available for Buddhism. In 1995, 23.2 percent of the population were Buddhist, 19.7 percent Protestant, 6.6 percent Catholic, 0.5 percent Confucian, and only 0.6 percent Ch'ŏndogyo. Almost half (49.3 percent) reported no religion.

5. We define stem family as any family that includes a married couple and one or more parents regardless of the number of generations, or whether the married couple have children. The most common stem family has three generations.

6. Dr. Kim teaches at Inje University in Kimhae, and thus could conveniently conduct and supervise interviews there.

7. Metropolitan cities (*kwangyŏk si*) are generally cities with a population over a million that have been made administratively separate from their surrounding province. South Korea presently has five metropolitan cities in addition to the "special city" (*t'ŭkpyol si*) of Seoul.

8. Masan was a sleepy town of 158,000 in 1965, but by 1975 was an industrial city of 372,000. Pusan grew similarly from 1,521,000 in 1965 to 2,519,000 in 1975.

9. The term *chungsanch'ŏng* means literally "those with middling amounts of property" and so tends to refer to a slightly higher social level than the term "middle class" usually implies in English.

10. We did not formally ask informants their educational status until halfway through the interviews. Of the twenty-seven for whom we have data, 6.4 percent ended their schooling with the ninth grade, 14.9 percent with the twelfth grade, 4.3 percent with trade school, 17.0 percent with four years of college, and 14.9 percent (most of whom were professors) with a graduate education.

11. Dr. Kim conducted twenty-two interviews, and Ms. Lee twenty-five. Before participating in this project, Ms. Lee already had experience in surveying and interviewing. Before conducting interviews, Dr. Kim discussed with her the kinds of responses expected from the interviewees and how to redirect the interviewees' attention to the issues when necessary. Ms. Lee accompanied Dr. Kim on about ten of his twenty-two interview sessions to learn how to conduct an anthropological interview, and Dr. Kim directly supervised about five of her twenty-five interviews.

12. "Stem form" consists of a married couple with or without children (most had children) coresiding with at least one parent.

13. For this question we excluded unmarried informants coresident with their parents.

14. The question of secular change in coresidence will be dealt with below.

15. Thirteen percent of the lower-middle-class families and 16.6 percent of the lower-class families were stem. As the lower-class percentage includes only one case, it is not significantly different from the lower-middle-class percentage.

16. These seven informants included those whose parents were dead at the time of the interview, but who reported living with their parents from the time of their marriage until the time of their parents' death. Thus, at the time of the interviews, not all of these families were in stem form.

17. *Chubu* and *anae* both mean wife, but in different senses. Anae, a homely word of native Korean origin, means literally "she inside" and is used mostly frequently by husbands to refer to their own wives in a humble, but also often affectionate, sense. (It would be uncultured to use this term of somebody else's wife, unless that person was an intimate friend.) Chubu, on the other hand, is of Chinese origin and means literally "ruling wife." The chubu is the woman in the house who is in a position of authority. One of the most popular women's magazines in Korea is titled *Chubu saenghwal,* which could be translated accurately (if awkwardly) as "House Mistress's Life." We use mistress here, of course, in the old sense of "woman of authority," and not in the derived sense of "illicit sexual companion."

18. Since several of our young female informants gave us a very positive assessment of stem families and their desire to live in them, however, avoidance of stem family form must be viewed as a tendency rather than a norm.

19. This is so much the case that middle-class housewives (*chungsanch'ŭng chubu*) are sometimes criticized as "familistic and antisocial" and thus incapable of contributing fully to the national economy and society (Mun 1992).

20. Those in services were all lower class.

21. At the exchange rates prevailing at the time of the interview this would come to about $25 per person, leading to an estimated cost for the food alone in the range of $15,000.

22. The period of mourning actually ends with the second anniversary when the *taesang* rite is held at the tomb of the deceased.

23. When Koreans say "Christian" (*kidokkyo*) they generally mean Protestant. Catholics are allowed to do the traditional bows of chesa, but Protestants are not.

24. Some informants expressed skepticism about whether Christianity promotes filial piety, however.

25. The Civil Code before 1989 provided that the eldest son *must* succeed to the position of head of household and that the person who succeeds to that position should receive twice what other children receive, regardless of other considerations. The revised code removed the provision preventing the eldest son from partitioning, and allowed parents to reward other children regardless of their birth order or gender.

26. Six of our informants spontaneously mentioned suffering for the sake of one's parents as an aspect of filial piety.

Chapter 9

This chapter has benefited greatly from helpful comments and suggestions by David Barnard, L. Keith Brown, Charlotte Ikels, and John Traphagan. It has also benefited from valuable research assistance by Yasumi Moroishi.

1. On the state promulgations *Senji katei kyōiku shidō ni kansuru ken* issued in 1942 and *Ie no hongi* issued in 1943, see Sekiguchi et al. (2000).

2. Reported in the television broadcast NHK special "Shirikon barē no chōsensha" (The challengers of Silicon Valley), Nov. 26, 2000.

Chapter 10

Research for this chapter was supported by a variety of funding agencies. I am appreciative of the Wenner-Gren Foundation for Anthropological Research, the Northeast Asia Council of the Association for Asian Studies, and the Michigan Exploratory Center for the Demography of Aging, which supported fieldwork during 1998. Fieldwork in the summer of 2000 was supported by grant AG016111 from the National Institute on Aging to study religion, well-being, and aging in Japan. I am particularly grateful to Dr. Tamotsu Kawamura of Iwate University for his help in locating some of the data used in this chapter.

1. As is customary, names of all informants are pseudonyms in order to protect their privacy.

2. Tōhoku is the name collectively used for the northernmost six prefectures of the main island of Honshū: Akita, Aomori, Fukushima, Iwate, Miyagi, and Yamagata.

3. See Traphagan (2000a) for a discussion of urban-rural migration and Iwate Prefecture. Also see Fukurai (1991) for a detailed discussion of migration patterns in Japan as a whole.

4. Traditionally, the man would take the wife's name and become listed on her family register. Increasingly, although a man may be willing to coreside with his wife's family, it is common for him to retain his family name and for the wife to take his name.

5. This information is taken from an interview conducted by Jennifer Mc-Dowell, who worked as a research assistant on my grant from the National Institute on Aging.

6. I have never run into a male who has complained about the reverse. Typically a man who marries into his wife's family does so with the expectation that he will take on the responsibility as successor and with the expectation that he has come into the household with the wife's approval for his taking on this role.

7. As Clark (1999) points out, this by no means suggests the woman has sev-

ered relations with her natal household and may still have very close interpersonal ties with her consanguineal kin. However, there is a sense that she has become a part of her husband's household and has specific responsibilities, including provision of health care to his parents, based upon her position in the household.

8. Fujiwara-san (junior) indicated that there are other reasons for building a two-generation house, one being avoidance of heavy inheritance taxes. Fujiwara-san (senior) indicated his son would receive all of the inheritance, in return for which he expected that, should the need arise, his son would take care of his parents in the future.

9. Portions of the dialogue from this interview also appear in Traphagan (2003).

10. As Jenike (1997) notes, the amount of work involved in caring for a hospitalized family member is considerably more than is typical in the United States. Family members, usually a daughter or daughter-in-law, are expected to stay with the hospitalized person day and night and to bring food and to help in bathing and other needs.

Chapter 11

This chapter is based on chapters 1 and 4 of my doctoral dissertation (Jenike 2002), the research for which was funded by the Japan Foundation. I am grateful to Hayashi Wakako and the staff of the day care center in Suginami for allowing me access to their facility, and to Toda Risaku for his initial introduction. I am indebted to Leng Leng Thang, Mariko Tamanoi, John Traphagan, David Plath, and Takako Sodei for advice during fieldwork; and to Mariko, John, Charlotte Ikels, Francesca Bray, Susan Phillips, and Douglas Hollan for their suggestions on earlier drafts. I am especially grateful to the seniors at the center whose company and friendship I so enjoyed.

1. Personal names have been changed to protect privacy.

2. According to the 1998 basic survey of national life, 50.3 percent of seniors aged 65 and over living at home were residing with an adult child, 32.3 percent were living with a spouse, and 13.2 percent were living alone, with the remaining 4.2 percent living with family members other than a son or daughter. In 1995, 67 percent of those aged 85 and over were living with an adult child, down from 81 percent in 1975 (Kōseishō 2000: 20–21).

3. For modified versions of this pattern of succession and inheritance see Kitaoji (1971).

The most important principle was neither primogeniture nor preservation of the bloodline, but the perpetuation of the family line through the recruitment of two permanent *ie* members—a married couple—in each generation (Bachnik 1983; Befu 1962; Kondo 1990; Plath 1964).

4. Sometimes nicknames are adopted to solve the confusion. For example, Mrs. Furusaki's (age 88) great-grandchildren call her daughter, who lives on the second floor of their home, *ton-ton obāchan*, because of the noise she makes when she walks up and down the stairs. Mrs. Furusaki, who lives on the first floor, is simply called *obāchan*.

5. The applicability of this statement to an elder's experience in areas outside of Tokyo is in question. Unlike in rural communities, or older urban communities, there is a greater occurrence of displacement for elderly residents in Tokyo. Often the elderly of Tokyo have moved from their native communities to Tokyo as an older adult in order to reside with their children. Even for those who have resided all their adult lives in Tokyo, their communities have radically changed during the postwar period, from rural to urban. Elderly in Tokyo, therefore, often suffer from disruptions in their social network, and do not share common experiences, life histories, or identities with their neighbors as do elderly in rural communities. On rural elderly, see Bernstein (1996) and Traphagan (2000a); for a comparative study of urban and rural elderly, see Kumagai (1987).

6. The government deems one to two six-hour days per week sufficient respite for family caregivers and adequate social interaction for seniors. Dependent seniors in need of further assistance can apply for a home helper from their local social welfare office or hire one from a private firm. Although there are private and nonprofit alternatives for home helper service, I knew of only the public program for day care service at the time of my fieldwork.

7. The haiku I include were composed at the day care center as part of a class. The haiku teacher would correct these poems to include the convention of a seasonal reference. I present the uncorrected versions for they more accurately convey the seniors' intent.

8. Shortcomings of day care service stem largely from inexperienced staff and an inflexible, institutional structure dictated by bureaucrats and national guidelines rather than by those actually working with the seniors. From my observations, the main drawback of day care compared to organizations led by seniors themselves is the lack of autonomy and agency allowed participating seniors. The day care I volunteered at was at times run like a day care for children. This was not the case, though, at long-established day care centers, with older, more experienced staff.

References

Ahern, Emily Martin. 1973. *The Cult of the Dead in a Chinese Village*. Stanford, CA: Stanford University Press.

Akita-ken nōgyō kyōdō kumiai chūō kai (Akita Prefecture Farming Cooperative Central Association). 1999. *Kennai shichōson betsu no nōka jinko to nōgyō rōdō chikara no dōkō* (Trends in City, Town, and Village Farm Population and Farm Labor Strength within the Prefecture). Akita: Akita-ken nōgyō kyōdō kumiai chūō kai.

Anbäcken, Els-Marie. 1997. *Who Cares? Culture, Structure, and Agency in Caring for the Elderly in Japan*. Stockholm East Asian monographs no. 9. Stockholm: Stockholm University.

Arichi Tōru. 1977. *Kindai Nihon no kazokukan: Meiji hen* (Modern Japanese Views of the Family: Meiji Period). Tokyo: Kōbundō.

Ariyoshi, Sawako. 1984. *The Twilight Years*. Trans. Mildred Tahara. New York: Kodansha.

Asahi shinbun, Akita shikyoku (Asahi Daily, Akita Branch Office), ed. 2000. *Jisatsu: Jisatsuritsu zenkoku ichi—Akita kara no hōkoku* (Suicide: National Suicide Rate Number One—Report from Akita). Akita: Mumyōsha shuppan.

Asahi Shinbun Japan Almanac 1999. 1998. Tokyo: Asahi shinbunsha.

Bachnik, Jane M. 1983. Recruitment strategies for household succession: Rethinking Japanese household organization. *Man* 18: 160–82.

Becker, Gary. S. 1981. *A Treatise on the Family*. Cambridge, MA: Harvard University Press.

Befu, Harumi. 1962. Corporate emphasis and patterns of descent in the Japanese family. In *Japanese Culture: Its Development and Characteristics*, ed. Robert J. Smith and Richard K. Beardsley, 34–41. Chicago: Aldine.

Bellah, Robert N. 1991. Father and son in Christianity and Confucianism. In *Beyond Belief: Essays on Religion in a Post-Traditional World*, 76–99. Berkeley: University of California Press.

Benedict, Ruth. 1946. *The Chrysanthemum and the Sword.* Boston: Houghton Mifflin.

Bernstein, Gail Lee. 1996. *Haruko's World: A Japanese Farm Woman and Her Community.* 2nd ed. Stanford, CA: Stanford University Press.

Bethel, Diana Lynn. 1992. Life on Obasuteyama, or, Inside a Japanese institution for the elderly. In *Japanese Social Organization,* ed. Takie Sugiyama Lebra, 109–34. Honolulu: University of Hawaii Press.

Bourdieu, Pierre. 1990. *The Logic of Practice.* Trans. Richard Nice. Stanford, CA: Stanford University Press.

Brandt, Vincent S. R. 1971. *A Korean Village between Farm and Sea.* Cambridge, MA: Harvard University Press.

Brinton, Mary C. 1992. Christmas cakes and wedding cakes: The social organization of Japanese women's life course. In *Japanese Social Organization,* ed. Takie Sugiyama Lebra, 79–107. Honolulu: University of Hawaii Press.

Brown, Keith. 1966. Dōzoku and descent ideology in Japan. *American Anthropologist* 68: 1129–51.

Cai Fang and Zhang Chewei. 2000. *2000 Nian: Zhongguo renkou wenti baogao—Nongcun renkou wenti jiqi zhili* (Year 2000: Report on China's Population Problems—Rural Population Problems and Their Solutions). Beijing: Shehui kexue wenxian chubanshe.

Caldwell, John C. 1981. The mechanisms of demographic change in historical perspective. *Population Studies* 35(1): 5–27.

———. 1982. *Theory of Fertility Decline.* New York: Academic Press.

Calhoun, Michael. 2001. *The Silver Market: New Opportunities in a Graying Japan and United States.* New York: Japan Society.

Campbell, John Creighton. 1992. *How Policies Change: The Japanese Government and the Aging Society.* Princeton, NJ: Princeton University Press.

Central Intelligence Agency. 2001. *The World Factbook 2001.* Jan. 2, 2002. [www.cia.gov/cia/publications/factbook/index/html].

Chai, Ch'u, and Winberg Chai. 1965. *The Sacred Books of Confucius and other Confucian Classics.* New Hyde Park, NY: University Books.

Chan, Angelique. 1997. An overview of the living arrangements and social support exchanges of older Singaporeans. *Asia-Pacific Population Journal* 12(4): 35–50.

Chang Chung-li. 1955. *The Chinese Gentry: Studies on Their Role in Nineteenth-Century Chinese Society.* Seattle: University of Washington Press.

Chang, Yun-Shik. 1989. From filial piety to the love of children. In *The World Community in Post-Industrial Society: Changing Families in the World Perspective,* ed. The Korean Christian Academy, 77–94. Seoul: Wooseok Publishing Co.

Chattopadhyay, Arpita, and Robert Marsh. 1999. Changes in living arrangement and familial support for the elderly in Taiwan: 1963–1991. *Journal of Comparative Family Studies* 30(3): 523–37.

Chen, Ivan. 1910. *The Book of Filial Duty.* New York: Dutton.

Chen, Theodore H. E., and Wen-hui C. Chen. 1959. Changing attitudes towards parents in Communist China. *Sociology and Social Research* 43: 175–82.

Chen Yiping. 1998. Nongcun laonian renkou juzhu yu huanjing zhuangkuang fenxi: Yi Guangdong boluo weili (An analysis of living arrangements and environment of rural elderly: A case study of a Guangdong rural community). *Xibei renkou* (Northwest Population Journal) 72(2): 36–38.

Chen Yunpiao. 1997. Puning, Xilong de laoren shanyang fangshi yu chihuotou chutan (A preliminary study of old-age support and meal rotation in Xilong, Puning). *Zhongshan daxue xuebao* (Journal of Zhongshan University) (Social science edition) 2: 62–67.

China Daily. 1998. Guangdong: "No burial in ground." (Apr. 7).

Cho Chŏngmun. 1997. Han'guk sahoe ch'injok kwan'gye ŭi yanggyehwa kyŏnghyang e kwanhan yŏn'gu (A study of the trend toward bilateralization of Korean society's kinship system). *Han'guk yŏsŏnghak* (Korean Women's Studies) 13(1): 87–114.

Ch'ü T'ung-tsu. 1965. *Law and Society in Traditional China.* Paris: Mouton.

Chun, Kyung-soo. 1984. *Reciprocity and Korean Society: An Ethnography of Hasami.* Seoul: Seoul National University Press.

Clark, Scott. 1999. My other house: Lifelong relationships among sisters of the Hayashi family. In *Lives in Motion: Composing Circles of Self and Community in Japan*, ed. Susan Orpett Long, 41–58. Ithaca, NY: Cornell East Asia Series.

Cohen, Myron L. 1976. *House United, House Divided: The Chinese Family in Taiwan.* New York: Columbia University Press.

———. 1988. Souls and salvation: Conflicting themes in Chinese popular religion. In *Death Ritual in Late Imperial and Modern China*, ed. Watson and Rawski 1988: 180–202.

———. 1992. Family management and family division in contemporary rural China. *China Quarterly* 130: 357–77.

———. 1998. North China rural families: Changes during the Communist era. *Etudes Chinoises* 17(1–2): 60–154.

Collcutt, Martin. 1991. The legacy of Confucianism in Japan. In *The East Asian Region*, ed. Rozman 1991: 111–54.

Cornell, Laurel L. 1991. The deaths of old women: Folklore and differential mortality in nineteenth-century Japan. In *Recreating Japanese Women, 1600–1945*, ed. Gail Lee Bernstein, 71–87. Berkeley: University of California Press.

Council for Economic Planning and Development, ROC. 1997. *Taiwan Statistical Data Book, 1997.* Taipei: CEPD.

Counts, Dorothy, and David R. Counts. 1985. *Aging and Its Transformations: Moving towards Death in Pacific Societies.* Pittsburgh: University of Pittsburgh Press.

Cowgill, Donald O. 1974. Aging and modernization: A revision of theory. In *Late*

Life: Communities and Environmental Policy, ed. Jaber F. Gubrium, 123–46. Springfield, IL: Charles C. Thomas.

Cowgill, Donald O., and Lowell Holmes, eds. 1972. *Aging and Modernization.* New York: Appleton-Century-Crofts.

Dalian ribao (Dalian Daily). 1997. A heart of gold. (July 29).

Davis, Deborah. 1993. Urban households: Supplicants to a socialist state. In *Chinese Families in the Post-Mao Era*, ed. Davis and Harrell 1993: 50–76.

Davis, Deborah, and Stevan Harrell, eds. 1993. *Chinese Families in the Post-Mao Era.* Berkeley: University of California Press.

Davis-Friedmann, Deborah. 1991. *Long Lives: Chinese Elderly and the Communist Revolution.* 2nd ed. Stanford, CA: Stanford University Press.

De Groot, J.J.M. 1964. *The Religious System of China.* Vol. 1, book 1. Taipei: Literature House, Ltd. (originally published 1892).

De Vos, George. 1980. Afterword. In *The Quiet Therapies: Japanese Pathways to Personal Growth*, ed. David K. Reynolds, 113–32. Honolulu: University of Hawaii Press.

Dean, Kenneth. 1997. Ritual and space: Civil society or popular religion? In *Civil Society in China*, ed. Timothy Brook and B. Michael Frolic, 172–92. Armonk, NY: M. E. Sharpe.

Deuchler, Martina. 1992. *The Confucian Transformation of Korea: A Study of Society and Ideology.* Cambridge, MA: Council on East Asian Studies, Harvard University.

Dickson, Bruce. 1997. *Democratization in China and Taiwan.* Oxford: Clarendon Press.

Directorate-General of Budgets, Accounting, and Statistics, ROC. 1996. *Statistical Yearbook of the Republic of China, 1995.* Taipei: DGBAS.

Doi Takeo. 1971. *Amae no kōzō* (The Anatomy of Dependence). Tokyo: Kōbundō.

———. 1973. *The Anatomy of Dependence.* Trans. John Bester. New York: Kodansha.

Doolittle, Justus. 1865. *Social Life of the Chinese: With Some Account of Their Religious, Governmental, Educational, and Business Customs and Opinions.* Vol. 1. New York: Harper and Brothers Publishers.

Dore, Ronald P. 1984. *Education in Tokugawa Japan.* London: Athlone Press.

Ebrey, Patricia Buckley, trans. 1991. *Chu Hsi's Family Rituals: A Twelfth-Century Chinese Manual for the Performance of Cappings, Weddings, Funerals, and Ancestral Rites.* Annotation and intro. by Patricia Buckley Ebrey. Princeton, NJ: Princeton University Press.

Editing Department. 2000. Taejosanim ŭi karŭch'im (The Great Founder's Teachings: The Ethics between Parents and Offspring). Apr. 16, 2001 [http://ns.chent'ae.or.kr/kmkang.2008/2.htm].

Eisenstadt, Shmuel N. 1956. *From Generation to Generation: Age Groups and Social Structure.* Glencoe, IL: Free Press.

————. 1996. Some observations on the transformation of Confucianism (and Buddhism) in Japan. In *Confucian Traditions in East Asian Modernity: Moral Education and Economic Culture in Japan and the Four Mini-Dragons,* ed. Wei-ming Tu, 175–85. Cambridge, MA: Harvard University Press.

Ember, Melvin, and Carol Ember. 1983. *Marriage, Family, and Kinship: Comparative Studies of Social Organization.* New Haven, CT: HRAF Press.

Fan Ying, comp. 2000. *Binzang gaige shehuixue* (The Sociology of Funeral and Interment Reform). Guangzhou: Guangdong sheng shehuixue xuehui.

Fei Xiaotong (Fei Hsiao-t'ung). 1939. *Peasant Life in China.* London: Routledge and Kegan Paul.

————. 1986. *Jiangcun jingji* (Yangzi Village Economics). Nanjing: Jiangsu renmin chubanshe. A translation of Fei Xiaotong 1939.

————. 1992. *From the Soil: The Foundations of Chinese Society.* Trans. Gary G. Hamilton and Wang Zheng. Berkeley: University of California Press.

Films for the Humanities. 1990. *Aging in Japan: When Traditional Mechanisms Vanish.* A production of NHK. 45 min. videocasette. Produced by Seichi Koike, directed by Keishi Tanaka.

Formanek, Susanne, and Sepp Linhart, eds. 1997. *Aging: Asian Concepts and Experiences, Past and Present.* Vienna: Verlag der Oesterreichischen Akademie der Wissenschaften.

Fortes, Meyer. 1984. Age, generation, and social structure. In *Age and Anthropological Theory,* ed. David I. Kertzer and Jennie Keith, 99–122. Ithaca, NY: Cornell University Press.

Foucault, Michel. 1980. *Power/Knowledge: Selected Interviews and Other Writings 1972–1977,* ed. and trans. Colin Gordon et al. New York: Pantheon.

Freedman, Maurice. 1958. *Lineage Organization in Southeastern China.* London: Athlone.

————. 1967. Ancestor worship: Two facets of the Chinese case. In *Social Organisation: Essays Presented to Raymond Firth,* ed. Maurice Freedman, 85–103. London: Frank Cass.

Fukurai, Hiroshi. 1991. Japanese migration in contemporary Japan: Economic segmentation and interprefectural migration. *Social Biology* 38(1): 28–50.

Giddens, Anthony. 1984. *The Constitution of Society: Outline of the Theory of Structuration.* Cambridge, Eng.: Polity Press.

Gluck, Carol. 1985. *Japan's Modern Myths: Ideology in the Late Meiji Period.* Princeton, NJ: Princeton University Press.

Goldstein, Melvyn C., and Yachun Ku. 1993. Income and family support among rural elderly in Zhejiang Province, China. *Journal of Cross-Cultural Gerontology* 8(3): 197–224.

Goldstein, Melvyn C., Yachun Ku, and Charlotte Ikels. 1990. Household composition of the elderly in two rural villages in the People's Republic of China. *Journal of Cross-Cultural Gerontology* 5(2): 119–30.

Goode, William J. 1963. *World Revolution and Family Patterns.* New York: Free Press.

Greenhalgh, Susan. 1988. Families and networks in Taiwan's economic development. In *Contending Approaches to the Political Economy of Taiwan,* ed. Edwin A. Winckler and Susan Greenhalgh, 224–45. Armonk, NY: M. E. Sharpe.

———. 1994. The peasant household in the transition from socialism: State intervention and its consequences in China. In *The Economic Anthropology of the State,* ed. Elizabeth M. Brumfiel, 43–64. Lanham, MD: University Press of America.

Gu, Edward. 2001. Market transition and the transformation of the health care system in urban China. *Policy Studies* 22(3/4): 197–215.

Gu Xinghuan et al. 1993. Financing health care in rural China: Preliminary report of a nationwide study. *Social Science and Medicine* 36(4): 385–91.

Guangzhou ribao (Guangzhou Daily). 1998a. Yangcheng xingjie binyiguan mie dou you (Ram City's star-class funeral parlor in a blink has everything). (Apr. 10): 1.

———. 1998b. Guangzhou shi binzang guanli guiding (Guangzhou city funeral management regulations). (July 16): D2.

Gui, Shixun. 1988. A report from mainland China: Status and needs of rural elderly in the suburbs of Shanghai. *Journal of Cross-Cultural Gerontology* 3(2): 149–67.

Guo Yuhua. 1997. Daiji guanxi zhongde gongping luoji ji qi bianqian (The logic of fairness and the changes in intergenerational relations). Institute of Sociology, Chinese Academy of Social Sciences, manuscript.

Haboush, JaHyun Kim. 1995. Filial emotions and filial values: Changing patterns in the discourse of filiality in late Choson Korea. *Harvard Journal of Asiatic Studies* 55(1): 129–77.

Hai Xiao. 1998. Mu song ernü shang fating (A mother sues her children). *Fazhi shijie* (The World of Law) 11: 46–47.

Hamabata, Matthews. 1990. *Crested Kimono: Power and Love in the Japanese Business Family.* Ithaca, NY: Cornell University Press.

Hara, Hiroko, and Mieko Minagawa. 1996. From productive dependents to precious guests: Historical changes in Japanese children. In *Japanese Childrearing: Two Generations of Scholarship,* ed. Shwalb and Shwalb 1996: 9–30.

Hardacre, Helen. 1986. *Kurozumikyo and the New Religions of Japan.* Princeton, NJ: Princeton University Press.

————. 1989. *Shinto and the State, 1868–1988.* Princeton, NJ: Princeton University Press.

Harrell, Stevan. 1993. Geography, demography, and family composition in three southwestern villages. In *Chinese Families in the Post-Mao Era,* ed. Davis and Harrell 1993: 77–102.

Harris, Phyllis Braudy, and Susan Orpett Long. 1993. Daughter-in-law's burden: An exploratory study of caregiving in Japan. *Journal of Cross-Cultural Gerontology* 8(2): 97–118.

Harris, Phyllis Braudy, Susan Orpett Long, and Miwa Fujii. 1998. Men and elder care in Japan: A ripple of change? *Journal of Cross-Cultural Gerontology* 13(2): 177–98.

Hashimoto, Akiko. 1993. Family relations in later life: A cross-cultural perspective. *Generations* 17(4): 24–26.

————. 1996. *The Gift of Generations: Japanese and American Perspectives on Aging and the Social Contract.* New York: Cambridge University Press.

Hashimoto, Akiko, Hal L. Kendig, and Larry C. Coppard. 1992. Family support to the elderly in international perspective. In *Family Support for the Elderly,* ed. Akiko Hashimoto, Hal L. Kendig, and Larry C. Coppard, 293–308. Oxford: Oxford University Press.

Hayami Yukiko. 1997. Taijidekiruka "enkō oyaji"? (Can "Enkō" men be banished?). *Aera* 11: 23–25.

Hermalin, Albert I. 1997. Drawing policy lessons for Asia from research on ageing. *Asia-Pacific Population Journal* 7(3): 5–12.

Hobsbawm, Eric, and Terence Ranger, eds. 1983. *The Invention of Tradition.* Cambridge, Eng.: Cambridge University Press.

Hochschild, Arlie R. 1979. Emotion work, feeling rules, and social structure. *American Journal of Sociology* 85: 551–75.

Horiuchi, Shiro. 2000. Greater lifetime expectations. *Nature* 405 (June 15): 744–45.

Hsieh Ji-chang. 1985. Meal rotation. In *The Chinese Family and Its Ritual Behaviour,* ed. Hsieh Ji-chang and Chuang Ying-chang, 70–83. Monograph series B, no. 15. Taipei: Institute of Ethnology, Academia Sinica.

Hsu, Francis L. K. 1998. Confucianism in comparative context. In *Confucianism and the Family,* ed. Slote and De Vos 1998: 53–71.

Hu, Yow-Hwey. 1995. Elderly suicide risk in family contexts: A critique of the Asian family care model. *Journal of Cross-Cultural Gerontology* 10(3): 199–217.

Huang, Philip C. 1996. *Civil Justice in China: Representation and Practice in the Qing.* Stanford, CA: Stanford University Press.

Huang Shumin. 1992. Reexamining the extended family in Chinese peasant society: Findings from a Fujian village. *Australian Journal of Chinese Affairs* 27: 25–38.

Hunt, Lynn. 1988. The sacred and the French Revolution. In *Durkheimian Sociology: Cultural Studies*, ed. Jeffrey C. Alexander, 25–43. Cambridge, Eng.: Cambridge University Press.

Ikels, Charlotte. 1990. Family caregivers and the elderly in China. In *Aging and Caregiving: Theory, Research, and Policy*, ed. David E. Biegel and Arthur Blum, 270–84. Newbury Park, CA: Sage Publications.

———. 1993. Settling accounts: The intergenerational contract in an age of reform. In *Chinese Families in the Post-Mao Era*, ed. Davis and Harrell 1993: 307–34.

———. 1996. *The Return of the God of Wealth: The Transition to a Market Economy in Urban China*. Stanford, CA: Stanford University Press.

Int'ŏnet han'gyŏre (Internet Hankyoreh). 1998. Pŏpwŏon: Pumo pongyang "Hyodo Sangsok kiyŏbun" ch'ŏt injŏng (Courts: First recognition of "Filial piety added share of inheritance" for caring for parents). *Int'ŏnet han'gyŏre* (Sept. 29, 1998). Apr. 16, 2001 [http://hani.co.kr/han/L980929/00929521.html].

Ishida, Takeshi. 1984. Conflict and its accommodation: *Omote-ura* and *uchi-soto* relations. In *Conflict in Japan*, ed. Krauss, Rohlen, and Steinhoff 1984: 16–38.

Isono Seiichi and Isono Fujiko. 1958. *Kazoku seido* (The Family System). Tokyo: Iwanami shoten.

Jacka, Tamara. 1997. *Women's Work in Rural China: Change and Continuity in an Era of Reform*. Cambridge, Eng.: Cambridge University Press.

Janelli, Roger L., and Dawnhee Yim Janelli. 1982. *Ancestor Worship and Korean Society*. Stanford, CA: Stanford University Press.

———. 1997. The mutual constitution of Confucianism and capitalism in South Korea. In *Culture and Economy: The Shaping of Capitalism in Eastern Asia*, ed. Timothy Brook and Hy van Luong, 107–24. Ann Arbor: University of Michigan Press.

Janelli, Roger L., with Dawnhee Yim. 1993. *Making Capitalism: The Social and Cultural Construction of a South Korean Conglomerate*. Stanford, CA: Stanford University Press.

Jankowiak, William R. 1988. The soul of Lao Yu. *Natural History* 12: 4–11.

———. 1993. *Sex, Death, and Hierarchy in a Chinese City: An Anthropological Account*. New York: Columbia University Press.

Jenike, Brenda Robb. 1997. Gender and duty in Japan's aged society: The experience of family caregivers. In *The Cultural Context of Aging: Worldwide Perspectives*, 2nd ed., ed. Jay Sokolovsky, 218–38. Westport, CT: Bergin & Garvey.

———. 2002. From the family to the community: Renegotiating responsibility for the care of the elderly in Japan. Ph.D. dissertation. University of California, Los Angeles.

———. 2003. Parent care and shifting family obligations in urban Japan. In

Demographic Change and the Family in Japan's Aging Society, ed. John W. Traphagan and John Knight, 177–201. Albany: State University of New York Press.

Ji Jianlin. 1999. Committed suicide in the Chinese rural areas. *Update on Global Mental and Social Health* (Newsletter of the World Mental Health Project). Boston: Department of Social Medicine, Harvard Medical School.

Jia Aimei. 1988. New experiments with elderly care in rural China. *Journal of Cross-Cultural Gerontology* 3: 139–48.

Jing, Jun. 1996. *The Temple of Memories: History, Power, and Morality in a Chinese Village.* Stanford, CA: Stanford University Press.

Johnson, Frank A. 1993. *Dependency and Japanese Socialization: Psychoanalytic and Anthropological Investigations in Amae.* New York: New York University Press.

Johnson, Kay Ann. 1983. *Women, the Family, and Peasant Revolution in China.* Chicago: University of Chicago Press.

Johnston, Reginald F. 1986. *Lion and Dragon in Northern China.* New York: Oxford University Press.

Judd, Ellen R. 1989. *Niangjia*: Chinese women and their natal families. *Journal of Asian Studies* 48: 525–44.

————. 1994. *Gender and Power in Rural North China.* Stanford, CA: Stanford University Press.

Kang Insun. 1990. Masan, Ch'angwŏn ŭi nodongja kyegŭp ŭi kajok saenghwal (The family life of the working class in Masan and Ch'angwŏn). In *Hanguk kajok ron* (A Treatise on the Korean Family), 129–46. Seoul: Yŏsŏng Han'guk Sahoe Yŏn'guhoe.

Kasuga Keichiro. 1993. Gaikokujin hanayome to chihō jichitai (Foreign brides and rural self-government bodies). In *Gendai no esupuri* (Today's Spirit), ed. Watanabe Fumio, 99–106. Tokyo: Shibundo.

Kawai Hayao. 1986. Violence in the home: Conflict between two principles—maternal and paternal. In *Japanese Culture and Behavior*, ed. Takie S. Lebra and William P. Lebra, 297–306. Honolulu: University of Hawaii Press.

————. 1997a. "Enjo kōsai" to iu mūbumento (A social movement called "assisted companionship"). *Sekai* (The World) 632: 137–48.

————. 1997b. Nihon no kyōiku no soko ni arumono (At the root of Japanese education). *Chūō kōron* (Central Review) 11: 54–67.

————. 1997c. "Chichioya no fukken" nado dekinai (The impossible restoration of fathers). *Bungei shunjū* 10: 262–68.

Kawakami Ryōichi. 1999. *Gakkō hōkai* (The Disintegration of Schools). Tokyo: Sōshisha.

Kawano, Satsuki. 1995. Gender, liminality, and ritual in Japan: Divination among single Tokyo women. *Journal of Ritual Studies* 9(2): 65–91.

276   REFERENCES

Kawashima Takeyoshi. 1950. *Nihon shakai no kazokuteki kōsei* (The Family Structure of Japanese Society). Tokyo: Nihon hyōronsha.

————. 1957. *Ideorogii toshite no kazoku seido* (The Family System as Ideology). Tokyo: Iwanami shoten.

Keisatsuchō (National Police Agency). 1999. *Keisatsu hakusho* (National Police Agency White Paper). Jan. 1, 2002 [http://www.npa.go.jp/hakusho/h11/h11s3.html].

Keith, Jennie. 1992. Care-taking in cultural context: Anthropological queries. In *Family Support for the Elderly*, ed. Akiko Hashimoto, Hal L. Kendig, and Larry C. Coppard, 15–30. New York: Oxford University Press.

Keith, Jennie, Christine L. Fry, and Charlotte Ikels. 1990. Community as Context for Successful Aging. In *The Cultural Context of Aging: Worldwide Perspectives*, ed. Jay Sokolovsky, 245–61. New York: Bergin & Garvey.

Kelly, William W. 1993. Finding a place in metropolitan Japan: Ideologies, institutions, and everyday life. In *Postwar Japan as History*, ed. Andrew Gordon, 189–216. Berkeley: University of California Press.

Kendall, Laurel. 1985. *Shamans, Housewives, and Other Restless Spirits: Women in Korean Ritual Life*. Honolulu: University of Hawaii Press.

————. 1996. *Getting Married in Korea: Of Gender, Morality, and Modernity*. Berkeley: University of California Press.

Kiefer, Christie W. 1987. Care of the aged in Japan. In *Health, Illness, and Medical Care in Japan: Cultural and Social Dimensions*, ed. Edward Norbeck and Margaret Lock, 89–109. Honolulu: University of Hawaii Press.

————. 1990. The elderly in modern Japan: Elite, victims, or plural players? In *The Cultural Context of Aging: Worldwide Perspectives*, ed. Jay Sokolovsky, 181–96. New York: Bergin and Garvey.

Kiire Katsumi. 1999. *Kōkō ga hōkai suru* (The Disintegration of High Schools). Tokyo: Sōshisha.

Kim, Choong Soon. 1988. *Faithful Endurance: An Ethnography of Korean Family Dispersal*. Tucson: University of Arizona Press.

Kim Han'gon. 1994. Yŏsŏng ŭi chiwi wa ch'ulsannyŏke kwanhan chilchŏk yŏn'gu (A qualitative study of the position of women and reproduction). *Han'guk in'guhakhoeji* (Journal of the Korean Demographic Society) 17(2): 21–43.

Kim, Seung-kyung. 1997. *Class Struggle or Family Struggle: The Lives of Women Factory Workers in South Korea*. Cambridge, Eng.: Cambridge University Press.

Kinsella, Sharon. 1995. Cuties in Japan. In *Women, Media, and Consumption in Japan*, ed. Lise Skov and Brian Moeran, 220–54. Honolulu: University of Hawaii Press.

Kipnis, Andrew B. 1995. Within and against peasantness: Backwardness and filiality in rural China. *Comparative Studies in Society and History* 37(1): 110–35.

———. 1997. *Producing Guanxi: Sentiment, Self, and Subculture in a North China Village.* Durham, NC: Duke University Press.

Kishida Shū. 2000. *Gensō ni ikiru oyakotachi* (Parents and Children Living in an Illusion). Tokyo: Bungei shunjū.

Kitaoji, Hironobu. 1971. The structure of the Japanese family. *American Anthropologist* 73(5): 1036–57.

Knodel, John, and Nibhon Debavalya. 1992. Social and economic support systems for the elderly in Asia: An introduction. *Asia-Pacific Population Journal* 7(3): 5–12.

Kodomo no taiken katsudō kenkyū kai (Society for Studying Children's Experiences and Activities). 2000. *Kodomo no taiken katsudō ni kansuru kokusai hikaku chōsa* (An International Survey of Children's Experiences and Activities). Nagano: Kodomo no taiken katsudō kenkyū kai.

Kondo, Dorinne K. 1990. *Crafting Selves: Power, Gender, and Discourses of Identity in a Japanese Workplace.* Chicago: University of Chicago Press.

Koo, Hagan. 1990. From farm to factory: Proletarianization in Korea. *American Sociological Review* 55(5): 669–81.

Korea National Commission for UNESCO. 1960. *Korea: Its Land, People, and Culture of All Ages.* Seoul: Hakwon sa.

Korea National Statistical Office. 1961. *Korea Statistical Yearbook.* Seoul: Economic Planning Board.

———. 1995, 1998, 1999. *Korea Statistical Yearbook.* Seoul: National Statistical Office.

Kōseishō (Ministry of Health and Welfare). 1989. *Ten-Year Gold Plan for the Welfare of the Aged* (English trans.). Tokyo: The Foundation of Social Development for Senior Citizens.

———. 1995. *New Gold Plan.* Tokyo.

———. 1996. *Kōsei hakusho, Heisei 8 nen han* (White Paper on Public Welfare, 1996 Edition). Tokyo.

———. 2000. *Kōsei hakusho, Heisei 12 nen han* (White Paper on Public Welfare, 2000 Edition). Tokyo.

Koyano, Wataru. 1989. Japanese attitudes toward the elderly: A review of research findings. *Journal of Cross-Cultural Gerontology* 4(4): 335–45.

———. 1997. Myths and facts of aging in Japan. In *Aging: Asian Concepts and Experiences, Past and Present,* ed. Formanek and Linhart 1997: 213–27.

Koyano, Wataru, et al. 1994. The social support system of the Japanese elderly. *Journal of Cross-Cultural Gerontology* 9(3): 323–33.

Krauss, Ellis S. 1974. *Japanese Radicals Revisited: Student Protest in Postwar Japan.* Berkeley: University of California Press.

Krauss, Ellis S., Thomas P. Rohlen, and Patricia G. Steinhoff, eds. 1984. *Conflict in Japan.* Honolulu: University of Hawaii Press.

Kumagai, Fumie. 1987. Satisfaction among rural and urban Japanese elderly in three-generation families. *Journal of Cross-Cultural Gerontology* 2(3): 225–39.

Kumagai, Hisa A., and Arno K. Kumagai. 1986. The hidden "I" in *amae. Ethos* 14: 305–21.

Kutcher, Norman. 1999. *Mourning in Late Imperial China: Filial Piety and the State.* Cambridge, Eng.: Cambridge University Press.

Kwŏn Yŏnggi. 2000. Han'gugin ŭi nohu saenghwal (The lives of elderly Koreans), *Wŏlgan Chosŏn* 2000 nyŏn 1 wŏl t'ŭkpyŏl purok (Monthly Chosun, Jan. 2000, special appendix). Apr. 15, 2001 [http://monthly.chosun.com/html/199912/199912310098_1.html].

Kwong, Paul, and Guoxuan Cai. 1992. Ageing in China: Trends, problems and strategies. In *Ageing in East and South-East Asia*, ed. David Phillips, 105–27. London: Edward Arnold.

Lanham, Betty B. 1979. Ethics and moral precepts taught in schools of Japan and the United States. *Ethos* 7(1): 1–18.

Lavely, William R., and Xinhua Ren. 1992. Patrilocality and early marital co-residence in rural China: 1955–85. *China Quarterly* 130: 378–91.

Lebra, Takie Sugiyama. 1976. *Japanese Patterns of Behavior.* Honolulu: University of Hawaii Press.

———. 1984a. *Japanese Women: Constraint and Fulfillment.* Honolulu: University of Hawaii Press.

———. 1984b. Nonconfrontational strategies for management of interpersonal conflicts. In *Conflict in Japan*, ed. Krauss, Rohlen, and Steinhoff 1984: 41–60.

———. 1998. Confucian gender role and personal fulfillment for Japanese women. In *Confucianism and the Family*, ed. Slote and De Vos 1998: 209–27.

Lee, Chulwoo. 1996. Law, culture and conflict in a colonial society: Rural Korea under Japanese rule. Ph.D. dissertation. London School of Economics and Political Science.

Lee, Kwang-kyu (Yi Kwanggyu). 1989. The practice of traditional family rituals in contemporary Korea. *Journal of Ritual Studies* 3(2): 167–83.

———. 1997. *Korean Family and Kinship.* Seoul: Jipmoondang Publishing Company.

Legge, James. 1885. *Li Ji Book I.* Oxford: Oxford University Press. Cited in Laurence Thompson, *Chinese Religion: An Introduction.* Belmont, CA: Wadsworth Publishing Company, 1996.

————. 1933. *The Four Books.* Trans. and with notes. Shanghai: The Chinese Book Company.

Lett, Denise. 1998. *In Pursuit of Status: The Making of South Korea's "New" Urban Middle Class.* Cambridge, MA: Harvard University Press.

Leung, Joe C. B. 1997. Family support for the elderly in China: Issues and challenges. *Journal of Aging and Social Policy* 9(3): 87–101.

Li Ruojian. 1999. Butong zhiye beijing laoren shenghuo ji yanglao moshi de xuanze (The life of elderly people of different occupational backgrounds and their choice of eldercare patterns). *Renkou yanjiu* (Population Research) 23(2): 61–64.

Lifton, Robert Jay. 1970. *History and Human Survival: Essays on the Young and Old, Survivors and the Dead, Peace and War, and on Contemporary Psychohistory.* New York: Random House.

Lin Jiang. 1995. Changing kinship structure and its implications for old-age support in urban and rural China. *Population Studies* 49: 127–45.

Lin Yueh-hua (Lin Yaohua). 1947. *The Golden Wing.* London: Oxford University Press.

Liu, Xian, Jersey Liang, and Shengzu Gu. 1995. Flows of social support and health status among older persons in China. *Social Science and Medicine* 41(8): 1175–84.

Lock, Margaret. 1993. *Encounters with Aging: Mythologies of Menopause in Japan and North America.* Berkeley: University of California Press.

————. 1996. Centering the household: The remaking of female maturity in Japan. In *Re-Imaging Japanese Women,* ed. Anne E. Imamura, 73–103. Berkeley: University of California Press.

Logan, John, Fuqin Bian, and Yanjie Bian. Unpublished. Tradition and Change in the Urban Chinese Family: The Case of Living Arrangements.

Logan, John, and Glenna Spitze. 1995. Self-interest and altruism in intergenerational relations. *Demography* 32: 353–64.

Long, Susan O. 1987. *Family Change and the Life Course in Japan.* Ithaca, NY: East Asia Program, Cornell University.

————. 2000. *Caring for the Elderly in Japan and the U.S.: Practices and Policies.* London: Routledge.

Madsen, Richard. 1984. *Morality and Power in a Chinese Village.* Berkeley: University of California Press.

————. 1990. The politics of revenge in rural China during the Cultural Revolution. In *Violence in China: Essays in Culture and Counterculture,* ed. Jonathan N. Lipman and Stevan Harrell, 175–201. Albany: State University of New York Press.

Martin, Linda G. 1988. The aging of Asia. *Journal of Gerontology* 43(4): 99–113.

————. 1990. Changing intergenerational family relations in East Asia. *Annals of the American Academy of Arts and Sciences* 510: 102–14.

Maruyama Masao. 1992. *Chūsei to hangyaku: Tenkeiki Nihon no seishinshiteki isō* (Loyalty and Treason: The Typology of Intellectual History in Japan during Transformation Periods). Tokyo: Iwanami shoten.

Masataka Nobuo. 1999. *Ikuji to Nihonjin* (Childrearing and the Japanese). Tokyo: Iwanami shoten.

Mason, Karen O. 1992. Family change and support of the elderly in Asia: What do we know? *Asia-Pacific Population Journal* 7(3): 13–32.

Meijer, Marinus J. 1971. *Marriage Law and Policy in the Chinese People's Republic.* Hong Kong: Hong Kong University Press.

Michael, Robert T., Victor R. Fuchs, and Sharon R. Scott. 1980. Changes in the propensity to live alone: 1950–1976. *Demography* 17(1): 39–56.

Ministry of Agriculture and Fisheries, Republic of Korea. 1977. *Yearbook of Agriculture and Forestry Statistics, 1977.* Seoul: Ministry of Agriculture and Fisheries.

Mitscherlich, Alexander. 1969. *Society without the Father: A Contribution to Social Psychology.* Trans. Eric Mosbacher. New York: Harper.

Morgan, S. Philip, and Kiyosi Hirosima. 1983. The persistence of extended family residence in Japan: Anachronism or alternative strategy? *American Sociological Review* 48: 269–81

Mun Okp'yo. 1992. Tosi chungsanch'ŭng ŭi kajok saenghwal kwa chubu ŭi yŏkhal. (The urban middle-class family and the role of the housewife). In *Tosi chungsanch'ŭng ŭ saenghwal munhwa,* ed. Mun Okp'yo 1992: 57–103.

————, ed. 1992. *Tosi chungsanch'ŭng ŭi saenghwal munhwa* (The Social Culture of the Urban Middle Class). Seoul: Chŏngsin munhwa yŏn'guwŏn.

Murakami Ryū. 1997. Joshi kōsei to bungaku no kiki (High school girls and the crisis of literature). *Bungakukai* (Literary World) 51: 282–97.

Nakane, Chie. 1967. *Kinship and Economic Organization in Rural Japan.* New York: Humanities Press.

Nakanishi Shintarō. 2000. Enhenka sareru wakamonotachi: Shakai shisutemu no hōkai to chisei no henyō (The marginalization of youth: The breakdown of a social system and changes in the intellectual landscape). *Sekai* (The World) 5: 87–93.

Nelson, Laura C. 2000. *Measured Excess: Status, Gender, and Consumer Nationalism in South Korea.* New York: Columbia University Press.

Nishiyama Akira. 1999. *Adaruto chirudoren: Jishinwa naikedo ikiteiku* (Adult children: Living without Confidence). Tokyo: Shūeisha.

Niwa Fumio. 1962. The hateful age. In *Modern Japanese Stories: An Anthology*, ed. and trans. Ivan Morris, 320–48. Tokyo: Charles Tuttle.

Noda Masaaki. 1999. "Shōnen A" fubo no shuki o yomu (Reading the memoirs of Youth A's parents). *Sekai* (The World) July: 130–36.

Ogasawara, Yuko. 1998. *Office Ladies and Salaried Men: Power, Gender, and Work in Japanese Companies.* Berkeley: University of California Press.

Ogawa, Naohiro. 1990. Economic factors affecting the health of the elderly. In *Improving the Health of Older People: A World View,* ed. Robert L. Kane, J. Grimley Evans, and David Macfadyen, 627–45. New York: Oxford University Press.

Okamoto Takiko. 1996. *Nihon no kōreisha fukushi* (Welfare for the Elderly in Japan). Tokyo: International Longevity Center of Japan.

Pak Pujin. 1994. Han'guk nongch'on kajok ŭi munhwajŏk ŭimi wa kajok kwan'gye ŭi pyŏnhwa e kwanhan yŏn'gu (A study of changes in the cultural meaning of the Korean rural family and family relationships). Ph.D. dissertation. Seoul National University.

Papanek, Hanna. 1989. Family status-production work: Women's contribution to social mobility and class differentiation. In *Gender and the Household Domain: Social and Cultural Dimensions,* ed. Maithreyi Krishnaraj and Karuna Chanana, 97–116. New Delhi: Sage Publications.

Parish, William L., and Martin K. Whyte. 1978. *Village and Family in Contemporary China.* Chicago: University of Chicago Press.

Parsons, Talcott. 1971. *The System of Modern Societies.* Englewood Cliffs, NJ: Prentice-Hall.

Peak, Lois. 1989. Learning to become part of the group: The Japanese child's transition to preschool life. *Journal of Japanese Studies* 15: 93–123.

Pharr, Susan J. 1980. *Political Women in Japan: The Search for a Place in Political Life.* Berkeley: University of California Press.

Pihl, Marshal R. 1994. *The Korean Singer of Tales.* Cambridge, MA: Harvard University Press.

Plath, David W. 1964. Where the Family of God is the family: The role of the dead in Japanese households. *American Anthropologist* 66: 300–317.

———. 1972. Japan: The after years. In *Aging and Modernization,* ed. Cowgill and Holmes 1972: 133–50.

———. 1980. *Long Engagements: Maturity in Modern Japan.* Stanford, CA: Stanford University Press.

———. 1983. Ecstasy years: Old age in Japan. In *Growing Old in Different Societies: Cross-Cultural Perspectives,* ed. Jay Sokolovsky, 147–53. Acton, MA: Copley Press.

———. 1988. The age of silver: Aging in modern Japan. *The World & I* (Mar.): 505–13.

Potter, Sulamith Heins, and Jack M. Potter. 1990. *China's Peasants: The Anthropology of a Revolution.* Cambridge, Eng.: Cambridge University Press.

Rawski, Evelyn S. 1988a. A historian's approach to Chinese death ritual. In *Death Ritual in Late Imperial and Modern China*, ed. Watson and Rawski 1988: 20–34.

———. 1988b. The imperial way of death: Ming and Ch'ing emperors and death ritual. In *Death Ritual in Late Imperial and Modern China*, ed. Watson and Rawski 1988: 228–53.

Reader, Ian. 1991. *Religion in Contemporary Japan*. Honolulu: University of Hawaii Press.

Rofel, Lisa. 1999. *Other Modernities: Gendered Yearnings in China after Socialism*. Berkeley: University of California Press.

Rogers, Carol. 1975. Female forms of power and the myth of male dominance: A model of female/male interaction in peasant society. *American Ethnologist* 2: 726–56.

Rohlen, Thomas P. 1989. Order in Japanese society: Attachment, authority, and routine. *Journal of Japanese Studies* 15: 5–40.

Rosaldo, Michelle Zimbalist. 1974. Women, culture, and society: A theoretical overview. In *Women, Culture, and Society*, ed. Michelle Zimbalist Rosaldo and Louise Lamphere, 17–42. Stanford, CA: Stanford University Press.

Rozman, Gilbert. 1991a. The East Asian region in comparative perspective. In *The East Asian Region*, ed. Rozman 1991: 3–42.

———. 1991b. Comparisons of modern Confucian values in China and Japan. In *The East Asian Region*, ed. Rozman 1991: 157–203.

———, ed. 1991. *The East Asian Region: Confucian Heritage and Its Modern Adaptation*. Princeton, NJ: Princeton University Press.

Saitō Tamaki. 1998. *Shakaiteki hikikomori: Owaranai shishunki* (Social Withdrawal: The Never-Ending Adolescence). Tokyo: PHP Kenkyūjo.

Sanday, Peggy R. 1974. Female status in the public domain. In *Women, Culture, and Society*, ed. Michelle Zimbalist Rosaldo and Louise Lamphere, 189–206. Stanford, CA: Stanford University Press.

Saunders, Peter, and Xiaoyuan Shang. 2001. Social security reform in China's transition to a market economy. *Social Policy and Administration* 35(3): 274–89.

Schooler, Carmi. 1996. William Caudill and the reproduction of culture: Infant, child, and maternal behavior in Japan and the United States. In *Japanese Childrearing*, ed. Shwalb and Shwalb 1996: 139–63.

Scott, James C. 1985. *Weapons of the Weak: Everyday Forms of Peasant Resistance*. New Haven, CT: Yale University Press.

———. 1990. *Domination and the Arts of Resistance: Hidden Transcripts*. New Haven, CT: Yale University Press.

Sekiguchi Yūko et al. 2000. *Kazoku to kekkon no rekishi* (The History of Family and Marriage). Tokyo: Shinwasha.

Selden, Mark. 1993. Family strategies and structures in rural North China. In *Chinese Families in the Post-Mao Era*, ed. Davis and Harrell 1993: 139–64.

Sengoku Tamotsu. 1998. *Nihon no kōkōsei: Kokusai hikaku de miru* (Japanese High School Students in International Perspective). Tokyo: NHK shuppankai.

Serizawa Shunsuke. 2000. *Tsuiteiku chichioya* (The Following Father). Tokyo: Shinchōsha.

Sher, Ada E. 1984. *Aging in Post-Mao China: The Politics of Veneration*. Boulder, CO: Westview Press.

Shi, Leiyu. 1993. Family financial and household support exchange between generations: A survey of Chinese rural elderly. *The Gerontologist* 33(4): 468–80.

———. 1994. Elderly support in rural and suburban villages: Implications for future support systems in China. *Social Science and Medicine* 39(2): 265–77.

Shwalb, David W., and Barbara J. Shwalb, eds. 1996. *Japanese Childrearing: Two Generations of Scholarship*. New York: Guilford Press.

Siu, Helen F. 1989a. *Agents and Victims in South China: Accomplices in Rural Revolution*. New Haven, CT: Yale University Press.

———. 1989b. Recycling rituals: Politics and popular culture in contemporary rural China. In *Unofficial China: Popular Culture and Thought in the People's Republic*, ed. Perry Link, Richard Madsen, and Paul G. Pickowicz, 121–37. Boulder, CO: Westview Press.

Slote, Walter H. 1998. Psychocultural dynamics within the Confucian family. In *Confucianism and the Family*, ed. Slote and De Vos 1998: 37–51.

Slote, Walter H., and George A. De Vos, eds. 1998. *Confucianism and the Family*. Albany: State University of New York Press.

Smith, Henry DeWitt, II. 1972. *Japan's First Student Radicals*. Cambridge, MA: Harvard University Press.

Smith, Robert J. 1974. *Ancestor Worship in Contemporary Japan*. Stanford, CA: Stanford University Press.

———. 1996. The Japanese (Confucian) family: Tradition from the bottom up. In *Confucian Traditions in East Asian Modernity: Moral Education and Economic Culture in Japan and the Four Mini-Dragons*, ed. Wei-ming Tu, 155–74. Cambridge, MA: Harvard University Press.

Sŏng Kyut'ak. 1995. Hyŏndae Han'gugin i insikhanŭn hyo: Naeyong punsŏk (Filial piety as conceived by modern Koreans: Measures and dimensions). In *Hyo sasang kwa mirae sahoe* (Filial Piety and Future Society), 577–613. Seoul: Han'guk Chŏngsin Munhwawŏn.

Sŏngsan hyodo taehagwŏn taehakkyo (Sungsan Hyo University of Graduate Studies). n.d. Apr. 16, 2001 [www.hyo.ac.kr].

Sorensen, Clark. 1983. Male, female, inside, outside: The division of labor in rural central Korea. In *Korean Women: View from the Inner Room*, ed. Laurel Kendall and Mark Peterson, 63–79. New Haven, CT: Eastrock Press.

———. 1986. Migration, the family, and the care of the aged in rural Korea: An investigation of a village in the Yongsŏ region of Kangwŏn Province, 1918–1983. *Journal of Cross-Cultural Gerontology* 1(2): 139–61.

———. 1988a. *Over the Mountains Are Mountains: Korean Peasant Household and Their Adaptations to Rapid Industrialization*. Seattle: University of Washington Press.

———. 1988b. The Myth of Princess Pari and the self-image of Korean women. *Anthropos* 83: 409–19.

———. 1990. Modernization and filial piety in contemporary Korea. *The World & I* (Jan.): 640–51.

———. 1994. Education and success in South Korea. *Comparative Education Review* 38(1): 10–35.

Stacey, Judith. 1983. *Patriarchy and Socialist Revolution in China*. Berkeley: University of California Press.

Statistics Bureau, Management and Coordination Agency. 1994. *Jyūmin Nihon daichō jinkō idō hōkoku nenpō* (Annual Report on the Internal Migration in Japan [Derived from the Basic Resident Registers]). Tokyo: Nihon tōkei kyokai.

Steinhoff, Patricia G. 1984. Student Conflict. In *Conflict in Japan*, ed. Krauss, Rohlen, and Steinhoff 1984: 174–213.

———. 1991. *Tenko: Ideology and Societal Integration in Prewar Japan*. New York: Garland Publishing.

Suginami-ku (Suginami Ward). 1996. *Kōreisha fukushi no shiori* (Guide to Senior Citizen Welfare). Tokyo: Suginami-ku.

Sunbogŭm sinmun (Pure Evangelical Church Newspaper). 2000. Sasŏl: Noin chŏngch'aege himŭl kiurija (Editorial: Let's put our effort toward policies for the aged). Feb. 22, 2001 [http://fgic.or.kr/times/200925/sasul.html].

Suzuki, Hikaru. 2000. *The Price of Death: The Funeral Industry in Contemporary Japan*. Stanford, CA: Stanford University Press.

Takahashi Junko. 1998. Enjokōsai sotsugyōsei no yūutsu (The gloom of enjokōsai graduates). *Aera* 11: 6–9.

Takahashi Kōichi, Tōkyō no fukushi kenkyūkai, and Tōkyō jichi mondai kenkyūkai, eds. 1994. *Zusetsu: Tōkyō no fukushi jittai, 1995 nen han* (Explanatory Diagrams: Actual Conditions of Welfare in Tokyo, 1995 Edition). Tokyo: Hōbunsha.

Takeda, Choshu. 1976. Family religion in Japan: The *ie* and its religious faith. In *The Realm of the Extra-Human: Ideas and Actions*, ed. Agchananda Bharati, 473–82. Chicago: Aldine.

Takeji, Kamiko. 1999. Reinterpreting mate selection in contemporary Japan. In *Lives in Motion: Composing Circles of Self and Community in Japan*, ed. Susan Orpett Long, 27–40. Ithaca, NY: Cornell East Asia Series.

Thang, Leng Leng. 1997. *Ikigai* and longevity among the elderly in Okinawa. In *Aging: Asian Concepts and Experiences, Past and Present*, ed. Formanek and Linhart 1997: 257–69.

Thornton, Arland, and T. E. Fricke. 1987. Social change and the family: Comparative perspectives from the West, China, and South Asia. *Sociological Forum* 2 (Fall): 746–79.

Thornton, Arland, and Hui-sheng Lin. 1994. *Social Change and the Family in Taiwan*. Chicago: University of Chicago Press.

Tobin, Joseph J., David Y. H. Wu, and Dana H. Davidson. 1989. *Preschool in Three Cultures: Japan, China, and the United States*. New Haven, CT: Yale University Press.

Tokyo Metropolitan Government. 1993. *Social Welfare in Japan*. Tokyo: Tōkyō-to.

Traphagan, John W. 1998a. Contesting the transition to old age in Japan. *Ethnology* 37(4): 333–50.

———. 1998b. Reasons for gateball participation among older Japanese. *Journal of Cross-Cultural Gerontology* 13(2): 159–75.

———. 2000a. The liminal family: Return migration and intergenerational conflict in Japan. *Journal of Anthropological Research* 56: 365–85.

———. 2000b. *Taming Oblivion: Aging Bodies and the Fear of Senility in Japan*. Albany: State University of New York Press.

———. 2003. Contesting coresidence: Women, in-laws, and health care in rural Japan. In *Demographic Change and the Family in Japan's Aging Society*, ed. John W. Traphagan and John Knight, 203–26. Albany: State University of New York Press.

Tsurumi, Kazuko. 1970. *Social Change and the Individual: Japan before and after Defeat in World War II*. Princeton, NJ: Princeton University Press.

Tsurumi Shunsuke. 1991. Senjiki Nihon no seishinshi, 1931–1945 (An intellectual history of wartime Japan, 1931–45). In *Gendai Nihon shisōshi: Tsurumi Shunsuke shū* (Contemporary Intellectual History of Japan: Works of Tsurumi Shunsuke), vol. 5: 3–189. Tokyo: Chikuma shobō.

Tu, Wei-ming. 1996. Epilogue. In *Confucian Traditions in East Asian Modernity: Moral Education and Economic Culture in Japan and the Four Mini-Dragons*, ed. Wei-ming Tu, 343–49. Cambridge, MA: Harvard University Press.

Turner, Victor. 1977. *The Ritual Process: Structure and Anti-Structure*. Ithaca, NY: Cornell University Press.

Ueno Chizuko. 1994. *Kindai kazoku no seiritsu to shūen* (The Rise and Fall of the Modern Family). Tokyo: Iwanami shoten.

untitled

Unger, Jonathan. 1993. Urban families in the eighties. In *Chinese Families in the Post-Mao Era*, ed. Davis and Harrell 1993: 25–49.

United States Bureau of the Census. 1999. *World Population Profile, 1998*. Report WP/98. Washington, D.C.: U.S. Government Printing Office.

Van der Sprenkel, Sybille. 1962. *Legal Institutions in Manchu China*. London: Athlone Press.

Vogel, Ezra, and Suzanne Vogel. 1968. Permissive dependency in Japan. In *Comparative Perspectives on Marriage and the Family*, ed. Kent H. Geiger, 68–77. Boston: Little, Brown.

Wakefield, David. 1998. *Fenjia: Household Division and Inheritance in Qing and Republican China*. Honolulu: University of Hawaii Press.

Walraven, Boudewijn. 1994. *Songs of the Shaman: The Ritual Chants of the Korean Mudang*. London: Kegan Paul International.

Wang, Danyu. 1999. Flying from the nest: The household formation in a village in northeastern China. Ph.D. dissertation. Brown University.

———. 2000a. Complex households, a fading glory: Household formation during the collective period in the PRC. *Journal of Family History* 25(4): 527–44.

———. 2000b. Stepping on two boats: The urban strategies of Chinese peasants and their children. *International Review of Social History Supplement: On Households' Survival Strategies* 8: 181–98.

Wang Laihua, Bai Hongguang, and Jia Dezhang. 1997. Laonian shenghuo baozhang yu dui shequ fuwu de yilai (Livelihood guarantees for the elderly and their dependence on community services). *Shehuixue yanjiu* (Sociological Studies) 3: 119–25.

Wang Xuede et al., eds. 1987. *Wafangdian minjian geyao* (Wafangdian Folk Lyrics). Liaoning: Wafangdian Culture Center.

Wang Yilong. 1999. Wangcun diaocha: Nongcun laoren jiating quanwei de shangshi jiqi yanglao wenti (Wang Village survey: The loss of the rural elderly's authority and their old-age support). *Shehui* (Society) 7: 24–26.

Ware, James R., trans. 1955. *The Sayings of Confucius: The Teachings of China's Greatest Sage*. New York: The New American Library.

Watson, James L. 1975. *Emigration and the Chinese Lineage*. Berkeley: University of California Press.

———. 1982. Of flesh and bones: the management of death pollution in Cantonese society. In *Death and the Regeneration of Life*, ed. Maurice Bloch and Jonathan Parry, 155–86. Cambridge, Eng.: Cambridge University Press.

———. 1987. From the common pot: Feasting with equals in Chinese society. *Anthropos* 82: 389–401.

———. 1988. The structure of Chinese funerary rites: Elementary forms, ritual sequence, and the primacy of performance. In *Death Ritual in Late Imperial and Modern China*, ed. Watson and Rawski 1988: 3–19.

Watson, James L., and Evelyn S. Rawski, eds. 1988. *Death Ritual in Late Imperial and Modern China*. Berkeley: University of California Press.

Watson, Rubie S. 1988. Remembering the dead: Graves and politics in Southeastern China. In *Death Ritual in Late Imperial and Modern China*, ed. Watson and Rawski 1988: 203–27.

Wei Zhong. 1997. Jiangsu nongcun yanglao baozhang moshi de duice yanjiu (Research on the models of old-age insurance in rural Jiangsu). *Xuehai* (Sea of Learning) 4: 85–90.

White, Gordon. 1998. Social security reforms: Toward an East Asian model? In *The East Asian Welfare Model: Welfare Orientalism and the State*, ed. Roger Goodman, Gordon White, and Huck-ju Kwon, 175–98. London: Routledge.

White, Merry. 1993. *The Material Child: Coming of Age in Japan and America*. Berkeley: University of California Press.

White, Merry, and Robert A. LeVine. 1986. What is an *Ii Ko* (good child)? In *Child Development and Education in Japan*, ed. H. Stevenson, H. Azuma, and K. Hakuta, 55–62. New York: W. H. Freeman.

Whyte, Martin K. 1988. Death in the People's Republic of China. In *Death Ritual in Late Imperial and Modern China*, ed. Watson and Rawski 1988: 289–316.

———. 1992. Introduction: Rural economic reforms and Chinese family patterns. (Symposium on rural family change.) *China Quarterly* 130: 317–22.

———. 1997. The fate of filial obligations in urban China. *The China Journal* 38: 1–31.

———. 2001. Zhongguo jiating zhong de shanyang yiwu: Xiandaihua de beilun (Filial obligations in Chinese families: Paradoxes of modernization). *Zhongguo xueshu* (China Scholarship) 4(8): 255–77.

Whyte, Martin K., and William L. Parish. 1984. *Urban Life in Contemporary China*. Chicago: University of Chicago Press.

Whyte, Martin K., and Xu Qin. 2003. A comparative study of support for aging parents from daughters versus sons. In *China's Revolutions and Intergenerational Relations*, ed. Martin K. Whyte, 167–95. Ann Arbor: University of Michigan Center for Chinese Studies.

Wolf, Margery. 1972. *Women and Family in Rural Taiwan*. Stanford, CA: Stanford University Press.

———. 1975. Women and suicide in China. In *Women in Chinese Society*, ed. Margery Wolf and Roxanne Witke, 111–41. Stanford, CA: Stanford University Press.

———. 1985. *Revolution Postponed: Women in Contemporary China*. Stanford, CA: Stanford University Press.

Wŏlgan Chosŏn (Monthly Chosun), ed. 2001. *The Chosun Almanac.* Seoul: Chosŏn ilbo sa.

World Bank. 1997. *World Development Report.* New York: Oxford University Press.

World Health Organization. 2001. *Mental Health and Brain Disorders.* (Suicide rates and absolute numbers of suicides by country [as of 2001]). Jan. 3, 2002 [www.who.int/mental_health/Topic_Suicide/suicide1.html].

Wöss, Fleur. 1993. Pokkuri temples and aging: Rituals for approaching death. In *Religion and Society in Modern Japan,* ed. Mark R. Mullins, Shimazono Susumu, and Paul L. Swanson, 191–202. Berkeley: Asian Humanities Press.

Xu Changhong. 1996. Nongcun yanglao jiufen tanwei (On the disputes concerning rural old-age support). *Shehui gongzuo* (Social Work) 3: 30–31.

Xue Xingli, Xin Xiangmu, and Liu Guiyuan. 1998. Nongcun laonian renkou yanglao wenti de shizheng fenxi yu jiben duice: Dui Shandong nongcun de wenjuan diaocha (Fact analysis and related strategies on the issue of old-age support for the rural elderly: Surveys in rural Shandong). *Shehui xue* (Sociology Studies) 4: 169–72.

Yan, Yunxiang. 1996. *The Flow of Gifts.* Stanford, CA: Stanford University Press.

———. 1997. The triumph of conjugality: Structural transformation of family relations in a Chinese village. *Ethnology* 36: 191–212.

———. 2003. *Private Life under Socialism: Individuality and Family Change in a Chinese Village, 1949–1999.* Stanford, CA: Stanford University Press.

Yang, C. K. 1961. *Religion in Chinese Society: A Study of Contemporary Social Functions of Religion and Some of Their Historical Factors.* Berkeley: University of California Press.

Yang, Haiou, and David Chandler. 1992. Intergenerational relations: Grievances of the elderly in rural China. *Journal of Comparative Family Studies* 23(3): 431–54.

Yangcheng wanbao (Ram City Evening News). 2000. "Qipai" binyiguan xiazhou kaichang ("Imposing" funeral parlor to open next week) (Sept. 1): A2.

Yao Yuan 1999. Zhengfu zai jiating yanglao zhong de diwei he zuoyong (The status and role of the government in the family care of the elderly). *Xibei renkou* (Northwest Population) 2: 8–11.

Yi Chŏngok and Han Yŏnghye. 1995. Haebang hu Han'guk kajok ŭi pyŏnhwa (Changes in the Korean family after liberation). In *Kwangbok 50 nyŏn kinyŏm nonmunjip 4: Sahoe* (Collected Essays Commemorating the Fiftieth Anniversary of the Restoration of Independence, vol. 4: Society), 129–71. Seoul: Han'guk haksul chinhŭng chaedan.

Yi Hyojae. 1983. *Kajok kwa sahoe* (Family and Society). Revised ed. Seoul: Kyŏngmun sa.

Yi Kaok et al. 1994. *Noin saenghwal silt'ae punsŏk mit chŏngch'aek kwaje* (An Analysis of the Actual Living Conditions of the Aged and Policy Needs). Seoul: Han'guk pogŏn sahoe yŏn'guwŏn.

Yi Kwanggyu (Kwang-kyu Lee). 1978. Han'guk ch'injok ch'egye e mich'in chungguk ŭi kyŏnghyang (Chinese influences on Korean kinship). *Illyuhak nonjip* (Anthropological Papers) 4: 97–137.

Yim, Dawnhee. 1998. Psychocultural features of ancestor worship in modern Korean society. In *Confucianism and the Family*, ed. Slote and De Vos 1998: 163–86.

Yoneyama, Shoko. 1999. *The Japanese High School: Silence and Resistance*. London: Routledge.

Young, Richard, and Fuki Ikeuchi. 1997. Religion in "The Hateful Age": Reflections on pokkuri and other geriatric rituals in Japan's aging society. In *Aging: Asian Concepts and Experiences, Past and Present*, ed. Formanek and Linhart 1997: 229–55.

Yu, Sang Duk. 1997. South Korean teachers' struggle for education reform. In *Korea Briefing: Toward Reunification*, ed. David R. McCann, 69–82. Armonk, NY: M. E. Sharpe.

Yuzawa Yasuhiko. 1995. *Zusetsu kazoku mondai no genzai* (Illustrated Contemporary Problems of the Family). Tokyo: NHK Books.

Zeng Yi et al. 1994. Leaving the parental home: Census-based estimates for China, Japan, South Korea, United States, France and Sweden. *Population Studies* 48: 65–80.

Zhang, Hong. 2001. Eldercare issues in contemporary China. *Chinese Sociology and Anthropology* 34(1): 3–26.

Zhang Junliang. 1995. Nongcun jiating yanglao cunzai de wenti (The problem of family support for the rural elderly). *Caijin kexue* (Finance and Science) 5: 27–30.

Zheng Caixiong and Zhou Huilin. 2001. Funeral reform springs to life. *China Daily* (Mar. 29): 3.

Zhuang Kongshao. 1996. *Yin chi* (The Silver Wing). Taipei: Guiguan Books.

Zito, Angela. 1997. *Of Body and Brush: Grand Sacrifice as Text/Performance in Eighteenth-Century China*. Chicago: University of Chicago Press.

Index

adult day care, Japanese, 217–18, 220, 228–30, 239; availability of, 241; and coresidence, 232–38; experiences in, 231–38; shortcomings of, 266n8

Aging in Japan: When Traditional Mechanisms Vanish (film), 219

Agonshū (Japanese sect), 189

agriculture: in China, 18, 38–39, 64; in Japan, 199–201, 206; in Korea, 138–40, 157, 261n3a; mechanization of, 138–39; women in, 140

Ahern, Emily, 39

Akita (city; Japan), 199

Akita Prefecture (Japan), 200–202

ancestors: coresidence with, 205–6; gaze of Japanese, 187–90, 197; and status, 189; and suicide, 7; tablets for, 90, 92–93, 99–100

ancestor worship: in China, 22, 35–36, 59, 80, 90, 92–93, 99–100, 106, 134–35; and Christianity, 150, 172–74, 263n23; and eldest sons, 138, 149–50, 173–74; in Japan, 204–6, 221; in Korea, 129, 133–34, 137–38, 149–50, 156, 165, 171–74; state opposition to, 22, 80, 92

Ariyoshi, Sawako, 223–24

Asian care model, 76–77

authority: criticism of, 189–92; of daughters-in-law, 170–71, 234; of elderly, 59–60, 64, 80–81, 83, 85, 140, 222, 234, 237, 241; inheritance of, 190–91; parental, 165–66, 214; passive resistance to, 192–93; and transcendence, 191. *See also* patriarchy

The Ballad of Narayama (film), 4, 224–25

Baoding (Hebei): filial support in, 110–16; survey data from, 109–10; *vs.* Taiwan, 117–22

Basic Living Preservation Law (Korea), 153

Bellah, Robert, 191

Benedict, Ruth, 220

birth rates. *See under* population

Brandt, Vincent, 136

Brinton, Mary, 226

Buddhism: in China, 35, 89–90, 95, 99–100, 104, 255n2; Ch'ŏnt'ae (Tiantai), 145; death ritual in, 89–90, 95, 99–100, 104, 172; in Japan, 221; in Korea, 145, 153–55, 172, 175, 262n4

burial: *vs.* cremation, 88, 93, 96, 172; double, 92, 100–101; for overseas Chinese, 93; surreptitious, 103, 105. *See also* death ritual

businesses: in China, 39–40, 64–65, 107–8, 120, 124–27; in China *vs.* Taiwan, 124–25; collective, 64–65, 126; family-run, 65, 107–8, 120, 124–25, 127, 257n4; inheritance of, 40; in Japan, 194; in Korea, 143–44; state-run, 40; in Taiwan, 107–8, 124–25, 257n4

cadres, Chinese, 256n7; and death ritual, 95, 98–102; intervention by, 62, 73, 83–84. *See also* government officials

Canada, 14

capital: social, 159–60, 204, 222–23, 240; symbolic, 5, 134, 204, 240

Catholicism. *See* Christianity

chaebŏl corporations, 162, 178

Chang, Yun-Shik, 139

Ch'angwŏn (Korea), 160–62, 164

Chen Yunpiao, 55–58

Chiang Kai-shek, 260*n*22

child care: conflicts over, 213, 215; as domestic role, 226; by elderly, 29, 36, 71, 73, 85, 114, 227; and low birth rates, 139

children, 183, 195; as expression of filial piety, 165, 174; and sacrificial mother, 187–88; socialization of, 184–87. *See also* youth

China. *See* China, imperial; China, People's Republic of; Hong Kong; Taiwan

China, imperial, 31, 98; ancestor worship in, 90, 106; Buddhism in, 89–90; daughters in, 106–7; daughters-in-law in, 20–21, 106; death ritual in, 13, 21, 89–91; family in, 18–22, 106–7; marriage in, 36, 80, 251*n*4

China, People's Republic of (PRC), 16–127; agriculture in, 18, 38–39, 64; ancestor worship in, 22, 35–36, 59, 80, 92–93, 99–100; authority of elderly in, 59–60, 64, 80, 83, 85, 222, 237; Buddhism in, 35, 95, 99–100, 104, 255*n*2; businesses in, 39–40, 64–65, 107–8, 120, 124–27; Confucianism in, 18, 34–35, 38, 58, 89–90, 106–8, 111, 190–91; coresidence in, 16–33, 66–67, 76–85, 87, 111–12, 116, 124, 252*n*6, 258*n*10; criticism of authority in, 190; daughters in, 34–37, 50–52, 55–56, 61, 65, 106, 108, 111, 116; daughters-in-law in, 25–32, 38, 50, 53, 55–57, 80, 84, 103–4, 118–20; death ritual in, 13, 22, 36, 88–105; economic development in, 11, 63, 68–69, 107, 125–27; economic reforms in, 125–27, 258*n*9; economy of, 18, 38–39, 43, 45–46, 61, 64–65, 68–69; education in, 25, 107, 124, 257*n*3; elderly living alone in, 63–87; employment in, 58, 110–11, 117–18, 120, 124–26; family in, 12–13, 15, 22–25, 31, 106–27; family-planning policy in, 8, 13, 34, 82, 110, 126, 252*n*1; film from, 11; foreign brides from, 206; health care in, 15, 36, 48, 50, 52, 64–65, 78, 80–83, 115, 126, 253*n*1, 254*n*7; holidays in, 48–49, 51, 94, 97–98, 100, 103, 105; housing in, 28–29, 39, 42, 52, 70, 77–78, 94, 124, 126–27; industrialization in, 76–78, 84, 107, 124; inheritance in, 5, 39–40, 110–11, 121–22, 124,

127; land in, 10, 23, 39–40, 44–49, 52, 60–61, 65, 83, 92; laws in, 13, 22, 41, 51, 78–79, 88, 92–93, 95, 122, 252*n*4; life expectancy in, 9, 82; lineage organizations in, 35–36, 58–59, 61–62, 92; marriage in, 22, 31–32, 58, 65, 67, 78, 82–83, 88, 111–12, 122, 252*n*4; meal rotation in, 53–62; migration in, 18, 63–65, 67–68, 77, 84; modernization in, 12, 24–25, 40, 84, 106–27; mothers-in-law in, 169; and overseas Chinese, 93; population of, 7–8, 13, 18, 34; religion in, 35–36, 102, 255*n*2; ritualistic coresidence in, 16–33; socialist family virtues in, 24–25; socialist *vs.* postsocialist family in, 252*n*5; sons in, 6, 51, 56, 59, 69–70, 79, 82, 84, 86, 108–9, 112, 121–23; sons *vs.* daughters in, 34–52; suicides in, 14–15, 77–80, 87; *vs.* Taiwan, 1, 107–9, 117–22, 257*n*3; urbanization in, 6, 77–78, 84, 107, 124; Western influence in, 108–9. *See also* cadres, Chinese; Chinese Communist Party; collectivization; decollectivization; government, Chinese (PRC)

Chinese Communist Party (CCP), 91–92, 108, 111, 256*n*7

Chinhae Kim (lineage), 130–31, 134–35

Ch'ŏndogyo (Religion of the Heavenly Way), 154, 261*n*4

Chosŏn dynasty (Korea), 143, 155

Christianity: and ancestor worship, 150, 172–74, 263*n*23; Catholic, 262*n*4, 263*n*23; in China, 35–36, 102, 255*n*2; and Ch'ŏndogyo, 261*n*4; *vs.* Confucianism, 191; and death ritual, 102; and filial piety, 175, 178, 263*n*24; in Korea, 145, 150, 154, 163, 172–75, 178, 261*n*4, 262*n*4; Protestant, 163, 262*n*4, 263*n*23

Chun, Kyung-soo, 136

Ch'ungch'ŏng Province (Korea), 157

Ch'usŏk (Harvest Moon Festival), 143, 173

Ch'ü T'ung-tsu, 91

civil codes, 22; Japanese (1947), 204; Japanese (Meiji; 1898), 204, 220–21; Korean, 156, 165, 261*n*1b, 263*n*25

class, socioeconomic, 170, 172; and coresidence, 167–68; elite, 91, 137, 155–56, 190; and filial piety, 159–60, 164, 176–78, 180; and filial piety tourism, 174; of intervie-

wees, 164–65; in Japan, 191, 196; terms for Korean, 262*n*9; urban middle (*chungsanch'ŭng*), 163–64
Classic of Filial Piety (*Xiaojing*), 3, 156, 257*n*1
Cohen, Myron, 43, 59–60, 86, 252*n*3, 253*n*4
collectivization (PRC): of businesses, 64–65, 126; and changes in family, 23; elderly under, 36, 58, 81, 83; health care under, 81–82; and household division contracts, 45; and intergenerational relations, 80; and meal rotation, 58. *See also* decollectivization
communism, 22, 36, 58, 190. *See also* Chinese Communist Party
Confucianism, 1–4; and CCP, 111; in China, 18, 34–35, 38, 58, 89–90, 106–8, 111; Chinese *vs.* Japanese, 190–91; *vs.* Christianity, 191; and death ritual, 89–90; and education, 156, 184; in Japan, 182, 184, 187–88, 190–91, 204, 220; in Korea, 144, 153–57, 159–60, 178–79, 181, 262*n*4; and mother, 187; in Taiwan, 107–8
Confucius (Kongzi), 3, 21, 37; lineage of, 61–62
consumption, 176, 178–81
Coppard, Larry, 76
coresidence: and adult day care, 232–38; alternatives to, 146; with ancestors, 205–6; attitudes toward, 85, 115, 120–22, 259*n*16, 263*n*18; in China, 16–33, 66–67, 76–85, 87, 111–12, 116, 124, 252*n*6, 258*n*10; in China *vs.* Taiwan, 120–23, 125; and class, 167–68; conflicts over, 207–14; with daughters, 111, 204–5, 233, 235; with daughters-in-law, 31–32, 168–71, 235; with daughters *vs.* sons, 142; decline in, 116; delayed, 221; and divorce, 169; as filial piety, 18–22, 30–33, 165–66; and great-grandparents, 217–18; and health care, 80, 82; and housing policy, 14; and inheritance, 147–48, 177, 204–5; and intergenerational relations, 30, 32–33, 112, 209; and isolation of elderly, 235–36, 238; in Japan, 199, 204–14, 216–18, 221–22, 228, 232–38; in Korea, 140, 146, 154–55, 165–69, 177, 180–81; *vs.* living

alone, 63–87, 233; and marriage, 31–32, 111–12; ritualistic, 16–33; rotating, 38, 252*n*6; with sons, 111, 199, 204–6, 216, 233, 235; and suicide, 80, 87; in Taiwan, 120–23, 125, 258*n*10; and vulnerability, 76–85
Cornell, Laurel, 4
cremation, 91–92, 102, 255*n*3; *vs.* burial, 88, 93, 96, 172
Cultural Revolution (PRC), 35–36, 91–92, 96, 258*n*9

Dachuan (Gansu), 56–57, 59–62
Daoism, 89, 255*n*2
daughters: adoption of, 65; in China *vs.* Taiwan, 121–23, 125; coresidence with, 111, 142, 204–5, 233, 235; and economic change, 61, 237; elder care by, 47, 67, 106–7, 118–20, 143, 146, 150–51, 215; employment of, 237; expectations of, 34–37, 50–52; filial piety of, 34–52, 137–38, 157; health care by, 47, 265*n*7; and inheritance, 204; among Mainlanders, 260*n*24; and meal rotation, 55–56, 61; and migration, 143; roles of, 116, 143, 226–27; *vs.* sons, 34–52, 116, 137–38, 142, 260*n*19; in Taiwan, 121–23, 125, 260*n*24; and Western influence, 108
daughters-in-law: authority of, 170–71, 234; changed status of, 80, 148–49; changing attitudes of, 84; in China *vs.* Taiwan, 118–20, 123; coresidence with, 31–32, 168–71, 235; and death ritual, 103–4; elder care by, 50, 118–20, 140, 147, 215, 223–24; eldest, 154; employment of, 58, 237; expectations of, 20–21, 25–32, 106; filial piety of, 38, 137–38; hospital care by, 265*n*8; independence of, 26–27; and meal rotation, 53, 55–57; modern models for, 25; and mothers-in-law, 6, 28–30, 136, 146, 169–71, 213, 215; and patriarchy, 169–71; roles of, 19–20, 227
Davis, Deborah, 70
Davis-Friedmann, Deborah, 36
death pollution, 89–90, 93, 96–98
death ritual, 13, 88–105; actions associated with, 93, 256*n*5; Buddhist, 89–90, 95, 99–100, 104, 172; for cadres, 98–102;

and Christianity, 102; and Confucianism, 89–90; and daughters-in-law,
103–4; described, 98–100; and economy,
254*n*6, 257*n*13; and filial piety, 21,
88–105, 133–34, 146, 165, 171–72, 205;
and government officials, 89–91, 98; in
Hong Kong, 93, 256*n*5; in hospitals,
97–98; and inheritance, 256*n*10; loosening of restrictions on, 93–94, 97–98,
104–5; and mourning, 18, 21; paper
goods burned in, 90, 92–95; and place
of death, 96–98; and power of elderly,
36; public *vs.* private, 92–93, 105; and
reputation, 254*n*6; in rural areas, 93,
96–97, 105; and the state, 22, 88–93, 105;
and status, 90–91, 98–102; and traditionality of deceased, 102–4; in urban
areas, 88, 91, 93, 172–73
Debavalya, Nibhon, 76
decollectivization: and cadres, 84; and
elder care, 65–66, 79–80; and health
care, 81–82; and household division contracts, 46; and meal rotation, 60–61
Deng Xiaoping, 36, 82, 258*n*5
dependence: economic, 117–18, 171; of elderly, 41, 59–60, 77, 83, 220, 237, 241; and
elderly as burden, 223; and meal rotation, 54; of oldest-old, 218, 227, 240;
permissive (*amae*), 222–23; on sons,
260*n*19; in urban areas, 83. *See also* independence
dingti system (inheritance of state job),
110–11
divorce, 169, 183
domestic sphere, 171; cycle of roles in,
225–27
Doolittle, Justus, 5

Eastern Han dynasty, 54
Ebrey, Patricia, 89
economic development: in China, 11, 63,
68–69, 107, 125–27; and communica-
tions, 132, 139; and daughters, 61, 237;
and flow of resources, 259*n*14; in Korea,
132, 138–40, 160–63; and living alone,
63, 68–69; and media, 132, 139; and state
policy, 138–40; and transportation, 139.
See also industrialization
economic resources: and coresidence, 63,

68–69, 78; and death ritual, 254*n*6,
257*n*13; and dependence *vs.* independence, 74, 79, 81, 83, 112, 115, 117–18, 123,
150, 171; in developed *vs.* developing
countries, 259*n*14; and filial piety, 5–7;
as incentives, 5–6, 43; and power of elderly, 40–41, 51–52; of urban *vs.* rural elderly, 70–71
economy: Chinese, 18, 38–39, 43, 45–46,
61, 64–65, 68–69; Chinese reforms of,
125–27, 258*n*9; Chinese *vs.* Taiwanese,
107, 257*n*3; effects on elderly of, 13–14;
export-oriented, 13, 130, 138; and generation gap, 236; global, 23; and household
division contracts, 43, 45–46; Japanese,
129–33, 194, 199–200, 236; Korean, 130,
138, 161, 261*n*2b; market, 58, 107, 253*n*1;
rural, 18, 38–39, 43, 45–46, 61, 64–65,
68–69; and the state, 13–14, 138–40; and
women, 58, 120, 124, 140
education: in China, 25, 124; in China *vs.*
Taiwan, 107, 257*n*3; Chinese-language,
156; Confucian, 156, 184; and filial piety,
135, 158; and generation gap, 236, 254*n*9;
in Japan, 184–86, 193–94, 201, 236,
254*n*9; in Korea, 135, 139–41, 150, 154,
156, 158, 165, 175, 261*n*3b, 262*n*10; in media, 25; and migration, 139, 201; and
modernization, 124, 156; nationalist, 184;
and roles of women, 141; and status of
elderly, 10
Eisenstadt, S. N., 189–90
elder care: Asian model of, 76–77; as commodity, 181; by daughters, 47, 67,
118–20, 143, 146, 150–51, 215; by daughters-in-law, 50, 118–20, 140, 147, 215,
223–24; and decollectivization, 65–66,
79–80; by eldest sons, 199, 204, 206; by
family, 34, 52, 157, 183–84, 219–20, 231;
and family-planning policy, 34; as filial
piety, 157, 165–68, 175; financial, 35,
112–13, 167; in Hong Kong, 78; in hospitals, 265*n*10; and household chores, 113,
118–20, 123; and housing, 147; and industrialization, 76–78, 84; and inheritance, 142, 147–48; insurance for long-
term, 227–28, 241; and intergenerational
relations, 34; and land, 142, 146, 148;
media on, 155, 168; and migration, 77,

84; physical, 158; physical *vs.* emotional, 239; public programs for, 219, 227–31; and rehabilitation services, 230; and social support, 228–30, 241; in Taiwan, 76, 78; types of, 118; and urbanization, 77–78, 84; by women, 24–25, 219. *See also* adult day care, Japanese; health care; institutional care

elderly: abuse of, 58–59, 79, 83–84, 142–43, 148, 153, 180, 237, 255*n*11; activities of, 60, 218, 226–27, 238–41; and age hierarchy, 185–86, 193–94, 238; aid to grown children from, 40, 114, 259*n*14; bargaining power of, 7, 39, 76, 83; childless, 66; community services for, 219, 227–31, 241–42; and filial piety tourism, 172, 174–75, 181; geographical distribution of, 8; health of, 233, 239–42; household chores done by, 71, 73, 79–80, 85, 114, 148; independent living arrangements of, 40–41, 63–87, 147, 265*n*2; isolation of, 235–36, 238–40; marginalization of, 37–41, 84; married, 110, 117; motivations for living alone of, 41, 68–76; numbers of children of, 110, 117; oldest-old, 217–42; overmedication of, 228; as percentage of population, 8, 34, 201–3, 218–19; public programs for, 227–31, 241; roles of, 218, 225–27, 233, 240–41; rural *vs.* urban, 40, 64, 70–71, 78, 201–3, 266*n*5; social participation by, 128, 131, 147, 151–52, 228–30, 238, 241, 266*n*5; traditional beliefs of, 102–4; in urban areas, 10, 40, 52, 83, 238; vulnerability of, 76–85

employment: in China, 58, 110–11, 120, 124, 126; in China *vs.* Taiwan, 117–18, 120, 124–25; and coresidence, 142, 147; of elderly, 110, 226, 228; and generation gap, 237; and industrialization, 138–39; in Japan, 193, 200, 206, 226, 228, 233, 237; in Korea, 138–42, 147, 154, 162, 164, 170; of men *vs.* women, 259*n*12; and passive noncompliance, 193; state-controlled, 110–11; of unmarried men, 206; wage labor, 23, 28, 84, 112; of women, 58, 120, 124, 140–42, 170, 226, 237

Falun Gong, 255*n*2

family: branch (*bunke*), 204; businesses run by, 65, 107–8, 120, 124–25, 127, 257*n*4; conjugal, 10, 79–81, 84, 108, 156, 254*n*10; as consumption unit, 125; continuity of, 225, 265*n*3; democratic, 183, 186; elder care by, 34, 52, 157, 184–85, 219–20, 231; extended, 10, 15, 69, 108, 123, 217–18, 225, 236; genealogies of, 35; and great-grandparents, 217–18; hierarchy in, 36, 182–97; and individualism, 182–83, 186; isolation of elderly in, 235–36, 238–40; and law, 13, 156, 182–83; and life expectancy, 183; membership of elderly in, 59–60; and modernization, 106–27, 157; multigenerational, 57, 70–71, 111, 221; natal, 10, 143, 265*n*7; networked (*wangluo jiating*), 112, 116; nuclear, 10, 69–71, 111, 123, 143, 145, 155, 160, 166, 181–83, 185, 188, 194, 206, 213–16, 221; patriarchal, 12, 183, 188, 251*n*4; patrilocal, 165–66; power relations in, 182–97; reputation of, 102, 134, 158, 254*n*6; roles in, 183, 204, 218, 225–27, 237–38, 241; samurai, 204; and socialism, 107–8; socialist *vs.* postsocialist, 252*n*5; and the state, 12–13, 17–18, 21–26, 36, 52, 76–77; stem, 66–67, 117, 154–57, 160, 165–71, 181–82, 213–16, 263*n*18; stem, defined, 262*n*5; stem *vs.* joint, 111; support of elderly by, 9–10, 36, 52, 64, 66, 76–77, 84, 222, 241; Taiwanese, 257*n*4; traditional, 18–22, 203–7; unity of, 28–29; and urbanization, 107, 155, 160, 183; and Westernization, 182–83; and youth, 189–90, 194. See also *ie*

Family Law (1947; Japan), 182, 186–87

family-planning policy: Chinese, 8, 13, 34, 82, 110, 126, 252*n*1; Korean, 139–40

Family Rituals (Zhu Xi), 89, 155

father: domestic role of, 226; industrious Japanese, 187–88. *See also* patriarchy

fengshui (geomancy), 90–91, 101

filial piety: awards for, 133, 143, 157–58, 175; causes of changes in, 7–14; Chinese term for, 2–3; *Classic* of, 3, 156, 257*n*1; decline of, 27–30, 58, 113–14, 145; defined, 2–3; and elderly living alone, 73, 75–76; forms of, 150; and generation

gap, 114–15, 176; Japanese terms for, 183–84, 194–96, 205, 213, 216, 220, 222–23; lack of decline in, 115, 122; maintenance of, 159–60; models of, 38, 106; motivations for, 4–7, 10, 158; movements against, 190; national campaigns for, 150; and negotiated solutions, 216; as normative feeling, 186; performance of, 165–74; popular concepts of, 157–58; practice of, 2, 27–30; pragmatic adaptations in, 157–60, 174–80; standards for, 159; subversion of resistance to, 186; traditional, 18–22, 133–38; "twenty-four tales" of, 106; vs. unfiliality, 3–4, 75–76, 175–76
Filial Piety Cultural Center, 144–45
film, 11–12, 219, 224–25. See also media
"five guarantees," 55, 65–66, 72
folktales: Japanese, 4, 11, 224–25; Korean, 135–37, 149, 151, 157
Foreign Export Zones (Korea), 161
Fortes, Meyer, 225
Foucault, Michel, 189
France, 171
Fujiwara family, 207–10, 213–14
Fumio, Niwa, 224
funerals. See death ritual

Gansu Province (China), 2, 35, 56–57, 59–62
gender: division of labor by, 140–43, 170–71; and family roles, 204, 226; and filial piety, 140–43, 158; hierarchies of, 12–13, 185–86; and isolation of elderly, 238; and sacrificial Japanese mother, 187; and the state, 23; and suicide, 7, 14–15; and Western influence, 108
Germany, 195
gerontocide, 224. See also Koryŏjang story; Obasuteyama
ghosts, wandering, 75
The Golden Wing (Lin Yaohua), 54
Gold Plan (1989; Japan), 228–29, 241
Goldstein, Melvyn, 70, 74, 84
Goode, William J., 108, 155, 258n6
government, Chinese (PRC): and ancestor worship, 22, 80, 92; benefits from, 78, 87, 124; businesses run by, 40; and death ritual, 22, 88–93, 105; and employment,

110–11; family policy of, 12–13, 17–18, 21–26, 31, 36, 52, 76–77; and family support of elderly, 36, 52, 76–77; "five guaranteed items" from, 55, 65–66; and meal rotation, 55; and patriarchy, 23–24; on religion, 255n2; vs. Taiwan, 108
government, Japanese, 184; and foreign brides, 206–7; programs for elderly of, 227–31, 241
government, Korean: and agriculture, 261n3a; and Confucianism, 156; and economic development, 138–40; on filial piety, 143–46
government, local, 46–47, 87, 255n1
government, Taiwanese, 108, 258n5
government officials, 89–91, 98. See also cadres, Chinese
great-grandparenthood, 217–42
Great Learning, 156
Greenhalgh, Susan, 84, 86
Guangdong Province (China), 2, 55, 57–58, 92, 255n3
Guangzhou (Guangdong), 88–105
guanxi (personal relationships), 114
guilds, 91
Guomindang (GMD), 108
Guo Yuhua, 55–56, 58–59
Gu Xinghua, 81

Haboush, JaHyun Kim, 137
Hashimoto, Akiko, 1, 3–4, 76, 182–97
health care: in China, 15, 36, 48, 50, 52, 64–65, 78, 80–83, 115, 126, 253n1, 254n7; in hospitals, 265n8; in Japan, 204, 219; and living alone, 15, 70–72, 86; and longevity, 8–10; medical savings plans for, 52; providers of, 47, 118–19, 265n7; and rehabilitation services, 228, 230; state-provided, 14, 55, 65–66, 78
Hebei Province (China), 2, 55–56, 58–59, 106–27
Heilongjiang Province (China), 79
Hobsbawm, Eric, 30
Hochschild, Arlie, 186
holidays: Chinese, 48–49, 51, 94, 97–98, 100, 103, 105; Japanese, 205; Korean, 132, 143, 173. See also life cycle: celebrations of
Home Sweet Home (film), 11–12

Hong Kong, 14, 78, 93, 256*n*5
Honshū (Japan), 199, 264*n*2b
hospitals, 97–98, 265*n*8
household: chores in, 71, 73, 79–80, 85, 113–14, 118–20, 123, 148; formation of, 16, 18; headship of, 204–5; and housing policy, 14; independent, 251*n*3; multi-generational, 17, 63, 66–67, 70, 221; nuclear *vs.* multigenerational, 70–71; production by, 22–23; registration of, 156, 253*n*2; traditional complex, 18–22. *See also* family
household division: avoidance of, 61; contracts for, 6–7, 16, 35, 41, 43–50, 58; and dependence of elderly, 60; early, 16, 23, 25, 28–29, 31; and elderly living alone, 67; and meal rotation, 53–54, 57–58; serial, 86; stigmatization of, 18–19; terms for, 253*n*4
housing: changing styles of, 28–29; in China, 39, 42, 52, 94, 127; in China *vs.* Taiwan, 124; conflicts over, 208–9; and household division contracts, 43, 46–47, 49; in Japan, 130, 183, 232; in Korea, 139, 147, 154, 162; and meal rotation, 53; multigenerational, 265*n*8; new, 70, 77; parental help with, 114; policy on, 14; private, 126; separate, 40–41, 63–87, 115, 221; shortage of, 78, 124; and taxes, 265*n*8; two-story, 39. *See also* coresidence; residence
Hu, Yow-Hwey, 14–15, 77–78
Huangcun (Fujian), 54–55, 57
Hubei Province (China), 2, 63–87
Huhhot (Inner Mongolia), 98
Hunan Province (China), 84
Hyundai Heavy Industries, 162

ie (Japanese stem family), 6, 182, 184, 222, 225, 265*n*3; and ancestor worship, 205; and Confucianism, 204; continuing importance of, 220–21; and disempowerment of Japanese youth, 194, 196; and filial piety, 203–4, 216
Ikels, Charlotte, 1–15, 70, 84, 88–105
ikigai (social participation, purpose of life), 228–29
Imamura Shōhei, 4, 224
income, 158, 261*n*2b; in China *vs.* Taiwan,

117–18, 123; and collectivization, 81; of elderly, 51–52, 112, 115; of elderly living alone, 68–69, 74, 86; and household division contracts, 50; and industrialization, 131; in rural *vs.* urban areas, 69–70; and wage labor, 23, 28, 84, 112; women's managment of, 171
independence: and consumption, 179; of daughters-in-law, 26–27; economic, 28, 74, 79, 81, 83, 112, 115, 123, 150; of elderly, 6–7, 9, 40–41, 52, 64, 68–69, 115, 117, 228; and separate living arrangements, 68–69, 84–86; and socialism, 126; in Taiwan *vs.* Baoding, 123; of women, 112, 251*n*3
individualism, 22, 69, 114, 182–83, 186
industrialization: of China *vs.* Taiwan, 107; and decline of filial piety, 145; and elder care, 76–78, 84; and employment, 138–39; export-led, 130, 138; and family change, 160; in Japan, 129–33, 200; in Korea, 138–40, 153–55, 160–63; and modernization, 124; and roles of women, 140–41, 151; of rural areas, 129–33. *See also* economic development
inheritance: and American Occupation, 221; of authority, 190–91; changes in, 124, 127, 146; in China *vs.* Taiwan, 121–22, 124; and coresidence, 147–48, 177, 204–5; by daughters, 204; and death rituals, 256*n*10; differential, 6, 142, 150; and elder care, 142, 147–48; of family businesses, 40; and filial piety, 5–6, 158, 176–78, 180; of household headship, 204–5; of land, 39–40; laws on, 5, 13, 142, 177, 204; and power of elderly, 39; by sons, 6, 138, 150; of state jobs (*dingti* system), 110–11; taxes on, 265*n*8; traditional patterns of, 204–5, 221–22
Inheritance Law (China; 1985), 5
institutional care: in China, 85; in Japan, 193, 224, 227–31; in Korea, 128, 148, 167–68, 177, 179–80; in old-age homes (*yangnoweŏn*), 128, 148; in retirement communities, 168, 179; in the West, 76, 128
insurance, 52, 87; long-term care, 227–28, 241

intergenerational relations: and authority, 189–93; case studies of, 207–13; in China, 34, 58, 109, 113–14; in China *vs.* Taiwan, 123, 125; and collectivization, 58, 80; and coresidence, 30, 32–33, 112, 209; in developed *vs.* developing countries, 259*n*14; and disempowerment of Japanese youth, 196; and extended old age, 217–42; factors in, 25–27, 38, 78, 223, 228, 254*n*9; and filial piety, 216; and generation gap, 114–15, 176, 236–37, 242, 254*n*9, 259*n*15; hierarchy in, 28, 193–94; in Japan, 188–89, 199, 207–13, 222; in Korea, 135–36, 142–43, 146; and media, 149, 151; *meiwaku* (burden) avoidance in, 223; and obedience, 165–66, 185–86; obedience in, 26–27, 37; power in, 184, 194–95; and ritualistic coresidence, 30, 32–33; and separate living arrangements, 64, 71–72; of sons *vs.* daughters, 138; and suicide, 87; in urban areas, 83; in U.S., 259*n*17

Islam, 255*n*2

Iwate Prefecture (Japan), 201–2, 206

"Iyagarase no nenrei" (The hateful age; Fumio), 224

Janelli, Roger, 1, 5, 128–52

Jankowiak, William, 98

Japan, 1, 3, 182–242; adult day care in, 217–18, 220, 228–39, 241, 266*n*8; age-based roles in, 225–27; agriculture in, 199–201, 206; American Occupation of, 182, 184; ancestor worship in, 204–6, 221; bureaucracy in, 231; children in, 183–88, 195; Christianity in, 191; Confucianism in, 182, 184, 187–88, 190–91, 204, 220; coresidence in, 199, 204–14, 216–18, 221–22, 228, 232–38; daughters in, 204–5, 226–27, 233, 235, 237; daughters-in-law in, 213, 215, 223–24, 227, 234–35, 237; death ritual in, 13, 205; economy of, 129–33, 194, 199–200, 236; education in, 184–86, 193–94, 201, 236, 254*n*9; elder care in, 76; eldest sons in, 198; family in, 6, 13, 182–97, 203–7, 216–22, 225, 231, 236, 265*n*3; film from, 11, 219, 224–25; folktales of, 4, 11, 224–25; foreign brides in, 206–7; health

care in, 204, 219; housing in, 130, 183, 232; industrialization in, 129–33, 200; inheritance in, 6, 190–91, 204–5, 221–22; institutional care in, 193, 224, 227–31; and Korea, 156, 161; laws in, 204, 220–21; life expectancy in, 9, 183, 202–3, 217–19, 237, 240–42; marriage in, 182–83, 198–216; migration in, 200–203, 264*n*3; nationalism in, 184, 220; population of, 8, 201–3, 218–25; sons in, 198–217, 221, 224, 233, 235; suicides in, 14–15, 201, 223; unmarried men in, 206; urbanization in, 6. *See also* government, Japanese

Jenike, Brenda Robb, 1, 9, 217–42

Jia, Aimei, 68, 84

Ji Jianlin, 15

Jing, Jun, 1, 35, 53–62

Johnston, Reginald, 43

Jōnai (Japan), 199–200

Kanegasaki (Japan), 200

Kaohsiung (Taiwan), 110

Kawashima Takeyoshi, 187

Keelung (Taiwan), 110

keirō kaikan (Japanese senior centers), 229, 231–32

Keith, Jennie, 78

Kendig, Hal, 76

Kiefer, Christie, 223

Kim, Sung-chul, 1, 153–81

Kimhae (Korea), 160, 162, 164

kinship: and cycle of roles, 225–27; patrilineal *vs.* bilateral, 108; terms for, 226. *See also* family

Kitakami (Japan), 200, 207

Knodel, John, 76

kōkō (filial piety), 184, 194, 196

Kōkutsu no hito (The Twilight Years; Ariyoshi), 223–24

Korea, 128–81; adaptation to social change in, 158–60; agriculture in, 138–40, 157, 261*n*3a; ancestor worship in, 129, 133–35, 137–38, 149–50, 156, 165, 171–74; children in, 165, 174, 195; class in, 137, 155–56, 159–60, 163–65, 167–68, 170, 172, 174, 176–78, 180, 262*n*9; Confucianism in, 144, 153–57, 159–60, 178–79, 181, 262*n*4; coresidence in, 140, 146, 154–55,

165–69, 177, 180–81; currency crisis
(1997) in, 261n2b; daughters in, 142–43,
150–51, 157; daughters-in-law in, 136–38,
140, 146–49, 154, 168–71; death ritual in,
13, 133–34, 146, 165, 171–73; economic
development in, 138–40; economy of,
130, 138, 161, 261n2b; education in, 135,
139–41, 150, 154, 156, 158, 165, 175,
261n3b, 262n10; family in, 13, 154–56,
160, 166–68; family-planning policy in,
139–40; folktales of, 4, 135–37, 149, 151,
157; government policies in, 129–30, 133,
138–40; holidays in, 132, 143, 173; housing in, 139, 147, 154, 162; industrialization in, 138–40, 153–55, 160–63; inheritance in, 5–6, 142, 147–48, 150, 158,
176–78, 180; institutional care in, 128,
148, 167–68, 177, 179–80; and Japan,
156, 161; land in, 130, 135, 142, 146, 148;
laws in, 153, 156, 165–66, 179, 261n1b,
263n25; life expectancy in, 9, 145, 155,
171; lineage organizations in, 130–31,
134–35, 146; marriage in, 131, 137, 151, 155,
165, 260n19; migration in, 132, 138–39,
143, 149, 154, 158, 162–63, 166, 261n2a;
modernization in, 12, 151, 153–56,
159–60; and North Korea, 161–62; population of, 7–8, 126, 132, 139–40, 155; religion in, 154, 261n4; sons in, 116,
137–38, 142–43, 147, 149–50, 154–55,
165–66, 168, 173–74, 263n25; suicides in,
14–15, 136; urbanization in, 6, 132–33,
138–40, 153–54, 160–63. See also government, Korean
Korean War, 161
Koryŏ dynasty (Korea), 155
Koryŏjang story, 135–36, 149, 151, 157
Koyano, Wataru, 223
Ku, Yachun, 70, 74, 84
Kurozumikyō (religion), 192
Kyŏnggi Province (South Korea), 163

labor: costs of, 161; gendered division of,
140–43, 170–71; and stem family, 157;
wage, 23, 28, 84, 112; of women, 76–77,
141, 169–70. See also employment
land: contract, 44; and cremation, 92; and
economic change, 23, 61, 130; and elder
care, 52, 142, 146, 148; elders' control of,

10, 83; and household division contracts,
44, 49; inheritance of, 39–40; leased, 47;
and meal rotation, 60–61; redistribution
of, 60–61, 65; responsibility, 44–49; for
ritual expenses, 135; scarcity of, 61; village-owned, 39–40
law: civil, 22, 156, 165, 204, 220–21, 261n1b,
263n25; on death ritual, 92–93, 95; on
elder care, 41, 51, 78–79, 153, 254n8; family, 156, 182–83; inheritance, 142, 177,
204; and local customs, 255n1; on marriage, 13, 22, 78, 88, 122; on parental authority, 165–66; sumptuary, 179
Lebra, Takie, 192, 204
Lee, Kwang-kyu, 146
Lee, Ryungyŏng, 164
Legge, James, 3
Liaoning Province (China), 2, 16–33
life cycle: celebrations of, 32, 165, 171–75,
177, 179–81; roles in, 225–27
life expectancy: and age distribution,
202–3; in China, 9, 82; and health care,
8–10; in Japan, 9, 183, 202–3, 217–19,
237, 240–42; in Korea, 9, 145, 155, 171;
and lack of role models, 237, 241–42;
and oldest-old, 217–19, 240
Liji (Book of Rites), 38
Lijia (Shandong), 6, 34–52; elderly in,
38–41
lineage, 5, 188–90; of Confucius, 61–62
lineage organizations, 130–31; ancestral
halls of, 35, 134–35, 146; and communism, 58, 92; and status of elderly, 36,
59, 61–62
Lin Yaohua, 54
literacy, 10, 154
Liu Guiyuan, 68
Lock, Margaret, 192, 226

mandate of heaven, 190
Mao Zedong, 12, 82, 107–8
marriage: and coresidence, 31–32, 111–12;
costs of, 58, 82–83; and domestic role,
226; of elderly, 110, 117; of eldest sons,
198, 206, 215; vs. filial piety, 165,
198–216; and household division contracts, 44, 47; laws on, 13, 22, 78, 88, 122,
252n4; and living alone, 63; patrilocal,
165–66, 251n1; traditional, 36, 80, 140,

251n4; traditional vs. modern, 155, 165, 182–83; uxorilocal, 65, 67, 131, 137, 151, 204, 208, 210, 214, 260n19, 264nn4,6; of widows, 121–23

Marriage Law (1950; China), 22, 78, 88, 122, 252n4

Marxism, 22, 108

Masan (Korea), 160–62, 262n8; interviews in, 164

Matsumoto-san, 210–13, 215–16

May Fourth movement (China), 107

meal rotation, 53–62, 66; frequency of, 54–57; public opinion on, 54, 62; reasons for, 57–62

media: ancestor worship in, 35; and economic development, 132, 139; education through, 25; on elder abuse, 79, 180; on elder care, 155, 168; and filial piety, 143–46, 158; funerals in, 173; images of elderly in, 227, 241; and intergenerational relations, 149, 151; and interviewees, 164; on oldest-old, 235; and the state, 25; on traditionalism, 203

Meiji period (Japan), 184

meiwaku (burden) avoidance, 223

Mencius, 3

mental health: of elderly, 237–40; of oldest-old, 240

migration: in China, 18, 63–65, 67–68, 77, 84; and elderly living alone, 63–65, 67–68; and funerals, 13; in Japan, 200–203, 264n3; in Korea, 132, 138–39, 143, 149, 154, 158, 162–63, 166, 261n2a; rural-urban, 18, 139, 162, 200, 261n2a; to U.S., 133

Miller, Eric T., 1, 6, 34–52, 236

Miyagi Prefecture (Japan), 201–2

Mizusawa (Japan), 200, 206–13, 215

modernization, 10–12; adaptations to, 159–60; in China, 12, 24–25, 40, 84, 106–27; in China vs. Taiwan, 123–25; and education, 124, 156; and family change, 23, 106–27, 157; in Japan, 194; in Korea, 12, 151, 153–56, 159–60; of marriage, 155, 165, 182–83; theories of, 258n6; of women, 24–25. See also industrialization; urbanization

Morioka (Japan), 199, 200

mothers, 190, 226; sacrificial, 185, 187–88

mothers-in-law, 226; and daughters-in-law, 6, 28–30, 136, 146, 169–71, 213, 215

Myŏngsim pogam (Precious Mirror for Enlightening the Mind), 156

Naeari (South Korea), 128–52; in 1970s, 133–38; in 1990s, 146–49

naikan (type of psychotherapy), 191

nationalism, 1, 12, 261n4; Japanese, 184, 220

neo-Confucianism, 191

New Reform Party (Shinshintō; Japan), 235

New Territories (Hong Kong), 93

New Village movement (Korea), 129

New Year: Chinese, 48–49, 51; Korean, 173

noin munje ("problems of the aged"), 144

North Korea, 161–62

Obasuteyama ("Throw-Out-Granny Mountain"), 4, 11, 224–25

obedience: and gender, 186, 251n2; in intergenerational relations, 26–27, 37, 165–66, 185–86; and Japanese youth, 184–89, 196, 220; and mother-child bond, 185, 187–88; passive resistance to, 192–93

Ogawa, Naohiro, 76

overseas Chinese, 93

oyakōkō (filial piety), 183–84, 194–95, 205, 213, 216, 220, 222–23

Pak Pujin, 146

parents: aid to grown children from, 114, 259n14; alienation from, 195; authority of, 27, 165–66, 183, 214. See also elderly

Pari Kongju myth, 137, 157

Parish, William, 92–93, 98

Park Chung Hee, 138, 161, 179

Parsons, Talcott, 125

patriarchy, 12; Chinese, 23–24, 251n4; Japanese, 182–83, 188, 194, 220–21, 236–37; Korean, 156, 169–71; and the state, 23–24

patrilineality, 108, 116, 123, 125, 131, 220–21

pensions, 13; in China, 23, 39–40, 42, 44, 54–56, 64, 67, 69, 71, 78, 83, 112, 124, 126, 253n1; in China vs. Taiwan, 117–18, 123–24; and elderly living alone, 64, 67, 69, 71, 78; of men vs. women, 259n12; in

rural areas, 23, 54, 112, 124, 126; in Taiwan, 117–18, 123–24, 260*n*23; in urban
areas, 55–56, 83, 253*n*1
Philippines, 206
Pingyuan (Zhejiang), 70
Plath, David, 220, 222–26
pokkuri (swift death) temples, 223
popular culture, 18; elderly in, 223–25; filial
piety in, 21–22, 157–58. *See also* media
population, 7–10, 18; aging, 8, 34, 201–3,
218–25; and birth rates, 7–8, 126, 132,
139–40, 155, 183, 203. *See also* family-
planning policy
power: and child-rearing, 213; of elderly, 7,
36, 39–41, 51–52, 76, 83; in family,
182–97, 199; in intergenerational relations, 184, 194–95; and resistance to authority, 192–93; and sacrificial Japanese
mother, 187; of women, 169–71. *See also*
patriarchy
PRC. *See* China, People's Republic of
Precious Mirror for Enlightening the Mind
(*Myŏngsim pogam*), 156
primogeniture, 182, 221, 265*n*3
"problems of the aged" (*noin munje*), 144
property: in China *vs.* Taiwan, 121–23, 125;
division of, 16, 43–50, 57; of elderly, 36,
51–52, 136, 142–43; religious, 93; and the
state, 22, 127; in Taiwan, 108, 121–23,
125. *See also* land
Protestantism. *See* Christianity
psychotherapy, 191–92
public sphere: death ritual in, 92–93, 105;
and domestic roles, 226; participation of
elderly in, 128, 131, 147, 151–52, 228–29,
238, 266*n*5
Pumo ŭnjung kyŏng (Sutra of Parental
Grace), 155
Pure Evangelical Church, 145
Pusan (South Korea), 132, 160–62, 164,
262*n*8

Qingming festival (China), 94, 97–98, 100,
103, 105

Ranger, Terence, 30
reincarnation, 90
religion: in China, 35, 62, 89, 255*n*2; in
Japan, 192; in Korea, 129, 145, 154,
261*n*4. *See also* ancestor worship; Buddhism; Christianity; Confucianism
residence: in China *vs.* Taiwan, 258*n*10;
creative arrangements for, 146; of grown
children, 35, 110–11, 117, 132; in household registration book, 253*n*2; and
parental authority, 214; patrilocal,
165–66, 251*n*1; rotating, 38, 252*n*6; separate, 40–41, 63–87, 115, 221; uxorilocal,
65, 67, 131, 137, 151, 204, 208, 210, 214,
260*n*19, 264*nn*4,6
responsibility system (PRC), 44–49
retirement, 110–11, 227–28, 253*n*1
retreatism, 192–93, 196
ritual: disputes over, 150; and filial piety,
21, 135; and identity, 31; and land, 135;
outlawing of, 92–93; and power of elderly, 36; revival of, 31. *See also* ancestor
worship; death ritual; life cycle: celebrations of
ritualism, resistance through, 192–93
ROC. *See* Taiwan
Rogers, Carol, 171
Rohlen, Thomas, 185
rōjinkai (*rōjin kurabu*; senior citizens
clubs), 229, 231–32
Rosaldo, Michelle, 171
rural areas, 2, 16–87, 198–216; aging population in, 8, 201–3; death ritual in, 13, 93,
96–97, 105; economy of, 18, 38–39, 43,
45–46, 61, 64–65, 68–69; elderly in, 10,
34, 40, 78, 225; filial piety in, 34–52,
157–58; income in, 69–70; industrialization of, 129–33; living alone in, 69–70;
meal rotation in, 54; migration from, 18,
139, 162, 200, 261*n*2a; pensions in, 23,
54, 112, 124, 126; ritual in, 171; sent-
down youth in, 258*n*9; suicide in, 14–15;
vs. urban, 40, 69–70, 83, 111, 131–32,
266*n*5; welfare system in, 55, 65, 252*n*6

Samsung Prize for Filial Piety, 158
Sendai (Japan), 200–201
senior centers, Japanese (*keirō kaikan*), 229,
231–32
senior clubs, Japanese (*rōjinkai*; *rōjin
kurabu*), 228, 231–32, 238
Seoul (South Korea), 132, 161, 163; Metropolitan Region of, 132

"sevens, doing the," 99, 104
Shaanxi Province (China), 84
shamanism, 255*n2*
Shancun (Zhejiang), 70
Shandong Province (China), 2, 34–52, 68
Shanghai (China), 8, 70–71
Shenzhen Special Economic Zone (China), 11
Shichirō, Fukuzawa, 224
Shōhei, Imamura, 4, 224
Showa period (Japan), 184
Shower (film), 11
Sichuan Province (China), 70
Silver Human Resource Centers (Japan), 228
silver towns (*silbŏ t'aun*), 168, 179
The Silver Wing (Zhuang Kongshao), 54
Sim Ch'ŏng, story of, 137, 157
Singapore, 14, 77
socialism, 64, 107–8, 110–11, 124–27
social relations: of elderly, 128, 131, 147, 151–52, 228–30, 238, 241, 266*n5*; and roles of women, 143
Sŏnggyun'gwan Confucian Academy, 156
Sŏng Kyut'ak, 158–59
Sŏngsan University Graduate School of Filial Piety, 145
sons: adopted, 56; changing attitudes of, 84; in China vs. Taiwan, 108–9, 121–23; competition between, 79; coresidence with, 111, 199, 204–6, 216, 233, 235; vs. daughters, 41–43, 51, 116, 137–38, 142–43, 260*n19*; and elderly living alone, 69; expectations of, 34–37; and family planning policy, 252*n1*; graded responsibilities of, 138; and household division contracts, 43–50; incomes of, 70; increased number of, 82; and industrialization, 155; inheritance by, 6, 138, 150; and meal rotation, 55–56, 59; necessity of, 112; only, 34–35, 51, 56, 59; support of parents by, 42–50, 67, 72–73, 118–20, 260*n19*; traditional roles of, 106–9; youngest, 86
sons, eldest: and ancestor worship, 138, 149–50, 173–74; coresidence with, 198, 233, 235; elder care by, 199, 204, 206; Japanese, 198–217, 221, 224; Korean, 147,

149–50, 154, 165–66, 168, 263*n25*; marriage with, 198–99
sons-in-law, married-in: Japanese (*mukoyōshi*), 204, 208, 210, 214, 264*nn4,6*; Korean, 131, 137, 151
Sorensen, Clark, 1, 137, 153–81
South Korea. *See* Korea
South Kyŏngsang Province (Korea), 157, 160–63
spirit mediums, 95, 103
the state: and filial piety, 89, 106, 158; role of, 12–14; suport for elderly from, 78, 180. *See also* government
status: and ancestors, 189; and Confucianism, 156; and consumption, 179–80; of daughters-in-law, 80, 148–49; and death ritual, 90–91, 98–102; of elderly, 10, 36, 59–62, 83, 219; and filial piety, 134–35, 158; in Korea, 156; and marriage, 165; and modernization, 12; redefinitions of, 160; and ritual, 172, 181; and urbanization, 10; and women, 23, 141, 170
Stone Mill village (Liaoning), 16–33
Suginami Ward (Tokyo), 228, 231–32
suicide: and coresidence, 80, 87; by elderly, 7, 14–15, 77–79, 87, 136, 201, 223, 255*n11*; and gender, 7, 14–15; and living alone, 79
Sutra of Parental Grace (*Pumo ŭnjung kyŏng*), 155
Sweden, 15

Tai, Mount, 35
Taichung (Taiwan), 110
Tainan (Taiwan), 110
Taipei (Taiwan), 110
Taishō period (Japan), 220
Taiwan (Republic of China; ROC): businesses in, 107–8, 124–25, 257*n4*; vs. China, 1, 107–9, 117–22, 257*n3*; Confucianism in, 107–8; coresidence in, 120–23, 125, 258*n10*; daughters in, 121–23, 125, 260*n24*; daughters-in-law in, 118–20, 123; economy of, 107, 117–18, 123, 257*n3*; education in, 107, 257*n3*; elder care in, 76, 78; employment in, 117–18, 120, 124–25; foreign investment from, 257*n13*; government of, 108,

258*n5*; household division in, 43; life expectancy in, 9; Mainlanders in, 117–19, 124, 260*nn*22,24; meal rotation in, 60; modernization in, 12, 107, 123–25; pensions in, 117–18, 123–24, 260*n*23; population growth in, 7–8; *vs.* PRC, 1, 107–9, 257*n*3; sons in, 108–9, 121–23; suicide in, 7, 14–15; survey data from, 109–10; traditionalism in, 107–8, 117, 120, 122–23
Tōhoku region (Japan), 200–203, 264*n*2b
Tokugawa period (Japan), 184
Tokyo (Japan), 200, 266*n*5
tourism, 35, 200; filial piety, 172, 174–75, 181
tradition: in China *vs.* Taiwan, 117, 120, 122–23, 125; and death ritual, 102–4; and family, 18–22, 203–7; and inheritance, 204–5, 221–22; invention of, 30; in Japan, 203; and marriage, 36, 80, 140, 155, 165, 182–83, 251*n*4; revival of, 31; in Taiwan, 107–8, 117, 120, 122–23
transportation, 132, 139, 143, 161
Traphagan, John W., 1, 192, 198–216, 221, 223
Tsurumi, Kazuko, 192
The Twenty-four Tales of Filial Piety, 25

Ulsan (South Korea), 162
Unger, Jonathan, 69–70, 85
United States: children in, 195; elder care in, 128, 151–52; eldest sons in, 198; filial piety in, 52; independence of elderly in, 9, 228; influence of, 151–52; intergenerational relations in, 259*n*17; Korean migration to, 133; suicide in, 14–15
urban areas, 2, 88–127, 153–81, 217–42, 262*n*7; adaptations to, 159–60; age-based roles in, 225; age distribution in, 8, 201–3; in China *vs.* Taiwan, 107–8; death ritual in, 13, 88, 91, 93, 172–73; elder care in, 34, 117–22; elderly in, 10, 40, 52, 64, 70–71, 78, 83, 201–3, 238, 266*n*5; family change in, 107; filial piety in, 50, 158–59; incomes in, 69–70; living alone in, 69–70; meal rotation in, 54; middle class in, 163–64; migration to, 18, 139, 162, 200, 261*n*2a; pensions in, 55–56, 83, 253*n*1; *vs.* rural, 40, 69–70, 83,

111, 131–32, 266*n*5; suicide in, 14–15; survey data from, 109–10; in Taiwan, 107–8, 260*n*23
urbanization, 6, 10; in China *vs.* Taiwan, 107; and elder care, 77–78, 84; and family, 107, 155, 160, 183; in Korea, 132–33, 138–40, 153–54, 160–63; and modernization, 124; and roles of women, 140
uxorilocal marriage. *See under* marriage

villages, 5, 133, 154; enterprises in, 39, 64–65; "single-surname" (*tongsŏng purak*), 131; teams in, 46–47, 64. *See also* Baoding; Huangcun; Jōnai; Lijia; Naeari; rural areas; Stone Mill village; Xiaoyangcun; Zhongshan

Wakefield, David, 43
Wang, Danyu, 1, 16–33
Wang Huizu, 255*n*1
Wang Yilong, 85
Watson, James, 93, 97, 256*n*5
the West: influence of, 108–9, 182; institutional care in, 76, 128; suicide in, 14; and Taiwan, 107–8. *See also* United States
Westernization, 145, 182–83
Whyte, Martin King, 1, 12, 92–93, 98, 106–27
widow remarriage, 5, 121–23
Wolf, Margery, 7
Wŏlgan Chosŏn (periodical), 144
women: changing roles of, 140–43, 151; death ritual for, 101; domestic roles of, 226–27; elder care by, 24–25, 216, 219; and eldest sons, 198–99; employment of, 58, 120, 124, 140–42, 170, 226, 237, 259*n*12; and filial piety, 192; as foreign brides, 206–7; and housing, 29; independence of, 112, 251*n*3; and independent household, 251*n*3; and industrialization, 140–41, 151; labor of, 76–77, 141, 169–70; and local religion, 62; model, 25; modern filial, 24–25; and natal family, 10, 143, 265*n*7; nontraditional, 226; power of, 169–71; remarriage of, 5, 121–23; rights of, 22–24; secret funds of, 141; and status, 23, 141, 170; terms for, 263*n*17; three rules of obedience for,

251*n*2. *See also* daughters; daughters-in-law; mothers; mothers-in-law
work units (PRC), 94, 111, 126
World Revolution and Family Patterns (Goode), 108
World War II, 107
Wuhan (Hubei), 69

xiao (filial piety), 2–3
Xiaoyangcun (Hebei), 55–56, 58–59
Xilong (Guangdong), 55, 57–58
Xin Xiangmu, 68
Xue Xingli, 68

yangban (Korean nobility), 156, 181
yangnowŏn (old-age homes), 128, 148
Yan Yunxiang, 79
Yim, Dawnhee, 1, 5, 128–52

Yokohama (Japan), 210–13, 215
youth: disempowerment of Japanese, 182–97; obedience of, 184–89, 196, 220; resistance to authority of, 189–90, 192–93; sent-down Chinese, 258*n*9

Zhang, Hong, 1, 6–7, 63–87, 236, 259*n*16
Zhang Junliang, 70
Zhejiang Province (China), 70, 74, 84–85
Zhongshan (Hubei), 6–7, 63–87; economy of, 64–65; housing in, 69, 77; living arrangements of elderly in, 66–68; uxorilocal marriage in, 65, 67
Zhou Enlai, 100
Zhuang Kongshao, 54–57
Zhu Xi, 89, 155
Zuoshi yaoyan (Precepts for Local Administrative Officials; Wang Huizu), 255*n*1